The Council of Europe and Sport

Basic Documents

This publication was realised with the cooperation of the

INTERNATIONAL OLYMPIC COMMITTEE
FIFPRO

Source of the Documents:

COUNCIL OF EUROPE

Partners of the ASSER International Sports Law Centre

L&L ABOGADOS
LARRAURI & LÓPEZ ANTE

LNA LAWYERS WORLDWIDE
LEGAL NETLINK ALLIANCE

LCA
avvocati e commercialisti d'impresa
studio associato

With Us, The Solution Is Well Within Reach...
TOLUN Consulting Sport Law Center

DF Advocates
Deguara Farrugia Advocates

C/M/S/ Derks Star Busmann
ATTORNEYS AT LAW CIVIL LAW NOTARIES TAX ADVISERS

TW TaylorWessing

DE KEERSMAEKER VROMANS
THE BRUSSELS OFFICE OF THE
ASSER INTERNATIONAL SPORTS LAW CENTRE

WILKENS C.S.
TRANSLATORS & INTERPRETERS

T.M.C. ASSER INSTITUUT
ASSER International Sports Law Centre

The Council of Europe and Sport

Basic Documents

Edited by

Robert C.R. Siekmann

and

Janwillem Soek

T•M•C•Asser press

Published by T·M·C·Asser press
P.O. Box 16163, 2500 BD The Hague, The Netherlands
<www.asserpress.nl>

T·M·C·Asser press' English language books are distributed exclusively by:

Cambridge University Press, The Edinburgh Building, Shaftesbury Road,
Cambridge CB2 2RU, UK,
or
for customers in the USA, Canada and Mexico:
Cambridge University Press, 100 Brook Hill Drive, West Nyack, NY 10994-2133, USA
<www.cambridge.org>

ISBN 90-6704-239-0
ISBN 978-90-6704-239-0

Cover photograph: Hans Erni, "Seven Sprinters", 1994. Tempera on paper, 76 x 57 cm.

T.M.C. Asser Instituut – Institute for Private and Public International Law, International Commercial Arbitration and European Law

Institute Address: R.J. Schimmelpennincklaan 20-22, The Hague, The Netherlands; Mailing Address: P.O. Box 30461, 2500 GL The Hague, The Netherlands; Tel.: +3170 342 0300; Fax: +3170 3420 359; Internet: www.asser.nl.
Over fourty years, the T.M.C. Asser Institute has developed into a leading scientific research institute in the field of international law. It covers private international law, public international law, including international humanitarian law, the law of the European Union, the law of international commercial arbitration and increasingly, also, international economic law, the law of international commerce and international sports law.
Conducting scientific research, either fundamental or applied, in the aforementioned domains, is the main activity of the Institute. In addition, the Institute organizes congresses and postgraduate courses, undertakes contract-research and operates its own publishing house.
Because of its inter-university background, the Institute often cooperates with Dutch law faculties as well as with various national and foreign institutions. The Institute organizes *Asser College Europe*, a project in cooperation with East and Central European countries whereby research and educational projects are organized and implemented.

FOREWORD

The Council of Europe is undoubtedly the body, which during forty years (since 1967) has made the most substantial contribution to paving the way for a European sports model. It was the first international intergovernmental organisation to take initiatives and to offer an institutional framework for the development of sport at European level and to establish numerous legal instruments.

The Council of Europe is aware that sport has a distinctive role to play as a force for social integration, tolerance and understanding. It is open to all, regardless of age, language, religion, culture, or ability. It is the single most popular activity in modern society. Sport provides the opportunity to learn to play by commonly agreed rules, to behave admirably both in victory and in defeat and to develop, not only the physical being, but also social competences and ethical values. Its contribution to education is increasingly acknowledged. Sport has a key contribution to bring to the promotion of the core values of the Council of Europe: democracy, human rights and the rule of law.

The Council of Europe continues to play an active role in European sports affairs in order to establish international standards for states parties to the European Cultural Convention, to assist public authorities, in co-operation with national sports organisations, to promote and develop sport that is open to everyone, without discrimination, and run in a healthy, safe and ethical environment. The upcoming Enlarged Partial Agreement on Sport is expected to strengthen the intergovernmental co-operation within the Council of Europe and to become an enhanced platform of co-operation between the public authorities and the Sport movement.

The present publication entitled *The Council of Europe and Sport: Basic Documents* is the second volume in the Asser series of collections of documents on international sports law, containing material on the intergovernmental (inter-state) part of international sports law. The first volume was devoted to the European Union. In previous other publications, NGO material, i.e., statutes and constitutions, doping rules and regulations and arbitral and disciplinary rules and regulations of the international sports organisations were published.

A reference book such as this is an extremely valuable tool for both legal practice and research purposes in the field of sport, law and policy, in this case focusing on the Council of Europe.

Strasbourg, November 2006

Dr. Ralf-René Weingärtner
Director for Youth and Sport
Council of Europe

TABLE OF CONTENTS

LIST OF ACRONYMS

ANMP	National Association of Portuguese Municipalities
ANOC	Association of National Olympic Committees
CCTV	closed-circuit video equipment
CDDS	Committee for the Development of Sport
CDEJ	European Steering Committee for Youth
CDMM	Steering Committee on the Mass Media
CDS	Council for the Development of Sport
CLRAE	Congress of Local and Regional Authorities of Europe
CM	Committee of Ministers
CO-DBP	Council of Europe in the field of biological and landscape diversity
COE	Council of Europe
CONI	Comitato Olimpico Nazionale Italiano
CwC	Compliance with Commitments
D.C.O.	Doping Control Officer
DCF	Doping Control Form
DG IV	Council of Europe's Directorate of Youth and Sport
DS-DO	Group on the European Anti-Doping Charter for Sport
EC	European Community
ECRI	European Commission against Racism and Intolerance
EEA	European Economic Area
EFPM	European Fair Play Movement
ENGSO	European Non Governmental Sports Organisation
ENs	European Standards
EOC	European Olympic Committees
ESC	European Sports Charter
ETS	European Treaty Series
EWS	European Women and Sport
EYES	European Year of Education through Sport
FA	National Football association
FESU	European Forum for Urban Security
FIFA	International Federation of Football Associations
GAISF	General Association of International Sports Federations
GLP	Good Laboratory Practice
GO	Governmental organisation
GR-C	Group on Education, Culture, Sport, Youth and Environment
GRECO	Council of Europe Group of States against Corruption
IAAF	International Amateur Athletic Federation
IF	International Federation
IMSC	International Military Sports Council
INOCSA	Interim National Olympic Committee of South Africa
IOC	International Olympic Committee
ISDC	International Standard for Doping Control
ISO	International Organisation for Standard
MINEPS III	Third International Conference of Ministers and Senior Officials responsible for Physical Education and Sport
NGO	Non-governmental organisation
NOC	National Olympic Committee

OECD	Organisation for Economic Co-operation and Development
PAS	Publicly Available Specification
Rec	Recommendation
T-DO	Monitoring Group of the Anti-Doping Convention
T-RV	Standing Committee of the European Convention on Spectator Violence
TREVI	European Community group of law enforcement ministers and officials
UEFA	Union des Associations Européennes de Football
UNEP	United Nations Environment Programme
UNESCO	United Nations Educational, Scientific and Cultural Organization
VAT	Value Added Tax
WADA	World Anti-Doping Agency
WFSGI	World Federation of the Sporting Goods Industry
WHO	World Health Organisation

THE COUNCIL OF EUROPE AND SPORT: AN INTRODUCTION*

by Stanislas Frossard**

1. Introduction

If a European Sports model exists, the Council of Europe is unquestionably the body that has made the most substantial contribution to pave its way. The Council of Europe was the first international intergovernmental organisation to take initiatives, to establish legal instruments, and to offer an institutional framework for the development of sport at European level.

The Council of Europe was the first international organisation established in Europe after the Second World War. With 46 Member States, the Council of Europe currently represents the image of a 'wider Europe'. The main objective of the Council of Europe is to strengthen democracy, human rights and the rule of law.

The extensive work of the Council of Europe on sport is evident through the main texts on sport, such as the European Sports Charter and the Code of Sports Ethics, the European Convention on Spectator Violence and the Anti-Doping Convention.

The Sports Charter and the Code of Sports Ethics strive to support national sport policies and to promote sport for all as a means of improving the quality of life, of facilitating social integration and of contributing to social cohesion, particularly among young people. With respect to these core values of the Council of Europe, this kind of action contributes to the dissemination and the promotion of the core values in the whole of society, *through* sport.

The Conventions on violence and doping attempt to counter certain negative aspects of sport and contribute to enforcing the Council of Europe's core values *in* sport.

Sport is a cultural, social and economic phenomenon of unparalleled importance, and it is, therefore, natural that the Council of Europe should give it considerable attention. The first stage of the Council of Europe's work in this field was marked by the adoption of the Committee of Ministers' Resolution on Doping of Athletes in 1967.

The European Cultural Convention (1954) provided the basis for international co-operation in the field of education, culture, European heritage, sport and youth

---

* The text is an updated and elaborated version of *Council of Europe's Work on Sport* by Mesut Özyavuz, formerly, Deputy Head, Sports Department, Council of Europe, in: *The International Sports Law Journal* (ISLJ) 2003/3 pp. 25-27.

** Sport Department, Directorate of Youth and Sport, Council of Europe.

activities. Sport co-operation within the Council of Europe is organised in partnership with national governmental and non-governmental bodies in the framework of the *Committee for the Development of Sport (CDDS)*, which was established in 1977 and in force until 2005. The CDDS used to meet annually in Strasbourg to adopt its programme and discuss current topical questions in sport. Bringing together all the 49 States Parties to the European Cultural Convention, the CDDS established and managed a pan-European work programme, and prepared the *Conferences of European Ministers responsible for Sport*. These conferences, which meet on average every other year, give political guidelines for the direction of future co-operation in the field of sport.

In 2005, the Committee of Ministers of the Council of Europe decided to renew the framework of co-operation for sport within the Council of Europe and to consider the creation of a partial agreement on sport to succeed the CDDS. A feasibility study was prepared in 2006 on various factors and the 17th Informal Meeting of Sports Ministers in Moscow in October 2006 decided that partial agreement would be the only possible way to continue and to deepen the work of the CDDS, and to give a new perspective to the pan-European sport co-operation within the Council of Europe. Partial agreement will allow all interested States to join, but all States party to the European Cultural Convention will continue to take part in ministerial conferences. Partial agreement will also provide a framework for an enhanced co-operation with international sport organisations, in order to address issues related to the good governance of sport in Europe.

2. General Instruments and Themes

On 24 September 1976, *the European Sport for All Charter* was adopted by European States. From this date, sports policies in Europe had a common programme based on the fundamental belief of the role of the Council of Europe in the values of sport.

The European Sports Charter, adopted as a recommendation of the Committee of Ministers of the Council of Europe in 1992 (revised in 2001), provides the framework for sports policy to which all European countries have put their names. It is a reference for public authorities and sports organisations alike.

In adopting the Charter, governments have made a commitment to give their citizens, in co-operation with the sports movement, the opportunity to practise sport under well-defined conditions, set out in 13 Articles. According to the Charter, sport must be healthy, safe, fair, tolerant and fulfilling; respectful of the environment; protective of human dignity; and accessible to everybody through the widest possible co-operation and the appropriate distribution of responsibilities between governmental and non-governmental organisations. *The Code of Sports Ethics* complements the Charter, placing fair play at the centre of the intrinsic value of sport. This is aimed particularly at children and young people, directly or indirectly, in order to influence and promote their experience and knowledge of sport, and at governments, sports organisations and individuals such as parents, teachers, coaches, umpires, doctors, journalists and top sports people, who often serve as role models.

The role that sport can play in strengthening *social cohesion* is another area where the Council of Europe – supported by the Committee of Ministers' adoption of a Recommendation (No. R(99)9) on the role of sport in furthering social cohesion) – contributes to the democratisation process, particularly among young people. Considerable emphasis has been put on providing sports programmes for minority groups, such as migrants, refugees, the unemployed, prisoners and young delinquents, and people with disabilities. The programmes are either implemented in close co-operation with central, regional or local government or entrusted to the voluntary sports sector in the countries concerned. Social cohesion through sport has a significant and very important role to play in the reconstruction and reconciliation process in regions of conflict.

As all children have *Physical Education* as a compulsory subject at school, it is a vital part of a child's learning process and also the way that many children are introduced to sport and games and other physical activities. Not surprisingly, therefore, the Conference of European Ministers responsible for Sport and the Committee for the Development of Sport (CDDS), are continuously interested in this topic and wish to take steps to improve the opportunities for Physical Education, the quality of teaching and the experiences dispensed during the classes. This includes giving children with disabilities equal opportunities for physical education during their school time.

At the 16th Informal Meeting of Sports Ministers in Warsaw in September 2002, on the basis of a European survey commissioned by the CDDS, there was an intensive and in-depth discussion of measures that could be taken at European level, as well as national steps, to achieve the goals of improving opportunities and the quality of physical education. These measures resulted in the adoption by the Committee of Ministers of Recommendation No. R(2003)6.

Aware of the primary importance of *sports legislation* to ensure democratic principles and accountability, and equal access to sports facilities and activities, the CDDS elaborated and put in place numerous legal instruments (resolutions, recommendations and conventions) to help governments and national sports organisations to establish democratic sports laws and rules.

The Council of Europe and the CDDS are conscious that democratising global sport is one of the main challenges to be faced in the coming years and for this reason this issue was discussed on the agenda of the Ministerial Conference on modernising sports governance, which took place in 2004. These deliberations facilitated the preparation of Recommendation No. R(2005)8 of the Committee of Ministers to Member States on the principles of good governance in sport, which was adopted in 2005.

3. Violence and Racism

The Council of Europe fights to control the negative aspects of sport, in particular, *violence* and *doping*, through two sports Conventions: binding legal instruments which, in the case of doping, operate equally outside the boundaries of Europe.

Although particularly acute today, the problem of *violence* has been a matter of concern to sports officials for a very long time. As early as 1983, the Council of Europe expressed its determination to take action against the increase in violence – both on and off the sports field. It was in this year that the Parliamentary Assembly adopted its recommendation on cultural and educational methods of reducing violence.

The Heysel disaster gave added urgency to the Council of Europe's work in this field. Shortly afterwards, Member States set out to find the best means of combating violence and developing international co-operation. The events at Heysel required an urgent response; and it was in this dramatic context that the *European Convention on Spectator Violence and Misbehaviour at Sports Events and, in particular, at Football Matches* was signed in Strasbourg on 19 August 1985. Some 41 States have now ratified this Convention.

This Convention provides governments with measures and remedies for the control, prevention and, where necessary, punishment of violence, as well as educational measures to prevent outbreaks of violence. The Standing Committee monitors compliance with set measures and issues practical recommendations. Among the principal measures recommended by the Convention, notably under Article 4, are:

- deploying public order resources in stadia and along the transit routes used by spectators;
- separating rival groups of supporters;
- strictly controlling ticket sales;
- excluding trouble-makers from stadia and matches;
- prohibiting the introduction and restricting the sale of alcoholic drinks in stadia;
- conducting security checks, particularly for objects likely to be used for violence;
- clearly defining responsibilities between organisers and the public authorities; and
- designing football stadia in such a way as to guarantee spectator safety.

In addition to the Convention, numerous Recommendations have been adopted by the Standing Committee, covering the following aspects:

- ticket sales (efficient management of ticket production, sale and distribution of tickets, key factors for overall football match safety);
- identification and treatment of offenders;
- stewarding (reducing police numbers in football stadia);

- efficient crowd management inside stadia, taking account of spectator safety and security (clear definition of responsibilities, appropriate stadia design, measures concerning the sale of alcoholic drinks, and so on);
- action against racism and xenophobia;
- police co-operation and information exchange; and
- social and educational measures to prevent violence in sport.

The Convention on spectator violence encourages close international co-operation among States and close co-operation among the relevant national sports authorities.

The Standing Committee is the body responsible for monitoring the implementation of the Convention. UEFA and FIFA are both associated with the Committee's work. During major international championships – the World Cup, European Championships, and others – the Standing Committee sets up an *ad hoc* working group to assess the security measures adopted and, after the major event in question, to draw conclusions from the implementation of such measures.

Major sports events are often marred by racist behaviour. Such behaviour must be firmly condemned; given the educational role sport has to play in promoting mutual respect, tolerance and fair play, and combating discrimination.

Following the proposal of the Standing Committee, Recommendation No. R(2001)6 of the Committee of Ministers was adopted on the prevention of racism, xenophobia and racial intolerance in sport. It urges governments of Member States to adopt effective policies and measures aimed at preventing and combating racist, xenophobic, discriminatory and intolerant behaviour in all sports, particularly in football.

In January 2003, the Standing Committee of the Convention adopted Recommendation No. R(2003)1 on the role of social and educational measures in preventing violence in sport. Drawing on the experience of recent major championship events, it recommends adopting measures to improve the welcoming and coaching of supporters. Fan coaching activities and projects, fan embassies, and fan coaches are the cornerstones of the recommended prevention policies.

Long-term activities are also recommended, including encouraging football clubs to broaden co-operation with fans and supporters' clubs and to acknowledge the role of the latter in their social environment. Finally, local authorities are encouraged to play a major role in developing youth projects for preventing violence.

A Round Table on sport, tolerance and fair play was organised in 1996. As part of the follow-up to this event, many European States have appointed national ambassadors for sport, tolerance and fair play. To date, 22 States have appointed such ambassadors, who are persons who are known and respected by their fellow citizens. Their role is to promote fair play in sport in their respective countries and implement programmes to encourage tolerance in sport, in order to guide and inspire national programmes encouraging all citizens to practice sport fairly and with respect for the other players.

4. Doping

Doping is not only contrary to the values of sport and the principles for which it stands, such as fair play, equal chances, fair competition and healthy activity, but it also endangers the health and life of athletes.

Doping in sport is not a new phenomenon, but it has grown, expanded geographically and become more visible in recent years. It is a genuine problem for many competitive sports and jeopardises the health of millions of young athletes across the world.

The Council of Europe realises the extent of this problem and continues to fight against it. The Anti-Doping Convention which opened for signature on 16 November 1989 in Strasbourg and entered into force on 1 March 1990, demonstrates this commitment. It expresses the contracting parties' political will to combat doping in sport in an active and co-ordinated manner. To date, the Convention has been ratified by 49 countries.

The main objective of the Convention is to promote the harmonisation, at national and international levels, of the measures to be taken against doping. The Convention does not claim to create a uniform model for anti-doping, but sets a certain number of common standards and regulations requiring that the parties adopt legislative, financial, technical, educational and other measures.

The spirit of the Convention derives from the political desire to help safeguard the ethics of sport and to preserve the integrity of 'clean' sport.

By adopting the principles and objectives of the Convention, the contracting parties undertake, in their respective constitutional provisions, to put into place a national anti-doping policy to:

- create a national co-ordinating body;
- reduce the trafficking of doping substances and the use of banned doping agents;
- reinforce doping controls and improve detection techniques;
- support education and information programmes;
- guarantee the efficiency of sanctions taken against offenders;
- collaborate with sports organisations as well as at international level; and
- use accredited anti-doping laboratories.

An additional Protocol to the Convention, concerning the mutual recognition of anti-doping controls, was opened for signature in September 2002 and has been ratified by 21 States and signed by 11 States to date.

A project on monitoring compliance with commitments started in 1998. It studies Member States' implementation of the Convention. Advisory visits are organised to help the countries put in place the policies and programmes necessary to carry out the requirements laid down in the basic texts. Evaluation visits are organised and the resulting evaluation reports are published.

Furthermore, each party must complete a detailed annual questionnaire on their national anti-doping policy.

The recently adopted (2002) Protocol to the Anti-Doping Convention includes an article which makes it an obligation for parties to be available for evaluation, thus making it one of the few international conventions with a stringent control system.

The Anti-Doping Convention was the first international legal reference instrument in the fight against doping. It is open to all countries. The body responsible for monitoring the implementation of the convention is the Monitoring Group. Other bodies, for example, UNESCO, the World Anti-Doping Agency (WADA), the International Olympic Committee (IOC) and international sports federations, are involved in its work. Several other non-European countries regularly participate as 'observers' in the activities of the Monitoring Group of the Convention, including China, Japan, New Zealand, South Africa and the United States.

Following the Lausanne Conference on Doping in Sport in February 1999, a new body was established in November 1999 in the fight against doping: the World Anti-Doping Agency (WADA). The Council of Europe played an active role in the creation of this agency, which is the first joint venture between the sports movement and the public authorities in this field, and its expertise contributes substantially to the work of the WADA, in particular, for the elaboration of the World Anti-Doping Code and its standards. Since WADA was established, the Council of Europe set up a co-ordination body (the *ad hoc* Committee European Coordination Forum for WADA) to co-ordinate the European governmental position within the governing bodies of WADA.

The UNESCO Round Table of Sports Ministers decided in January 2003 (which decision was confirmed by the UNESCO Executive Committee in April 2003) that the Council of Europe's Anti-Doping Convention will serve as the basis for the future global instrument against doping, which will be prepared for the next MINEPS IV Conference (Sports Ministers Conference of UNESCO), to take place just before the Athens Olympic Games in 2004 and to be adopted, if possible, before the Winter Olympic Games in 2006. Indeed, the General Conference of the UNESCO adopted the International Convention against doping in sport in October 2005, and this Convention is expected to enter into force at the beginning of 2007. The Monitoring Group of the Anti-Doping Convention intends to co-operate with the UNESCO Convention, supporting the development of the monitoring system and drawing the attention of the UNESCO Conference of Parties to issues of relevance that will have been identified and discussed within the Monitoring Group.

5. Conclusion

The European Sports Charter and the Conventions are permanent constituents of the Council of Europe's sports programme.

Thus, many different subjects have been treated over the years. Once these programmes are finalised the Committee passes the responsibility to the Member States to follow up the work at national level. Examples of areas – other than those mentioned above – where the Council of Europe is involved are:

- sport and physical education for children and young people;
- sports facilities;
- the promotion of sport;
- sport policy, management and economy;
- the economic impact of sport; and
- sport and the environment.

To conclude, the Council of Europe is aware that sport has a distinctive role to play as a force for social integration and co-operation. It is open to all, regardless of age, language, religion, culture or ability. It is the single most popular activity in modern society. Sport provides the opportunity to learn to play by commonly agreed rules, to behave admirably both in victory and in defeat and to develop, not only the physical being, but also social competences and ethical values. Its potential for improving health, but also in education is increasingly acknowledged.

The Council of Europe continues to play an active role in European sports affairs to establish international standards for States Parties to the European Cultural Convention, to help public authorities, in co-operation with national sports organisations, to promote and develop sport that is open to all, without discrimination, and run in a healthy, safe and ethical environment.

Chapter 1
APARTHEID

1.1. Resolution in relation to Apartheid (84/9)

The European Ministers responsible for Sport, meeting in Malta for their 4th Conference from 15 to 16 May 1984

Invite the Committee of Ministers of the Council of Europe to ensure that there are exchanges of information on national policies with regard to all discriminatory practices in sport, including apartheid.

1.2. Written Declaration No. 108 (1984) on Sport in South Africa

The undersigned members of the Assembly,

1. Reaffirming their belief in the importance of individual human rights in all fields of human activity, including sport;
2. Drawing attention to the fact that full autonomy was given by the south African Government in 1976 to all sports federations in that country and to the National South African Olympic Committee;
3. Noting that, since that date, racial integration has become a general feature of sport in South Africa and of South African teams seeking to compete internationally;
4. Regretting the lack of recognition of this progress by many countries in the world, including member countries of the Council of Europe, and the continuing refusal of the International Olympic Committee to allow South Africa to compete in the Olympic Games;
5. Gravely concerned that the first to suffer from such an attitude on the international level are the blacks, coloured and Indians in South Africa and that the first to gain are those interested in maintaining apartheid in that country;
6. Wishing to prevent a reactionary backlash in South Africa that might undermine the 1976 decision on the autonomy of sport and the progress being made towards political freedom in other fields;
7. Call on member states of the Council of Europe and in particular on the Conference of European Ministers responsible for Sport to take a lead in recognising the independence of sport in South Africa and its freedom from racial discrimination; and to press for the admission of South African athletes, regardless of their colour, to international sport;
8. Resolve nevertheless to continue to press for the further reduction of apartheid and other forms of racial discrimination in South Africa.

1.3. Resolution on Apartheid in Sport (86/9)

The European Ministers responsible for Sport, meeting in Dublin for their 5th Conference from 30 September to 2 October 1986

Considering the principles of human rights and fundamental freedoms laid down in the European Convention on Human Rights;
Gravely concerned that the policies and practices of apartheid in South Africa which are universally condemned invariably have an impact upon sports and infringe those rights and freedoms;
Recalling their previous statements condemning all discriminatory practices in sport, and in particular apartheid;
Reaffirming their unqualified support for the Olympic principle that no discrimination be allowed on the grounds of race, religion or political affiliation and their belief that merit and interest should be the sole criteria for participation in sports activities;
Welcoming the decisions of the IOC and of most international sports federations to exclude South Africa from all international sports activities;
Recognising that participation in apartheid sports activities condones and strengthens apartheid;
Aware of the efforts of some sportsmen inside South Africa to eradicate apartheid through peaceful means;
Believing that sports federations can play a positive role;

1. Strongly condemn apartheid practices in sports in South Africa;
2. Resolve to take all possible action to encourage those sports federations which have not yet done so to break all sports links with South Africa and exchange information regularly on the progress towards this goal;
3. Agree not to provide financial or other assistance to enable sports bodies, teams or individuals to participate in sports activities in South Africa;
4. Invite the Committee of Ministers of the Council of Europe to ask the CDDS, in the period up to the 6th Conference, to consider what steps could be taken in the future to further the objective of eradicating apartheid in sports, in co-ordination with other initiatives which might be taken by the Council of Europe on the subject of apartheid.

1.4. Resolution on Apartheid in Sport (89/5)

The European Ministers responsible for Sport, meeting at Reykjavik for their 6th Conference from 30 May to 1 June 1989

Recalling their previous statements and resolutions condemning all discriminatory practices in sport, and in particular apartheid;
Noting the report prepared by the CDDS submitted to the Conference;
Noting the declaration of the International Olympic Committee against apartheid in sport adopted on 21 June 1988;
Noting also Section 13 of Recommendation N° 4 unanimously adopted by the 2nd International Conference of Ministers and senior officials responsible for sport and physical education of Unesco on 25 November 1988, which strongly condemned "the practice of apartheid and all other forms of discrimination in sport and urged member states of Unesco and sports federations:

1. to make every effort to ensure that the principles formulated by the United Nations condemning apartheid are respected in physical education and sport;
2. to take all possible measures to discourage their nationals from taking part in sports contests organised by countries practising a policy of apartheid and in sports contacts with individuals and teams representing those countries, (for example by withholding financial aid, visas, etc.);

3. to step up their support to the victims of apartheid in physical education and sport inside and outside South Africa;"

Reaffirming that the participation in sports events by representatives from countries practising apartheid and other discriminatory practices in sport condones and strengthens such discriminatory practices;

Concerned by the fact that many national and international sports bodies have continued sports contacts with countries practising apartheid and other discriminatory practices in sport,

Undertake to forward the text of this resolution to sports organisations in their countries and to confirm their request to the Committee of Ministers of the Council of Europe that the CDDS should produce information periodically on progress with regard to this issue.

Chapter 2
BOXING

2.1. Recommendation No. 1047 (1986) on the Dangers of Boxing

The Assembly,
Recalling its Recommendation No. 963 (1983), on cultural and educational means of reducing violence, and the European Convention on Spectator Violence and Misbehaviour at Sports Events and in particular Football Matches;
Determined to draw a distinction between sport and legitimised gladiatorial violence, and therefore gravely concerned at the justification of many of the aspects of boxing (and especially professional boxing) as a sport in modern, civilised society;
Drawing attention to the immediate and long-term effects of boxing, in particular on the mental health of boxers, and to the adverse social consequences with regard to the spectators;
Supporting the recommendations made, for example by the World Medical Association, the British Medical Association and the American Medical Association, for stricter measures in the current practice of the sport in order to protect boxers;
Insisting on the need for world-wide co-operation of governments, the independent boxing associations and other national and international sporting bodies, including the International Olympic Committee, for ensuring the implementation of these recommendations in both amateur and professional boxing;
Drawing a distinction between commercial and non-commercial aspects of boxing;
Deploring the promotion of boxing for commercial gain (as, for example, indicated by the proliferation of international boxing bodies) and the unscrupulous advantage often taken of potential boxers from poorer social backgrounds;
Believing, that governments and the mass media have a duty to inform the public of the potential harmful effects of boxing, both as a sport and as an entertainment, and of the dangers it poses to society and human life, and that national parliaments have a special responsibility in this context;
Welcoming the fact that most amateur boxing associations and several member states have already imposed restrictions on boxing;
Recommends that the Committee of Ministers initiate through the Steering Committee for the Development of Sport a full inquiry, on a European level and in association with the boxing federations, medical bodies and other appropriate organisations, into the direct and indirect effects of boxing, and that this inquiry be charged, within a specified deadline, with making concrete proposals for such medical, technical, fiscal and other changes as would bring about:

1. increased and improved education about the medical and social risks of boxing in general;
2. increased safety (perhaps, for example, through the introduction of compulsory regular brain scans);
3. decreased risks (perhaps, for example, through automatic bans on boxers with any brain abnormalities);
4. restraints on the commercial aspects of boxing and on media coverage.

Reply by the Committee of Ministers:

The Committee of Ministers has examined Assembly Recommendation No. 1047 on the dangers of boxing.

1. It shares the Assembly's concerns on this subject, while noting that this is a controversial issue.
2. It recalls that several national studies on boxing have already been carried out outside the Council of Europe and that in the framework of the "Sport for all: sporting injuries and their prevention" project, case studies are being carried out, some of them related to boxing.
3. That being the case, it thinks it suitable to await the results of the above-mentioned project before considering the suitability of carrying out a full study on boxing.
4. It has transmitted Recommendation No. 1047 (1986) to the Steering Committee for the Development of Sport so that it may be taken into account in the preparation of the final conclusions and recommendations of the current project.

Chapter 3
CHILDREN AND YOUNG PEOPLE

3.1. European Manifesto on Young People and Sport
Adopted by the Ministers' Deputies on 12 October 1995

Article 1 – Aim

1. The aim of this Manifesto is to foster policies that encourage young people to develop positive attitudes towards participation in sport and physical activity in accordance with the European Sports Charter and the European Code of Ethics, and thus lay the foundation for their lifelong practice.
2. Society as a whole in co-operation with all partners concerned has a duty to provide young people with the opportunities for the achievement of this aim. To this end:
    a. Public authorities, together with the sports organisations concerned, are responsible for providing the necessary leadership in the development and promotion of a sports policy for young people;
    b. Public authorities at all levels have a responsibility to contribute to the range of opportunities through appropriate legislative or regulatory frameworks, financial support, the provision of facilities and any other appropriate measure.

Article 2 – Definitions

1. The European Sports Charter defines sport as "all forms of physical activity which, through casual or organised participation, aim at expressing or improving physical fitness and mental well-being and forming social relationships, or obtaining results in competition at all levels".
2. The notion of sport in this Manifesto is based on the ideals of humanism and tolerance which characterise the Council of Europe. For young people, physical activity is a natural form of movement involving challenge and enjoyment based on play. For the purpose of this Manifesto, the term young people covers all individuals considered as minors under the national legislation of each member State of the Council of Europe.

Article 3 – Scope

1. Sport in all its forms shall be accessible to all young people without any discrimination, offering both girls and boys equal opportunities, and taking account of any special requirements at different ages or of groups with special needs.
2. Participation in sport should aim in particular at:
    a. Developing mental, physical and social qualities;
    b. Understanding ethical values and fair-play, discipline and rules;
    c. Respecting oneself and others, including minority groups;
    d. Learning tolerance and responsibility, for instance organisational, as prerequisites for life in a democratic society;
    e. Learning self-control, gaining self-esteem and developing self-achievement;
    f. Acquiring healthy life-styles.
3. The overall well-being of the young person comes before any other consideration (such as performance, prestige, commercial exploitation); while each should be helped to reach his or her potential safely, the roles of training and competition should be kept in due proportion.

Article 4 – The foundation: families and schools

1. The home and family are the first unit of socialisation for children and have a unique role to play in encouraging them to develop an active and healthy life-style.
2. The school has the vital task of providing sound physical activity and sport so as to ensure a healthy balance between physical and intellectual activities. Sport can make a contribution to the quality of school life in general.
   a. All young people should be able to receive physical education and acquire basic skills in sport and thus be encouraged, either within or outside the curriculum, to engage in sport or daily physical activity.
   b. Schools should provide a safe and healthy environment for physical exercise and sport.
   c. Schools should try to respond to acceptable new trends in sport when they have educational value and offer young people a wide range of possible outlets.

Article 5 – Towards lifelong involvement

1. To ensure a progression into a lifelong involvement in physical activity and sport, the assistance of other partners is necessary and public authorities should encourage the creation of such partnerships.
2. Sports clubs and sports organisations including school sport associations play a vital role in providing opportunities for young people to improve their levels of performance through training and competitive events and in promoting and facilitating lifelong participation.
3. Other voluntary or community organisations provide a further important means of attracting the interest of young people towards sport.
4. Commercial organisations can also provide additional opportunities for young people to try a wide range of activities, thereby complementing those outlets provided by the statutory and voluntary sectors.

Article 6 – Programmes

1. Appropriate and well-balanced programmes should be made available to provide opportunities for all young people to become involved in sport and physical activity. Programmes should aim at combining physiological and mental development with the acquisition of skills and values.
2. The range of programmes should reflect the needs and encourage the potential of all young people at various stages of growth and development and reflect their differing abilities.
3. Programmes should provide opportunities for exchanges between young people through sport.

Article 7 – Leadership

1. All sports activities, inside or outside schools, should be led and directed by qualified and proficient leaders, teachers and coaches, whether they are working on a voluntary or professional basis. These, as well as the managers of sport facilities should be aware of their responsibilities and of the specific needs of young people.
2. Leaders should treat young people with respect, transmit them a message of tolerance and fairness, involve them in decision-making processes in respect of the organisation of their sports activities and encourage them to gain experience in leadership roles.
3. The competent authorities should take appropriate steps to ensure that these teachers, coaches, leaders and managers receive regular in-service training in addition to their initial training.

Article 8 – Facilities and equipment

1. All schools should have the necessary and appropriate facilities and equipment for the practice of physical activities and sport.
2. Reciprocal and co-ordinated use of school and community facilities both indoor and outdoor should be promoted, with a view to maximising the use of public funds and facilitating contacts.
3. Use of and access to natural spaces and outdoor facilities, in both urban and rural areas, should be encouraged along with respect for the environment, to ensure sustainable use of such natural resources.
4. All young people should be able to have easy access to facilities and these should be suitable for use by those with disabilities or other special needs.
5. Planners, designers and managers of sport facilities should receive professional training and/or qualifications to enable them to respond to the needs and demands of young people.

Article 9 – Resources

Governments should ensure that appropriate support and resources are made available from public funds and encourage involvement by the other partners for the attainment of the aims and purposes of this Manifesto.

3.2. Recommendation No. R (95) 16 of the Committee of Ministers to Member States on Young People and Sport

Adopted by the Committee of Ministers on 12 October 1995 at the 545th meeting of the Ministers' Deputies

The Committee of Ministers, in application of Article 15b of the Statute of the Council of Europe,

Recalling the 1989 United Nation's Convention on the Rights of the Child, and referring to Articles 28 and 29, and in particular Article 31, which provides among other things that states parties recognise "the right of the child ... to engage in play and recreational activities appropriate to the age of the child" and encourage "the provision of appropriate and equal opportunities for ... recreational ... activity";

Referring to the European Sports Charter, and in particular to its Article 5, Building the Foundation, as well as to the Code of Sports Ethics which give specific guidance on how to conduct physical activities and sports with young people, and which were adopted by the Committee of Ministers as Recommendations No. R (92) 13 and No. R (92) 14;

Considering the importance of the development and balanced training of physical, intellectual, artistic and moral faculties for any person;

Stressing the contribution which education through sport can make to the fulfilment of the aims of the Vienna Declaration, to social integration, and to health improvement, to the building of character, to the understanding of ethics, to respect for the environment, and to cultural tolerance and international exchanges;

Recalling Committee of Ministers' Resolution (72) 30 on the Hygiene of Sports Installations and Recommendation No. R (87) 9 on the Eurofit tests of physical fitness for young people of school age;

Considering that the proper provision by society of opportunities for all young people to take part in physical activities can not only encourage a constructive use of leisure time, but can also help fight some of society's problems such as intolerance, aimlessness, violence, alcohol abuse, illicit drug use, etc.;

Concerned that the time allotted to physical education or other physical activities in general in the school system is often insufficient to enable the children to benefit, either for their physical development or their mental equilibrium, from the educational programmes that are provided, and that young people who are not involved in sport or physical activities have low levels of physical fitness;
Determined therefore to encourage in their own countries the building of new partnerships to enable young people to learn, create and express themselves through physical activities and sport;
Recalling the work done by other European organisations on youth and sport and acknowledging the unique and irreplaceable contribution of non-governmental sports organisations to providing opportunities for the practice of sport;
Having regard to the Resolution on the European Manifesto on Young People and Sport adopted at the 8th Conference of European Ministers responsible for Sport (Lisbon, 17-18 May 1995);
Anxious to follow up the principles set out in the above-mentioned resolution,
Recommends that the governments of member states draw inspiration from the principles and ideas set out in the manifesto appended to the present recommendation when framing and implementing policies and activities in the area of youth and sport in their respective countries.

Appendix to Recommendation No. R (95) 16
European Manifesto on Young People and Sport
Article 1 – Aim

1. The aim of this manifesto is to foster policies that encourage young people to develop positive attitudes towards participation in sport and physical activity in accordance with the European Sports Charter and the European Code of Ethics, and thus lay the foundation for their lifelong practice.
2. Society as a whole, in co-operation with all partners concerned, has a duty to provide young people with opportunities for the achievement of this aim. To this end:
   - 2.1. public authorities, together with the sports organisations concerned, are responsible for providing the necessary leadership in the development and promotion of a sports policy for young people;
   - 2.2. public authorities at all levels have a responsibility to contribute to the range of opportunities through appropriate legislative or regulatory frameworks, financial support, the provision of facilities and any other appropriate measure.

Article 2 – Definitions

1. The European Sports Charter defines sport as “all forms of physical activity which, through casual or organised participation, aim at expressing or improving physical fitness and mental well-being and forming social relationships, or obtaining results in competition at all levels”.
2. The notion of sport in this manifesto is based on the ideals of humanism and tolerance which characterise the Council of Europe. For young people, physical activity is a natural form of movement involving challenge and enjoyment based on play. For the purpose of this manifesto, the term “young people” covers all individuals considered as minors under the national legislation of each member state of the Council of Europe.

Article 3 – Scope

1. Sport in all its forms shall be accessible to all young people without any discrimination, offering both girls and boys equal opportunities, and taking account of any special requirements at different ages or of groups with special needs.

2. Participation in sport should aim in particular at:
   2.1. developing mental, physical and social qualities;
   2.2. understanding ethical values and fair-play, discipline and rules;
   2.3. respecting oneself and others, including minority groups;
   2.4. learning tolerance and responsibility (for instance by taking on organisational responsibilities, as prerequisites for life in a democratic society;
   2.5. learning self-control, gaining self-esteem and developing self-achievement;
   2.6. acquiring healthy lifestyles.
3. The overall well-being of the young person comes before any other consideration (such as performance, prestige, commercial exploitation); while each should be helped to reach his or her potential safely, the roles of training and competition should be kept in due proportion.

Article 4 – The foundation: families and schools
1. The home and family are the first unit of socialisation for children and have a unique role to play in encouraging them to develop an active and healthy lifestyle.
2. The school has the vital task of providing sound physical activity and sport so as to ensure a healthy balance between physical and intellectual activities. Sport can make a contribution to the quality of school life in general.
   2.1. All young people should be able to receive physical education and acquire basic skills in sport and thus be encouraged, either within or outside the curriculum, to engage in sport or daily physical activity.
   2.2. Schools should provide a safe and healthy environment for physical exercise and sport.
   2.3. Schools should try to respond to acceptable new trends in sport when they have educational value and offer young people a wide range of possible outlets.

Article 5 – Towards lifelong involvement
1. To ensure a progression into a lifelong involvement in physical activity and sport, the assistance of other partners is necessary and public authorities should encourage the creation of such partnerships.
2. Sports clubs and sports organisations including school sport associations play a vital role in providing opportunities for young people to improve their levels of performance through training and competitive events and in promoting and facilitating lifelong participation.
3. Other voluntary or community organisations provide a further important means of attracting the interest of young people towards sport.
4. Commercial organisations can also provide additional opportunities for young people to try a wide range of activities, thereby complementing those outlets provided by the statutory and voluntary sectors.

Article 6 – Programmes
1. Appropriate and well-balanced programmes should be made available to provide opportunities for all young people to become involved in sport and physical activity. Programmes should aim at combining physiological and mental development with the acquisition of skills and values.
2. The range of programmes should reflect the needs and encourage the potential of all young people at various stages of growth and development and reflect their differing abilities.

3. Programmes should provide opportunities for exchanges between young people through sport.

Article 7 – Leadership

1. All sports activities, inside or outside schools, should be led and directed by qualified and proficient leaders, teachers and coaches, whether they are working on a voluntary or professional basis. These, as well as the managers of sport facilities, should be aware of their responsibilities and of the specific needs of young people.
2. Leaders should treat young people with respect, transmit to them a message of tolerance and fairness, involve them in decision-making processes in respect of the organisation of their sports activities and encourage them to gain experience in leadership roles.
3. The competent authorities should take appropriate steps to ensure that these teachers, coaches, leaders and managers receive regular in-service training in addition to their initial training.

Article 8 – Facilities and equipment

1. All schools should have the necessary and appropriate facilities and equipment for the practice of physical activities and sport.
2. Reciprocal and co-ordinated use of school and community facilities both indoor and outdoor should be promoted, with a view to maximising the use of public funds and facilitating contacts.
3. Use of and access to natural spaces and outdoor facilities, in both urban and rural areas, should be encouraged along with respect for the environment, to ensure sustainable use of such natural resources.
4. All young people should be able to have easy access to facilities and these should be suitable for use by those with disabilities or other special needs.
5. Planners, designers and managers of sport facilities should receive professional training and/or qualifications to enable them to respond to the needs and demands of young people.

Article 9 – Resources

Governments should ensure that appropriate support and resources are made available from public funds and encourage involvement by the other partners for the attainment of the aims and purposes of this manifesto.

3.3. Resolution on the European Manifesto on Young People and Sport (95/1)

Adopted by the Ministers' Deputies on 12 October 1995

The European Ministers responsible for Sport, meeting in Lisbon for their 8th Conference from 17 to 18 May 1995,

Recalling the Resolutions adopted at their previous Conferences on the theme of young people and sport;

Considering that while young people have a natural propensity for movement and physical activities, the change towards a sedentary life-style all over Europe, is reducing the time spent on such movement and activities;

Believing that balanced physical, intellectual and artistic development and education is basic and important for everybody;

Stressing the contribution which education through sport can make to the fulfilment of the aims of the Vienna Declaration, to social integration, and to health improvement, to character development, to the understanding of ethics, to respect for the environment, and to tolerance and international understanding;
Recalling Committee of Ministers' Resolution (72) 30 on the Hygiene of Sports Installations and Recommendation N° R (87) 9 on the Eurofit tests of physical fitness for young people of school age;
Considering that the proper provision, by society as a whole, of opportunities for all young people to take part in physical activities can not only lead to a constructive use of leisure time, but can also help alleviate some of society's problems such as intolerance, aimlessness, aggressiveness, alcohol and other substance abuse, etc.;
Concerned that the time allotted to physical education or other physical activities in many schools is often insufficient to enable the child to benefit from the educational programmes that are provided, and that young people who are not involved in sport or physical activities have low levels of physical fitness;
Determined therefore to encourage in their own countries the building of new partnerships to enable young people to learn, create and express themselves through physical activities and sport;
Recalling the 1989 United Nation's Convention on the Rights of the Child, in particular Articles 29 and 31;
Referring to the European Sports Charter, and in particular to its Article 5, Building the Foundation, as well as to the Code of Sports Ethics which give specific guidance on how to conduct physical activities and sports with young people, and which were adopted by the Committee of Ministers as Recommendations N° R (92) 13 and N° R (92) 14;
Recalling the work done by other European organisations on youth sport and acknowledging the unique contribution of non-governmental sports organisations to providing opportunities for young people to practice sport;
Recalling its Declaration on the significance of sport for society adopted at this Conference and in particular the evidence produced on the socialising role of sport and physical activities and their influence on health;

1. Adopt the European Manifesto on Young People and Sport appended hereto as a means of complementing and extending the principles laid down in Article 5 of the European Sports Charter;
2. Agree to contribute to its wide dissemination amongst all partners concerned by it;

Invite the Committee of Ministers:

1. to consider the Manifesto with a view to its adoption as a Recommendation to member states;
2. to ask the Committee for the Development of Sport to monitor the implementation of the ideas set out in the Manifesto.

3.4. Recommendation No. 1292 (1996) of the Committee of Ministers to member states on Young People in High-level Sport

The Assembly is concerned at the involvement of young people in high-level sport at too early an age.
Sport has a primary role in the mental as well as physical development of children and young people and therefore should be an integral part of the general educational process for democratic society.

Elite sport however is aimed exclusively at top level performances, that only very few can hope to achieve, and has its own further risks:

1. physical and physiological risks (such as the overloading of the respiratory, cardiovascular and neuromuscular systems);
2. psychological risks (such as the strain caused by the "win at all costs" mentality and "dropping-out" as a result of early commitment to intense training);
3. reduced possibilities for children involved in intense training to attend normal school, especially during competition periods.

Some internationally agreed texts, either on young people or on sport, have referred to the need for protection of young people, but without formulating precise recommendations. For example the recent European Manifesto on Young People and Sport, adopted by the European Ministers responsible for Sport in May 1995, states that "the level and intensity of training and competition should be appropriate to the age and physical and mental development of the child".

Certain sports federations have shown concern at the early age at which some young people enter competition and have taken steps to raise it (for example, the International Gymnastics Federation and the Women's Tennis Association). The Assembly welcomes such moves and calls on sports federations and on the International Olympic Committee to review national and international competition systems involving young people with a view to raising minimum age-limits or, where already appropriate, enforcing them.

The Assembly sees several advantages in drawing a clearer distinction between juvenile and adult competition classes. This could be achieved by raising the age-limits for participation in certain competitions to 16 or 18 years, depending on the sport, particularly in international competitions and championships.

The Assembly also believes that legislation on the basic rights of the child should be reviewed in a number of countries in order to ensure that sport is part of the normal development of children and that young athletes are better protected from training abuse. The Assembly stresses the responsibility of parents and families in this regard.

The Assembly therefore recommends that the Committee of Ministers call on governments, in co-operation with sports clubs and federations, to:

1. make a clear policy distinction between sport for young people in general (sport for all) and elite or high-level sport;
2. encourage the drawing up of internationally agreed, gender-sensitive guidelines and appropriate minimum age-limits as regards training methods, rules and restrictions for young people in individual sports, with special attention to those sports where competition level can be reached at a very early age, for instance gymnastics, swimming and ski jumping, or to those sports known to be dangerous, such as boxing;
3. introduce, in particular, fixed minimum age-limits for participation in international competitions and championships, between 16 and 18 years, depending on the type of sports involved;
4. ensure that the most talented young athletes receive a sufficient basic education, follow reasonable training and competition schedules and have the opportunity to be children and grow up as members of society wilt the possibility of developing other skills;
5. pay closer attention to the training of coaches, in technical matters and in their wider moral responsibilities, their competence being ensured by national sports organisations and, at the local level, municipalities and sports clubs.

The Assembly also recommends that the Committee of Ministers:

1. encourage continuing research on the subject of young people in high-level sport in order to be able to assess the evolution in sport for young people, especially in some sports;

2. collect and disseminate through appropriate networks information on this and on sports structures and programmes for young people.

3.5. Recommendation Rec (2003) 6 of the Committee of Ministers to member states on improving physical education and sport for children and young people in all European countries

Adopted by the Committee of Ministers on 30 April 2003

The Committee of Ministers, under the terms of Article 15.b of the Statute of the Council of Europe,
Considering that the aim of the Council of Europe is to achieve a greater unity between its members, notably by means of common action in social and cultural matters;
Bearing in mind the conclusions of the European Ministers responsible for Sport at their 16th Informal Meeting in Warsaw on 12 and 13 September 2002 on improving physical education and sport for children and young people in all European countries;
Having taken note of the report on European sports co-operation and of Recommendation 1565 (2002) adopted by the Parliamentary Assembly, and welcoming the Assembly's support for the work of the Council of Europe in the field of sport;
Having taken due note of the conclusions of other international conferences and meetings on physical education and sport for children and young people in recent years, such as the adoption of the Declaration of Punta del Este at the 3rd Unesco Conference of Ministers and Senior Officials responsible for Physical Education and Sport in 1999 and the World Summit on Physical Education in Berlin in 1999;
Aware of the findings of recent surveys that point to a serious decline in several countries in the quality of, and the time allocated to, the teaching of physical education and sport to children and young people in schools, together with reduced opportunities to participate in recreational sport out of school;
Conscious of the importance of, and the known benefits that result from, the provision of regular and adequate physical education and sport in the school curriculum for all age groups;
Noting that lessons in physical education and sport also provide a context for teaching important values upheld by the Council of Europe, such as tolerance and fair play, experience in winning and losing, social cohesion, respect for the environment and education for democratic citizenship;
Acknowledging the importance of the role of the non-governmental sports movement in providing recreational sports activities for children and young people often organised by volunteers in their leisure time, which not only improve health and physical prowess, but also introduce children and young people to the wider community and prepare them for the responsibilities of adult life;
Approving the suggested measures for national, regional and local action plans and for the Pan-European programmes to improve the quality and quantity of sports and physical education activities offered to children and young people in all European countries as set out in the Appendix;
Bearing in mind that the European Union has designated 2004 as the European Year of Education through Sport,

Recommends that the governments of member states:

1. study ways in which the provision of physical education and sport can be improved in their countries for all children and young people, including those with disabilities;

2. investigate and consider whether, in the light of the findings of recent international surveys, there is a need at national level:
   - to redefine the role and purpose that physical education and sport should fulfil within the school curriculum;
   - to consider the need to improve the quality of physical education and sport available for children and young people in schools and ensure the necessary time, for example, three hours of physical education classes for each child each week, to achieve the goals set;
   - to promote the ideal of one hour of physical activity each day for children and young people, including both physical education and sport in the school environment and recreational sport outside of school;
   - to examine the following areas: the curriculum, the status of the subject, the financial resources available, the availability and condition of facilities, gender and disability issues;
   - to take action, in the light of their findings, to improve the motivation and status of physical education teachers in order to attract and keep young people in the profession;
   - to improve the quality of training and retraining for those teaching physical education and sport, in order to increase the number of well-trained physical education teachers in European countries and to revise and improve their training programmes where possible;
   - to introduce campaigns which strive for a more active lifestyle for children and young people, while also taking steps to improve recreational facilities and sports programmes in the community;
3. co-operate with and contribute to pan-European programmes which:
   - encourage an active lifestyle;
   - exchange information and experience in this area;
   - work towards a co-ordinated health strategy for children and young people;
   - aim to develop standard tools for measuring and monitoring health and fitness levels;
4. consider ways of implementing the measures proposed in the Appendix, possibly in the context of the European Year of Education through Sport in 2004, and examine the progress in this field at the 10th Conference of Ministers responsible for Sport in Budapest in 2004.

Instructs the Committee for the Development of Sport (CDDS) that within the context of the "Compliance with Commitments" project pertaining to the European Sports Charter, emphasis should be placed on evaluating the provision of physical education and sport for children and young people and the implementation of the conclusions of the 16th Informal Meeting of European Ministers responsible for Sport.

Appendix to Recommendation Rec(2003)6

Agreed measures for improving physical education and sport for children and young people in all European countries

I. Preface

   1. The conclusions adopted by the 16th Informal Meeting of European Ministers responsible for Sport point clearly to the need for national, regional and local Action Plans and pan-European programmes to improve the quality and quantity of physical education programmes for children and young people throughout Europe.

2. Physical education and sport hold a unique position in the educational world, firstly because they contribute to the harmonious development of body and mind and secondly because the practice of sport, as understood by Sport for All, has wide-ranging effects for the quality of adult life when school days are over. It also provides an obvious framework for educating children and young people in the importance of tolerance and fair play and in practising social cohesion.
3. The drop in physical activity and sport in a number of children and young people has been a contributory element to the rise in obesity, diabetes mellitus, and high levels of blood pressure among this group of the population. These factors have never been observed before at such an early age. Unhealthy children are already making considerable demands on national health budgets. They are, it is to be feared, destined to grow into unhealthy adults, placing an even greater strain on these budgets. Programmes and policies which include physical education and sports provision are indispensable in halting this trend.
4. Improved access to sport and physical education for children and young people to participate in sport during their school life makes it more likely that they will continue sports activities into adult life. Governments are urged to involve all the responsible sectors in formulating a list of objectives and/or a list of activities to be included in national action plans or European programmes working to improve the quality and quantity of physical education and sport, available in and out of schools.
5. The following measures are grouped around the spheres that influence the lives of children and young people and thus include home and family, school, the local community and the national policies of the member states of the CDDS.

II. Targeting the group – Children and young people

1. Policies and programmes must centre on the needs of the children and young people themselves. It has to be remembered that they are not "mini adults".
2. Consultation with young people is essential to involve them in the decision-making processes and the development of programmes. Some European countries have developed models and good practices, with extensive consultation machinery, where children and young persons play an active part in the planning and implementation of the programmes affecting them, which can serve as case studies.

III. Suggested Policies and Action

A. Within the home and family

1. Activities that can be done as a family should be actively supported. Parental support for children's activities is crucial – if only to ensure that children and young persons have access to the facilities and programmes. Parents should be encouraged to become involved in the schools and sports clubs working with their children. Parents can serve on the different governing bodies to ensure that children and young people obtain the maximum benefit from physical education and sport.
2. Marketing techniques and the different media can be used to inform parents of the importance of physical activity, so that they, in their turn, become active and serve as role models for their children and young people.

3. Parents can take steps to encourage their children to increase the amount of leisure time spent in physical activities and sport, while restricting the period spent watching television or using a personal computer.

B. Within the School

1. It is agreed that the number of hours of physical education in the curriculum should move towards a compulsory legal minimum of 180 minutes weekly, in three periods, with schools endeavouring to go beyond this minimum where this is possible. Children and young people should, however, have one hour of physical activity every day, which would include physical education and sports lessons in or out of school time, and other out-of-school exercise (for example, walking or cycling to school).
2. The concept of the school as a place that promotes heath at all levels should be developed. Physical education should be a core curriculum component, with close links to other academic subjects. The role of schools as centres for teaching a healthy lifestyle to both pupils and the wider community should be underlined and reinforced by, for example, increasing the opportunity for the use of school sports facilities outside school hours.
3. It is important to encourage schools to make it tempting for children and young people to spend their recreation time outdoors playing different games. In many schools the free access to the sports facilities during breaks and after school, under the qualified guidance of physical education teachers or trainers, has awakened the interest of children and young people in physical activity and sport.
4. The quality of physical education and sports training should be improved by promoting and providing in-service training through model training packages aimed at both physical education teachers and non-specialists. Appropriate steps to monitor performance could be introduced. Schools with a particularly good record might be encouraged to help other local schools in the area to attain similar high levels in physical education and sport.
5. Schools and local authorities should be given guidelines on how they can improve the environment around schools to encourage walking and cycling. It is important to set up local networks of "safe houses"[1] on popular walk-to-school routes, where children can go if they are in trouble from bullying, etc.
6. Establishing "safe routes and zones" for a certain distance around all schools, where walking and cycling have priority and where car travel is difficult or even impossible, would encourage children to come to school "under their own steam".
7. Schools should introduce all children and young people, especially school-leavers, to local sports clubs and facilities. Teaching personnel should help young people to find a recreational physical activity that they enjoy. Local clubs might offer several free sessions to school-leavers. Young people should know what is available locally, how they can

[1] A "safe house" is a place where a child can go if in need of protection, for example, from bullying.

continue to play sport after their school days are over and be aware of which activities they prefer and find stimulating.

C. Within the local community

1. A funding programme for community-wide physical activity projects could be set up, in co-operation with both the local authorities and non-governmental sports associations. Such a fund could aim at increasing participation in sport and physical activity and tackling social exclusion.
2. Networks of local and regional physical activity and leisure co-ordinators should be developed in order to stimulate community-level actions. They can work across institutional boundaries and facilitate links between all local bodies, including schools.
3. The improvement of the local sporting environment should be made a priority in order to facilitate formal and informal physical activity. It should include non-club based informal activity, for example street sport, in deprived areas, staffed by trained volunteers. Children and young persons should be consulted when assessing the local needs. Ideas could include new, multifunctional, flexible community sports facilities, such as:
   - skate parks and adventure playgrounds;
   - facilities aimed at girls;
   - the provision of basketball hoops in cities.
4. The idea of "home zones", promoting safe play in the locality, with measures to slow or ban traffic could be extended.
5. Sports fields should not be taken to provide land for building purposes, especially in areas where there are few sports facilities.

IV. The Development of National Policies

1. Each country will have its own specific problems in this area, and will need to select and implement its own priorities, develop both short- and long-term plans and lay down clearly the lines of responsibility in each area. Short-term plans could prioritise:
   - minimum standards in the quality and quantity of physical education in schools;
   - improving the training of physical education teachers, trainers and volunteer helpers;
   - upgrading facilities.

   Long-term plans could include:
   - developing inter-regional co-operation;
   - developing co-operation between local and national authorities;
   - further training programmes for the above-mentioned groups, for example, teachers;
   - ensuring equal treatment in the area of gender and for those with disabilities.
2. Increased inter-sectorial activity between government departments would ensure co-operation between all the parties involved in promoting physical activity for children and young people. Committees or working groups including representatives from all the relevant areas – sport, education, transport, environment and health – would help to steer co-ordinated action.

3. It is important to consider the needs of pedestrians and cyclists, especially in connection with walking and cycling to school (where and when the climate permits) which has beneficial effects for the natural environment and sustainable development.
4. The proved connection between the physical activity and health of children and young persons makes effective links between the government departments concerned imperative in this important area of co operation.
5. The ministries responsible for sport can take initiatives to make recreational sport more attractive to a wider range of people, with less emphasis on competition and more on the importance of lifelong physical activity.
6. Funding for physical activity programmes aimed at under-privileged children and young persons should be increased. This should include programmes for such groups as children and young people with disabilities, migrants and refugees.
7. Marketing techniques should be employed, for example, through work with various forms of media, including television, the printed press, and the organisation of national campaigns.

V. The European Dimension

1. There is a need for an integrated European health strategy that would serve as the basis of a health project for children and young people. It could be built on intergovernmental co-operation within the Council of Europe and between the Council of Europe and other European and international bodies. There should be special emphasis on activities during the European Year of Education through Sport in 2004.
2. Europe-wide programmes and campaigns encouraging an active lifestyle, discouraging excessive sedentary activities and taking account of the international nature of youth culture could be envisaged. Ways to counter the influence of video games and television, both of which add to the problem of a sedentary lifestyle, could be investigated and research done into the reasons why some children and young people find physical education boring or unsatisfying.
3. Regular surveys that monitor and evaluate the level of physical activity among children and young people should be established. Making provision for a pan-European survey on physical education policies and practices every five years would help to maintain interest in this area, give deeper insight into the question and chart progress and compliance with the applicable articles of the European Sports Charter. These measures would help to ensure that this remains a priority area. The simplified series of tests in Eurofit for children could be used more often.
4. Activities at both the European and national levels should interact and take account of the priorities as established by surveys. Co-operation between member states and European networks should be encouraged in order to share information, the results of research and national experiences on promoting physical activity.

3.6. Recommendation Rec (2003)8 on the promotion and recognition of non-formal education/learning of young people

Adopted by the Committee of Ministers on 30 April 2003 at the 838th meeting of the Ministers' Deputies

The Committee of Ministers, under the terms of Article 15.b of the Statute of the Council of Europe,

Having regard to the objectives of the Council of Europe in the youth field and in the field of education;

Having regard to the Final Declaration adopted by the 5th Conference of European Ministers responsible for Youth in Bucharest (27-29 April 1998), in particular the reference to non-formal education, and to the Final Declaration of the 6th Conference (Thessaloniki, 7-9 November 2002);

Having regard to Recommendation 1437 (2000) of the Parliamentary Assembly on non-formal education;

Having regard to the experience and achievements of the youth sector of the Council of Europe regarding non-formal education/learning, in particular the work of the European Steering Committee for Youth (CDEJ) and the Symposium on Non-Formal Education held at the European Youth Centre in Strasbourg from 12 to 15 October 2000;

Having regard to Recommendation Rec(2002)6 of the Committee of Ministers to member states on higher education policies in lifelong learning;

Having regard to the activities undertaken since 1999 by the Council of Europe in the field of education for democratic citizenship, and Recommendation Rec(2002)12 on this issue, adopted by the Committee of Ministers;

Considering the important role attached to non-formal learning in the Lisbon process and the present debate on lifelong learning in the European Union as well as in the White Paper of the European Commission "A new impetus for European youth"; taking into consideration the ongoing co-operation between the Council of Europe and the European Union in this field;

Convinced that lifelong learning has an important role to play in reducing social inequality and social exclusion, and in promoting active participation in democratic life; and that non-formal education/learning can contribute to secure all the knowledge and capacities which young people need to succeed in contemporary societies;

Convinced of the necessity to mobilise the full learning potential within children and young people, in view of the social and cultural transformations resulting from the emergence of knowledge-based economies and societies in Europe and the world as a whole,

1. Recommends that the governments of member states:
   a. reaffirm that non-formal education/learning nowadays constitutes a fundamental dimension of the lifelong learning process, and therefore work towards the development of effective standards of recognition of non-formal education/learning as an essential part of general education and vocational training, and this with regard to:
      1. the qualification of professional and voluntary staff in charge of offers of non-formal education/learning;
      2. the quality of the education/learning offer itself;
      3. the monitoring of learning progress made by participants within non-formal education/learning programmes, both individually and as part of a group;
   b. support the creation and the use of a European portfolio as a description tool aiming to record experiences, skills and knowledge (learning outcomes) acquired through non-formal education/learning, bearing in mind the example of the European Language Portfolio;
   c. promote equal opportunities for all young people, in particular for the socially-disadvantaged groups, by creating equitable conditions of access to non-formal

education/learning in order to fully develop its potential with regard to reducing social inequality and social exclusion;

d. actively encourage innovative non-formal education/learning experiences by supporting the effective dissemination of relevant documentation about good practice, training methods and achievements of non-formal education/learning;

e. introduce support measures for non-formal education/learning initiatives aiming to encourage young people's commitment and contribution to the promotion of values such as active citizenship, human rights, tolerance, social justice, inter-generational dialogue, peace and intercultural understanding;

f. actively engage the non-formal education/learning sector, alongside the formal educational and vocational training systems, in the development of a common European area for lifelong learning;

g. actively use the potential of non-formal education/learning as a complementary means of facilitating the integration of young people in society, by supporting their increased participation, in particular those from transition countries, in relevant European exchange programmes;

h. promote dialogue between actors of formal and non-formal education/learning and encourage better understanding of different approaches concerning non-formal education/learning in the different European countries;

i. support and further develop existing research work in the field of non-formal education/learning, as well as the use of its results; encourage the gathering and diffusion of examples of good practice in the field of non-formal education/learning, at national and European levels; and further support existing co-operation between the Council of Europe and the European Union in this respect;

j. make non-formal education/learning a significant element of national youth policies, and of European co-operation in this field;

k. secure sufficient human and financial resources for the implementation and the recognition of non-formal education/learning programmes and their outcomes, with a view to enabling non-formal education/learning to have an adequate space within the learning community;

2. Invites the Secretary General of the Council of Europe to transmit this recommendation to the governments of those states parties to the European Cultural Convention which are not members of the Council of Europe.

Chapter 4
COMMITTEE FOR THE DEVELOPMENT OF SPORT (CDDS)

4.1. Resolution on past and future work of the CDDS, 1981 to 1984, and 1984 to 1986 (84/11)

The European Ministers responsible for Sport, meeting in Malta for their 4th Conference on 15 and 16 May 1984,

Recalling the resolutions adopted at their 3rd Conference;
Thanking the CDDS for its work on the subjects identified at that conference as priorities for European sports co-operation;
Thanking the Clearing House for its continuing contribution to this co-operation;
Endorsing the conclusions of this work as submitted in the background paper for Theme I of this Conference;
Reaffirming their conviction that the Council of Europe and the European Cultural Convention, with their possibilities for political, practical and technical forms of co-operation, should remain the principal framework for European intergovernmental co-operation in sport;
Warmly thank the Maltese government for its hospitality during this Conference and gratefully accept the offer of the Irish government to host the 5th Conference in 1986 at Dublin;
Invite the Committee of Ministers of the Council of Europe to request the Committee for the Development of Sport (CDDS), within agreed budgetary resources, to continue to provide policy-makers with help in implementing the provisions of the European Sport for All Charter adopted at the 1st Conference by giving special attention to the following areas, where appropriate in co-operation with the international sports organisations:

1. with regard to Article 1:
   proposing long term policies for sports development in the 1990s, the balance to be achieved between policies designed to further on the one hand top level competitive sport and on the other recreational sport, taking into account the impact of international sport on national sports policies;
2. with regard to Article 2:
   the funding of sport, and the desired relationship between public provision, the voluntary contribution and the commercial sector; and to suggest ways and methods of achieving harmonious and balanced partnerships, based on clearly stated roles for governments, sports organisations and private initiatives;
3. with regard to Article 3:
   to make a co-ordinated European study of the economic and financial importance of sport, including its economic impact on other areas of policy making, planning and cultural life;
4. with regard to Article 4:
   to propose ways of intensifying co-operation between public and voluntary bodies, both at national and European levels, taking into account their relationships with the commercial sector;
5. with regard to Article 5:
   to propose ways of maintaining the ethical values of sport, for example, by helping the effective implementation of the European Anti-Doping Charter for Sport adopted at this Conference, and of Recommendation R (84) 8 on the reduction of Spectator

Violence at Sporting Events; and to study the influence of commercial pressures, including the impact of TV rights, on sport, and to prepare if necessary a revised sports sponsorship code;

6. with regard to Articles 6 and 8:
to study the roles of public, voluntary and commercial bodies in the provision of sports facilities and in the recruitment, training and employment of the personnel needed for sports development policies for the late 1980s and 1990s.

4.2. Proposals of the Strategy Group on the future priorities and work of the CDDS
Adopted by the Bureau at its Meeting on 28-29 October 2003

Proposals
Taking into account the SWOT analysis of the CDDS (see appendix), and with the aim of succeeding at all political levels, from Ministers to the decision-making bodies of the Council of Europe, the following proposals are put forward by the Strategy Group[2]:

1. To increase the internal and external visibility of the CDDS and its work:
   - To publish a web bulletin on the sport policy of the Council of Europe, the aims, activities and work of the CDDS; (user-friendly language and presentation will be key elements).
   - To reinforce the presentation and visibility of the CDDS's mission and vision for senior policy-makers in member States, taking into account new political tendencies both in Europe and its member states.
   - To publish the main policy documents of the CDDS in one brochure: European Sports Charter, Code of Sports Ethics, Spectator Violence Convention, Anti-Doping Convention, Additional Protocol.
   - To improve and modernise the CDDS Web portal and add the CDDS policy guidelines and activities to the CoE Intranet resources, create links to CDDS member states relevant Web pages.
   - To improve continuous relationships between CDDS delegates and their Permanent Representatives in Strasbourg.
2. To improve reciprocal links between the Secretariat – CDDS – Bureau:
   - In order to give member countries and their representatives a better understanding of the machinery of the Council of Europe, to provide schematic material demonstrating the co-existence, functioning and co-operation of various Council of Europe authorities, bodies and forums (Secretary General, Summits, Committee of Ministers, Rapporteur Group on Education, Culture, Sport, Youth and Environment (GR-C), Parliamentary Assembly, Congress of Local and Regional Authorities of Europe, other steering committees, Directorate of Strategic Planning, Permanent Representations, etc.).
   - As part of an induction process, equip the Bureau members and CDDS delegations with a dossier comprising procedural rules and regulations, tasks and timetable of the year.

[2] Completely new proposals are in italic; proposals which have been identified by the Strategy Group as the first or main priorities are in bold; proposals which can be implemented with adjustments to existing practice are in ordinary type.

3. To involve CDDS delegations more actively in the work of the CDDS:
   - To invite CDDS delegations to participate more actively in the preparation of CDDS activities (a theme for CDDS meeting, Sport Ministers Conference, etc.) to be reinforced by more informal regular email contact through such things as the bulletin/newsletter.
   - To assess the sport policy and national priorities of the CDDS delegations (possibly by means of a tour de table at annual CDDS meetings, cf. 6.2 and 6.3) and to ensure that draft CDDS sport policy guidelines complement such needs and priorities.
   - To make more use of the geographical groups to propose or to report (e.g. in preparation the EYES 2004 project – to spot best practices in the region).
   - To secure an active partnership with national sports NGOs in the preparation and execution of the CDDS programme.
   - To ask delegations to show what is the "added value" for and from sport in the Council of Europe; for and from the CDDS in member States; for such or such a project in the CDDS programme?
4. To work more with harmonised data collecting through mutual communication – politicians need facts:
   - To update and report constantly on changes in national sport structures, umbrella organisations, new people in GOs and NGOs (for example by distributing the List of Sports Ministers and Officials).
   - To have statistics on NGOs in the member States (number and % of NGOs, memberships, public funding to sport) and promote Compass project towards comparative data in sport (need to look at how this links with the new budget line in the EU for 4 major research projects on the impact of sport in education but which looks in depth at the structure of the 25 sport systems).
   - To publish a list of definitions – sport, national umbrella organisation, sport federation, club, participation, youth, etc.
   - To carry out studies on sport legislation and other similar measures in member states on the implementation of ESC and two Conventions.
   - To carry out further studies on value of sport, value of volunteers, role of NGOs.
   - To collect data on best practices in the member states in different areas of the sport sector.
5. To improve evaluation and follow-up of the CDDS work:
   - To develop benchmarks (indicators) for the European Sports Charter, Anti-Doping Convention, Spectator Violence Convention. Indicators dealing with educational matters to be focused in relation also to the two Conventions.
   - To revise the handbook for the Compliance with Commitments (CwC) project to facilitate its implementation by evaluation or advisory visits teams and monitor follow-up of the reports and recommendations.
   - To provide regular study (analytical surveys) on progress made by the CDDS member states, when the necessary measures have become established.
   - To support and assist "Sprint countries" and to improve existing programmes and field actions (bearing in mind that the CDDS is not an operational body).
6. To improve the management of the CDDS Agenda:
   - To propose for the agenda items which can be adopted without discussion.
   - To allow more possibilities for involvement by all delegations in agenda item discussions.

- To include a tour de table on topical questions in member states with a view to identifying common problems.
- To improve the form of the documents that makes them simpler to understand and more attractive (avoid including draft decisions in the annotated agenda of the CDDS meeting).
- CDDS members to work more closely with national members of the Parliamentary Assembly and their Permanent Representatives to strengthen the political aspect and profile of the work of the CDDS.
- To involve Bureau members in the discussions of specific items in the CDDS.
- To use small, ad hoc working groups for exchanges of views etc. (for example Sprint co-ordination group) during CDDS meetings.
- To prepare working documents in good time for national consultation before meetings.

Chapter 5
DEMOCRACY

5.1. European Crossroads – Sport, Front Door to Democracy
Strasbourg, 13-14 May 2004

Conclusions
Concerned about the situation in the youth sport in Europe, presented in facts and figures by the ENGSO Youth Committee;
Having reconsidered the current European policies in youth sport, outlined by the Heads of the leading umbrella sport institutions and organisations: the Council of Europe, the European Commission and, the European Non Governmental Sports Organisation;
Encouraged by the strategy of the Canadian government in promoting youth and sport internationally;
Having re-assessed the important contribution sport can make to the development of personal skills and qualities, as described by numerous top athletes, coaches and sport leaders;
Considering the conclusions from the three workshops: How to include young people in the decision-making process in sports organisations? How to motivate and recruit young people into sport leadership? How to prevent drop out of young people from sports clubs?
Noting the rich variety of interesting national practices in the field of youth sport, as presented by Azerbaijan, Bulgaria, Finland, France (Region Alsace in particular), Georgia, Germany, Hungary, Luxembourg, Netherlands, and the UK;
Encouraged by the very successful mutual co-operation among all the partners of the project: the Council of Europe, its Youth and Sport Directorate, the Committee for the Development of Sport (CDDS) and the CDDS Bureau, the Sport Unit of the European Commission, the European Non Governmental Sports Organisation ENGSO and its Youth Committee, the City of Strasbourg, its Office des Sports and Graine de Cirque, which ensured the success of the EC-COE joint project within the European Year of Education through Sport 2004,
The co-organizers of the European Crossroads Conference agree to follow up the tasks proposed by the participants of the European Crossroads in the following ways:

1. Provide dissemination of the Final Report of the European Crossroads to all the participants of the conference, all the CDDS delegations and the ENGSO member-organisations.
2. Present the Final Report of the European Crossroads and the video-film (complementary to the Report) to the Sports Ministers at the 10th Conference of European Ministers responsible for Sport in Budapest on 14-15 October 2004 and invite the Ministers, in the context of good governance issue, to foster policies that encourage young people to participate in sport, physical activity and decision-making processes (as specified also in Rec (2003) 6 of the Committee of Ministers of the Council of Europe to member states on improving physical education and sport for children and young people in all European countries).
3. Prepare publication of the Book on Good Practices in Youth Sport Policies in Europe in English and French (based on the material collected from as many countries as possible) and disseminate it to all the Council of Europe member countries, and encourage the translation of the Book in the national languages.

4. Encourage the CDDS delegations (in co-operation with their ENGSO partners) to pay increased attention to youth sport policies: development of leadership training programmes for young people, more active involvement of young people in decision-making processes, establishment of youth sport structures in their countries.
5. In the CDDS programmes in future to focus on activities targeted at such issues as the education of teachers, trainers and leaders and the development of sport policies to promote sport as a front door to democracy, and use the experience of the countries that have developed effective and favourable models.
6. Initiate better intersectoral co-operation within the CoE Youth and Sport Directorate, providing the inclusion of sport as an integral part of all youth work.
7. Initiate discussions for the preparation of common Partnership Agreements (or other appropriate measure) in this field between the Council of Europe and the European Commission, thus to maximise joint efforts and to provide more opportunities for joint activities in future.

Chapter 6
DEPRIVATION AND URBAN STRESS

6.1. Resolution on Sport for those Suffering from Deprivation and Urban Stress (81/6)
The European Ministers responsible for sport, meeting from 8 to 10 April 1981 in Palma de Majorca for their 3rd Conference,

Recalling the recommendation made at their 2nd Conference on "the importance of sport for social groups suffering from deprivation and urban stress" in the context of the European Sport for All Charter;
Welcoming the report of the seminar organised in Glasgow in 1980 on the topic of sport in areas of special need;
Resolve that they will give every support to positive efforts in their countries to identify the precise needs and to encourage the direction of more financial and human resources to these areas of special need;

Invite the Committee of Ministers of the Council of Europe:

1. to ask the CDDS:
   a. to continue its efforts on this topic;
   b. in particular to continue to support this aspect of the Council of Europe's Campaign for Urban Renaissance;
2. to recommend to the Governments of member states that they:
   a. should do all in their power to create the atmosphere and promote actively flexible financial and administrative conditions which encourage municipal authorities to carry out comprehensive policies to stimulate sport and physical recreation in areas of deprivation;
   b. consider how best policies and programmes can be co-ordinated to bring special emphasis to the needs of those living in areas of deprivation;
   c. encourage the development of relevant research with particular reference to the part that sport and physical recreation can play in helping alleviate poor living conditions;
   d. consider what special programmes can be devised and developed in their countries as a means of providing sport and recreation to those who are unemployed or underemployed;
   e. consider ways and means by which special attention can be paid to providing recreational opportunities in areas of deprivation in fulfilment of the Sport for All Charter.

Chapter 7
DISABLED PERSONS

7.1. Resolution on Sport for Handicapped Persons (81/5)

The European Ministers responsible for Sport, meeting from 8 to 10 April 1981 in Palma de Majorca for their 3rd Conference

Aware of the responsibilities of society towards the handicapped;
After analysing and discussing the ways in which sport can be adapted to different kinds of handicap;
Consider that sport is of paramount importance in preparing for life, restoring and maintaining health, rehabilitating motor functions and providing secondary prevention of neurophysiological accidents;
Recognise sport as a valuable means of education, rehabilitation, enhancement of leisure activities and social integration;

Undertake within their respective countries to:

1 set objectives for the development of adapted physical activities in conjunction with the bodies representing the handicapped, while paying attention to medical surveillance;
2 do their utmost to introduce physical activities and sport in the education, rehabilitation and preventive treatment of the handicapped;
3 encourage the setting-up of independent bodies responsible for the organisation of sports adapted to different kinds of handicap;
4 take measures to make sports facilities more easily accessible, encourage the training of specialist staff and promote research and public information;

Invite the Committee of Ministers of the Council of Europe to ask the Committee for the Development of Sport to design and implement as a matter of urgency a European programme aimed at easing the practice of sport by handicapped persons and in particular to:

1 lay down general guidelines and establish priorities;
2 centralise and disseminate through the Clearing House the results of the experience gained on this subject within each member State, paying particular attention to research and information;
3 provide international co-ordination of staff training and action;
4 advise governments on the development of specific programmes and give assistance where necessary;
5 assist in the co-ordination of the sports activities of bodies responsible for the handicapped in the fields of health, education rehabilitation and recreation;
6 take suitable measures to guide and support representative European voluntary organisations in order to prevent dissipation of effort and ensure a harmonious progression of action on behalf of the handicapped.

7.2. Resolution on Sport for the Handicapped and other Health Impaired Groups (84/7)

The European Ministers responsible for Sport, meeting in Malta for their 4th Conference on 15 and 16 May 1984,

Emphasising the need for special measures for groups whose participation in physical education and sport on an equitable basis is otherwise difficult or impossible;
Recalling the principles of the Sport for All Charter, and their Resolution N° 5/81 on "Sport for the Handicapped" adopted at their 3rd Conference, and in particular the need to implement a European programme aimed at easing the practice of sport by handicapped persons;
Aware of the health-promoting and rehabilitating effect of physical education and sport as well as its importance for the overall development of the personality and as a means of social integration;
Supporting the efforts of international sport organisations and bodies for the development of sport for the handicapped and other health impaired groups;
Invite the Committee of Ministers of the Council of Europe to recommend that the governments of member states continue their efforts to develop physical education and sport for the handicapped and other health impaired groups, in particular by:

1 when building or converting sports facilities, to ensure that there is suitable access for these groups, thus increasing their participation opportunities in physical education and sport;
2 seeing to it that sufficient financial support is given to the physical education and sport activities of such groups;
3 developing training for physical education, pre-school education and general education teachers so as to include sufficient instruction concerning the need and importance of adapted physical education and sport for the handicapped and other health impaired groups with the aim of integrating this education into general physical education and sports activities;
4 promoting the adequate representation of the above-mentioned groups in the decision-making bodies concerning physical education and sport;
5 encouraging national and local sports bodies and organisations to undertake research and pilot projects in order to improve the participation of such groups in physical education and sport;
6 to this end, promoting co-operation between administrators in different sectors, particularly in the fields of physical education and sport, health, social welfare and education;
7 furthering international research co-operation as well as exchanges of information and documentation concerning measures aimed at improving the situation of the handicapped and other health impaired groups in physical education and sport.

7.3. Resolution AP (84) 3 on a Coherent Policy for the Rehabilitation of Disabled People[3]

Adopted by the Committee of Ministers on 17 September 1984

2.4 Leisure, sport, holidays
  2.4.1 Integration measures
  2.4.1.1 Social measures
    2.4.1.1.1 Leisure time and holiday activities for disabled people should be integrated with ordinary leisure activities. Leisure activi-

[3] This is an extract from the Resolution concerning sport. This Resolution develops the decisions taken in Resolution AP (76)4 on the Possibilities of Leisure Activities and Holidays for the Disabled adopted by the Committee of Ministers on 16 November 1976.

ties for those with certain types of need could be organised in special clubs as a complement to ordinary leisure activities.

2.4.1.1.2 The participation of disabled people in all cultural, social, political and sports activities should be encouraged.

2.4.1.1.3 Sport should be recognised as one of the vital factors in the disabled person's rehabilitation, with particular respect to his integration into society.

2.4.1.1.4 Sports activities for disabled people should therefore be intensified and their further development encouraged by appropriate public relations methods, the training of staff, the planning of sports centres and the promotion of associations concerned with sports activities.

2.4.1.1.5 In accordance with the objective of rehabilitation, appropriate measures should be taken for practising sport in the company of the able-bodies.

2.4.1.1.6 Programmes for the training of leisure and holiday promoters should be adapted in order to allow disabled people to be trained for these careers.

2.4.1.2 Structural measures

2.4.1.2.1 Structural, technical and psychological obstacles which limit the enjoyment of leisure time, sport and holiday possibilities for disabled people should be removed; in particular, access to buildings. to means of transport and to leisure establishments should be facilitated.

2.4.1.2.2 Disabled people's dwellings should be adapted to their needs in order to give them the possibility of spending their leisure time in conditions which are as normal as possible and in privacy.

2.4.1.2.3 Tourist establishments, sporting facilities and places of entertainment at holiday centres (cinemas, swimming pools, sports grounds, etc.), should be planned and equipped to render them accessible to disabled people.

2.4.1.2.4 Psychological barriers and other obstacles to communication between all people, whether disabled or not, should be overcome by means of material aids and through social programmes.

2.4.1.2.4.1 Material aids should include, amongst others, the technical means which enable disabled people:

- to take a full part in all leisure activities
- to communicate with the surrounding world through information systems (telecommunications, computers, etc.) suitable adapted to needs.

2.4.1.2.4.2 Social programmes, undertaken jointly by universities, private initiatives, organisations concerned with the rehabilitation of disabled people with particular kinds of need and public authorities, should also endeavour to:

- develop individual technical aids to compensate for the disability;
- extend adaptations for accessibility to means of transport and communication.

2.4.2 Information measures

2.4.2.1 The general public, disabled people themselves and their families, and those providing services for disabled people should be informed of the existence of:

- technical aids and means of communication facilitating participation of disabled people in leisure, sport and holiday activities for all;
- leisure and sport facilities, vacation possibilities and holiday resorts specifically adapted for disabled people if needed.

2.4.2.2 An international exchange of information should be encouraged on new initiatives to make it easier for disabled people to organise their leisure time and their holidays.

2.4.2.3 Tourist and leisure guide books should include all possible information on the facilities available for disabled people in tourist establishments (hotels, restaurants, etc.) on the accessibility of nearby leisure possibilities for them (swimming pools, cinemas, theatres, etc.) and on sport facilities. They should indicate by symbols the accessibility to and in hotels, restaurants and other tourist and cultural establishments. The key to the symbols should be given in several languages.

2.4.2.4 Tourist guide books for special categories of disabled persons could be envisaged whenever necessary preferably as a complement to normal guide books. Ordinary guide books could contain special information for particular kinds of disability.

2.4.2.5 National and/or regional information centres should provide disabled people and tourist offices and agencies with information on holiday, leisure and sports possibilities for disabled people at home and abroad.

2.4.2.6 Financial assistance should be envisaged to encourage initiatives to develop and improve tourist, leisure and sport information for disabled people.

2.4.3 Other measures

2.4.3.1 School curricula and physical rehabilitation programmes for disabled children should enable them to become aware of life in society as early as possible in order to motivate them for leisure activities as soon as possible and, if necessary, to adapt their choices to their skills and capacities.

2.4.3.2 Programmes for disabled adults should encourage them to undertake creative and leisure activities, even outside the institution, in order to enable successful social integration.

2.4.3.3 Scientific and technical studies should be carried out to examine more thoroughly specific problems concerning leisure time and holiday facilities for disabled people and, among others, the adaptability of leisure materials to their disability.

2.4.3.4 Specific sporting activities during the rehabilitation process should be planned, introduced or developed, particularly:

- when the nature of the impairment or disability calls for

changes in the rules of certain sports, in the conditions under which they are practised or the equipment used;
- when for psychological reasons, the disabled person has serious difficulty in practising sport with able-bodies people or feels the need for a reassuring environment created by and for disabled people.

2.4.3.5 The practice of sport during the rehabilitation process should be carried out under appropriate medical supervision.

2.4.3.6 The training of staff specialised in leisure, sport activities and holidays for disabled persons should be envisaged.

3.8.3 Leisure, sport, holidays

3.8.3.1 The general public, disabled people themselves and their families and institutions for disabled people should be informed of the existence of:
- technical aids and means of communication facilitating participation by disabled people in leisure, sports and holiday activities for all;
- leisure and sports facilities. vacation possibilities and holiday resorts specifically for disabled people.

3.8.3.2 An international exchange of information should be encouraged on new initiatives to make it easier for disabled people to organise their leisure time and their holidays.

3.8.3.3 Tourist and leisure guide books should include all possible information on the facilities available for disabled people in tourist establishments (hotels, restaurants, etc.) on the accessibility of nearby recreation possibilities for them (swimming Pools, cinemas, theatres, etc.) and on sports facilities. They should indicate by symbols accessibility for disabled people at hotels, restaurants and other tourist and cultural establishments. The key to the symbols should be given in several languages.

3.8.3.4 Tourist guide books for disabled people with particular needs could be envisaged whenever necessary, preferably as a supplement to normal guide books. Ordinary guide books could contain special information for groups with particular needs.

3.8.3.5 National and/or regional information centres should provide disabled people and tourist offices and agencies with information about holiday, leisure and sports possibilities for disabled people at home and abroad.

3.8.3.6 Financial assistance should be envisaged to encourage schemes to develop and improve tourist, leisure and sports information for disabled people.

7.4. Resolution No. 1/86 the European Charter for Sport for All: Disabled Persons

5th Conference of European Ministers responsible for Sport, Dublin, 30 September-2 October 1986

Resolution No. 1/86 [...] having been adopted as Recommendation No. R(86)18 by the Committee of Ministers [...]

7.5. Recommendation of the Committee of Ministers to Member States of the European Charter on Sport for All: Disabled Persons (86/18)
Adopted by the Committee of Ministers on 4 December 1986

The Committee of Ministers, under the terms of Article 15b of the Statute of the Council of Europe,
Considering that the aim of the Council of Europe is to achieve a greater unity between its members, notably by means of common action in social and cultural matters;
Considering that in the member states nearly one person in every ten suffers from a variety of impairment, disability or handicap;
Bearing in mind its Resolution (76) 41 on the principles for a policy of sport for all and particularly Article 1 of the appendix thereto which states that "every individual shall have the right to participate in sport";
Having regard to Resolution N° 5/81 and Resolution N° 7/84 on sport for handicapped persons, adopted respectively at the 3rd (Palma de Majorca, 1981) and 4th (Malta, 1984) Conferences of European Ministers responsible for Sport;
Bearing in mind its Resolution AP (84) 3 adopted in the framework of the Partial Agreement in the Social and Public Health Field, on a coherent policy for the integration of disabled people which states, in paragraph 2.4 of its appendix, that "participation in sport should be encouraged", that "sport is a vital factor in rehabilitation and integration", and that "sports activities should be intensified and their further development encouraged by appropriate public relations methods, the training of staff, the planning of sports centres and the promotion of associations";
Considering that it is necessary to create a welcoming climate for disabled people, to recognise their right to be helped and to improve their position in society;
Considering that, in accordance with these ethical principles and the respect of each human being, the promotion and development of sport and physical recreation for all disabled persons is an important means of improving the quality of their life, as well as contributing to their rehabilitation and integration in society;
Considering that the European ministers responsible for sport, meeting for their 5th Conference in Dublin (1986), adopted a resolution defining such principles under the title of the "European Charter on Sport for All: disabled persons",

Recommends the governments of member states:

1 to take the action set out in Part A of the appendix to this recommendation;
2 to encourage and work closely with the sports organisations concerned to take action set out in Part B of the appendix to this recommendation;
3 to distribute this recommendation widely amongst all sports organisations and other bodies and organisations concerned with disabled persons.

Instructs the Secretary General to transmit this recommendation to:

1 the governments of states party to the European Cultural Convention which are not members of the Council of Europe;
2. the competent international sports organisations, and other organisations concerned with the needs of disabled persons.

Appendix
European Charter on Sport for All: disabled persons.

7.6. European Charter on Sport for All: Disabled Persons
Adopted by the Committee of Ministers on 4 December 1986

Part A
The governments of member states should:

1 take the necessary steps to ensure that all relevant public authorities and private organisations are aware of the sporting and recreational wants and needs, including in education, of all disabled persons – not only those who are physically or sensorially disabled and mentally handicapped, but also those who suffer from an organic or psychosomatic disorder;

2 orientate their policies for such persons so that they may have adequate opportunities to take part in recreational physical activities which will:
 a encourage their feeling of well-being and /or improve their physical condition;
 b provide self-fulfilling leisure-time occupations;
 c encourage social communication both between themselves and between them and able-bodied persons;

3 encourage the appropriate authorities to seek to ensure that public sports facilities are accessible to and usable by disabled persons and to incite these authorities:
 a to consider the need to set aside public money to help with the conversion of existing facilities to meet the building guidelines set down in the appendix to the explanatory memorandum to this recommendation or equivalent national standards;
 b to ensure so far as is possible that future sports facilities will meet these guidelines or equivalent national standards;
 c to take steps to familiarise architects and managers of sports facilities with the requirements of disabled people;

4 encourage co-operation between the various public authorities involved in sport for disabled persons, such as health, social welfare, education and sport departments, and their policies and actions;

5 encourage where appropriate the setting up of an umbrella body for the development of sport for all disabled persons, bringing together all appropriate and relevant interests and expertise;

6 encourage those financing sports activities for all disabled persons as an integral part of rehabilitation and as a continuation of it as well as for its wider general benefit;

7 encourage the development of sport and recreation for disabled persons as an integral part of rehabilitation and as a continuation of it as well as for its wider general benefit;

8 encourage research, as necessary, which will determine scientifically the physiological, psychological, social or other benefits of sport for different categories of disabled people, together with other research which may be deemed to be appropriate;

9 encourage educational authorities to take sufficient steps to provide adequate and real physical education for disabled children in schools, and to train to the required level those who may teach these children;

10 encourage the provision of opportunities for disabled persons who so desire to train as physical education teachers;

11 encourage the provision of training of disabled and able-bodied instructors to work with recognised competent sports organisations;
12 ensure that when sports policy is being decided the interests and views of disabled persons are given due consideration;
13 ensure, within their constitutional limits, that this recommendation is also observed by the appropriate regional and local authorities with competence in any of the areas mentioned above.

Part B
The governments of member states should encourage and work closely with the sports organisations concerned in order:
1 to develop appropriate activities at all levels of sport for disabled persons and to ensure in particular that recreational participation in sport is adequately provided for;
2 to consider ways in which disabled persons may be offered opportunities for integrating into traditional sports clubs and organisations;
3 to encourage disabled persons to contribute directly to the development of sports policies which concern them;
4 to ensure that in their policy-making and decisions the sporting interests of all disabled persons are taken into due account;
5 to recognise that disabled persons may aspire to elite sport and to participate in it according to their abilities and to ensure that the organisation of such competitions does not in any way lead to the exploitation, whether physical, psychological or financial, of possible participants;
6 to continue the efforts, at national, regional, and local levels, and within the competent international sports organisations to harmonise, simplify and, where appropriate, to reduce the classification categories and the eligibility criteria for participation at competitions between disabled persons;
7 to intensify efforts to enable disabled persons, insofar as they may desire to do so, to compete in the same events as the able-bodied, while preserving the principle of fair and equal competition;
8 to intensify the co-operation of their activities, with a view to eventual unification, both at international level and at national level, in the body described at Article 5 of Part A;
9 to develop policies designed to give the general public more information on sport for disabled people.

7.7. Recommendation No. R (97) 8 of the Committee of Ministers to Member States on Rehabilitation Through Sport for People with Disabilities in Bosnia and Herzegovina
Adopted by the Committee of Ministers on 2 June 1997, at the 594th meeting of the Ministers' Deputies

The Committee of Ministers, under the terms of Article 15.b of the Statute of the Council of Europe,
Considering that the aim of the Council of Europe is to achieve a greater unity between its members, notably by means of common action in social and cultural matters;
Considering that in Bosnia and Herzegovina there are thought to be half a million people, of both sexes and all ages, injured and maimed as the result of war-related activities;
Bearing in mind that in its Recommendation No. R (86) 18 on the European Charter on Sport for All: Disabled persons, it said that "the promotion and development of sport and physical

recreation for all disabled persons is an important means of improving the quality of their life, as well as contributing to their rehabilitation and integration in society", and wishing to see carried out in Bosnia and Herzegovina the principles set out in the recommendation;
Bearing in mind that in the appendix to its Recommendation No. R (92) 6 on a coherent policy for people with disabilities, it is said that "sport, including competitive sport, should be recognised as one of the vital factors in the rehabilitation [and integration process and that] sporting activities for people with disabilities should therefore be extended and their further development encouraged by appropriate public relations methods, the training of staff, the planning of sports centres and the promotion of associations concerned with sporting activities";
Having regard to Article 15 of the Revised European Social Charter (3 April 1996), by virtue of which the parties, with a view to ensuring persons with disabilities "the effective exercise of the right to independence, social integration and participation in the life of the community", undertake in particular "to promote their full social integration and participation in the life of the community in particular through measures, including technical aids, aiming to overcome barriers to communication and mobility and enabling access to transport, housing, cultural activities and leisure";
Recalling that at its 99th session, the Committee of Ministers "invited its Deputies to examine the future role of the Council of Europe in the civilian reconstruction" of Bosnia and Herzegovina, and that it has given priority to "activities aimed at bringing young people from different ethnic backgrounds together through cultural, educational and sports activities";
Considering that sports and recreation facilities have been destroyed in that country;
On the proposal of the Committee for the Development of Sport (CDDS), which has assembled a number of international and European partners to contribute to the carrying out of an action plan on rehabilitation through sport for people with disabilities in Bosnia and Herzegovina, noting that these partners come from national governments, as well as the intergovernmental, international and national non-governmental sports bodies, and the private sector, and that many of them have already indicated their decision to help implement this action plan;
Determined to lend its support to the implementation of this action plan,

Recommends that the governments of member states:

a. take cognisance of the action plan "Rehabilitation through sport for people with disabilities in Bosnia and Herzegovina" as set out in the publication Action Plan for Bosnia and Herzegovina: rehabilitation through sport and to study the possibility of providing, on a bilateral level, aid or assistance which would help realise or complement the realisation of the various projects set out in this plan. Such assistance could consist of direct contributions to the projects or indirect assistance, for example in the training of architects or planners of sports facilities in the rebuilding or restoration of sports facilities and other physical recreation areas with appropriate access for people with disabilities, on the basis of the norms set out in Recommendation No. R (86) 18;
b. bring the action plan to the attention of their central sports organisations, comprising both the able-bodied and people with disabilities, with a view to encouraging them, on a bilateral level, to take action to help ensure the rapid reintegration of sport in Bosnia and Herzegovina into the European sports family; and to bring it to the attention of other appropriate non-governmental organisations, such as those for refugees, so that those wishing to return to Bosnia and Herzegovina may obtain training in sport and recreation;
c. bring the action plan to the attention of their universities and other appropriate institutes of higher education and sports research, with a view to encouraging them, on a

bilateral level, to assist in the training, retraining and further training of sports leaders, instructors, coaches, and teachers of physical education, particularly in the field of sport and physical recreation for people with disabilities in Bosnia and Herzegovina, and in the provision of relevant educational and other materials in languages spoken in Bosnia and Herzegovina;

d. to co-ordinate the actions taken under a to c above with the plans of the various European institutions involved in the reconstruction of Bosnia and Herzegovina.

Instructs the Secretary General:

a. to bring this recommendation to the attention of the Parliamentary Assembly and the Congress of Local and Regional Authorities of Europe and to ask them to inform him of any follow-up given to the action plan (for example, in the case of the Congress, in the context of town-twinning agreements);

b. to transmit this recommendation to the European Commission; Unesco; the European Non-Governmental Sports Organisation (ENGSO); the International Olympic Committee; the International Paralympic Committee; the General Association of International Sports Federations; the European Olympic Committees; the World Federation of the Sporting Goods Industry (WFSGI); the International Military Sports Council; and the Union of European Football Associations;

c. to transmit this recommendation to the government and other appropriate authorities in Bosnia and Herzegovina.

Chapter 8
DOPING

8.1. Resolution on the Doping of Athletes (67/12)
Adopted by the Ministers' Deputies on 29th June 1967

The Committee of Ministers of the Council of Europe,
Considering that the aim of the Council of Europe is to achieve greater unity among its members for the purpose of safeguarding and promoting the ideals and principles which are their common heritage and of facilitating their economic and social progress;
Considering that sports activities now play an important role in the protection of health, in moral and physical training and in promoting international understanding;
Considering that the influence of sport on young people and adults has grown considerably as a result of modern information media and travel facilities;
Having regard to the value of the example set by champions and their behaviour, as well as their prestige in the eyes of most young people and many adults;
Considering the increasingly evil effects of certain practices known as "doping" which jeopardise the health and dignity of those who resort to it and offend against the spirit of fair play essential to all sports;
Considering that doping is the administration to or the use by a healthy person, in any manner whatsoever, of agents foreign to the organism, or of physiological substances in excessive quantities or introduced by an abnormal channel, with the sole purpose of affecting artificially and by unfair means the performance of such a person when taking part in a competition,

Recommends the governments of member states:
1. to persuade the sports associations and federations which organise competitions in their territory to take action if necessary with their international federations and, if they have not already done so, to issue regulations:
    a. condemning the use, or procedures to facilitate the use, in preparation for or during a sports competition, of the substances or processes employed for doping as defined in the Preamble to this Recommendation;
    b. penalising offenders by prohibiting them, temporarily or permanently, from taking part in, organising or acting in an official capacity at any sports competition;
    c. applying the regulations to any person who, in another member State, has been penalised in accordance with the provisions of paragraph b. above;
2. to take the appropriate measures at their disposal to achieve the objectives set forth in paragraph 1 above, if the regulations referred to in that paragraph have not, within three years from the date of this recommendation, been issued or effectively applied;
   Invites the governments of member states to keep it informed of action taken by them to implement this recommendation.

8.2. Recommendation of the Committee of Ministers to Member States concerning Doping in Sport (79/8)
Adopted by the Committee of Ministers on 20 April 1979

The Committee of Ministers, under the terms of Article 15b of the Statute of the Council of Europe,
Affirming that its Resolution (67) 12 on "Doping of athletes" remains a valid condemnation of the harm caused by the use of doping agents to the ethical and moral values of sport and to human dignity;
Recalling its Resolution (76) 41 on the "Principles for a policy of sport for all" (the "European Sport for All Charter") and in particular Article 5, which states that "methods should be sought to safeguard sport and sportsmen from exploitation for political, commercial or financial gain and from practices that are abusive and debasing, including the unfair use of drugs":
Considering that many of the problems raised by the taking of illicit substances for the purpose of artificially improving sporting performances are still unresolved, and that in some respects this evil practice has become more widespread since the adoption of Resolution (67) 12;
Bearing in mind the resolution on doping and health adopted at the 2nd Conference of European Ministers responsible for Sport at London in 1978, and that some member states have enacted national legislation forbidding the use of doping agents in sport;
Considering that the member states of the Council of Europe should take a lead in combating the problems of doping in sport, and that governments and the voluntary bodies of sport should work together to this end;

Recommends the governments of member states:

1. to give all the support in their power to the governing bodies of sport, athletes and all those associated with sport in their efforts to eradicate doping (as defined in Resolution (67) 12) in sport and to encourage them to take the steps necessary for the simplification and harmonisation of the various anti-doping regulations adopted by the sports federations;
2. to develop, in co-ordination with the governing bodies of sport, an educational campaign pointing out both to athletes and to coaches, directors and other people involved, the risks involved in using or advocating the use of doping agents, in particular that many such agents present serious long-term dangers to health; that their use does not always result in an improvement of performance; and that the way to success is not the use of doping agents but rather the development of each individual's personal qualities of character, physique and mind;
3. to set up systems for the control of the use of artificial stimulants in sport and to this end;
    a. to encourage the development and testing, in laboratories, of effective methods for detecting the use of illicit substances in sport, and in particular those substances the use of which is forbidden either by the international governing bodies of sport or by national legislation in those countries where such legislation exists;
    b. to increase their contribution to European co-operation in research into doping, and in particular into the detection and control of new substances capable of being used for the purpose of doping in sport;
    c. to encourage as a priority the creation of suitable laboratories for the comprehensive testing and control of sportsmen, and in particular:
        i. to ensure by whatever may be the most appropriate means in each country that sportsmen and federations can make effective and continuous use of such laboratories;

ii. to encourage international co-operation, both bilaterally and within the Council of Europe, so that those member states without such laboratories may have reasonable access to laboratories in other states and to the experience, skills and techniques necessary for them to set up such laboratories at a later stage;

iii. to encourage the harmonisation of technical procedures of high standard in these laboratories;

iv. to take steps to ensure that such laboratories are manned by properly qualified and experienced staff and to make provision for the training of personnel from other member states in the training programmes;

4. to consider, where this has not already been done, the creation of a national anti-doping committee (which could consist of representatives from the sports federations, national confederations of sport, governmental administrations responsible for sport and for public health) in order to provide the necessary liaison between the parties involved in the efforts to eradicate the problems of doping in sport;
5. to consider in what ways they might most suitably support those athletes or federations who as a result of taking a stand against the use of illicit substances in sport suffer material consequences;
6. to report to the Secretary General, by 1 March 1980, on measures taken in implementation of this recommendation.

8.3. Recommendation of the Committee of Ministers to Member States on the "European Anti-Doping Charter for Sport" (84/19)
Adopted by the Committee of Ministers on 25 September 1984

The Committee of Ministers, under the terms of Article 15b of the Statute of the Council of Europe,
Recalling its Resolution (67) 12 on the "Doping of Athletes" and Recommendation N° R (79) 8 on "Doping in Sport";
Bearing in mind the resolution on "Doping and Health" adopted at the 2nd Conference of European Ministers responsible for Sport, in London in 1978;
Emphasising that the use of doping agents is both unhealthy and contrary to the ethical values of sport and thus undermines the main purposes for which sport is supported financially by public authorities;
Concerned that the use of doping agents is becoming more common and spreading to more forms of sport and that ever-younger sportsmen and sportswomen use them;
Considering that governments have a general responsibility to counter the use of doping in sport;
Considering that doping in sport is a part of the problem of drug abuse in society;
Stressing that the elimination of this problem will require common action by public authorities and sports organisations, each acting within the sphere of its own responsibilities;
Recognising that a statement of principles on the roles of each partner will make a timely contribution to further endeavours in the anti-doping campaign, and that the text adopted by the European Ministers responsible for Sport at their 4th Conference, in Malta in 1984, under the title of the "European Anti-Doping Charter for Sport" is such a statement of principles,

Recommends the governments of member states:
1. to take the action set out in Part A of the appendix to this recommendation;
2. to take, in co-operation with the sports organisations, the action set out in Part B of the appendix to this recommendation;

3. to distribute this recommendation and its explanatory memorandum widely among all sports organisations and other interested parties;

Instructs the Secretary General to transmit this recommendation to the governments of states party to the European Cultural Convention who are not member states of the Council of Europe;
Instructs the Secretary General to transmit this recommendation to international sports organisations.

Appendix
European Anti-Doping Charter for Sport

8.4. European Anti-Doping Charter for Sport
Adopted by the Committee of Ministers on 25 September 1984

Part A
The governments of member states should:

1. Take all appropriate steps falling within their competence to eradicate doping in sport and in particular:
    a. to ensure that effective anti-doping regulations are implemented: for example, by applying the provisions of appropriate legislation in member states where it exists or by obliging sports organisations which have not yet done so to adopt and apply effective anti-doping regulations, for example by making it a condition for receiving public subsidies;
    b. to co-operate at international level:
        i. in measures designed to reduce the availability of doping agents;
        ii. in facilitating the carrying out of official doping controls decided on by international sports federations.
2. Set up and run, either individually or collectively, doping control laboratories of a high technical standard.
   The creation and operation of high-class doping control laboratories should include provision for the training and retraining of qualified staff and for an appropriate research programme.
   These laboratories should be of such a standard that they can be recognised, accredited and verified at regular intervals by the competent international organisations, especially insofar as such laboratories may be used for doping controls at international sports events held on the territory of the member state.
3. Encourage and promote research in doping control laboratories into analytical chemistry and biochemistry, and subsequently help with the publication of the results of research in order to disseminate such knowledge; and make suitable arrangements for the adoption of techniques, standards and policies as research shows to be necessary.
4. Devise and implement educational programmes and campaigns from school-age onwards drawing attention to the dangers and unfairness of doping and promoting the proper ethical and physical values of sport; and support the design of properly constructed physiological and psychological training programmes which would encourage the continual search for improved performances without using artificial aids or harming the participant's organism.
5. Assist with the financing of doping controls.

Part B
The governments of member states should offer their co-operation to the sports organisations, so that the latter take all measures falling within their competence to eradicate doping.

6. Sports organisations should be encouraged:
   a. to harmonise their anti-doping regulations and procedures, based on those of the International Olympic Committee (IOC) and the International Amateur Athletic Federation, and ensure that these regulations provide for an adequate protection of the rights of sports participants accused of contravening the anti-doping regulations, including the right to a fair examination in the proceedings which may lead to penalties being imposed;
   b. to harmonise their lists of banned substances, based on those of the IOC, and making appropriate provision for the specific anti-doping requirements of each sport;
   c. to make full and efficient use of the facilities available for doping controls;
   d. to include a clause in their regulations whereby, in order to be considered to be eligible to take part in any official event of that sports organisation or federation, an athlete would agree to submit at any time to any doping control decided on by an official properly and duly authorised by that federation or its superior federation;
   e. to agree on similar and substantial penalties for sportsmen or women caught using doping substances and for any other person providing, administering or facilitating the use of doping substances;
   f. to recognise that unduly high performance levels required in some events might result in the temptation to use drugs.

8.5. Resolution Doping in Sport (86/4)
The European Ministers responsible for Sport, meeting in Dublin for their 5th Conference from 30 September to 2 October 1986

Welcoming the several developments both at national and at international level reported to the conference on measures designed to implement the European Anti-Doping Charter for Sport adopted at their 4th Conference;
Thanking the international sports organisations for their co-operation in this matter;
Determined to do all in their power, both at governmental level and in co-operation with the sports movement, to eradicate doping in sport;
Welcoming the positive proposals made, inter alia, by the Canadian Minister responsible for Sport, on future action to widen the impact of the European Anti-Doping Charter for Sport, and accepting his offer to collaborate with the Council of Europe member states and other nations with this objective in view;

Resolve:
to encourage, in accordance with the principles set out in the European Anti-Doping Charter for Sport, the working out of measures, where necessary, in order to reduce trafficking in doping agents and to promote preventive aspects, including educational campaigns;
to encourage sports organisations and schools to carry out information and educational campaigns, so as to draw the attention of athletes and young people in general to the fact that doping is both dangerous and unfair, and defend the ethical and physical value of sport;
to offer their continued support to the many international and national sports organisations

which have acted in accordance with the principles set out in the European Anti-Doping Charter for Sport, and to urge other sports organisations to do so;
to draw the attention of the sports organisations to the desirability of uniform and effective regulations, procedures and penalties to be applied in a consistent manner; in this context, Ministers encourage sports organisations to impose an effective penalty, normally a life ban from international competitions, as already provided for in the regulations of some sports organisations, as for example the IOC; and, because of the particular problems raised by the availability of certain doping agents, for the need for them to take adequate counter-measures, for instance in proper testing programmes, including out-of-competition controls;
to invite the sports organisations to adapt their disciplinary procedures to follow the principles set out in the conference paper MSL-5 (86) B 3, particularly with regard to a fair hearing and an appeal body;
to express their confidence that the sports organisations will continue to deal with the problems of doping in sport in accordance with their seriousness; and to thank them for their continuing co-operation with the Council of Europe on this question;
to encourage the International Olympic Committee to include clearer criteria relative to the anti-doping campaign in its own eligibility rules and bye-laws;

Invite the Committee of Ministers:

1. to consider ways in which European co-operation could help with the resolution of problems connected with the distribution and availability of certain doping agents;
2. to study ways in which the Canadian authorities could be associated with future work on doping, including the proposals set out below;
3. to ask the CDDS to follow up as soon as possible the proposals made to the conference with a view to:
    a. enlarging the circle of countries or regions which could accept and begin to apply the principles laid down in the European Anti-Doping Charter for Sport;
    b. encouraging the sports organisations to take further action on the measures proposed for the harmonisation of their anti-doping regulations and procedures.

8.6. Recommendation of the Committee of Ministers to Member States on the Institution of Doping Controls without Warning outside Competitions (88/12)

Adopted by the Committee of Ministers on 21 June 1988

The Committee of Ministers, under the terms of Article 15b of the Statute of the Council of Europe,
Recalling its Resolution (67) 12 on the doping of athletes, its Recommendation N° R (79) 8 on doping in sport and, in particular, its Recommendation N° (84) 19 on the "European Anti-Doping Charter for Sport";
Bearing in mind Resolution N° 4/86 on doping in sport, adopted by the European Ministers responsible for Sport at their 5th Conference in Dublin on 2 October 1986;
Noting that many governments have taken action in accordance with the European Anti-Doping Charter for Sport, both in regard to their own competence and in offering their co-operation to sports organisations, so that many of them have taken measures falling within their competence;
Acknowledging that the organisers of most major national and international competitions regularly conduct doping controls at them, and that these controls constitute in themselves an important deterrent and educational tool in the anti-doping campaign;

Considering that the carrying out of doping controls at competitions will not by itself ensure the eradication of doping from sport;
Welcoming the decisions taken by the competent authorities – whether governmental or non-governmental – in several member states, and by some international sports federations, to institute doping controls not only at competitions, but also, without warning, during training;
Welcoming the fact that the majority of member states now have officially accredited doping-control laboratories and that they are now in a position to provide sports organisations with a continuous and adequate supply of analyses;
Desirous of seeing the principle of doping control outside competition extended in all member states on a harmonious basis, both between countries and between sports, and in a way which is equitable to all athletes, in accordance with the ethical principles and purposes of the European Anti-Doping Charter for Sport,
Recommends the governments of member states to take all the appropriate steps that may fall within their competence, and to offer their co-operation to their sports organisations so that they are encouraged to take all the appropriate steps falling within their competence, with a view to achieving the objectives set out in the appendix to this recommendation;
Instructs the Secretary General to transmit this recommendation to the governments of non-member states party to the European Cultural Convention;
Instructs the Secretary General to transmit this recommendation to international sports organisations.

Appendix to Recommendation N° R (88) 12 Objectives for doping controls without warning outside competitions

1. The setting up, in accordance with the principles of the European Anti-Doping Charter for Sport, of programmes for the carrying out of doping controls on a regular basis, not only at competitions or at events where new regional or world records are claimed, but also, without warning, at any appropriate time outside competitions.
2. The adaptation, or adoption where necessary, of doping regulations by sports organisations so that due provision and authority is made for doping controls without warning outside competitions; these regulations should be fair and equitable, respect the rights of suspected athletes and include the principle of hearing both sides; they should include the principle of the random selection of those to be tested and retested; the regulations should be consistent with the doping regulations and lists of banned substances etc. of the International Olympic Committee and should ensure that there is testing for banned substances, such as anabolic steroids, with long-term effects on performance; they should include provision for the application of appropriate penalties and/or procedures for dealing with cases which seem to reveal either a deliberate or an inadvertent breach of the regulations.
3. Seeking to ensure that regulations of sports organisations are compatible with the provisions of such relevant domestic legislation as may exist, so that effective random doping controls without warning outside competitions may be carried out.
4. Facilitating the task of those officially entrusted by those international sports federations concerned with the carrying out of random doping controls at short notice on the territory of a member state (for example in the granting of visas).
5. Encouraging the creation of voluntary registers whereby athletes who wish to be considered for selection in a representative competition would agree to undergo a duly authorised doping control at any time.
6. Continuing the principle of financial assistance, encouragement and inducement for doping controls on this wider basis.

7. The conclusion of agreements on a bilateral or multilateral basis which would allow athletes from one member state, training on the territory of another, to be tested, in accordance with the principles of this recommendation, by an authorised doping-control team of the latter member state or of an international sports organisation and which would ensure that consequent appropriate action would be taken as if the control had taken place on the athlete's own territory.
8. Taking appropriate steps to ensure that athletes are informed of the principles of the anti-doping campaign on this enlarged basis and that they, and others also concerned, are provided with educational material warning of the dangers of taking or providing doping substances, and explaining the ethical implications of doping abuse in sport.
9. Ensuring that the effectiveness of out-of-competition controls is not undermined by athletes having access to doping agents.

8.7. Resolution on Doping in sport and the draft Anti-doping Convention (89/1)

The European Ministers responsible for Sport, meeting at Reykjavik for their 6th Conference from 30 May to 1 June 1989

Welcome the adoption by the 1st Permanent World Anti-Doping in Sport Conference in Ottawa (26 to 29 June 1988) of the text, based on the European Anti-Doping Charter, and supported by the 2nd International Conference of Ministers and Senior Officials responsible for Sport and Physical Education organised by Unesco at Moscow (22 to 25 November 1988);
Note that the recommendation of the Unesco conference called for member states to examine the desirability of recognising and adopting the International Olympic Anti-doping Charter;
Endorse the principles of this Charter and those elements that relate to the role of governments, and support the efforts of the Canadian government to promote the world-wide endorsement of the Charter among governments;
Note that since the Sports Ministers at their 13th informal meeting at Athens, 1 and 2 June 1988, made their proposal for the preparation of an anti-doping Convention, some developments in international sport have further reinforced the need for concerted and effective international action to combat doping in sport, to be taken by public authorities and sports organisations acting in conjunction in their respective but complementary areas of responsibility;
Welcome the decision taken by the International Olympic Committee to set up an independent doping control team for international out-of-competition testing;

Appeal to all sports organisations:
1. to follow the International Olympic Anti-Doping Charter;
2. to introduce proper control and disciplinary procedures in line with that Charter;
3. to facilitate the work of the IOC independent out-of-competition doping control team;
4. to introduce medical care and supervision for their members which respects the rights of sportsmen and sportswomen;
5. to develop constructive educational campaigns;

Welcome the proposals made by the Committee for the Development of Sport with regard to a draft anti-doping Convention;
Resolve to continue their efforts to achieve world-wide agreements on effective anti-doping measures;
Consider that the draft anti-doping Convention is one such measure and hope that other states not participating in the Conference will examine this draft text favourably with a view to extending international co-operation and harmonisation on this subject;

Approve the draft texts of the anti-doping Convention and explanatory memorandum as examined by this Conference,

Invite the Committee of Ministers of the Council of Europe to:

1. adopt the text of this draft Convention (see Part I of this Volume) and to decide to open it for signature at an early date;
2. invite other states not members of the Council of Europe to accede to the Convention;
3. authorise the publication of the draft explanatory memorandum to the draft Convention;
4. instruct the Secretary General to transmit this resolution to the government of Canada;
5. instruct the Secretary General to transmit this resolution to the governments of states invited to accede to the European Cultural Convention and to the international sports organisations.

8.8. Anti-doping Convention
Strasbourg, 16 November 1989
European Treaty Series – No. 135

Preamble
The member States of the Council of Europe, the other States party to the European Cultural Convention, and other States, signatory hereto,
Considering that the aim of the Council of Europe is to achieve a greater unity between its members for the purpose of safeguarding and realising the ideals and principles which are their common heritage and facilitating their economic and social progress;
Conscious that sport should play an important role in the protection of health, in moral and physical education and in promoting international understanding;
Concerned by the growing use of doping agents and methods by sportsmen and sportswomen throughout sport and the consequences thereof for the health of participants and the future of sport;
Mindful that this problem puts at risk the ethical principles and educational values embodied in the Olympic Charter, in the International Charter for Sport and Physical Education of Unesco and in Resolution (76) 41 of the Committee of Ministers of the Council of Europe, known as the "European Sport for All Charter";
Bearing in mind the anti-doping regulations, policies and declarations adopted by the international sports organisations;
Aware that public authorities and the voluntary sports organisations have complementary responsibilities to combat doping in sport, notably to ensure the proper conduct, on the basis of the principle of fair play, of sports events and to protect the health of those that take part in them;
Recognising that these authorities and organisations must work together for these purposes at all appropriate levels;
Recalling the resolutions on doping adopted by the Conference of European Ministers responsible for Sport, and in particular Resolution No. 1 adopted at the 6th Conference at Reykjavik in 1989;
Recalling that the Committee of Ministers of the Council of Europe has already adopted Resolution (67) 12 on the doping of athletes, Recommendation No. R (79) 8 on doping in sport, Recommendation No. R (84) 19 on the "European Anti-doping Charter for Sport", and

Recommendation No. R (88) 12 on the institution of doping controls without warning outside competitions;

Recalling Recommendation No. 5 on doping adopted by the 2nd International Conference of Ministers and Senior Officials responsible for Sport and Physical Education organised by Unesco at Moscow (1988);

Determined however to take further and stronger co-operative action aimed at the reduction and eventual elimination of doping in sport using as a basis the ethical values and practical measures contained in those instruments,

Have agreed as follows:

Article 1 – Aim of the Convention

The Parties, with a view to the reduction and eventual elimination of doping in sport, undertake, within the limits of their respective constitutional provisions, to take the steps necessary to apply the provisions of this Convention.

Article 2 – Definition and scope of the Convention

1 For the purposes of this Convention:

a "doping in sport" means the administration to sportsmen or sportswomen, or the use by them, of pharmacological classes of doping agents or doping methods;

b "pharmacological classes of doping agents or doping methods" means, subject to paragraph 2 below, those classes of doping agents or doping methods banned by the relevant international sports organisations and appearing in lists that have been approved by the monitoring group under the terms of Article 11.1.b;

c "sportsmen and sportswomen" means those persons who participate regularly in organised sports activities.

2 Until such time as a list of banned pharmacological classes of doping agents and doping methods is approved by the monitoring group under the terms of Article 11.1.b, the reference list in the appendix to this Convention shall apply.

Article 3 – Domestic co-ordination

1 The Parties shall co-ordinate the policies and actions of their government departments and other public agencies concerned with combating doping in sport.

2 They shall ensure that there is practical application of this Convention, and in particular that the requirements under Article 7 are met, by entrusting, where appropriate, the implementation of some of the provisions of this Convention to a designated governmental or non-governmental sports authority or to a sports organisation.

Article 4 – Measures to restrict the availability and use of banned doping agents and methods

1 The Parties shall adopt where appropriate legislation, regulations or administrative measures to restrict the availability (including provisions to control movement, possession, importation, distribution and sale) as well as the use in sport of banned doping agents and doping methods and in particular anabolic steroids.

2 To this end, the Parties or, where appropriate, the relevant non-governmental organisations shall make it a criterion for the grant of public subsidies to sports organisations that they effectively apply anti-doping regulations.

3 Furthermore, the Parties shall:

a assist their sports organisations to finance doping controls and analyses, either by direct subsidies or grants, or by recognising the costs of such controls and analyses when determining the overall subsidies or grants to be awarded to those organisations;

b take appropriate steps to withhold the grant of subsidies from public funds, for training purposes, to individual sportsmen and sportswomen who have been suspended following a doping offence in sport, during the period of their suspension;

c encourage and, where appropriate, facilitate the carrying out by their sports organisations of the doping controls required by the competent international sports organisations whether during or outside competitions; and

d encourage and facilitate the negotiation by sports organisations of agreements permitting their members to be tested by duly authorised doping control teams in other countries.

4 Parties reserve the right to adopt anti-doping regulations and to organise doping controls on their own initiative and on their own responsibility, provided that they are compatible with the relevant principles of this Convention.

Article 5 – Laboratories

1 Each Party undertakes:

a either to establish or facilitate the establishment on its territory of one or more doping control laboratories suitable for consideration for accreditation under the criteria adopted by the relevant international sports organisations and approved by the monitoring group under the terms of Article 11.1.b; or

b to assist its sports organisations to gain access to such a laboratory on the territory of another Party.

2 These laboratories shall be encouraged to:

a take appropriate action to employ and retain, train and retrain qualified staff;

b undertake appropriate programmes of research and development into doping agents and methods used, or thought to be used, for the purposes of doping in sport and into analytical biochemistry and pharmacology with a view to obtaining a better understanding of the effects of various substances upon the human body and their consequences for athletic performance;

c publish and circulate promptly new data from their research.

Article 6 – Education

1 The Parties undertake to devise and implement, where appropriate in co-operation with the sports organisations concerned and the mass media, educational programmes and information campaigns emphasising the dangers to health inherent in doping and its harm to the ethical values of sport. Such programmes and campaigns shall be directed at both young people in schools and sports clubs and their parents and at adult sportsmen and sportswomen, sports officials, coaches and trainers. For those involved in medicine, such educational programmes will emphasise respect for medical ethics.

2 The Parties undertake to encourage and promote research, in co-operation with the regional, national and international sports organisations concerned, into ways and means of devising scientifically-based physiological and psychological training programmes that respect the integrity of the human person.

Article 7 – Co-operation with sports organisations on measures to be taken by them

1 The Parties undertake to encourage their sports organisations and through them the international sports organisations to formulate and apply all appropriate measures, falling within their competence, against doping in sport.

2 To this end, they shall encourage their sports organisations to clarify and harmonise their respective rights, obligations and duties, in particular by harmonising their:

a anti-doping regulations on the basis of the regulations agreed by the relevant international sports organisations;

b lists of banned pharmacological classes of doping agents and banned doping methods on the basis of the lists agreed by the relevant international sports organisations;

c doping control procedures;

d disciplinary procedures, applying agreed international principles of natural justice and ensuring respect for the fundamental rights of suspected sportsmen and sportswomen; these principles will include:

i the reporting and disciplinary bodies to be distinct from one another;

ii the right of such persons to a fair hearing and to be assisted or represented;

iii clear and enforceable provisions for appealing against any judgment made;

e procedures for the imposition of effective penalties for officials, doctors, veterinary doctors, coaches, physiotherapists and other officials or accessories associated with infringements of the anti-doping regulations by sportsmen and sportswomen;

f procedures for the mutual recognition of suspensions and other penalties imposed by other sports organisations in the same or other countries.

3 Moreover, the Parties shall encourage their sports organisations:

a to introduce, on an effective scale, doping controls not only at, but also without advance warning at any appropriate time outside, competitions, such controls to be conducted in a way which is equitable for all sportsmen and sportswomen and which include testing and retesting of persons selected, where appropriate, on a random basis;

b to negotiate agreements with sports organisations of other countries permitting a sportsman or sportswoman training in another country to be tested by a duly authorised doping control team of that country;

c to clarify and harmonise regulations on eligibility to take part in sports events which will include anti-doping criteria;

d to promote active participation by sportsmen and sportswomen themselves in the anti-doping work of international sports organisations;

e to make full and efficient use of the facilities available for doping analysis at the laboratories provided for by Article 5, both during and outside sports competitions;

f to study scientific training methods and to devise guidelines to protect sportsmen and sportswomen of all ages appropriate for each sport.

Article 8 – International co-operation

1 The Parties shall co-operate closely on the matters covered by this Convention and shall encourage similar co-operation amongst their sports organisations.

2 The Parties undertake:

a to encourage their sports organisations to operate in a manner that promotes application of the provisions of this Convention within all the appropriate international sports organisations to which they are affiliated, including the refusal to ratify claims for world or regional records unless accompanied by an authenticated negative doping control report;

b to promote co-operation between the staffs of their doping control laboratories established or operating in pursuance of Article 5; and

c to initiate bilateral and multilateral co-operation between their appropriate agencies, authorities and organisations in order to achieve, at the international level as well, the purposes set out in Article 4.1.

3 The Parties with laboratories established or operating in pursuance of Article 5 undertake to assist other Parties to enable them to acquire the experience, skills and techniques necessary to establish their own laboratories.

Article 9 – Provision of information

Each Party shall forward to the Secretary General of the Council of Europe, in one of the official languages of the Council of Europe, all relevant information concerning legislative and other measures taken by it for the purpose of complying with the terms of this Convention.

Article 10 – Monitoring group

1 For the purposes of this Convention, a monitoring group is hereby set up.

2 Any Party may be represented on the monitoring group by one or more delegates. Each Party shall have one vote.

3 Any State mentioned in Article 14.1 which is not a Party to this Convention may be represented on the monitoring group by an observer.

4 The monitoring group may, by unanimous decision, invite any non-member State of the Council of Europe which is not a Party to the Convention and any sports or other professional organisation concerned to be represented by an observer at one or more of its meetings.

5 The monitoring group shall be convened by the Secretary General. Its first meeting shall be held as soon as reasonably practicable, and in any case within one year after the date of the entry into force of the Convention. It shall subsequently meet whenever necessary, on the initiative of the Secretary General or a Party.

6 A majority of the Parties shall constitute a quorum for holding a meeting of the monitoring group.

7 The monitoring group shall meet in private.

8 Subject to the provisions of this Convention, the monitoring group shall draw up and adopt by consensus its own Rules of Procedure.

Article 11

1 The monitoring group shall monitor the application of this Convention. It may in particular:

a keep under review the provisions of this Convention and examine any modifications necessary;

b approve the list, and any revision thereto, of pharmacological classes of doping agents and doping methods banned by the relevant international sports organisations, referred to in Articles 2.1 and 2.2, and the criteria for accreditation of laboratories, and any revision thereto, adopted by the said organisations, referred to in Article 5.1.a, and fix the date for the relevant decisions to enter into force;

c hold consultations with relevant sports organisations;

d make recommendations to the Parties concerning measures to be taken for the purposes of this Convention;

e recommend the appropriate measures to keep relevant international organisations and the public informed about the activities undertaken within the framework of this Convention;

f make recommendations to the Committee of Ministers concerning non-member States of the Council of Europe to be invited to accede to this Convention;

g make any proposal for improving the effectiveness of this Convention.

2 In order to discharge its functions, the monitoring group may, on its own initiative, arrange for meetings of groups of experts.

Article 12

After each meeting, the monitoring group shall forward to the Committee of Ministers of the Council of Europe a report on its work and on the functioning of the Convention.

Article 13 – Amendments to the Articles of the Convention

1 Amendments to the articles of this Convention may be proposed by a Party, the Committee of Ministers of the Council of Europe or the monitoring group.

2 Any proposal for amendment shall be communicated by the Secretary General of the Council of Europe to the States mentioned in Article 14 and to every State which has acceded to or has been invited to accede to this Convention in accordance with the provisions of Article 16.

3 Any amendment proposed by a Party or the Committee of Ministers shall be communicated to the monitoring group at least two months before the meeting at which it is to be considered. The monitoring group shall submit to the Committee of Ministers its opinion on the proposed amendment, where appropriate after consultation with the relevant sports organisations.

4 The Committee of Ministers shall consider the proposed amendment and any opinion submitted by the monitoring group and may adopt the amendment.

5 The text of any amendment adopted by the Committee of Ministers in accordance with paragraph 4 of this article shall be forwarded to the Parties for acceptance.

6 Any amendment adopted in accordance with paragraph 4 of this article shall come into force on the first day of the month following the expiration of a period of one month after all Parties have informed the Secretary General of their acceptance thereof.

Final clauses

Article 14

1 This Convention shall be open for signature by member States of the Council of Europe, other States party to the European Cultural Convention and non-member States which have participated in the elaboration of this Convention, which may express their consent to be bound by:

a signature without reservation as to ratification, acceptance or approval, or

b signature subject to ratification, acceptance or approval, followed by ratification, acceptance or approval.

2 Instruments of ratification, acceptance or approval shall be deposited with the Secretary General of the Council of Europe.

Article 15

1 The Convention shall enter into force on the first day of the month following the expiration of a period of one month after the date on which five States, including at least

four member States of the Council of Europe, have expressed their consent to be bound by the Convention in accordance with the provisions of Article 14.

2 In respect of any signatory State which subsequently expresses its consent to be bound by it, the Convention shall enter into force on the first day of the month following the expiration of a period of one month after the date of signature or of the deposit of the instrument of ratification, acceptance or approval.

Article 16

1 After the entry into force of this Convention, the Committee of Ministers of the Council of Europe, after consulting the Parties, may invite to accede to the Convention any non-member State by a decision taken by the majority provided for in Article 20.d of the Statute of the Council of Europe and by the unanimous vote of the representatives of the Contracting States entitled to sit on the Committee.

2 In respect of any acceding State, the Convention shall enter into force on the first day of the month following the expiration of a period of one month after the date of the deposit of the instrument of accession with the Secretary General of the Council of Europe.

Article 17

1 Any State may, at the time of signature or when depositing its instrument of ratification, acceptance, approval or accession, specify the territory or territories to which this Convention shall apply.

2 Any State may, at any later date, by a declaration addressed to the Secretary General, extend the application of this Convention to any other territory specified in the declaration. In respect of such territory the Convention shall enter into force on the first day of the month following the expiration of a period of one month after the date of receipt of such declaration by the Secretary General.

3 Any declaration made under the two preceding paragraphs may, in respect of any territory mentioned in such declaration, be withdrawn by a notification addressed to the Secretary General. Such withdrawal shall become effective on the first day of the month following the expiration of a period of six months after the date of receipt of the notification by the Secretary General.

Article 18

1 Any Party may, at any time, denounce this Convention by means of a notification addressed to the Secretary General of the Council of Europe.

2 Such denunciation shall become effective on the first day of the month following the expiration of a period of six months after the date of receipt of the notification by the Secretary General.

Article 19

The Secretary General of the Council of Europe shall notify the Parties, the other member States of the Council of Europe, the other States party to the European Cultural Convention, the non-member States which have participated in the elaboration of this Convention and any State which has acceded or has been invited to accede to it of:

a any signature in accordance with Article 14;

b the deposit of any instrument of ratification, acceptance, approval or accession in accordance with Article 14 or 16;

c any date of entry into force of this Convention in accordance with Articles 15 and 16;

d any information forwarded under the provisions of Article 9;
e any report prepared in pursuance of the provisions of Article 12;
f any proposal for amendment or any amendment adopted in accordance with Article 13 and the date on which the amendment comes into force;
g any declaration made under the provisions of Article 17;
h any notification made under the provisions of Article 18 and the date on which the denunciation takes effect;
i any other act, notification or communication relating to this Convention.

In witness whereof the undersigned, being duly authorised thereto, have signed this Convention.

Done at Strasbourg, the 16th day of November 1989, in English and French, both texts being equally authentic, in a single copy which shall be deposited in the archives of the Council of Europe. The Secretary General of the Council of Europe shall transmit certified copies to each member State of the Council of Europe, to the other States party to the European Cultural Convention, to the non-member States which have participated in the elaboration of this Convention and to any State invited to accede to it.

Appendix

New Reference List of Prohibited Pharmacological Classes of Doping Agents and Doping Methods[4]
And its Appendix

Date of Entry Into Force : 31 March 2000

I. PROHIBITED CLASSES OF SUBSTANCES

A. Stimulants
Prohibited substances in class (A) include the following examples:
amineptine, amiphenazole, amphetamines, bromantan, caffeine*, carphedon, cocaine, ephedrines**, fencamfamin, mesocarb, pentetrazol, pipradrol, salbutamol***, salmeterol***, terbutaline***, … and related substances.

* For caffeine the definition of a positive is a concentration in urine greater than 12 micrograms per millilitre.

** For cathine, the definition of a positive is a concentration in urine greater than 5 micrograms per millilitre. For ephedrine, and methylephedrine, the definition of a positive is a concentration in urine greater than 10 micrograms per millilitre. For phenylpropanolamine and pseudoephedrine, the definition of a positive is a concentration in urine greater than 25 micrograms per millilitre.

4 Previously amended on 1 September 1990, on 24 January 1992, on 1 August 1993, on 1 July 1996, on 1 July 1997, on 15 March 1998 and on 15 March 1999.

*** Permitted by inhaler only to prevent and/or treat asthma and exercise-induced asthma. Written notification of asthma and/or exercise-induced asthma by a respiratory or team physician is necessary to the relevant medical authority.

NOTE: All imidazole preparations are acceptable for topical use. Vasoconstrictors may be administered with local anaesthetic agents. Topical preparations (e.g. nasal, ophtalmological, rectal) of adrenaline and phenylephrine are permitted.

B. Narcotics

Prohibited substances in class (B) include the following examples:

buprenorphine, dextromoramide, diamorphine (heroin), methadone, morphine, pentazocine, pethidine, … and related substances.

NOTE: codeine, dextromethorphan, dextropropoxyphene, dihydrocodeine, diphenoxylate, ethylmorphine, pholcodine, propoxyphene and tramadol are permitted.

C. Anabolic agents

Prohibited substances in class (C) include the following examples:

1. Anabolic androgenic steroids
   a. clostebol, fluoxymesterone, metandienone, metenolone, nandrolone, 19-norandrostenediol, 19-norandrostenedione, oxandrolone, stanozolol, … and related substances.
   b. androstenediol, androstenedione, dehydroepiandrosterone (DHEA), dihydrotestosterone, testosterone*, … and related substances.

Evidence obtained from metabolic profiles and/or isotopic ratio measurements may be used to draw definitive conclusions.

* The presence of a testosterone (T) to epitestosterone (E) ratio greater than six (6) to one (1) in the urine of a competitor constitutes an offence unless there is evidence that this ratio is due to a physiological or pathological condition, e.g. low epitestosterone excretion, androgen producing tumour, enzyme deficiencies.

In the case of T/E higher than 6, it is mandatory that the relevant medical authority conducts an investigation before the sample is declared positive. A full report will be written and will include a review of previous tests, subsequent tests and any results of endocrine investigations. In the event that previous tests are not available, the athlete should be tested unannounced at least once per month for three months. The results of these investigations should be included in the report. Failure to co-operate in the investigations will result in declaring the sample positive.

2. Beta-2 agonists

   bambuterol, clenbuterol, fenoterol, formoterol, reproterol, salbutamol*, terbutaline*, … and related substances.

* Authorized by inhalation as described in Article (I.A).

D. Diuretics

Prohibited substances in class (D) include the following examples:

acetazolamide, bumetanide, chlorthalidone, ethacrynic acid, furosemide, hydrochlorothiazide, mannitol*, mersalyl, spironolactone, triamterene, ... and related substances.

* Prohibited by intravenous injection.

E. Peptide hormones, mimetics and analogues

Prohibited substances in class (E) include the following examples and their analogues and mimetics:

1. Chorionic Gonadotrophin (hCG) prohibited in males only;
2. Pituitary and synthetic gonadotrophins (LH) prohibited in males only;
3. Corticotrophins (ACTH, tetracosactide);
4. Growth hormone (hGH);
5. Insulin-like Growth Factor (IGF-1);
   and all the respective releasing factors and their analogues;
6. Erythropoietin (EPO);
7. Insulin;

permitted only to treat certified insulin-dependent diabetes. Written certification of insulin-dependent diabetes must be obtained from an endocrynologist or team physician.

The presence of an abnormal concentration of an endogenous hormone in class (E) or its diagnostic marker(s) in the urine of a competitor constitutes an offence unless it has been proven to be due to a physiological or pathological condition.

II. PROHIBITED METHODS

The following procedures are prohibited:

1. Blood doping;
2. Administering artificial oxygen carriers or plasma expanders;
3. Pharmacological, chemical and physical manipulations.

III. CLASSES OF PROHIBITED SUBSTANCES IN CERTAIN CIRCUMSTANCES

A. Alcohol

Where the rules of a responsible authority so provide, tests will be conducted for ethanol.

B. Cannabinoids

Where the rules of a responsible authority so provide, tests will be conducted for cannabinoids (e.g. Marijuana, Hashish). At the Olympic Games, tests will be conducted for cannabinoids. A concentration in urine of 11-nor-delta 9-tetrahydrocannabinol-9-carboxylic acid (carboxy-THC) greater than 15 nanograms per millilitre constitutes doping.

C. Local anaesthetics

Injectable local anaesthetics are permitted under the following conditions:

a. bupivacaine, lidocaine, mepivacaine, procaine, and related substances, can be used but not cocaine. Vasoconstrictor agents may be used in conjunction with local anaesthetics;

b. only local or intra-articular injections may be administered;

c. only when medically justified.

Where the rules of a responsible authority so provide, notification of administration may be necessary.

D. Glucocorticosteroids

The systemic use of glucocorticosteroids is prohibited when administered orally, rectally, or by intravenous or intramuscular injection.

E. Beta-blockers

Prohibited substances in class (E) include the following examples:

acebutolol, alprenolol, atenolol, labetalol, metoprolol, nadolol, oxprenolol, propranolol, sotalol, … and related substances.

Where the rules of a responsible authority so provide, tests will be conducted for beta-blockers.

Summary of Urinary Concentrations above which IOC Accredited Laboratories must Report Findings for Specific Substances

caffeine	> 12 micrograms / millilitre
carboxy-THC	> 15 nanograms / millilitre
cathine	> 5 micrograms / millilitre
ephedrine	> 10 micrograms / millilitre
epitestosterone	> 200 nanograms / millilitre
methylephedrine	> 10 micrograms / millilitre
morphine	> 1 microgram / millilitre
19-norandrosterone	> 2 nanograms / millilitre in males
19-norandrosterone	> 5 nanograms / millilitre in females
phenylpropanolamine	> 25 micrograms / millilitre
pseudoephedrine	> 25 micrograms / millilitre
salbutamol (out-of-competition testing)	> 1000 nanograms / millilitre
T/E ratio	> 6

IV. OUT-OF-COMPETITION TESTING

Unless specifically requested by the responsible authority, out-of-competition testing is directed solely at prohibited substances in class I.C (Anabolic Agents), I.D. (Diuretics), I.E. (Peptide Hormones, Mimetics and Analogues), and II (Prohibited Methods).

LIST OF EXAMPLES OF PROHIBITED SUBSTANCES

CAUTION: This is not an exhaustive list of prohibited substances. Many substances that do not appear on this list are considered prohibited under the term "and related substances". Athletes must ensure that any medicines, supplement, over-the-counter preparation or any other substances they use does not contain any prohibited substance.

STIMULANTS:
amineptine, amfepramone, amiphenazole, amphetamine, bambuterol, bromantan, caffeine, carphedon, cathine, cocaine, cropropamide, crotethamide, ephedrine, etamivan, etilamphetamine, etilefrine, fencamfamin, fenetylline, fenfluramine, formoterol, heptaminol, mefenorex, mephentermine, mesocarb, methamphetamine, methoxyphenamine, methylendioxyamphetamine, methylephedrine, methylphenidate, nikethamide, norfenfluramine, parahydroxyamphetamine, pemoline, pentetrazol, phendimetrazine, phentermine, phenylephrine, phenylpropanolamine, pholedrine, pipradrol, prolintane, propylhexedrine, pseudoephedrine, reproterol, salbutamol, salmeterol, selegiline, strychnine, terbutaline,

NARCOTICS:
buprenorphine, dextromoramide, diamorphine (heroin), hydrocodone, methadone, morphine, pentazocine, pethidine,

ANABOLIC AGENTS:
androstenediol, androstenedione, bambuterol, boldenone, clenbuterol, clostebol, danazol, dehydrochlormethyltestosterone, dehydroepiandrosterone (DHEA), dihydrotestosterone, drostanolone, fenoterol, fluoxymesterone, formebolone, formoterol, gestrinone, mesterolone, metandienone, metenolone, methandriol, methyltestosterone, mibolerone, nandrolone, 19-norandrostenediol, 19-norandrostenedione, norethandrolone, oxandrolone, oxymesterone, oxymetholone, reproterol, salbutamol, salmeterol, stanozolol, terbutaline, testosterone, trenbolone,

DIURETICS
acetazolamide, bendroflumethiazide, bumetanide, canrenone, chlortalidone, ethacrynic acid, furosemide, hydrochlorothiazide, indapamide, mannitol (by intravenous injection), mersalyl, spironolactone, triamterene,

MASKING AGENTS:
bromantan, diuretics (see above), epitestosterone, probenecid,

PEPTIDE HORMONES, MIMETICS AND ANALOGUES:
ACTH, erythropoietin (EPO), hCG*, hGH, insulin, LH*, clomiphene*, cyclofenil*, tamoxifen*,
* Prohibited in males only

BETA BLOCKERS:
acebutolol, alprenolol, atenolol, betaxolol, bisoprolol, bunolol, carteolol, celiprolol, esmolol, labetalol, levobunolol, metipranolol, metoprolol, nadodol, oxprenolol, pindolol, propranolol, sotalol, timolol.

APPENDIX

Salbutamol

Salbutamol is classified as both a stimulant and an anabolic agent.

The intent of out-of-competition testing is to detect anabolic agents. The revised rules on salbutamol consider it as anabolic agent when its concentration is higher than 500 nanograms/millilitre and confirmed by enantiomeric analysis.

However, pending the acceptance of the enantiomeric analysis by a peer-reviewed journal, only concentrations higher than 1000 manograms/millilitre will be considered positive as an anabolic agent until further notice. Samples that contain less than this amount are not to be reported to the authorities for out-of-competition testing.

In-competition testing is designed to detect the use of salbutamol either as an anabolic agent or as a stimulant. Whether or not the administration of salbutamol is declared is an important issue for in-competition testing.

As always, it is the task of the authorities to interpret the laboratory finding. In order not to overload authorities with the need to confirm medical notifications of non-recent inhaled use, laboratories do not need to report concentrations lower than 100 manograms/millilitre.

All concentrations above correspond to free (non conjugated) salbutamol.

Ephedrines

The pharmacology and urinary pharmacokinetics of the ephedrines were reviewed. The consensus was that the revised cut-offs would detect all cases of doping where the ephedrines were ingested on the day of competition.

Explanatory Report

Introduction

- At the 13th Informal Meeting of the European Conference of Ministers responsible for Sport, held near Athens on 1 and 2 June 1988, the Sports Ministers, in the framework of a lengthy discussion on doping, agreed that, in order to maintain and improve the Council of Europe's lead in anti-doping work, it would be advisable to prepare an anti-doping convention which should be open for signature by non-member states of the Council of Europe. This should be based on earlier accepted texts of the Council of Europe, such as the European Anti-Doping Charter for Sport (Recommendation No. R (84) 19). A convention "would be a further encouragement to those already engaged in such work, a significant step towards a greater unity of approach and a signal of Europe's determination to keep up the work" it was already engaged in.
- The Bureau of the Committee for the Development of Sport (CDDS), at its meeting in September 1988, agreed to try to meet the wish of the Sports Ministers expressed in Athens to approve a text of the proposed convention at their 6th Conference to be held at Reykjavik on 31 May and 1 June 1989. The CDDS, with the help of its Expert

Group on the European Anti-Doping Charter for Sport (DS-DO), therefore worked on the preparation of the draft convention in the second half of 1988 and the first half of 1989, together with this explanatory report,

- The 6th Conference of European Ministers responsible for Sport at Reykjavik adopted Resolution No. 1 approving the text of the proposed draft convention and transmitted it, and the draft explanatory report, to the Committee of Ministers, inviting it to adopt it and open it for signature at an early date.
- The Committee of Ministers, meeting at Deputy level, adopted the text of the convention (No. 135 in the European Treaty Series) at its 428th meeting on 19 September 1989 and decided that it would be opened for signature on 16 November 1989 at the 85th Session of the Committee of Ministers.
- The Committee of Ministers also authorised the publication of this explanatory report on 19 September 1989.

Background

- The Convention is largely based on previous work of the Council of Europe on doping in sport. It behoves us, therefore, to set out this work and to comment on the texts which have been accepted in the past. It is to be noted that the resolutions and recommendations of the Committee of Ministers mentioned below were adopted unanimously.
- The first text to do with sport adopted by the Council of Europe was indeed on the subject of doping. The refusal of the first five riders in the 1966 world road-race championship to submit to a doping control and the death of a professional cyclist in the 1967 *Tour de France had* resulted in considerable public concern at the abuse of drugs in sport. The adoption by the Committee of Ministers in 1967 of Resolution (67) 12 on the doping of athletes was therefore particularly timely. It was the first international text of this kind on the subject. Later that year, the International Olympic Committee instituted its first doping controls, for the 1968 Olympic Games. Resolution (67) 12 provided a definition of doping that was accepted for several years – it talked of chemical or physiological manipulation – and was sufficiently broad to include types of doping which were not even thought of in 1967, such as "blood-doping". The resolution stressed the moral and ethical principles at stake for sport, and the health dangers for athletes. It recommended governments to persuade sports organisations to take the necessary steps to have proper and adequate regulations and to penalise offenders. Lastly, the resolution recommended governments to take action themselves if the sports organisations did not act sufficiently within three years.
- It is to be noted that several states legislated against doping in this period: Belgium and France in 1965, Italy and Turkey in 1971. Amongst sports bodies, the International Olympic Committee (IOC) had adopted anti-doping regulations in 1967; the Swiss Sports Association in the same year. The *Union cycliste internationale had* in fact been the first sports organisation to have anti-doping regulations (since 1965) and to set up a system of accredited laboratories.
- As the 1967 resolution clearly states two of the main principles which have guided the Council of Europe in all its subsequent work on doping, it is perhaps useful to examine them:

  a. *An insistence on the ethical and moral aspects*

     Doping is cheating.

     Doping is contrary to the values of sport and the principles for which it stands: fair play, equal chances, loyal competition, healthy activity. Doping endangers the health of athletes, as they are using substances in ways that they were not designed for; sport is meant to be a life-enhancing activity not one that imperils life. In Resolution (76) 41 on the principles for a policy for sport for all the European Sport for All Charter of 1975 – the practice of doping was described as "abusive and debasing".

b. *The responsibility of sports organisations*

– It is the governing bodies of sport who are responsible for organising all internal aspects of the competition, events and activities which they provide for their members. Doping is one of these aspects: it is upon them that the primary responsibility falls for drawing up doping regulations, providing doping controls, fixing penalties, etc., as with other aspects of discipline. Governments, desirous of respecting the autonomy of the voluntary sports movement, respect its capacity for self-regulation. Doping in sport is a legal offence only in countries which have legislated, and a "police force" for sport is not therefore practicable on a large scale. Furthermore, sport is international so there is a need for the international sports organisations to ensure equality of chances and obligations for all national federations. Governments would not, therefore, in principle intervene unless the sports' governing bodies failed to discharge their responsibilities.

– In the 1970s, action was taken by several national sports organisations (for example, in the Federal Republic of Germany, by the *Deutscher Sportbund;* in Norway, by the Norwegian Confederation of Sport) and most of the international sports federations involved in the Olympic Games aligned their own regulations on those which they had to follow when at the Olympic Games. But if procedures slowly improved, so also did doping techniques: the ingestion of anabolic steroids, to increase muscle mass and endurance; the use of peptide hormones (for example HCG) and the application of testosterone to improve strength/weight ratios. There were rumours of the use of blood-doping in endurance events, and news of the abuse of substances and procedures multiplied considerably in the late 1970s. The pioneering work into detection and analysis techniques undertaken at the first IOC – recognised laboratories, particularly the one at Cologne, financed by the Government of the Federal Republic of Germany, provided evidence of large-scale and often sophisticated abuse. Competitors were being encouraged to win – by friends, by their entourage – on the basis of rumours of success, and thinking that they would be unlikely to be tested, or if so, not detected.

– For the 2nd Conference of European Ministers responsible for Sport (London, 1978), the Committee for the Development of Sport commissioned a study from Prince Alexandre de Merode, President of the IOC Medical Commission, on the then situation. This study revealed wide discrepancies in the status and effectiveness of national and international regulations, inadequate testing, a lack of laboratories, and, lastly, that virtually no preventative work was being undertaken.

– At their 2nd Conference, the Sports Ministers held a major debate on ethical problems in sport, in which doping figured largely, and adopted, in a resolution on "Ethical and human problems in sport", a substantial text on doping. This text stated that governments should provide a co-ordinated policy and an overall medical care framework in which the doping controls of sports organisations could take place. The latter should increase and harmonise their work and begin educational campaigns. It was at the London Conference that the Norwegian Minister responsible for Sport announced his Government's support for the policy of the Norwegian Confederation of Sport, which would not tolerate the use of doping agents by Norwegian competitors, even if that meant that the price to be paid in the future was that Norwegian athletes would no longer win medals in major international events.

- This resolution provided the basis for the next recommendation of the Council of Europe – Recommendation No. R (79) 8 on doping in sport. This recommendation was to encourage the development of reliable detection tests, the creation of an adequate number of approved laboratories, the setting up of a proper programme of controls, providing proper health and medical checks for sports participants, international standardisation of regulations and the institution of strict penalties.
- Once again, the recommendation was faithful to the principle of the separation of competences between governments and sports organisations, but also suggested areas for co-operative work in the development of educational programmes, and in the creation and use of doping control laboratories. Member states were to co-operate in helping set up such laboratories: in 1978-79 there were too few of them – only three IOC-approved laboratories in the then twenty-two states participating in sports co-operation.
- In the aftermath of Recommendation No. R (79) 8, and in the period when the recommendation was influencing national policy, the 11th Olympic Congress at Baden-Baden in 1981 sent a further message from the united sports movement. The athletes described doping as the greatest and most evil scourge of modern sport and called for life bans on all those involved in its administration or use.
- This appeal from Baden-Baden was a spur to further work within the Council of Europe. In considering the desirability of a new initiative, the CDDS was aware of three favourable circumstances:
- governments had made their opposition to doping clear, not only in Recommendation No. R (79) 8, but also, more recently, at the 3rd Conference of Ministers responsible for Sport (Palma de Mallorca, April 1981) when the eradication of doping was specified as the priority topic for their co-operation with international sports organisations;
- sports organisations were aware of their members' urgent appeals, and needed the help of public authorities, for example, with finance and technical facilities;
- lastly, laboratories were confident that they could detect most abuses. Many new laboratories were in the process of being set up and/or accredited by the IOC. Technical facilities and scientific techniques would soon be adequate: it merely required the will to use them.

17. It was in those circumstances that a meeting of CDDS doping experts, mainly laboratory heads, asked the CDDS, in 1981, to prepare a convention on doping in sport. In 1981-2, however, a convention was not a political feasibility: the CDDS suggested, in 1982, and the 9th Informal Meeting of Sports Ministers held in Paris on 27 January 1983 approved, that efforts should be directed towards consolidating all its past work and the work of all the various parties concerned (government, sport, medicine, science) into a new, revised comprehensive strategy. This was the origin of the European Anti-Doping Charter for Sport. This charter would not have the status of a legally binding convention, but that of a recommendation. The intention and hope was, however,

that it would have a moral, political and practical impact rather higher than that of an ordinary recommendation.

18. The European Anti-Doping Charter for Sport was drawn up by an expert group of the CDDS, under the chairmanship of Prince Alexandre de Merode (Belgium). Accompanying this statement of principles were an explanatory memorandum and four annexes listing useful and practical information for doping strategies/policies. It was submitted by the CDDS to the 4th Conference of European Ministers responsible for Sport in Malta (May 1984), approved by the Sports Ministers there in Resolution No. 1, and adopted by the Committee of Ministers in September 1984 as Recommendation No. R (84) 19.

19. In 1984, the General Association of International Sports Federations and the International Olympic Committee both adopted resolutions in support of the charter, as did the Association of European National Olympic Committees in 1985.

20. The Doping Charter, as it is commonly called, has also been cited as a reference text by international public bodies, including the Commission of the European Communities, the World Health Organisation and Unesco.

21. With regard to acceptance by other states, progress was made at the 5th Conference of European Ministers responsible for Sport, in Dublin in October 1986. The Canadian Minister responsible for Sport made proposals, welcomed by the conference, on ways to widen its impact, and offered his help to collaborate with the Council of Europe with this objective in view. In Resolution No. 4 of the Dublin Conference, the Sports Ministers asked for action to enlarge "the circle of countries or regions which could accept and begin to apply the principles" of the charter.

22. A first start was made when, in December 1986, Canada was admitted as an observer in the CDDS work on doping, followed, in March 1988, by the admission of the United States of America.

23. Meanwhile, the Vice-Chairman of the CDDS expert group, Sir Arthur Gold, had been appointed chairman of a working group on doping set up by the (pan-) European Sports Conference. At the 8th European Sports Conference in Athens, in October 1987, participants adopted a declaration on doping which indicated very complementary avenues of thought. Just before that conference, the leaders of sports organisations from socialist countries had issued an appeal in which they asked for internationally accepted rules and obligations on doping, and in particular for out-of-competition controls. In November 1988, the leaders issued an appeal from Budapest, requesting the IOC to set up an international itinerant team for such doping controls.

24. In June 1988, the first Permanent World Conference on Anti- Doping in Sport took place in Ottawa. Co-chaired by Canada and the International Olympic Committee and prepared by a working group composed of representatives from Canada, the United States Olympic Committee and the Chairman and Vice-Chairman of the DS-DO, this conference adopted a series of statements, including an International Anti-Doping Charter. This charter was very largely based on the European charter (Recommendation No. R (84) 19) and was later endorsed by the IOC and became the International Olympic Anti-Doping Charter. Furthermore, at the 2nd International Conference of Ministers and Senior Officials responsible for Sport and Physical Education, organised by Unesco in Moscow in November 1988, the Ministers present adopted a recommendation (No. 5) in support of the International Olympic Anti-Doping Charter. This recommendation referred to the European Anti-Doping Charter.

25. Thus, by the end of 1988, the Conference of European Sports Ministers' resolution adopted in Dublin in October 1986, proposing to enlarge "the circle of countries or

regions which could accept and begin to apply the principles laid down in the European Anti- Doping Charter for Sport", had been carried through with several non-Council of Europe states, and international sporting and intergovernmental organisations endorsing an international charter based on the European one.

26. Meanwhile, on 21 June 1988, the Committee of Ministers had, on the proposal of the 13th Informal Meeting of Sports Ministers (see paragraph 1), adopted Recommendation No. R (88) 12 on the institution of doping controls without warning outside competitions, extending the principles of the charter to this important area of anti-doping work.

The Convention

a. *Reasons for preparing a convention*

27. As the preceding paragraphs will have shown, a major task in the anti-doping campaign is to secure international harmonisation, not only between sports but also between countries. The adoption of the International Olympic Anti-Doping Charter (paragraph 24) was a major step forward in this respect as far as sport is concerned. The Convention provides the counterpoint for public authorities, acknowledging their general responsibility for actively participating in this work as partners with and of sport. The main harmonisation provided by this Convention will be in providing a common backdrop for each country's specific policy. It is not the intention of most of the governments of the signatory states to organise controls themselves, but to ensure that they are carried out by the appropriate authorities. By adopting a common backdrop and framework, governments will help athletes who will know that they are subject to the same policy and procedures no matter which country they come from.

28. Developments in all aspects of doping in the past few years have also brought the topic increasingly into the news: incidents at the Olympic Games in 1988 and the Tour de France in 1988 have dominated the news for days at a time. Athletes themselves have become more conscious of the problem and many have taken initiatives themselves to compete in dope-free sport. The growing number of controls (47 069 analyses in IOC-accredited laboratories in 1988, 2,45% of which were analytically positive A-samples) has also brought, perhaps inevitably, an increase in controversy, appeals and, on occasions, recourse to civil law. Both sports organisations and the athletes who are controlled need to have clear unambiguous regulations and rules, objective analyses and impartial procedures for dealing with infringements. Most laboratories are supported by public funds: governments will therefore seek assurance that they are both properly and adequately used.

29. The pressures of top-class international sport and the rewards for success are now substantial. The length and sophistication of the training required, the intensity and continuity of competition, the psychological demands on an élite performer are very considerable. Such people are provided with technical backup of high standard coaches, trainers, medical and paramedical personnel are available, and they too are required constantly to keep up to date with the latest professional literature. The influence of the "peer group factor" should not be ignored either – both on athletes and on the auxiliary personnel. In these circumstances, the word- of-mouth recommendations of colleagues, the need to do well in a competition for which one is not 100% physically or psychologically ready, and the desire to beat the next person by any means are some of the factors that may trigger the temptation to use – or be ready to use – an artificial aid; often, to use dope, and thus to cheat. By having commonly agreed standards, such as those in the Convention, the pressures are somewhat reduced and thus contribute to a more controlled and acceptable situation.

30. The dividing line between scientific advance and scientific manipulation can often be a fine one, and it is here that ethical considerations can help to provide a clearer view of what should and should not be allowed. The athlete has a body, an organism, which is as inviolate as any other person's; he is engaged in a pursuit of bodily perfection in technical or artistic ways; he requires – at high level – a very high degree of physical fitness, co-ordination, skill and technique. The joy of sport has always been in using these gifts and talents in a way which pushes the boundary of performance just that little bit further- this applies whether the athlete is competing against his or her own self at a recreational level or at top international level. This physical prowess and skill is totally abnegated if it is buoyed up or replaced by pharmaceutical, chemical or physiological experimentation and manipulation. The pharmacological laboratory should not replace the human body. The Convention affirms this position and states clearly that the legitimate search for improved performance can only be sought within agreed limits, and in the respect of each individual human being.

31. Experience often shows that the suppression of an undesirable social phenomenon is not always the result of repressive or controlling actions. Repression often leads to such phenomena going underground and becoming even more difficult to control. On the other hand, to acknowledge the existence of a problem, to discuss it and to provide educational material for target groups at potential risk is in itself a measure of prevention and potential cure. It may be doubted if doping will ever be completely eliminated from sport, any more than society will ever be free of cheating, but the efficacy of the anti-doping campaign will be much improved if the strict and necessary control measures are complemented by long-term educational work. The Council of Europe has always acknowledged this and the Convention turns this appreciation into a commitment, and a commitment in which public authorities have a major role to play in carrying it out.

b. *Main features of the Convention*

32. The Convention, expressing the political will of the Parties to counter doping in sport, recognises that effective action has to be both multilateral and co-operative. Thus, a number of common standards are set out whereby all Parties engage to take an agreed set of measures – legislative, financial, technical, educational, etc. – and a series of common policy measures are set out for implementation by all the bodies concerned within the state, both by governments themselves and by governments in support of sports organisations. One of the main aims of the Convention therefore is to encourage further international harmony and consensus, particularly within the sports organisations themselves, but also, and acting in support of them, the public authorities.

33. Because of the wide variety of constitutional arrangements within the states which have participated in the elaboration of the Convention, and because the Convention is an open one – that is, it is not restricted to Council of Europe member states or states which have acceded to the European Cultural Convention and therefore may attract, it is hoped, other Parties – the Convention tries to avoid setting out a rigid model for legislation or implementation. The Convention recognises that many actors will be involved and that Parties will use the structures and bodies which are most appropriate to it. There will be a common lead by all Parties' governments, and common action by all states: the intermediate features and responsibilities will be individual (see paragraphs 49-51). it is also for this reason that the Convention has purposely avoided making detailed provisions. It sets out a series of basic Common principles, the implementation of which will be up to the appropriate national authorities.

34. It is not the purpose of the Convention to lay down obligations which will be applied with equal rigour to all sports at all levels. It will be for each Party's authorities to judge which sports and which levels require attention and action at various times. However, the Convention ensures that all sports and all sports people will be treated on an equal basis. The spread of doping abuse throughout sport means that authorities will be concerned not only with the top level of high-profile sports but also with the possible misuse of drugs in mass or recreational sport. Each Party will decide its own priorities and emphasis, but public authorities and various sports have the obligation to be able to show, and prove, claims to be free of drug abuse.

35. The Convention tries to strike a balance between understanding the many and complex factors which lead to doping in sport and the somewhat simplistic solution of merely punishing those sports participants found positive. Awareness of the problems of athletes and the pressures on them, the need for them to have rights as well as responsibilities, and the need to search for the person behind the competitor who often encourages or prescribes the use of doping agents, are some of the features of the text.

c. *Text of the Convention*

Preamble

36. The text invites "other states" which do not participate in the work of the Council of Europe on sport (that is, the member states of the Council of Europe and the states which are party to the European Cultural Convention)[5] but which participated in the elaboration of this Convention, that is to say Canada and the United States of America, to join in this international instrument. The text itself has been examined by a group of experts into which those two non-member states have been admitted as observers. Furthermore, Canada, Hungary and Poland took part as observers in the 6th Conference of European Ministers responsible for Sport which approved the draft text of this Convention.

37. Second paragraph. Not all sports are safe at all times for all participants. Injuries may happen. There are particular dangers for young sports people in some sports at elite level, if they are encouraged to excess. The Convention therefore stresses that sport should play an important role in the protection of health, and in developing moral and physical qualities. The fact that sport is organised on an international basis, through the international sports organisations, also provides unique scope for international co-operation and understanding between countries and people.

38. Third paragraph. Evidence is appearing of the spread of doping in sport to more and more sports, and to ever lower levels of sports and at all ages. Some of this may be pure inadvertence, but not all. Public authorities are concerned by the implications of this – not only from the ethical viewpoint, but also because of its possible connections with the general misuse and abuse of drugs in society; in particular, they will wish to help provide a better protection for young people. If abuse is more strictly controlled at top level, which is always a focus for emulation and attention, sports people at other levels will find it easier to resist the spread of abusive practices. Furthermore, governments have a general obligation to take the measures they consider appropriate to protect

[5] Member states of the Council of Europe (1989): Austria, Belgium, Cyprus, Denmark, Finland, France, the Federal Republic of Germany, Greece, Iceland, Ireland, Italy, Liechtenstein, Luxembourg, Malta, the Netherlands, Norway, Portugal, San Marino, Spain, Sweden, Switzerland, Turkey, the United Kingdom. States which have acceded to the European Cultural Convention (1989): Holy See, Hungary, Poland, Yugoslavia.

public health. Top-level sport is subject to intense public attention, and must therefore expect intense scrutiny as well.

39. Fifth paragraph. The international sports federations are responsible for the organisation of the activities under their aegis. They have consistently stressed their democratic, independent, non-governmental nature and their desire to carry out their duties free from political interference. As mentioned in paragraph 24, the International Olympic Committee has adopted its own Anti-Doping Charter in 1988, and most international sports organisations have adopted regulations, etc. which follow those of the IOC. At its 1988 General Assembly, the General Association of International Sports Federations adopted a declaration which, inter alia, stressed the need "to respect the moral and physical well- being of competitors" and stated that: "Sport is about health and honesty and doping is unhealthy and dishonest."

40. Sixth paragraph. Public authorities have a general duty to protect the interests of society as a whole and to protect the health of citizens, including sports people. They should ensure that sport contributes to the wholesome development of each person. Education and information are of special value in preventing the use of doping in sport. The scope for action by public authorities will depend, partly, on each country's constitution, sports legislation and tradition. The voluntary sports organisations, which are independent at international level, but whose degree of autonomy varies from state to state at national level, similarly have varying degrees of scope of action in the anti-doping campaign. It is not possible to specify a precise division of responsibilities for all countries, and in nearly all countries these responsibilities would in practice be shared, each partner contributing to the campaign in the way that it was best able to. The two main areas of complementary responsibility are the need to ensure fair competition and the need to preserve a healthy activity, as stated in paragraph 9 of this report. Articles 3 to 8 of the Convention indicate how these "complementary responsibilities" may be effectively shared and divided.

41. Eighth and ninth paragraphs. See paragraphs 3 and 7 to 26 of this report.

42. Tenth paragraph. As mentioned in paragraph 24, the 2nd Unesco International Conference of Ministers and Senior Officials responsible for Physical Education and Sport adopted a recommendation on doping which brings the principles of the European Anti-Doping Charter, the Ottawa Anti-Doping Charter, and the IOC Anti-Doping Charter into operation at world level as far as public authorities are concerned. This constitutes the first world- wide intergovernmental agreement on doping. The Convention too follows the principles set out in these international texts.

43. Eleventh paragraph. The Convention is conceived as an instrument to intensify international co-operation and harmonisation in the anti-doping campaign. Its essence derives from the political desire to help safeguard the ethics of sport and to preserve the underlying purpose of the Sport For All philosophy. The Convention is not an instrument for bringing about sophisticated technical changes, but a reassertion, at a crucial moment in sport's history, of certain lasting principles.

Article 1 – Aim

44. The aim of the Convention is to reduce and eliminate doping, as far as possible, from sport. This can only be done within the law and states can only commit themselves as far as their existing confidential constraints allow (see paragraphs 50 and 51).

Article 2 – Definition and scope

45. The definition of doping adopted in Resolution (67) 12 (see paragraph 7 above) is now considered by experts to be unsatisfactory in some respects. The international sports

organisations have not yet provided a universal definition, preferring to specify practices or the use of certain substances which are forbidden. The two criteria used by such organisations are:

- practices (that is, all methods) or substances (that is, all doping agents) which have an effect on performance (which includes using such practices or substances to improve training or recuperation from training) to obtain an unfair advantage;
- practices or substances which have either adverse effects on the health of those who take them or which normally healthy persons (which competitors should be) would not need.

This is summarised in Article 2.1.a.

46. The International Olympic Committee (IOC) is to be regarded as the relevant international organisation to be used for reference, as its list of banned classes and methods is now recognised by virtually all international sports federations, including non- Olympic sports, and stems from sport itself. It is the current IOC list (April 1989) which is reproduced in the appendix to the Convention as the reference list, and it is future revisions of it which the Monitoring Group will examine and approve. The word "approve" was chosen as it implies a formal decision and endorsement. As indicated in Article 11.1.b, the drafters have provided for a mechanism allowing speedy approval by the Monitoring Group of new lists, so that they may become legally applicable for the Parties' own purposes. As a transitional measure, the reference list reproduced in the appendix shall apply only between the time of entry into force of the Convention and the time when the Monitoring Group is able to approve a list under the procedure set forth in Article 11. 1.b. Thereafter, the appendix to the Convention shall cease to be effective and the applicable list shall be the list approved by the Monitoring Group (Article 2.2).

47. For the IOC list of banned pharmacological classes of agents and related compounds to be used practically in each country, it is highly desirable to draw up national lists, for doctors and others who look after the health of sportsmen and women, which show indicatively – but as fully as possible – pharmaceutical preparations which are available in each country and which contain (or do not contain) compounds of these banned classes. These lists have to be national as it is at national level that authorisations are given to put pharmaceutical preparations on the market, and some preparations have different trade names in different countries. National authorities will, however, need to be vigilant not only with regard to imports of preparations not available in that country, containing banned classes or related compounds, but also with regard to individual, non-commercial preparations containing them.

48. It is not the drafters' intention that the Convention is to be applied indiscriminately to ail sports and to all levels of sport. Certain sports are assumed to be dope-free. Some sports have a history of fairly consistent drug abuse. National authorities will decide their own priorities and make appropriate selections and decisions: the provisions of the Convention may in some countries be progressively applied to an increasing number of sports. The Convention will be applied realistically, concentrating firstly on sports where doping is known to exist. As dope controls multiply, other sports will provide evidence as to whether or not doping exists in that sport. In most states, membership of an approved sports association or participation in an organised event will automatically confer the obligation to be ready to undergo an authorised doping control. However, the spread of sport and events outside the control of recognised federations means that not all participants are subject to such obligations. The use of the adverb "regularly" in

Article 2.1.c is designed to bring these participants within the remit of the Convention where it is appropriate, while not prescribing an unduly heavy obligation to control purely casual participants. For sports using animals, the definition should bear in mind the explanation given in paragraph 72 of this explanatory report.

Article 3 – Domestic co-ordination

49. There are likely to be several governmental departments or agencies involved in the anti-doping campaign: the departments responsible for sport, physical education, public health, medical care, police and customs, universities and research, veterinary services, etc. They will need to work together constructively to achieve the best results.

50. As stated earlier in this report, inter alia in paragraphs 9.b and 40, the Convention does not propose a single operative method, and it does not intend that governments should usurp or otherwise take over or assume responsibilities which have traditionally been exercised by sports organisations. It is up to each state to decide how responsibilities will be allocated. However, Parties assume, vis-à-vis other Parties, the obligations laid down in the Convention and for this purpose may wish to establish or maintain a national responsible body. In many states, such a consultative or co-ordinating body already exists; if so, it might continue to be responsible for these matters. Experience has shown the usefulness of such a body, which has some degree of authority over individual sports in order to ensure national consistency between sports in anti-doping matters.

51. Article 3.2, may be particularly useful for states which may have already entrusted by law some responsibilities in sport and/or in doping matters to an overall (national in most countries) sports organisation, for states whose legal framework may prevent or hinder the assumption of direct governmental responsibilities, as well for those states whose tradition it is to entrust all sports questions to their national sports organisations.

Article 4 – Availability and use

52. In the IOC list of banned pharmacological classes of agents, there are six main classes: stimulants, narcotics, anabolic steroids, betablockers, diuretics and peptide hormones and analogues. Many of the drugs in the stimulant class – such as amphetamines and related compounds – are protected by strict pharmacists' regulations, and others – such as the ephedrines – are often present in preparations for colds and hay fever which can be bought, quite correctly, directly over the counter. Narcotics are already protected in all phases of their production, distribution and supply by the rigorous provisions of the 1971 Vienna Convention on psychotropic substances. Beta-blockers and diuretics should only be administered under strict medical control.

53. The main area for further restriction lies in the anabolic steroids. This class of drugs is closely related to the male hormone testosterone, which is a natural product. Used unnaturally or in unnatural quantities, it increases muscle bulk, strength and power and, in some circumstances, competitiveness. Used in training periods, it increases the training load which can be assumed and speeds recovery time. In many states, the possession of anabolic steroids is already regulated via the need for a valid and appropriate prescription. Methods which may be appropriate for states to consider besides those mentioned in Article 4, paragraph 1 ("legislation, regulations or administrative measures"), include: strict control of medical ethics and the pharmacists' code; collaboration between the police, customs, veterinary services and public health inspectors; control of private gymnasiums and fitness centres; co-operation between police and customs authorities

and sports organisations; inspection of sports teams' luggage at border controls, etc. A principal objective should be to try and dismantle the channels by which sports people are supplied, increasingly by "outsiders", with illicit consignments of steroids and to punish severely those who organise this trafficking. A future area of concern may lie in the peptide hormone and analogue class.

Article 4 (paragraphs 2 and 3)

54. In addition to direct measures, states may offer various forms of encouragement to sports organisations to reduce the use of doping agents in sport. These may take various forms:
   - financial encouragement and/or penalisation (Articles 4.2, 4.3.a and 4.1b);
   - practical (for example, in facilitating the granting of visas for international itinerant random dope-control teams) (Article 4.3.c);
   - reciprocal standardisation (Article 4.3.d).

55. Paragraph 2 can be applied by states or by central sports organisations which grant subsidies to individual federations in such a way that the criterion may be judged with particular reference to the effectiveness of the regulations applied by the sport to the élite (national level and higher) sector. In the case of very widespread sports and/or sports with a large recreational practice, it would be unrealistic to expect anti-doping regulations to be applied at all levels and at all times with the rigour required for national or international purposes (see also paragraph 48). In order to take account of the special situation of some non- governmental umbrella organisations whose resources derive mainly from public money (CONI in Italy, for example), this article should be applied in such a way that the practice of sport in general is not prejudiced.

56. Paragraph 3.a respects the situation of those states who provide grants to sports organisations without conditions. In addition, governments may underwrite the entire cost of doping controls and analyses or offer partial grants and subsidies to encourage sports organisations to undertake them on a worthwhile scale.

57. Paragraph 3.b is to be interpreted in the sense of withholding financial support from public funds, whether directly or indirectly through sports organisations, to sportsmen and sportswomen (including, where appropriate, to those categories of sports officials mentioned in Article 7.2.e). It does not apply to subsidies granted by sports organisations from non-public sources (though they are encouraged to adopt similar guidelines) nor does it imply that suspended sportsmen and sportswomen are not allowed to benefit from indirect public help (in having access, for example, to a sports facility for training purposes).

Article 4, paragraph 4

58. Some states have adopted legislation by virtue of which, inter alia, public authorities may themselves organise doping controls. This is particularly the case where the public authorities feel that the sports organisations are not fulfilling or shouldering their responsibilities adequately (sub-paragraphs 9.b and 27). Article 4.4 not only recognises this possibility, but it also provides a further encouragement for sports organisations to regulate their own affairs satisfactorily. The conduct of doping controls by public authorities is subject to the same principles and standards as those set out in the Convention and carried out by the sports organisations.

Article 5 – Laboratories

59. The creation of doping control laboratories is an essential part of a coherent anti-doping strategy (see paragraphs 8, 10, 14, 16, 17 and 28 above). Their complexity is such

that, in the vast majority of cases, such laboratories will be attached to an institution benefiting from public funds (hospital, university, etc.). A number of elements for the recognition of doping laboratories are relevant, in particular the criteria established by the International Olympic Committee. Their criteria are followed by virtually all sports organisations. It is their criteria which the Monitoring Group will examine and approve.

60. It is important that laboratories not only reach high technical standards, but that they also abide by an ethical code. Here too the IOC's ethical code provides an internationally accepted safeguard. This code includes safeguards to ensure that controls are not carried out with the sole purpose of screening athletes (for example, before an international competition) but that appropriate action is taken subsequently.

61. Not all states will either wish to have or need a laboratory (a minimum of 2 000 analyses per year is necessary for reasonable economy of operation). In such cases, access to an accredited laboratory in another country must be sought and subsidised in the same way as a laboratory on its own territory, as indicated in Article 5.1.b.

62. Research is an essential part of such laboratories' work (see paragraph 10) and should be incorporated in their assignment and taken into account in staff allocation. The rapid publication of research results is important: publication is a criterion for scientific consideration and for the divulgation of new techniques and/or discoveries, whether relating to analysis or to new doping methods. The development of new detection methods should be made operational and applied in all laboratories as soon as possible.

Article 6 – Education

63. The drafters of the Convention have consistently underlined the importance of effective, preventative work and medical care for athletes as a necessary complement to control (see paragraphs 11, 13, 30, 31 and 35). Education is primarily an area for governmental action, as it must start with young people in schools, when and where they have their first contacts with sport and games in physical education classes. Anti-doping education is a part of general moral and civic education as well as a specific element in the education of sport ethics and fair play. For both the current and the future generations of sportsmen and sportswomen, practical emphasis will doubtless be given to the dangers to health (see also paragraph 76 in this context).

64. However, the necessary complementary role of sports organisations and clubs in education is vitally important, both for young athletes, their parents, and, not least, in educating officials, coaches and medical personnel in the dangers of doping to sport. The regional sports organisations referred to are those within a single country with the authority to act in this way.

65. Medical practitioners need the encouragement of the last sentence of Article 6.1, in order to help them combat the pressures that they too are subject to in the modern, highly competitive sports world (see paragraphs 29 and 35 above).

66. The drafters of the Convention considered that the rights and obligations of the patient and doctor could be summarised as follows:

a. doctors had the right to treat their patients in the way they considered most appropriate (sport did not seek to dictate treatment; even if it did, doctors would not and could not accept it);

b. patients had the responsibility to inform their doctors if they were practising sportsmen and sportswomen and had thus to abide by certain regulations;

c. sports doctors had a responsibility to know the medical and anti-doping regulations of the sports organisation(s) to which they were affiliated;

d. doctors could offer alternative therapies, and it was for the patient to judge the consequences for his or her eligibility to participate in sport;

e. the "workload" often required of a modern, top-level sports person was not a sufficient reason for prescribing medical preparations containing banned substances if the medically indicated therapy was a period of rest.

The drafters noted that the freedom to practise emphasised in subparagraph a would hardly be limited in practice, as, for virtually all medical conditions, there were pharmaceutical preparations available which did not contain any banned classes.

67. A further weapon in the anti-doping campaign is supported in Article 6.2. If biochemical manipulation is to be avoided (see paragraphs 29 and 30 above), science must contribute its dose towards the constant and legitimate search for improved performance. That men and women should consequently seek new barriers or limits to conquer is normal and praiseworthy, but not at any price.

Article 7 – Co-operation with the sports organisations in measures to be taken by them

68. Within the sharing of responsibilities set out in the preamble and Article 3, there are a number of policy and operational matters for which the sports organisations have sole or prime competence: the adoption of regulations, lists of banned classes and methods, control procedures, punishments, the organisation of controls, etc. The purpose of this article is not only to encourage sports organisations to adopt and implement a series of measures which, together, will constitute the effective application of anti-doping regulations called for in Article 4.2; but also to indicate the strong desire for national and international compatibility and harmonisation between sports and countries, with due respect for the rights of persons who may fall foul of these regulations. As indicated earlier (paragraphs 46 and 59), the harmonisation referred to in Article 7.2.a, b and c is to be sought on the basis of the regulations, etc. adopted by the IOC. Parties are conscious that they cannot make demands of the sports organisations; they can, however, and, when they feel it appropriate, must encourage them to undertake certain courses of action, relying on their good sense to turn those principles into practical regulations.

69. Article 7.2.d implies that sports organisations should adapt – or if necessary, adopt – regulations which would give expression to the concept of natural justice, or due process. The principles to be followed are those set down in, for example, the International Covenant on Civil and Political Rights of the United Nations (1966) and, for the member states of the Council of Europe, in the Convention for the Protection of Human Rights and Fundamental Freedoms (1950), or in the procedures adopted by the IOC. In particular, their disciplinary procedures will need to ensure:

a. that the reporting (accusatory) and disciplinary (judging) bodies are distinct. The laboratory or the medical commission should not be the bodies or persons which impose penalties;

b. the suspected athlete should be present, and/or be assisted or represented by a person of his/her choosing, at a hearing which should be fair, and he/she should have the right to speak;

c. there should be clear and enforceable provisions for appealing against any judgement made, and that appeal should be heard with regard to the principles in sub-paragraphs a and b above.

70. The provisions of Article 7.2.d. iii (paragraph 69.c above) should not be interpreted as interfering with the right and duty of sports organisations to organise and prepare for their events properly and fairly. The power to order the disqualification of a sportsman – whether from a result obtained in competition or suspension from future events in

that competition, or as a result of an out-of-competition control – is a necessary power, if only to ensure that athletes who do not use dope can participate in fair and equal competition. If a convicted athlete wishes to appeal, he may do so, after the competition, but the power of the sports organisation to order its affairs may be likened to those powers which enable courts to grant injunctions, temporary or otherwise.

71. Article 7.2.e and f introduces elements of consistency between sports and between nations: to ensure that penalties are not disregarded by seeking alternative jurisdictions, and to ensure that those who encourage or abet the abuse of drugs (see paragraphs 29, 30, 35 and 65) are also subject to similar and proportionate penalties. Any such penalties imposed should also be rendered public.

72. The inclusion of "veterinary doctors" is a reminder that sports involving the use of animals must also apply doping regulations to those animals in order to ensure fair competition. In many countries, drug abuse discovered in such an animal (for example, the horse in modern pentathlon) is treated by regarding the horse as a part of the competitor. It will have been noticed, from the phrase in this paragraph "sports involving the use of animals" and from the definition given in Articles 2. 1.a and 2.1.c, that the Convention was not drawn up with the primary intention of applying to sports that are mainly or solely contests between animals (like horse-racing or greyhound racing), as distinct from human beings. However, co-operation between the responsible authorities and in particular the veterinary experts and laboratories – should continue or be developed in these sports in order to decide and implement effective anti-doping measures, including the detection of attempts to sabotage another animal, appropriate for sports using animals.

73. Article 7.3.a and b repeats the basic principles of Recommendation No. R (88) 12. One international federation organises its own out-of-competition controls; many national anti- doping commissions prefer to organise them on a national basis. The Convention leaves it to the appreciation of each Party to judge what is the most "effective scale" in a way that is equitable for the various sports and for potential competitors. Penalties should also be effective: athletes have responsibilities as well as rights. It is important that suspended athletes wishing to re-enter competition are regularly tested during the period of their suspension, so that, if and when they do so, it is on a fair and equal basis. The purpose of out-of-competition testing is to detect those who abuse drugs during training, thus demonstrating their willingness even determination – to cheat. The emphasis will therefore concentrate on deterring the use of anabolic steroids and other classes of drugs with long-term effects, such as peptide hormones.

74. Following the principles alluded to in paragraph 69, out-of- competition controls should not unreasonably interfere with the private life of a sportsman or sportswoman (see, for example, Article 17 of the International Covenant on Civil and Political Rights).

75. As stated at paragraph 56, governments may decide to finance such out-of-competition controls and analyses either wholly or partly. It is to be anticipated that the emphasis of doping control will progressively shift from competition to out-of-competition controls. The sports organisations have procedures for the imposition of penalties following out-of-competition controls, proposed by the IOC, which take account of ordinary therapeutic needs during training.

76. Article 7.3.f is a further reflection of the concern expressed in Article 6.2, namely that the pressures of modern elite sport may lead to excesses. Many sports organisations already provide guidelines to protect competitors (for example, in age-limits for various levels of competition, frequency of competition, restrictions on particular events at various ages), and such guidelines should be developed so that young sportsmen,

their parents and their coaches are provided with a clear set of practical and reasonable ambitions which will not cause unnecessary harm to the competitor's body or growth patterns. This would remove any temptation to steal a march on other competitors by taking dope. In this context, it is also important to stress that nationalist pressures are also amongst those which may contribute to such temptations. The provision of scientifically prepared training guidelines – based primarily on biomechanical and physiological studies – would provide a necessary start in this direction.

Article 8 – International co-operation

77. Articles 8.1 and 8.2.c are logical extensions of the principle of Articles 3 and 4 in the context of an international instrument. A main channel for such co-ordination will naturally be the Monitoring Group set up by virtue of Article 10.

78. Most international sports organisations already apply regulations giving effect to the principle of only ratifying records when negative doping control reports are submitted. The drafters discussed the desirability of obliging national record claims to be subject to a similar requirement, but the practical difficulties of having a doping control team at every event, in every sport at which a national record might be claimed would be too great. In some countries where the emphasis is on out-of- competition controls, it would also be retrograde. However, the drafters considered that it was important that this explanatory report should mention the desirability of having such a condition, where practical, for national records, at least in high-profile sports or events. The regional records referred to are those of a grouping of countries.

79. Article 8.2 is similarly a logical extension of the principle of Article 7 towards the independent international sports organisations.

80. Articles 8.2b and 8.3 seek to ensure that all Parties have equal access to high-quality laboratories, as provided for in Article 5.

Article 9 – Provision of information

81. The purpose of this article is not primarily to check the effectiveness of the Convention but, through the offices of the Secretary General, to exchange information and experiences between Parties and observers. The meetings of the Monitoring Group (Article 10) are also suitable occasions for providing and exchanging such information.

Articles 10 and 11 – Monitoring Group

82. The purpose of setting up a Monitoring Group, composed of representatives of the Parties, is to facilitate the smooth running of the Convention.

83. In particular, the Monitoring Group is empowered to approve and update the list of banned pharmacological classes of agents and methods referred to in Article 2.1 and the criteria for accreditation of laboratories referred to in Article 5.1.a.

After the transitional period during which the list of banned pharmacological classes of agents and methods appended to the Convention shall be the applicable list, the ordinary procedure for approval of the list, as set forth in Article 11.1.b, shall be followed. The scope of the Convention under the terms of Article 2.1 shall therefore be determined by the decisions of approval by the Monitoring Group.

84. The drafters did not think it useful to have transnational criteria for accreditation of laboratories; hence, the first set of criteria shall be the one approved by the Monitoring Group under the ordinary procedure of Article 11.1.b.

85. In both cases, the Monitoring Group shall fix the date for the relevant decisions to enter into force.

Article 13 – Amendments to the Articles of the Convention

86. The Committee of Ministers, which adopted the original text of the Convention, is also competent to adopt any amendments.
In accordance with paragraph 1, the initiative for amendments may be taken by the Committee of Ministers itself, by the Monitoring Group and by a Party (whether a member state of the Council of Europe or not).
Any proposal for amendment which has not originated with the Monitoring Group should be submitted to it, in accordance with paragraph 3, for an opinion.
Any amendment shall enter into force upon acceptance by ail Parties.

Articles 14 to 19 – Final clauses

87. The provisions contained in Articles 14 to 19 are, for the most part, based on the "Model final clauses for conventions and agreements concluded within the Council of Europe", which were approved by the Committee of Ministers of the Council of Europe at the 315th meeting of their Deputies in February 1980.

88. The provision of Article 14 is intended to enable the maximum number of interested states, not necessarily members of the Council of Europe, to become Parties as soon as possible. The Convention is open for signature by the member states of the Council of Europe, by the other states party to the European Cultural Convention, as well as by non-member states which have participated in its elaboration. The last provision is intended to apply to two non- member states, Canada and the United States of America, which were actively associated with the elaboration of the Convention. They may sign the Convention, just as the member states of the Council of Europe, before its entry into force. According to Article 15, the Convention enters into force when five states, including at least four member states of the Council of Europe, have expressed their consent to be bound by it.

89. Non-member states other than those referred to in Article 14.1 may, by virtue of Article 15, be invited by the Committee of Ministers to accede to the Convention, but only after its entry into force and after consultation of the Parties.
Notes on the Appendix to the Convention
Back to the commentaries on the Convention
The list is based on the banning of pharmacological classes of agents.
This definition has the advantage that new drugs, some of which may be especially designed for doping purposes, are also banned.
The following list represents examples of the different classes of doping agents to illustrate the doping definition. Unless indicated, all substances belonging to the banned classes may not be used for medical treatment, even if they are not listed as examples. Action will be taken if substances of the banned classes are detected in the laboratory. It should be noted that the presence of the drug in the urine constitutes an offence, irrespective of the route of administration.

Explanations

I. Doping classes

A. Stimulants

Stimulants comprise various types of drugs which increase alertness, reduce fatigue and may increase competitiveness and hostility. Their use can also produce loss of judgement, which may lead to accidents to others in some sports. Amphetamine and related compounds have the most notorious reputation in producing problems in sport. Some deaths of sportsmen have resulted even when normal doses have been used under conditions of maximum physical activity. There is no medical justification for the use of "amphetamines" in sport.

One group of stimulants is the sympathomimetic amines of which ephedrine is an example. In high doses, this type of compound produces mental stimulation and increased blood flow. Adverse effects include elevated blood pressure and headache, increased and irregular heart beat, anxiety and tremor. In lower doses, they are often present ephedrine, pseudoephedrine, phenylpropanolamine, norpseudoephedrine, for exemple – in cold and hay fever preparations which can be purchased in pharmacies and sometimes from other retail outlets without the need of a medical prescription.

Thus no product for use in colds, flu or hay fever purchased by a competitor or given to him should be used without first checking with a doctor or pharmacist that the product does not contain a drug of the banned stimulants class.

- Beta 2 agonists

The choice of medication in the treatment of asthma and respiratory ailments has posed many problems. Some years ago, ephedrine and related substances were administered quite frequently. However, these substances are prohibited because they are classed in the category of "sympathomimetic amines" and therefore considered as stimulants.

The use of only the following beta-2 agonists is permitted in aerosol form: bitolterol, orciprenaline, rimiterol, salbutamol, terbutaline.

B. Narcotic analgesics

The drugs belonging to this class, which are represented by morphine and its chemical and pharmacological analogues, act fairly specifically as analgesics for the management of moderate to severe pain. This description, however, by no means implies that their clinical effect is limited to the relief of trivial disabilities. Most of these drugs have major side effects, including dose-related respiratory depression, and carry a high risk of physical and psychological dependence. There exists evidence indicating that narcotic analgesics have been and are abused in sports, and therefore a ban has been issued and maintained on their use during the Olympic Games. The ban is also justified by international restrictions affecting the movement of these compounds and is in line with the regulations and recommendations of the World Health Organisation regarding narcotics.

Furthermore, it is felt that the treatment of slight to moderate pain can be effective using drugs – other than the narcotics – which have analgesic, anti-inflammatory and antipyretic actions. Such alternatives, which have been successfully used for the treatment of sports injuries, include anthranilic acid derivatives (such as mefenamic acid, floctafenine, glafenine, etc.), phenylalkonoic acid derivatives (such as diclofenac, ibuprofen, ketoprofen, naproxen, etc.) and compounds such as indomethacin and sulindac. Athletes and team doctors are also reminded that aspirin and its newer derivatives (such as diflunisal) are not banned, but are cautioned against some pharmaceutical preparations where aspirin is often associated to a banned drug such as codeine. The same precautions hold for cough and cold preparations which often contain drugs of the banned classes.

Note: Dextromethorphan is not banned and may be used as an antitussive; diphenoxylate is also permitted.

C. Anabolic steroids

This class of drugs includes chemicals which are related in structure and activity to the male hormone testosterone, which is also included in this banned class. They have been misused in sport, not only to attempt to increase muscle bulk, strength and power when used with increased food intake, but also in lower doses and normal food intake to attempt to improve competitiveness.

Their use in teenagers who have not fully developed can result in stunted growth by affecting growth at the ends of the long bones. Their use can produce psychological changes, liver damage and can adversely affect the cardiovascular system. In males, their use can reduce testicular size and sperm production; in females, their use can produce masculinisation, acne, development of male-pattern hair growth and suppression of ovarian function and menstruation.

D. Beta-blockers

The therapeutic indications for the use of beta-blocking drugs have been reviewed and it has been noted that there is now a wide range of effective alternative preparations available in order to control hypertension, cardiac arrhythmias, angina pectoris and migraine. Due to the continued misuse of beta-blockers in some sports where physical activity is of no or little importance, the right has been reserved to test those sports which are deemed appropriate. These are unlikely to include endurance events which necessitate prolonged periods of high cardiac output and large stores of metabolic substrates in which beta-blockers would severely decrease performance capacity.

E. Diuretics

Diuretics have important therapeutic indications for the elimination of fluids from the tissues in certain pathological conditions. However, strict medical control is required.

Diuretics are sometimes misused by competitors for two main reasons, namely: to reduce weight quickly in sports where weight categories are involved, and to reduce the concentration of drugs in urine by producing a more rapid excretion of urine to attempt to minimise detection of drug misuse. Rapid reduction of weight in sport cannot be justified medically. Health risks are involved in such misuse because of serious side-effects which might occur.

Furthermore, deliberate attempts to reduce weight artificially in order to compete in lower weight classes or to dilute urine constitute clear manipulations which are unacceptable on ethical grounds. Therefore, it has been decided to include diuretics on the list of banned classes of drugs.

N.B. For sports involving weight classes, the right is reserved to obtain urine samples from the competitor at the time of the weigh- in.

F. Peptide hormones and analogues

It is well known that the administration to males of human chorionic gonadotrophin (HCG) and other compounds with related activity leads to an increased rate of production of endogenous androgenic steroids and is considered to be equivalent to the exogenous administration of testosterone.

Corticotrophin has been misused to increase the blood levels of endogenous corticosteroids, notably to obtain the euphoric effect of corticosteroids. The application of corticotrophin is considered to be equivalent to the oral, intramuscular or intravenous application of corticosteroids (see section III.D).

The misuse of growth hormone in sport is deemed to be unethical and dangerous because of various adverse effects, for example, allergic reactions, diabetogenic effects, and acromegaly when applied in high doses.

All the respective releasing factors of the above-mentioned substances are also banned.

II. *Methods*

A. Blood doping

Blood transfusion is the intravenous administration of red blood cells or related blood products that contain red blood cells. Such products can be obtained from blood drawn from the same (autologous) or from a different (non-autologous) individual. The most common indications for red blood transfusion in conventional medical practice are acute blood loss and severe anaemia.

Blood doping is the administration of blood or related red blood products to an athlete other than for legitimate medical treatment. This procedure may be preceded by withdrawal of blood from the athlete who continues to train in this blood-depleted state.

These procedures contravene the ethics of medicine and of sport. There are also risks involved in the transfusion of blood and related blood products. These include the development of allergic reactions (rash, fever, etc.) and acute haemolytic reaction with kidney damage if incorrectly typed blood is used, as well as delayed transfusion reaction resulting in fever and jaundice, transmission of infectious diseases (viral hepatitis and Aids), overload of the circulation and metabolic shock.

Therefore, the practice of blood doping in sport is banned.

B. Pharmacological, chemical and physical manipulation

The use of substances and of methods which alter the integrity and validity of urine samples used in doping controls is banned. Examples of banned methods are catheterisation, urine substitution and/or tampering, inhibition of renal excretion, for example by probenecid and related compounds.

III. *Classes of drugs subject to certain restrictions*

A. Alcohol

Alcohol is not prohibited. However, breath or blood alcohol levels may be determined at the request of an international federation.

B. Marijuana

Marijuana is not prohibited. However, tests may be carried out at the request of an international federation.

C. Local anaesthetics

Injectable local anaesthetics are permitted under the following conditions:

a. that procaine, xylocaine, carbocaine, etc. are used but not cocaine;
b. only local or intra-articular injections may be administered;
c. only when medically justified (that is, the details including diagnosis, dose and route of administration must be submitted immediately in writing).

D. Corticosteroids

The naturally occurring and synthetic corticosteroids are mainly used as anti-inflammatory drugs which also relieve pain. They influence circulating concentrations of natural corticosteroids in the body. They produce euphoria and side-effects such that their medical use, except when used topically, requires medical control.

Since 1975, attempts have been made to restrict their use during the Olympic Games by requiring a declaration by the team doctors, because it was known that corticosteroids were being used non- therapeutically by the oral, intramuscular and even the intravenous route in some sports. However, the problem was not solved by these restrictions and therefore stronger measures, designed not to interfere with the appropriate medical use of these compounds, became necessary.

The use of corticosteroids is banned except for topical use (aural, opthalmological and dermatological), inhalational therapy (asthma, allergic rhinitis) and local or intra-articular injections.

Any team doctor wishing to administer corticosteroids intra- articularly or locally to a competitor must give written notification.

Note: The explanations given above are an edited version of those issued by the International Olympic Committee in 1989 with regard to its list of banned pharmacological classes of agents and methods.

For the list of banned pharmacological classes of agents and related compounds to be used practically in each country, it is highly desirable to draw up for doctors and others who look after the health of sportsmen and sportswomen national lists which show indicatively, but as fully as possible, the pharmaceutical preparations which are available in each country and which contain (or do not contain) compounds of these banned classes. These lists have to be national as it is at national level that authorisations are given to put pharmaceutical preparations on the market, and some preparations have different trade names in different countries. National authorities will, however, need to be vigilant with respect not only to imports of preparations not available in that country, containing banned classes or related compounds, but also with regard to individual, non-commercial, preparations containing them.

List of declarations made with respect to treaty no. 135
Anti-doping Convention
Complete chronology on: 04/06/00
By State

Denmark:
Declaration contained in a letter handed to the Secretary General at the time of signature, on 16 November 1989 – Or. Engl.
Until further notice the signature of Denmark of this Convention does not engage Greenland and the Faroe Islands.
Period covered: 01/03/90 –
The preceding statement concerns Article(s): 17

France:
Declaration contained in the instrument of approval deposited on 21 January 1991 – Or. Fr.
When depositing its instrument of approval of the Anti-Doping Convention, France declares that according to the provision of Article 17 of the Convention, the Convention shall apply to European and overseas departments of the French Republic.
Period covered: 01/03/91 –
The preceding statement concerns Article(s): 17

Greece:
Declaration contained in a letter from the Permanent Representation of Greece, dated 6 July 1994, registered at the Secretariat General, on 7 July 1994 – Or. Fr.
The Government of the Hellenic Republic declares that the accession of the Former Yugoslav Republic of Macedonia to the Conventions of the Council of Europe to which the Hellenic Republic is a Contracting Party does not imply the recognition of the Former Yugoslav Republic of Macedonia by the Hellenic Republic.
Period covered: 07/07/94 –
The preceding statement concerns Article(s): –

Netherlands:
Declaration contained in the instrument of acceptance, deposited on 11 April 1995 – Or.Engl.
The Kingdom of the Netherlands accepts the said Convention for the Kingdom in Europe.
Period covered: 01/06/95 –
The preceding statement concerns Article(s): 17

United Kingdom:
Declaration contained in a letter from the Permanent Representative, dated 28 September 1993 registered at the Secretariat General on 1 October 1993 – Or. Engl.
In accordance with Article 17 of the said Convention I hereby declare, on behalf of the Government of the United Kingdom, that the Convention shall apply to the Isle of Man, being a territory for whose international relations the Government of the United Kingdom are responsible.
Period covered: 01/11/94 –
The preceding statement concerns Article(s): 17

By the European Community
There are no statements made by the European Community with respect to this treaty.

8.9. Revised Rules of Procedures of the Monitoring Group of the Anti-Doping Convention

The Monitoring Group,
Having regard to the entry into force on 1st March 1990 of the Anti-Doping Convention,
Having regard to Articles 10 to 13 of the Convention,
Adopts the present revised Rules of Procedure:
Preliminary Article
For the purposes of the Rules of Procedure, the following definitions are used:

- "Convention" means the Anti-Doping Convention;
- "Group" means the Monitoring Group of the Convention;
- "Delegate" means the representative of a Party to the Convention;
- "Observer" means the observer of a member State of the Council of Europe, other State party to the European Cultural Convention or non-member State which has participated in the elaboration of the Convention, which has not ratified, accepted or approved the Convention, or of any State or sports organisation invited by the Group according to Article 10.4 of the Convention;
- "Votes cast" means the votes of the delegates voting for or against; delegates abstaining on a vote are considered as not having cast a vote.

Section I: Procedure in general
Article 1 – Appointment of Delegates

1. One or more delegates shall be appointed to the Group by the Governments, which shall communicate their names, addresses and working language to the Secretary General of the Council of Europe, whenever possible at least one month before the date fixed for the opening of the meeting. In the case of multi-member delegations, Governments shall indicate the head of the delegation.
2. Each delegate shall retain office until the Government or the delegate concerned has notified the Secretary General that the delegate has been replaced.

3. A delegate may be accompanied by one or more experts.
4. The provisions of this Article shall apply mutatis mutandis to observers.

Article 2 – Observers

1. An observer shall have no right to vote.
2. With the permission of the Chair, an observer may make oral or written statements on the subjects under discussion.

Article 3 – Meetings

1. The Group shall hold a meeting at least once a year. The Group shall fix the date of its meetings in consultation with the Secretary General.
2. Whenever a Party requests the Group to be convened according to Article 10.5 of the Convention, the Secretary General may fix the date of the meeting in consultation, if possible, with the Chair of the Group.
3. When a meeting has been convened, any request for postponement must reach the Secretary General at least four weeks before the date previously fixed for the opening of the meeting. A decision in favour of postponement shall be considered as having been taken when a majority of the delegates shall have notified the Secretary General of their agreement seven days before the date previously fixed.
4. In general meetings shall be held at the seat of the Council of Europe at Strasbourg.

Article 4 – Convocation

1. Meetings of the Group shall be convened by letter addressed by the Secretary General to the delegates and to the observers. Whenever there is a vacancy on the Group the letter of convocation shall be addressed to the Government concerned.
2. A copy of the letter of convocation addressed to the delegates and observers shall be sent to the Governments of the member States, the other States party to the European Cultural Convention and the non-member States which have participated in the elaboration of the Convention.
3. Letters of convocation shall, in general, be sent at least two months before the date fixed for the opening of the meeting.

Article 5 – Officers

1. The Chair and Vice-Chair shall be elected for a term of two years, by a majority of the votes cast. They shall be eligible for re-election for one more term of two years.
2. Elections shall be held at the end of the last meeting which precedes the expiry of the term of office concerned.
3. The Chair shall direct the work and preside at meetings of the Group.
4. The Chair shall retain the right to participate in the discussions of the Group and to vote.
5. If the Chair is absent or prevented from chairing, he or she shall be replaced by the Vice-Chair. If neither of these persons is able to carry out their duties, the Group shall designate one of its members to take the Chair in an acting capacity.
6. Should any of the above offices fall vacant before the completion of the relevant terms of office, the Group shall decide whether to hold an election for the vacant post at the beginning of its next meeting. Any person so elected shall complete the term of office of his or her predecessor.

Article 6 – Secretariat

1. The Secretary General of the Council of Europe or his/her representative may at any time make an oral or written statement on any matter under consideration.
2. The Secretary General shall provide the Group with the necessary staff and facilities.
3. The Secretariat shall be responsible for the material preparation and distribution of the working documents to be examined by the Group. Documents should normally be sent to delegates at least one month before the opening of the meeting.

Article 7 – Agenda

The agenda shall be adopted at the beginning of each meeting on the basis of a draft prepared by the Secretariat and annexed to the letter of convocation.

Article 8 – Languages

1. The official languages of the Group shall be those of the Council of Europe.
2. Any delegate or observer may, however, use a language other than an official language, provided that his/her delegation provides for interpretation into one of the official languages.
3. Any document to be considered by the Group submitted in a language other than one of the official languages shall be accompanied by a translation into one of the official languages.

Article 9 – Privacy of Meetings

Meetings shall be held in private.

Article 10 – Quorum

There shall be a quorum if a majority of the Parties are present.

Article 11 – Voting

1. Each Party to the Convention shall have one vote.
2. The Group shall take decisions on matters other than those mentioned in paragraphs 4 and 8 of Article 10 of the Convention by a majority of the votes cast. However, in the case of the written procedure for amending the reference list, Article 16, paragraph 2, of the present Rules of Procedure shall apply.
3. In case of doubt as to what rule applies to the taking of any decision, the Group shall decide by a two-thirds majority of votes cast.

Article 12 – Reconsideration of a decision

When a decision has been taken on any particular matter, such matter shall not be re-opened except at the request of a delegate approved by a two-thirds majority of the votes cast.

Article 13 – Decisions and Reports

1. The Secretariat shall prepare for decision under Article 11.1 of the Convention drafts which shall be adopted by the Group at the end of each meeting.
2. The Secretariat shall prepare a draft report after each meeting which shall be considered as adopted unless objections are formulated within one month of the date of its circulation.

In the event that objections are formulated, the report shall be adopted at the following meeting.

Section II: Miscellaneous Provisions

Article 14 – Consultation with other organisations or with experts

1. The Group may decide to invite intergovernmental or non-governmental organisations or bodies to appoint a person who will be available for consultation during a particular meeting or part of a meeting.
2. The Group may, in liaison with the Secretary General, appoint a consultant expert to make a report on one or more particular matters.

Article 15 – Meetings of groups of experts set up by virtue of Article 11.2 of the Convention

1. Experts for such meetings shall be nominated by the Group.
2. Articles 5 to 14 of the present rules of procedure shall apply, where applicable, and mutatis mutandis, to such meetings.

Article 16 – Procedure for amending the reference list

1. The reference list of banned pharmacological classes of doping agents and doping methods shall be amended in accordance with Article 11.1.b of the Convention.
2. Should the above list and/or explanatory notes require modification in a period exceeding three months before the next meeting of the Group, the following written (or electronic) procedure will be used:
   - the Secretariat shall transmit to the delegates for approval the draft decision(s), including the date of their taking effect, together with a postal voting form; observers may also be asked for their views;
   - delegates shall ensure that their votes reach the Secretariat within two weeks of the date of receipt of the draft decision(s); if no vote is received, the delegate is considered as not having cast a vote;
   - if a majority of the Parties approve the draft decision(s), a letter from the Secretariat will inform Parties and observers of this decision(s), and confirm the date at which this decision shall enter into force.

Article 17 – Amendment to the Rules of Procedure

1. These rules may be amended by the Group at any time, on the basis of draft amendments circulated at least one month before a meeting of the Group.
2. Amendments shall be adopted by a two-thirds majority of the votes cast.

8.10. Recommendation No. 1/94 of the Monitoring Group of the Anti-Doping Convention to Parties, on Standard Urine Sampling Procedures for Doping Control

Strasbourg 14-16 June 1994

The Monitoring Group of the Anti-Doping Convention, under the terms of Article 11.1.d of the Convention,

Whereas under Article 3 of the Anti-Doping Convention the Parties undertake to co-ordinate the policies and actions of their government departments and other public agencies concerned with combating doping in sport;

Whereas in Article 7 of the Convention the Parties undertake to encourage their sports organisations to harmonise their doping control procedures;

Considering that common operating standards for control procedures would ensure a fair and equitable system for athletes;

Considering that such standards could also provide a firm basis upon which to build bilateral and multilateral agreements for doping control between countries;
Considering that this would also encourage other sports organisations and countries to seek common standards;
Convinced of the need to establish a standard system of urine sample collection;
Having studied the Standard Operating Procedures of the International Olympic Anti-Doping Charter;
Having discussed this Recommendation with international and European sport organisations;
Recommends that Parties to the Anti-Doping Convention include or, where appropriate, strongly urge the national sports bodies concerned to include, in their Anti-Doping Regulations, the Standard Urine Sampling Procedures and annexes thereto appended to the present Recommendation.

8.11. Recommendation on Measures to restrict the availability of Anabolic Steroids (94/2)

Strasbourg 14-16 June 1994

The Monitoring Group of the Anti-Doping Convention, under the terms of Article 11.1.d. of the Convention,
Recalling Article 4.1 of the Convention which states that "the Parties shall adopt where appropriate legislation, regulations or administrative measures to restrict the availability (including provisions to control movement, possession, importation, distribution and sale) as well as the use in sport of banned doping agents and doping methods, and, in particular, anabolic steroids";
Concerned by the widespread abuse of anabolic/androgenic steroids in nearly all sports, and at all levels of sport, and by all ages of sports people;
Concerned equally by the even more widespread abuse of steroids in para-sporting circles and in fitness centres for purposes that may not be linked directly to sporting performance;
Considering that such abuse presents a challenge not only to sporting ethics but also to public health in general;
Considering that the illicit distribution of anabolic/androgenic steroids appears to be increasing, thus putting many young people at risk, and, giving rise to harmful physiological and psychological consequences associated with steroid abuse;
Convinced that international co-operation is necessary to reduce steroid abuse and the illicit trade in steroids;
Bearing in mind the legislation already adopted or proposed for adoption in Parties to the Anti-Doping Convention, and in other States associated with the Convention,

Recommends the Parties:

(i) to ensure, where such a framework does not already exists, that a legislative framework provides for efficient control of the supply and transfer of anabolic/androgenic steroids;

(ii) to ensure that these controls cover unauthorised manufacture, import or export, distribution, trade or transfer for gain of products containing such compounds; the controls should also contain appropriate provisions against unauthorised possession;

(iii) to ensure that the scale of penalties for contravening such controls are appropriate, bearing in mind the nature and scale of the offence;

(iv) to ensure that such controls and penalties also extend to veterinary steroids when diverted to or intended for human use;

(v) to consider ensuring that authorised producers, distributors, doctors, pharmacists and veterinarians keep appropriate records of their several holdings and transfers of such steroids.

Explanatory Memorandum to Recommendation (94/2)

A. Present situation

1. Article 4.1 of the Anti-Doping Convention states: "The Parties shall where appropriate adopt measures to restrict the availability (including provisions to control movement, possession, importation, distribution and sale) as well as the use in sport of banned doping agents and doping methods and, in particular, anabolic steroids".
2. Denmark, Norway and Sweden have adopted legislation making transfer, import or acquisition for the purpose of (financial) gain a crime. Canada has adopted legislation to reschedule anabolic steroids in the Food and Drugs Act, making it a criminal offence to import, export, traffic, manufacture or distribute all (human) steroid products, except by authorised persons or for authorised purposes. In Denmark and Sweden, use and in Norway, possession and use, remain unpenalised. Finland is contemplating similar legislation.
3. The United States of America has implemented the Steroid Control Act of 1990 which brings all steroids intended for human use under the provisions of the Controlled Substances Act. This criminalises production, trafficking, non-medical use, possession, or distribution of steroids with penalties of up to 20 years imprisonment, and/or $1m fine and/or asset forfeiture.
4. In most European countries other than those mentioned in paragraph 2 above, controls on anabolic steroids are exercised through existing medical drug control acts or regulations. These usually stipulate that obtaining drugs or pharmaceutical preparations containing steroid compounds is subject to appropriate medical prescriptions. However, it is believed that it is possible to obtain some such preparations in Belgium and Portugal over the counter (OTC) from a pharmacy. Unauthorised or unprescribed possession or use of such compounds is not usually penalised. Some doctors and pharmacists have however suffered penalties either under law or under their appropriate professional codes for illicit distribution of these drugs.
5. In addition, there is growing evidence of illicit trade in these substances in the world of organised crime, independent of medical/pharmaceutical circles.

B. Scale of problem

6. Steroid abuse is widespread at all levels and in all kinds of sport.
7. It is not, however, limited to organised sport. Anabolic steroids are commonly abused in gyms/fitness centres, etc., by people who want to `look good' and by people who have a professional need to remain/keep physically fit and strong. Such people are not necessarily covered by the testing programmes carried out by sports organisations.
8. Studies carried out in recent years indicate that millions of people in sporting and para-sporting circles are at risk from anabolic steroid abuse, and the illegal market in such substances is worth hundreds of millions of dollars.

C. Social and other consequences

9. Besides the undermining of sports ethics by drug abuse, there are 4 principal reasons why public authorities should be concerned at this high level of steroid misuse:
   (a) the young age at which much abuse starts. 14 years old is not unheard of; 16 years old is common; by 18 many are psychologically dependent. The role of sports heroes as models for impressionable young people is decisive here;

(b) the quantities that are often involved. Stacking (taking several different steroids simultaneously) and cycling (taking them in accordance with successive timetables) lead to excessively large quantities of steroids being misused, greatly in excess of any dose which might be considered therapeutic;

(c) the types of steroid being abused. Amongst these are a large number of steroids originally designed for veterinary use and therefore not suited for human ingestion, as well as various kinds of illicitly produced compounds, with varying levels of impurity.

(d) the health consequences of abuse. Apart from the pronounced physiological changes in both men and women which steroid abuse causes (such changes are well known and documented) and the risk of specific types of cancer and cardiological disorders, it can also cause unpleasant and dangerous psychological alterations, increasing aggressiveness and violence. There are also studies which show a strong degree of addictiveness/dependence on steroids which continues after the sporting or other original motivation/purpose has ceased.

D. Proposals

10. The Working Party on Legal Issues therefore proposed that the Monitoring Group should adopt a Recommendation to Parties with a view to Parties' instituting stricter controls on the availability of anabolic steroids. Because of the international nature of the `trade' in steroids, these controls should contain common provisions making illegal the unauthorised production, import/export, distribution, supply, transfer, sale and, where appropriate, possession of anabolic steroids, whether for human or veterinary use. Given the various legal situations in the different States, each Party should look for the most efficient legal means of achieving these goals and enforcing a control system with appropriate scope and penalties.

11. The Working Party, recalling that the term "anabolic steroids" appears in the text of the Convention (see Article 4.1) and is expanded upon in the Explanatory Report thereto (see "Notes on the Appendix to the Convention", section C), took the view that it is unnecessary, and would perhaps even be counterproductive, to enshrine a definition in the proposed draft Recommendation.

12. The same argument applies to appending a definitive list of the substances coming within the scope of the proposed text, since product development could easily render such a list out-of-date and therefore less effective.
However, reference is made to the Appendix to the Anti-doping Convention: "Reference list of pharmacological classes of doping agents and doping methods" (which is updated as needed by the Monitoring Group), "Androgenic/anabolic steroids".

13. Finally, consideration may have to given in the future to a similar Recommendation on the subject of certain polypeptide hormones, as and when concrete evidence of their abuse for sporting purposes becomes available.

8.12. Recommendation on Standard Urine Sampling Procedures for Doping Control in and out of Competition (95/1)

The Monitoring Group of the Anti-Doping Convention, under the terms of Article 11.1.d of the Convention,

Whereas under Article 3 of the Anti-Doping Convention the Parties undertake to co-ordinate the policies and actions of their government departments and other public agencies concerned with combating doping in sport;

Whereas in Article 7 of the Convention the Parties undertake to encourage their sports organisations to harmonise their doping control procedures;
Considering that common operating standards for control procedures would ensure a fair and equitable system for athletes;
Considering that such standards could also provide a firm basis upon which to build bilateral and multilateral agreements for doping control between countries;
Considering that this would also encourage other sports organisations and countries to seek common standards;
Convinced of the need to establish a standard system of urine sample collection;
Having studied the Sampling Procedures of the International Olympic Committee's Medical Code;
Having discussed this Recommendation with international and European sports organisations;
Having revised Recommendation N□ 1/94 adopted by the Monitoring Group in 1994, to include provision for standard urine sampling procedures for doping controls out of competition.
Recommends that Parties to the Anti-Doping Convention include, or where appropriate, strongly urge the national sports bodies concerned to include, in their Anti-Doping Regulations, the Standard Urine Sampling Procedures and annexes thereto appended to the present Recommendation.

Appendix
Standard urine sampling procedures for doping control in and out of competition

Introduction

1. The Anti-Doping Convention requires Contracting Parties to encourage their sports organisations to harmonise their procedures for doping control. The aims of achieving harmonisation are many fold:
   - Common operating standards for testing procedures would ensure a fair and equitable system for all athletes.
   - It could lead to the establishment of an international system of sample collection.
   - Minimum operating standards could also provide a firm basis upon which to build bilateral and multilateral anti-doping agreements between countries.
   - Sports organisations and countries would be encouraged to seek common standards.
   - Countries would be able to guarantee a level of competence within these standards.
2. By operating to common standards, testing programmes organised by International Sports Federations, of national governing bodies and by national anti-doping organisations could be intercommunicated. Working together, these parties could create and develop a more effective system of doping control.
3. The Anti-Doping Convention invites Contracting Parties to coordinate their anti-doping policies and actions (Art. 3.1, the Parties shall co-ordinate the policies and actions of their government departments and other public agencies concerned with combating doping in sport). As suggested in Art. 3.2 (they shall ensure that there is practical application of this Convention, and in particular that the requirements under Article 7 are met, by entrusting, where appropriate, the implementation of some of the provisions of this Convention to a designated governmental or non-governmental sports authority

or to a sports organisation), a designated national authority or organisation (whether in the public sector or within the sports movement) with clearly defined roles and responsibilities could undertake the implementation of practical elements of the Convention. In essence, a national anti-doping organisation should be established so as to operate independently of but in association with individual sports federations, both national and international. Furthermore, to achieve harmonisation national governing bodies and International Sports Federations should try to make maximum use of the common testing services offered by the national anti-doping organisation.

4. These Standard Sampling Procedures should be followed as far as is reasonably practicable in each case. A minor departure from them shall not invalidate the possible finding of a prohibited substance during analysis. Only a departure which reasonably casts doubt upon the validity of a positive analysis will be entertained.

5. These Standard Sampling Procedures apply only to the collection of urine samples.

Sampling procedures

1. SAMPLE COLLECTION TEAMS

1.1. Sample collection should be carried out by qualified staff (including independent sampling officers and medically qualified experts, hereafter called "doping control officers") properly trained and duly authorised. When recruited by the national anti-doping organisation (or agency or body; hereafter called "organisation"), these officials should be independent of the sport in which they are testing and from the persons being tested, though they should be familiar with the sport and its rules.

1.2. National anti-doping organisations should undertake training of appropriate individuals using a curriculum based on the procedures which follow.

1.3. Wherever possible a sample collection team should consist of a minimum of 2 doping control officers. In appointing the team to collect urine samples, the sex of the athlete(s) should be taken into account.

1.4. Doping control officers should carry an identity card issued by the national anti-doping organisation or international federation. In addition each doping control officer should have written authorization from the national anti-doping organisation or from the international federation to carry out the controls.

2. SELECTION PROCEDURES

2.1. In Competition

At competitions, the doping control officer and/or national anti-doping organisation is responsible for the selection of athletes. However, where the competition regulations of the relevant sports federation so require, this selection or pre-selection shall be made in conjunction with and in the presence of the nominated representative of that federation.

2.2. Out of Competition

Individual athletes may also be selected for out of competition testing at any time, in accordance with national procedures and/or International Federation regulations. The testing procedures may be initiated with no or little notice at any appropriate time. Controls shall be conducted in a way which is equitable for all sportsmen and sportswomen and which includes testing and retesting of persons selected, where appropriate, on a random basis.

3. NOTIFICATION AND DOPING CONTROL FORM

3.1. General

3.1.1. The doping control officer (or nominated representative of the Federation, or a person designated by the national anti-doping organisation) may notify the athlete in writing or orally. Oral notification must be confirmed in writing. The date and time of notification shall be noted on the Doping Control Form (DCF: Annex B2). The athlete should sign this form to acknowledge receipt of the notice as soon as the notice is presented.

3.1.2. The athlete's identification data shall be included on the form, together with advice that and/or conditions under which he/she may be accompanied to the Doping Control Station by a person of his/her choosing.

3.1.3. The possible consequences of failing to report for the control or for refusing to provide a sample (ie such failure or refusal being deemed to be equivalent to a positive result) shall be clearly stated on the notification form (cf. 8, 9 and 10 below, in order to keep the form manageable, any additional information which may be given should be put on a separate sheet attached to the form).

3.2. Procedure for notification of controls – in competition

3.2.1. Notification of the doping control test should normally take place immediately after the athlete has finished competing.

3.2.2. Notification and sample collection may be made earlier if appropriate. For example, in sports involving weight classes, testing may also take place at the time of the weigh-in.

3.3. Procedure for notification of controls – out of competition

3.3.1. Once liable for testing, athletes may be notified at any appropriate time that they are required to provide a urine sample.

3.3.2. The sample should be collected at the earliest opportunity (24 hours between notification and collection should be considered a maximum).

3.3.3. Following notification, every effort should be made to chaperone the athlete until the sample has been provided.

4. REPORTING FOR SAMPLE COLLECTIONS

4.1. General

4.1.1. The athlete may if so wished be accompanied to the Doping Control Station by a person of his/her choice (see 3.2.), provided this person is accessible and available within the time limit specified.

4.1.2. The date and time of reporting, together with the means of identification should be recorded on the Doping Control Form. Appropriate details relating to the accompanying person should also be noted.

4.1.3. Failure to report to the Doping Control Station within the agreed time limit shall be recorded and reported to the responsible authority for consideration.

4.1.4. Provision may be made for keeping the athlete under observation (escort, chaperone) between notification and reporting.

4.2. In Competition

4.2.1. At competitions, an athlete must report to the Doping Control Station at the time indicated on the notification (usually as soon as possible, and no later than one hour after notification).

4.2.2. At the request of the athlete and where there is good reason to do so (for example, presence required to attend a victory ceremony or press conference; to warm down; to receive treatment for an injury), the doping control officer or authorised representative may authorise a delay (for example, 60 minutes) in the reporting time. In such cases, the athlete will be kept under observation during this period.

4.3. Out of Competition

4.3.1. When providing a no notice sample, athletes will be kept under observation and will be required to provide a sample as soon as practically possible.

4.3.2. When providing a short notice sample out of competition, athletes will be required to report to the Doping Control Officer at a time and place mutually established, within the time allowed after notification.

5. PREMISES FOR DOPING CONTROL

5.1. General

5.1.1. Privacy and security should be maintained at all times at the place where the sample is collected.

5.1.2. Only one athlete at a time should be called to the area in which urine is to be provided. When the sample is passed, only the D.C.O. or other qualified person shall be present, except in specific circumstances provided for in the regulations.

5.1.3. Photographs etc. should not be taken during doping control procedures, unless they are required for official identification purposes.

5.2. In Competition

5.2.1. At competitions, an area should be specifically designated for doping control as close as possible to the competition/training area. Sports federations are advised to include provision for adequate premises in their requirements for facilities at major competitions.

5.2.2. Ideally the doping control premises should comprise a separate waiting and administration area adjacent to toilet facilities for the collection of samples (example attached at Annex A).

5.2.3. The following persons should be authorised to attend the Doping Control Station:

The athlete, an accompanying person, members of the sampling team and nominated representatives of the international and/or national federations, and, if required, an interpreter.

The chief doping control officer should authorise any additional presence.

5.3. Out of Competition

5.3.1. Sample collection should be made in as a discrete a way as possible, whether in a sports facility, training centre, athlete's home, or wherever the mutually established rendezvous may be (see 4.2.2.).

6. SAMPLE COLLECTION PROCEDURES

6.1. The sampling equipment used (see Annex B.1) must be able to guarantee the unique identification, security and integrity of the urine samples collected.

6.2. Sample collection procedures must be explained to the athlete.

6.3. When ready to provide a urine sample, the athlete will select a collection vessel (individually sealed) and shall urinate into it under the direct observation of the doping control officer or other designated person. A minimum volume of 75 ml is usually required. The amount shall be indicated by the doping control officer (in accordance with the national or international federation requirements).

6.4. In order to avoid any manipulation, the doping control officer should require the athlete to remove sufficient clothing to provide the observer with an unobstructed view of the passing of the sample.

6.5. a. The athlete shall select a pair of (pre-sealed) bottles or bottle containers and individual code numbers and break the seal to obtain the bottles.

b. Approximately 2/3rds of the urine sample will be poured into the first bottle and approximately 1/3rd into the second bottle.

c. Both bottles will be closed, sealed and coded with a unique identification method.

Either the athlete or, at his/her request, the doping control officer may carry out the procedures under b & c.

d. The codes of the bottles will be recorded on the Doping Control Form and cross-checked by the doping control officer, by the athlete and by any accompanying person.

6.6. If required by the international or national Federation, the specific gravity and pH of the urine will be measured using a residual volume of urine in the collection vessel. Details of the measurements should be recorded on the Doping Control Form. If the sample does not meet the relevant specifications, a further sample may be required.

Partial sample:

6.7. If insufficient urine has been provided by the athlete, the partial sample shall be poured into a bottle (as in 6.5 above). The bottle shall be closed, sealed and coded. The code shall be recorded on the Doping Control Form (or on a separate form provided for that purpose; cf. Annex B.2 § 15). The athlete must remain under the observation of a member of the doping control officer team until further urine has been provided and the sample collection procedures are complete.

6.8. When the athlete is ready to provide more urine, a further collection vessel should be selected by the athlete and the sample should be provided under the observation of the doping control officer. The doping control officer should check the seal number on the bottle against the codes previously recorded (before breaking the seal to open the bottle). The urine collected from the second collection shall be added to the urine collected from the first collection and the total volume checked. Once the required volume has been provided the procedures will continue as from 6.5. above. Otherwise the sealing of the sample as in 6.7. will continue until the required volume has been obtained.

Declaration of Medications:

6.9. The athlete shall be advised by the doping control officer that it is in his/her own interest to declare any medication or other substance taken in the relevant period prior to the control, the length of this period being specified in accordance with national/international regulations. The declaration should be recorded on the Doping Control Form by the athlete or the doping control officer. If the athlete declines to make a declaration, this shall be recorded on the Doping Control Form.

Such information must be treated in the strictest confidence by all who have access to it.

(With a view to respecting the athlete's privacy, anti-doping organisations might consider entering the declaration on a separate, sellable annex to the Doping

Control Form, which would be opened only if the sample gives rise to a positive finding.)

Completion of the Doping Control Form

6.10 The Doping Control Form will be completed by the doping control officer. Details relating to the athlete and sample identification data should be recorded and cross-checked by the athlete and by the doping control officer. If measured, the pH and specific gravity to the sample shall also be recorded (cf. 6.6.).

6.11 The athlete shall certify the accuracy of the information and correctness of procedures used by signing the Doping Control Form which should also be signed by the doping control officer. Additional signatures may be required if specified in national and international regulations.

6.12 Any reason for dissatisfaction identified by either party should be declared on the Doping Control Form before or at the time of signature. Standard Sampling Procedures should be followed as far as is reasonably practicable in each case. A minor departure from them shall not necessarily invalidate the possible finding of a prohibited substance during analysis. Only a departure which reasonably casts doubt upon the validity of a positive analysis will be entertained. A statement to this effect shall be included on the Doping Control Form and shall be drawn to the attention of the athlete prior to signature.

6.13 Copies of the Doping Control Form shall be available for:

6.13.1. the athlete;
6.13.2. the national anti-doping organisation;
6.13.3. the laboratory (with no information on the name or identification details of the athlete and accompanying representative);
6.13.4. the national sports federation where appropriate;
6.13.5. the international sports federation, where appropriate.

Chain of Custody: (Annex C1 and C2)

6.14. At the site of collection, samples should be securely packed for transport in a container which is then sealed. A chain of custody form should be used to record the contents and custody of the equipment in the container from the site of collection to the laboratory.

7. TRANSFER OF SAMPLES TO THE LABORATORY

7.1. All samples shall be sent to the laboratory by a method of despatch which is secure and which has been approved by the national anti-doping organisation.

7.2. Despatch shall take place as soon as reasonably possible after the controls have been completed. Samples must be held in a cold and secure place until they can be delivered to the laboratory.

8. REFUSAL

A refusal by an athlete to agree to doping control procedures should be noted on the Doping Control Form. If possible, the signature of the athlete and/or a witness to the refusal should be obtained.

9. FAILURE TO REPORT

If an athlete fails to report for sample collection at the agreed time, this should be noted on the Doping Control Form. Wherever possible attempts to contact the athlete within a reasonable timescale (e.g. one hour) should be made and noted.

10. PENALTIES

In general, a refusal or failure to report or a refusal to provide a sample or otherwise to comply with these standard sampling procedures shall be deemed to be equivalent to a positive test.

Annex A

Doping control station in competition

Facilities for Doping Control should provide privacy for competitors and security for the collection procedures. They should be situated close to the competition or training area. Access to the Doping Control Station is restricted to authorised personnel only (i.e. doping control officer, selected competitors and their accompanying officials, Federation Doping Control official). The entry door to the Doping Control Station must be secure.

Within the station three areas are required, a waiting area, administration area and an area for sample collection. (Ideally, there should be at least two inter-connecting rooms).

The waiting area should be equipped with chairs, clothes hangers and hooks, space for an adequate supply of non-alcoholic drinks (still and carbonated) in unopened containers and a rubbish bin. In addition reading materials, television or radio are helpful to create a relaxed atmosphere.

The administration area should contain table and chairs, wash basin, soap and towels. At major events involving sample collection over several days, a lockable freezer or refrigerator for storage of samples is useful. At least one W.C. is required in the sample collection area and separate sample collection areas should be provided for each sex being tested. Sufficient space is needed to accommodate the doping control officer and competitor in this area.

An Ideal Station

[...]

A Waiting Room
B Administration Room
C Sample Collection Room

An Alternative Arrangement

[...]

A Waiting Room
B Administration Room
C Sample Collection Room

Annex B1

Sampling equipment

1. Sampling equipment which is approved by national anti-doping organisations should include the following:
   - 1.1. Disposable urine collection vessels, individually sealed prior to use.
   - 1.2. Transparent bottles (of sufficient volume to ensure the total quantity of urine could be contained in 1 bottle, i.e. when collecting partial samples prior to subdivision), sealed prior to use.
   - 1.3. A unique sealing system which secures the bottles during transit and storage.
   - 1.4. Doping Control Forms to record identifying details for the samples, athlete and collection procedure. This form should consist of an original with 4 copies:

1.4.1. the athlete;
1.4.2. the national anti-doping organisation;
1.4.3. the laboratory (with no information on the name or identification details of the athlete and accompanying representative);
1.4.4. the national sports federation where appropriate;
1.4.5. the international sports federation, where appropriate.

Copies should be clearly indicated and differentiated by colour.
A checklist of the information required is attached at Annex B2

1.5. A secure container for transporting the sample bottles to and from the laboratory.
1.6. Measurement sticks for pH and specific gravity.
1.7. Chain of custody form(s).

2. There should be sufficient numbers of collection vessels, bottles and codes to allow the athlete to choose, provision for possible faulty equipment, breakages; provision for partial and second samples.

Annex B2
Doping control form/s
The Doping Control Form or Forms (for notification and for the collection procedure) should provide space for the following information:
Athlete's details:
Control details:

1. Athlete's name
In competition
Y/N

2. Sport
Out of Competition
Y/N

3. Country

4. Identification
Event/Team/Competition
Notification details and consequences of refusal, etc.:

5. Notification Date and Place

6. Notification Time

7. Signature of doping control officer (for notification)

8. Name of doping control officer

9. Signature of Athlete

10. Consequences of refusal (para 3.3)
"Failure to report for doping control and refusal to provide a sample are deemed to be equivalent to a positive result".

11. Procedural objections waiver (para 6.12)
"Standard Sampling Procedures should be followed as far as is reasonably practicable in each case. A minor departure from them shall not necessarily invalidate the possible finding of a prohibited substance during analysis. Only a departure which reasonably casts doubt upon the validity of a positive analysis will be entertained".
Collection Procedure details:
(repeat information under 5 & 6 if two forms are used)

12. Date and Place of Sample Collection

13. Time of Arrival at Doping Control Station

14. Event Code if at competition

15. Sex of Athlete

16. Total Volume of Urine

17. Partial Sample Seal Numbers (if taken)

18. Bottle Code A/B

19. Seal Numbers A/B

20. pH reading (if taken)

21. Specific gravity reading (if taken)

22. Declaration of Medications (see para 6.9)
"...it is in his/her own interest to declare any medication or other substance taken in the relevant period prior to the control, the length of this period being specified in accordance with national/international regulations".

23. Comments

24. Signature of Athlete

25. Signature of doping control officer (to certify procedures correct)

26. Signature of International Representative (if present)

27. Signatures of Accompanying Official and Person (if present)

RECOMMENDATION
A standard form with a consistent colour scheme should be used (for distribution of copies, cf. Annex B1, item 1.4).

Annex C1

Chain of custody

1. There should be a secure and documented chain of custody for the transport of sampling equipment from the despatch of the prepared equipment to the doping control officer and from the doping control officer to the laboratory. If the doping control officer opens the transport container on receipt to check the contents, the sample equipment within must remain sealed. The transport container should be resealed and the code noted.
2. Equipment (see Annex B 1, 1.1 – 1.3) should be received (by the doping control officer and the athlete) sealed.
3. Once the equipment has been used, it should be sealed in a manner distinct from the first sealing system (i.e. by colour/design or other means).
4. There should be restricted access to both types of seals. The first seals (from the organisation preparing the kit to the doping control officer) should not be available outside the organisation. A secure method of ordering, delivery and storage of the seals should be implemented, and the organisation should maintain an inventory of issue.
5. A copy of the chain of custody form should be sealed inside the kit.
   Prepared
   -> doping control officer
   doping control officer
   -> Laboratory
6. The chain of custody form should include the following information:
   6.1. Control code number
   6.2. Week number/date
   6.3. Number of samples collected, A and B bottle
   6.4. Competition (event code) or out of competition
   6.5. Sport/Federation
   6.6. Outer bag seal number on despatch – sealed by
   6.7. Outer bag seal number on receipt – received by
   6.8. Outer bag seal number on return – sealed by
   6.9. Sampling Kit custody details:
      6.9.1. seal numbers
      6.9.2. released by
      6.9.3. received by
      6.9.4. purpose
      6.9.5. date/time
   6.10. Bottle numbers (seal numbers indicate bottle contains urine)
   An example is attached at Annex C2
7. Completion of the form:
   7.1. On dispatch from the organisation responsible for preparing the kit, the date, seal number for transport and details of equipment enclosed in the transport container should be noted.
   7.2. On initial receipt, the breaking and re-sealing of the transport container by the doping control officer (or any official body, e.g. customs, security) should be noted and signed.
   7.3. The seal of the transport container should be broken at the collection point in the presence of witnesses (doping control officer, athlete or governing body official).

7.4. The bottle and seal numbers of all samples enclosed in the transport container should be noted on the form together with the seal number for the transport bag itself. A copy of the form must be enclosed.

7.5. Changes in custody of the transport container during transfer to the laboratory must be noted by signature acknowledging the seal number recorded to be correct.

7.6. Any further breaking and resealing of the transport container must be also noted and agreed by signature (e.g. by an official of Customs or security)

7.7. The chain of custody form may be photocopied and the copy given to signatories, the original should continue to accompany the transport container until its acceptance by:

7.7.1. the laboratory;

7.7.2. an official carrier which operates its own chain of custody documentation, with signature required for transfer of ownership

7.8. The original chain of custody form should then be returned to the authority initiating the control, who will have responsibility for checking the chain of custody is complete before forwarding a report of the analysis of the governing body/athlete. In the laboratory report of the analysis, it is suggested that date, time and seal numbers are noted.

Annex C2
Doping control

SAMPLE COLLECTION – CHAIN OF CUSTODY FORM

The sampling kit sealed as below contains urine samples collected from sports men/women as a part of a programme of doping control. These samples are of no commercial value. They are being transported to an International Olympic Committee accredited Laboratory for analysis. The urine samples have been collected and sealed at the place of collection. Maintenance of the chain of custody is essential to ensure the security and integrity of the urine samples. When custody of the sampling kit is transferred confirmation of receipt to the sealed container must be obtained by signature of the receiving party. A photocopy of this form should be retained as written receipt. If inspection of the sampling kit is required by Customs and Excise or other authority, acknowledgement of the sealing process by the inspecting authority will assist the maintenance of this chain of custody. Opening of the inner containers will invalidate the chain of custody unless appropriate record is appended which is recognised in a court of law. For further information about the contents of the sampling kit please contact: ....

1 Event Code:
2 No of samples collected:
A
B
3 Outer bag seal number from Laboratory:

Sealed by______________
4 Tick box as appropriate
Competition

OOCT

5 Sport / Federation:
6 Outer bag Seal number:
On receipt

Received by____
7
On return

Sealed by______
8 Sampling kit custody details:
Seal numbers
Released by
Received by
Purpose
Date/Time

9 Bottle numbers enclosed (seal number indicates bottle contains urine sample)
[...]

8.13. Recommendation on disciplinary measures to be taken with regard to members of the athlete's entourage in application of Article 7.2.e of the Anti-Doping Convention (96/1)

Adopted by the Monitoring Group of the Anti-Doping Convention at its 7th meeting, Strasbourg, 30-31 May 1996)

Part 1: Explanatory memorandum

1. In Article 7, Paragraph 1, of the Anti-Doping Convention, "the Parties undertake to encourage their sports organisations and through them the international sports organisations to formulate and apply all appropriate measures, falling within their competence, against doping in sport."
2. In Paragraph 2 of the same Article it is stated that "To this end, they shall encourage their sports organisations to clarify and harmonise their respective rights, obligations and duties, in particular by harmonising their: [...]
   "e. procedures for the imposition of effective penalties for officials, doctors, veterinary doctors, coaches, physiotherapists and other officials or accessories associated with infringements of the anti-doping regulations by sportsmen and sportswomen;".
3. For the purposes of the present draft Recommendation it is assumed that the group of persons (referred to throughout as the "athlete's entourage") includes team officials, medical and paramedical practitioners acting either for the team of for the individual athlete, and any other person who is acting, at the time of the commission of a doping offence, in a capacity of care or authority in relation to the athlete concerned. The category therefore includes parents or other relatives, friends or acquaintances who fulfil this condition, although it is obviously difficult to envisage how appropriate jurisdictions can be made to cover some people within this group.
4. Doping case-law to date shows that the imposition of sanctions on such persons is very much rarer than the sanctioning of athletes, a state of affairs which may not necessarily reflect the true situation. The reasons are easy to understand:
   - dope-testing programmes, both in and out of competition, are focused on athletes;

- the doping offence is relatively clearly definable, and the test is – in theory at least -a black-and-white matter based on the notion of strict liability;
- establishing the involvement of persons other than athletes in the commission of a doping offence would, on the other hand, depend on the results of an investigation procedure for collecting evidence, implying a disciplinary procedure which would be adversarial in nature;
- anti-doping agencies and sports governing bodies are already required to devote a major part of their resources to the judicial and quasi-judicial consequences of positive findings with respect to athletes, and could have difficulty in assuming the additional burden implicit in investigating and if appropriate sanctioning other people as well – even if in some cases this proves to be inevitable.

5. Nonetheless, increased attention to the involvement of others in doping offences is justified and necessary:
   - if the use of performance-enhancing substances and methods is wrong, then it is obviously wrong to incite or condone it, or to incite or condone related offences such as refusal to submit to an anti-doping control;
   - morally, such conduct is doubly wrong in circumstances where officials are in a position of responsibility and authority in relation to young people, and the competent authorities might wish to consider such offences as more serious, particularly from the point of view of sentencing (Two recent cases involving swimmers under the age of majority emphasise the need to take measures in this area.);
   - insofar as members of the athlete's entourage also have a duty of care in respect of the athlete's health, their involvement in doping offences is equally condemnable.
   - strategically, the imposition of sanctions on members of the athlete's entourage involved in doping offences may prove a more effective means of combating doping than limiting sanctions to athletes, who represent the end of the chain;
   - finally, however much stress the relevant regulations may rightly place on the athlete's personal responsibility to his sport and himself, one may question the fairness of a system whereby, to all intents and purposes, athletes are the only ones to undergo – frequently severe – sanctions whilst responsibility for the offence may well be more widely shared.

6. The Legal Issues Working Party of the Monitoring Group of the Anti-Doping Convention considered the issue of persons other than athletes involved in the commission of doping offences, initially on the basis of a discussion paper presented by the Canadian delegation. The Working Party made a number of observations concerning the legal and practical problems raised by the matter:
   - provisions for sanctioning doping-related offences other than doping or refusal to test were dealt with in a variety of ways in different countries and depending upon the circumstances of the offence. For example, it was inevitable that many such offences would come under criminal law as well as constituting breaches of disciplinary codes or codes of professional ethics, and the procedures in each domain, as well as the rules regarding the burden of proof, could be different;
   - means of encouraging participation in identifying offenders (promises of leniency, etc.) could be socially divisive and had to be handled with care; there was also a danger of frivolous or malicious denunciations, requiring provisions in the procedure to discourage them;

- the specific social conditions prevailing in sporting milieux could result either in "conspiracies of silence" whereby people protect their own, or alternatively in false accusations in fulfilment of grudges. It is unreasonable to suppose that bodies responsible for enforcing rules of this kind will have either time or the resources to conduct sophisticated investigations. It follows that the rules of evidence have to be kept simple and thus easy to manage.

7. In general it should be stated that the difficulty of establishing guilt – which is acknowledged should not in itself be a barrier to the adoption of a Recommendation on the subject. One important role of a Recommendation is to make it clearly known to members of the athlete's entourage that they bear a share of responsibility for doping offences committed by sportspersons in their charge, and that in certain circumstances they may be held accountable. The deterrent effect of rules is, by force of circumstance, more important than any gain realised by catching and punishing people.
8. The responsibility of people in the athletes' entourage is an important factor in the doping problem, and it is necessary in the interest of the fairness and effectiveness of anti-doping activity that more effort be dedicated to implementing the Convention's provisions in this regard.
9. A number of practical measures can be used to this end:
   - adequate investigation, as soon as a positive sample test is found, of the circumstances surrounding the commission of the offence. This, if incorporated in anti-doping regulations, could have a deterrent effect;
   - criminal proceedings under existing legislation on illegal possession or transfer of drugs and restricted substances, including legislation in accordance with the Monitoring Group's Recommendation 2/94 on measures to restrict the availability of anabolic steroids, should be brought as a matter of course in cases where grounds exist;
   - regulations should make it clear that sanctions will be applied under anti-doping regulations even if the relevant provisions of professional and other applicable codes of conduct differ with regard to the offence established;
   - Chapter VIII (Trafficking in Drugs) of the International Olympic Committee's Medical Code should be referred to or incorporated into sports organisations' anti-doping regulations.

Part 2:
Recommendation No. 1/96 to Parties on disciplinary measures to be taken with regard to members of the athlete's entourage in application of Article 7.2.e of the Convention
Under the terms of Article 11.d of the Convention;
Recalling that, in Article 7 of the Convention, the Parties "undertake to encourage their sports organisations and through them the international sports organisations to formulate and apply all appropriate measures, falling within their competence, against doping in sport", and that to that end, to harmonise (among other things) their "procedures for the imposition of effective penalties for officials, doctors, veterinary doctors, coaches, physiotherapists and other officials or accessories associated with infringements of the anti-doping regulations by sportsmen and sportswomen";
Welcoming, in this regard, Chapter VIII of the Medical Code of the International Olympic Committee on trafficking in drugs;
Considering that persons in the entourage of sportsmen and women, such as team managers, coaches, trainers, medical practitioners and any other person who occupies an equivalent position of responsibility towards them may be implicated in doping offences of which the sportsmen or women may be found guilty;

Convinced that the responsibility of people in athletes' entourages is an important factor in the doping problem, and that it is necessary in the interest of the fairness and effectiveness of anti-doping activity that more effort be dedicated to implementing the Convention's provisions in this regard;
Considering therefore that action should be taken to sanction any such persons who are found to be implicated in the commission of an offence;
Bearing in mind that the imposition of effective penalties may be dealt with in a variety of ways in different countries according to their respective legal traditions (applicability of criminal law, disciplinary or professional codes, rules concerning the burden of proof, quality of evidence etc.) and depending upon the circumstances of the offence,

RECOMMENDS to the States Parties that effective regulations in the matter of involvement of persons other than athletes in doping offences, irrespective of the legal framework in which they are established, should be based on the following elements:

1. the definition of offences consisting in inciting or deliberately condoning either:
   - the use of prohibited substances or methods as defined in the Convention (including the procurement or supply of prohibited substances); or
   - the contravention of anti-doping regulations including the avoidance of controls;
2. the designation of the persons who are in a position to be involved in the commission of a doping offence, and the assurance that all relevant persons are subject, either by contract or under the terms of an appropriate disciplinary code, to an obligation not to commit or be a party to such offences;
3. the establishment of appropriate mechanisms for the investigation of allegations related to such offences and of the circumstances surrounding positive sample tests;
4. the provision of appropriate sanctions either by way of legislation or through the regulations of sports organisations (e.g. withdrawal of recognition or licence (to be applicable throughout sport) or banning from relevant premises, etc. for an appropriate period) to be imposed on those found guilty of such offences;
5. the establishment of an independent mechanism to review decisions taken by the competent bodies in respect of such offences or to hear appeals against them.

8.14. Recommendation N° 1/97 to Parties on disciplinary measures to be taken with regard to members of the athlete's entourage and protection of minors, in application of Article 7.2.e of the Convention

Part 1: Explanatory memorandum

1. In Article 7, Paragraph 1, of the Anti-Doping Convention, "the Parties undertake to encourage their sports organisations and through them the international sports organisations to formulate and apply all appropriate measures, falling within their competence, against doping in sport."
2. In Paragraph 2 of the same Article it is stated that "To this end, they shall encourage their sports organisations to clarify and harmonise their respective rights, obligations and duties, in particular by harmonising their: [...]
   "e. procedures for the imposition of effective penalties for officials, doctors, veterinary doctors, coaches, physiotherapists and other officials or accessories associated with infringements of the anti-doping regulations by sportsmen and sportswomen;".

3. For the purposes of the present draft Recommendation it is assumed that the group of persons (referred to throughout as the "athlete's entourage") includes team officials, medical and paramedical practitioners acting either for the team of for the individual athlete, and any other person who is acting, at the time of the commission of a doping offence, in a capacity of care or authority in relation to the athlete concerned. The category therefore includes parents or other relatives, friends or acquaintances who fulfil this condition, although it is obviously difficult to envisage how appropriate jurisdictions can be made to cover some people within this group.
4. Doping case-law to date shows that the imposition of sanctions on such persons is very much rarer than the sanctioning of athletes, a state of affairs which may not necessarily reflect the true situation. The reasons are easy to understand:
   - dope-testing programmes, both in and out of competition, are focused on athletes;
   - the doping offence is relatively clearly definable, and the test is – in theory at least -a black-and-white matter based on the notion of strict liability;
   - establishing the involvement of persons other than athletes in the commission of a doping offence would, on the other hand, depend on the results of an investigation procedure for collecting evidence, implying a disciplinary procedure which would be adversarial in nature;
   - anti-doping agencies and sports governing bodies are already required to devote a major part of their resources to the judicial and quasi-judicial consequences of positive findings with respect to athletes, and could have difficulty in assuming the additional burden implicit in investigating and if appropriate sanctioning other people as well – even if in some cases this proves to be inevitable.
5. Nonetheless, increased attention to the involvement of others in doping offences is justified and necessary:
   - if the use of performance-enhancing substances and methods is wrong, then it is obviously wrong to incite or condone it, or to incite or condone related offences such as refusal to submit to an anti-doping control;
   - morally, such conduct is doubly wrong in circumstances where officials are in a position of responsibility and authority in relation to young people, and the competent authorities might wish to consider such offences as more serious, particularly from the point of view of sentencing;
   - insofar as members of the athlete's entourage also have a duty of care in respect of the athlete's health, their involvement in doping offences is equally condemnable.
   - strategically, the imposition of sanctions on members of the athlete's entourage involved in doping offences may prove a more effective means of combating doping than limiting sanctions to athletes, who represent the end of the chain;
   - finally, however much stress the relevant regulations may rightly place on the athlete's personal responsibility to his sport and himself, one may question the fairness of a system whereby, to all intents and purposes, athletes are the only ones to undergo – frequently severe – sanctions whilst responsibility for the offence may well be more widely shared.
6. The Legal Issues Working Party of the Monitoring Group of the Anti-Doping Convention considered the issue of persons other than athletes involved in the commission of doping offences, initially on the basis of a discussion paper presented by the Canadian delegation. The Working Party made a number of observations concerning the legal and practical problems raised by the matter:

- provisions for sanctioning doping-related offences other than doping or refusal to test were dealt with in a variety of ways in different countries and depending upon the circumstances of the offence. For example, it was inevitable that many such offences would come under criminal law as well as constituting breaches of disciplinary codes or codes of professional ethics, and the procedures in each domain, as well as the rules regarding the burden of proof, could be different;
- means of encouraging participation in identifying offenders (promises of leniency, etc.) could be socially divisive and had to be handled with care; there was also a danger of frivolous or malicious denunciations, requiring provisions in the procedure to discourage them;
- the specific social conditions prevailing in sporting milieux could result either in "conspiracies of silence" whereby people protect their own, or alternatively in false accusations in fulfilment of grudges. It is unreasonable to suppose that bodies responsible for enforcing rules of this kind will have either time or the resources to conduct sophisticated investigations. It follows that the rules of evidence have to be kept simple and thus easy to manage.

7. In general it should be stated that the difficulty of establishing guilt – which is acknowledged – should not in itself be a barrier to the adoption of a Recommendation on the subject. One important role of a Recommendation is to make it clearly known to members of the athlete's entourage that they bear a share of responsibility for doping offences committed by sportspersons in their charge, and that in certain circumstances they may be held accountable. The deterrent effect of rules is, by force of circumstance, more important than any gain realised by catching and punishing people.
8. The responsibility of people in the athletes' entourage is an important factor in the doping problem, and it is necessary in the interest of the fairness and effectiveness of anti-doping activity that more effort be dedicated to implementing the Convention's provisions in this regard.
   In the case of minors in sport the responsibility which is incumbent on the entourage is certainly more important. The protection of minors found guilty of a doping offence must be reinforced.
9. A number of practical measures can be used to this end:
   - adequate investigation, as soon as a positive sample test is found, of the circumstances surrounding the commission of the offence. This, if incorporated in anti-doping regulations, could have a deterrent effect;
   - criminal proceedings under existing legislation on illegal possession or transfer of drugs and restricted substances, including legislation in accordance with the Monitoring Group's Recommendation 2/94 on measures to restrict the availability of anabolic steroids, should be brought as a matter of course in cases where grounds exist;
   - regulations should make it clear that sanctions will be applied under anti-doping regulations even if the relevant provisions of professional and other applicable codes of conduct differ with regard to the offence established;
   - Chapter VIII (Trafficking in Drugs) of the International Olympic Committee's Medical Code should be referred to or incorporated into sports organisations' anti-doping regulations.

Part 2:
Recommendation No. 1/97 to Parties on disciplinary measures to be taken with regard to members of the athlete's entourage and protection of minors, in application of Article 7.2.e of the Convention

Under the terms of Article 11.d of the Convention;

Recalling that, in Article 7 of the Convention, the Parties "undertake to encourage their sports organisations and through them the international sports organisations to formulate and apply all appropriate measures, falling within their competence, against doping in sport", and that to that end, to harmonise (among other things) their "procedures for the imposition of effective penalties for officials, doctors, veterinary doctors, coaches, physiotherapists and other officials or accessories associated with infringements of the anti-doping regulations by sportsmen and sportswomen";

Welcoming, in this regard, Chapter VIII of the Medical Code of the International Olympic Committee on trafficking in drugs;

Considering that persons in the entourage of sportsmen and women, such as team managers, coaches, trainers, medical practitioners and any other person who occupies an equivalent position of responsibility towards them may be implicated in doping offences of which the sportsmen or women may be found guilty;

Convinced that the responsibility of people in athletes' entourages is an important factor in the doping problem, and that it is necessary in the interest of the fairness and effectiveness of anti-doping activity that more effort be dedicated to implementing the Convention's provisions in this regard;

Considering therefore that action should be taken to sanction any such persons who are found to be implicated in the commission of an offence;

Bearing in mind that the imposition of effective penalties may be dealt with in a variety of ways in different countries according to their respective legal traditions (applicability of criminal law, disciplinary or professional codes, rules concerning the burden of proof, quality of evidence etc.) and depending upon the circumstances of the offence;

Believing that athletes who are minors require special protection in such circumstances;

RECOMMENDS to the States Parties that effective regulations in the matter of involvement of persons other than athletes in doping offences, irrespective of the legal framework in which they are established, should be based on the following elements:

1. the definition of offences consisting in inciting or deliberately condoning either:
   - the use of prohibited substances or methods as defined in the Convention (including the procurement or supply of prohibited substances); or
   - the contravention of anti-doping regulations including the avoidance of controls;
2. the designation of the persons who are in a position to be involved in the commission of a doping offence, and the assurance that all relevant persons are subject, either by contract or under the terms of an appropriate disciplinary code, to an obligation not to commit or be a party to such offences;
3. the establishment of appropriate mechanisms for the investigation of allegations related to such offences and of the circumstances surrounding positive sample tests;
4. the provision of appropriate sanctions either by way of legislation or through the regulations of sports organisations (e.g. withdrawal of recognition or licence (to be applicable throughout sport) or banning from relevant premises, etc. for an appropriate period) to be imposed on those found guilty of such offences;
5. the establishment of an independent mechanism to review decisions taken by the competent bodies in respect of such offences or to hear appeals against them;

6. the invariable launching of an investigation, based on the above principles, amongst the entourage of an athlete who is a minor and found guilty of a doping offence.

8.15. Resolution on the approval of a new reference list of prohibited pharmacological classes of doping agents and doping methods (97/1)

The Monitoring Group of the Anti-Doping Convention;
Having regard to Article 2 of the Convention concerning the definition of doping and the scope of the Convention;
Pursuant to Article 11.1.a and b of the Convention, under which the Monitoring Group is responsible for approving the list, and any revision thereto, of pharmacological classes of doping agents and doping methods banned by the relevant international sports organisations;
Recalling that, in previous years, the Monitoring Group approved at its meetings the list of "Prohibited Classes of Substances and Prohibited Methods" drawn up by the International Olympic Committee;
Recalling that approval took the form of a simple decision by the Monitoring Group, under which the list applied to all its members;
Considering that adoption of the reference list, pursuant to Article 11.1.b of the Convention, in the form of a resolution will provide a sound legal basis for its application in the States Parties to the Convention;
Having studied the list of prohibited classes of substances and prohibited methods, as adopted by the Executive Board of the International Olympic Committee at its meeting on 17 November 1996, which took effect on 31 January 1997;
Decides to adopt the said list as the reference list of pharmacological classes of doping agents and doping methods appended to the Convention.
Appendix
A new reference list of prohibited pharmacological classes of doping agents and doping methods

8.16. Recommendation on standard operating procedures at doping control laboratories [procedures for non-analytical phases] (98/1)

The Monitoring Group of the Anti-Doping Convention, under the terms of Article 11.1.d of the Convention,

Whereas under Article 3 of the Anti-Doping Convention the Parties undertake to co-ordinate the policies and actions of their government departments and other public bodies concerned with combating doping in sport;
Whereas in Article 7 of the Convention the Parties undertake to encourage their sports organisations to harmonise their doping control procedures;
Considering that such standards could also provide a firm basis of confidence upon which to build bilateral and multilateral agreements on all aspects of doping control between organisations, bodies and countries party to the Convention;
Considering that this would also encourage other sports organisations and countries to seek common standards;
Convinced of the need to establish standard operating procedures at the laboratory phase;
Considering that such common operating standards would ensure a fair and equitable system for athletes;

Recalling its Recommendation No. 1/95 of the Monitoring Group of the Anti-Doping Convention to Parties;
Recalling its Recommendation No. 1/97 of the Monitoring Group of the Anti-Doping Convention to Parties;
Having studied the International Olympic Committee's Medical Code and relevant disciplinary procedures adopted within the international sports federations;
Having discussed this Recommendation with international and European sports organisations;
Recommends that Parties to the Anti-Doping Convention include, or where appropriate, strongly urge the national sports bodies concerned to include, in their Anti-Doping Regulations or other appropriate texts, Standard Operating Procedures at doping control laboratories based on those appended to the present Recommendation.

Appendix
Background

1. At its 2nd meeting (Paris, 17 – 18 October 1994), the Working Party on Legal Issues considered the question of overturning of positive results. Among the problems identified by the Working Party in connection with this issue were:
   - difficulties in the relationships between testing authorities and laboratories;
   - incompatibility of sanctions between, for example, national and international federations concerned with the same sport;
   - latitude in admitting the defence of inadvertent use;
   - problems associated with the chain of custody;
   - difficulties in interpreting "borderline" testosterone/epitestosterone ratios.

   At the end of its debate, the Working Party expressed agreement with the Secretariat's suggestion that a draft Recommendation should be prepared concerning standard operating procedures subsequent to sample collection.
2. The Working Party on Technical Questions debated the issue at its meeting on 17 November 1994, and added a number of further considerations:
   - the absence of internationally agreed rules and procedures in a number of important areas;
   - uncertainty as to who should initiate disciplinary proceedings against positive-testing athletes: the country of origin, or the country in which the sample had been taken?;
   - equal uncertainty about who takes financial responsibility for the growing costs of such proceedings;
   - the absence of an international mechanism of co-operation on the management of test results.

The Working Party considered that the proposed draft Recommendation should not simply take up the anti-doping procedures where Recommendation No. 1/95 left off, but should provide for certain matters before the sampling process, such as agreements as to the sharing out of responsibilities prior to events.

Objective

3. Recommendation No. 1/95 of the Monitoring Group deals with "Standard Urine Sampling Procedures for Doping Control". Its last operative paragraph is entitled: "7. TRANSFER OF SAMPLES TO THE LABORATORY". It is the purpose of this paper

to pursue the principles of Recommendation No. 1/95 to the subsequent phases of doping control, from the laboratory to, where relevant, the disciplinary procedures.

4. The purpose of the Monitoring Group in adopting Recommendation No. 1/95 was to provide national anti-doping agencies, national sports bodies and international sports federations with a common set of guidelines on the basis of which they can construct their detailed regulations: the preamble to the Recommendation says that "common operating control procedures would ensure a fair and equitable system for athletes; ... a firm basis [for] agreements for doping control between countries; ... encourage other sports organisations and countries to seek common standards". Based upon the procedures already developed by the International Olympic Committee (IOC), the International Amateur Athletic Federation (IAAF) and several national bodies within the Monitoring Group, the Recommendation provides a basis for the necessary further harmonisation of such procedures. Recommendation No. 1/94 was adopted by IOC Medical Commission (Harmonisation) and distributed to its corresponding partners as a source of inspiration and common guidelines.

5. The objective of this present text is to provide anti-doping organisations with a similar set of standard operating procedures for the subsequent phases of doping control: notably at the laboratory. It should be stressed that it is not the intention of this text to set down any proposals on the analytical techniques used in laboratories for the detection of prohibited substances or methods. That is a matter for the appropriate specialists. It is also understood that at all stages of operating procedures the analysis will be conducted according to Good Laboratory Practice (GLP). This text confines itself to the procedural aspects while the sample is at the laboratory.

Standard operating procedures at doping control laboratories
[procedures for non analytical phases]

1. Chain of custody from the doping control point to the Laboratory
   - 1.1 There should be a secure and documented chain of custody for the transport of sampling equipment from the despatch of the prepared equipment to the doping control officer and from the doping control officer to the laboratory. If the doping control officer opens the transport container on receipt to check the contents, the sample equipment within must remain sealed. The transport container should be resealed and the code noted. Only authorised personnel may handle specimens to be tested and they shall sign chain of custody forms to the document when the specimens are in their possession.
   - 1.2 Equipment should be received (by the doping control officer and the athlete) sealed.
   - 1.3 Once the equipment has been used, it should be sealed in a manner distinct from the first sealing system (i.e. by colour/design or other means).
   - 1.4 There should be restricted access to both types of seals. The first seals (from the organisation preparing the kit to the doping control officer) should not be available outside the organisation. A secure method of ordering, delivery and storage of the seals should be implemented, and the organisation should maintain an inventory of issue.
   - 1.5 A copy of the chain of custody form should be sealed inside the kit.
   - 1.6 The chain of custody form should include the following information:
     - 1.6.1 Control code number
     - 1.6.2 Week number/date
     - 1.6.3 Number of samples collected, A and B bottle/container

1.6.4 Competition (event code) or out of competition
1.6.5 Sport/Federation
1.6.6 Outer bag seal number on despatch – sealed by
1.6.7 Outer bag seal number on receipt – received by
1.6.8 Outer bag seal number on return – sealed by
1.6.9 Sampling Kit custody details:
1.6.9.1. seal numbers
1.6.9.2. released by
1.6.9.3. received by
1.6.9.4. purpose
1.6.9.5. date/time
1.6.10 Bottle/container numbers (seal numbers indicate bottle contains urine)
1.7 Despatch form indicating reception by the laboratory.

2. Reception and storage of the sample at the laboratory

2.1 Secure transport and containers
All samples shall be sent to the laboratory by a method of despatch or carrier which is secure and which has been approved by the national [competent] anti-doping organisation.

2.2 Despatch shall take place as soon as reasonably possible after the controls have been completed. An authorised person at the receiving laboratory shall verify the code number, seals, forms, total number of samples and shall sign the chain of custody form and the despatch form indicating receipt.

2.3 The sealed B-sample specimens shall be retained and placed in a properly secure long-term storage (4° C or less) for at least 90 days in the case of a result potentially positive. Within this period a governing body may request the laboratory to retain the specimen for an additional period of time. If no such request is submitted, the specimen may be discarded. However, specific national programmes may have longer storage requirements.

2.4 The B-sample bottles must be kept under locked conditions at all times. Any risk of exposure to sun light or other external factors that could deteriorate the sample must be avoided. Only the head of the laboratory (or a designated delegate) shall have access to the B-specimens.

2.5 The laboratory is responsible for the integrity of samples from the moment when the authorised person has signed the chain of custody and receipt form.

2.6 The laboratory shall use appropriate security measures and facilities to ensure limited and/or controlled access to the samples.

3. Sample Analysis

3.1 The analysis of the A-sample shall be performed as soon as reasonably possible after arrival at the Doping Control Laboratory.

3.2 The samples shall be screened in accordance with the standard analytical techniques and GLP.

3.3 Any declaration of the athlete about any medication or other substance taken in the relevant period prior to the control should be recorded on the Doping Control Form by the athlete or the doping control officer as stated in para. 6.9 of the Recommendation No. 1/95 and transmitted to the laboratory together with samples. If the athlete declines to make a declaration, this shall be recorded on the Doping Control Form.

3.4 Such information must be treated in the strictest confidence by all who have access to it.

3.5 In addition to the head of laboratory and the laboratory staff, only the head or authorised member of the Anti-Doping Commission/Anti-doping organisation shall be admitted to the laboratory during the A-sample analysis.

3.6. Proper chain of custody controls shall always be enforced during all testing and specimen handling. Only authorised personnel may handle specimens to be tested and they shall sign chain of custody forms to document when specimens are in their possession. Authorised technicians shall sign the chain of custody forms and be responsible for each specimen to be tested.

3.7 If the analysis of the A-sample is positive, the following procedures will be followed.

4. The quorum necessary for the destorage and analysis of the B sample

4.1 The B-sample can be destored and analysed after the responsible officer of the laboratory gives his/her authorisation, in accordance with the timescale agreed with the relevant organisation that authorised the control.

4.2 The destorage and analysis of the B-sample will be performed in the same laboratory having performed the A-sample, in the presence of the representative of the federation, the representative of the sports person with the positive A-sample, the head of the Anti-Doping Commission/Anti-doping organisation and the head of laboratory.

4.3 Before proceeding to the B-sample analysis the witnesses and the head of the laboratory should sign a report that describes the status of the sealing and coding of the B-sample. If the status of the sample is deemed acceptable by the head of the laboratory, the B-sample analysis will proceed.

4.4 A report on the analysis of the B-sample, including a document on the analytical results, will be passed to the responsible authority.

4.5 If the B-sample is positive, the head of laboratory may submit his opinion (in writing and duly signed/sealed) to the Anti-Doping Commission/Anti-doping organisation on whether there may be any mitigating circumstances surrounding the use of a banned substance or method.

5. Description of the form of the report of the analytical phase

5.1 The report shall contain the number of specimens assigned by the submitting authority, the specimen identification number and results of the screening analysis for banned substances and methods. All specimens negative on the initial test or negative on the confirmatory test shall be reported as negative. Only specimens confirmed positive will be reported positive for a specific banned substance or method. Results may be transmitted by various electronic means (e.g. teleprinters, facsimile or computer). The official report duly signed by the responsible technician and head of laboratory and countersigned by those entitled to be present and with an official stamp shall be sent by mail and sealed. Copies of all analytical results shall be available from the laboratory when requested by an appropriate authority.

5.2 The following reporting format for positive analytical results on sample B shall be used:

5.2.1 Administration

a) Code number
b) Name and date of competition/ out of competition/place of control
c) Name of collecting body
d) Date of receipt of samples at the laboratory
e) Confirmation that the seal of the box was intact

f) Confirmation that the seal of the bottle/container (sampling kit) was intact

5.2.2 Analytical results, for both A-and B-samples

a) pH, density and appearance of the sample, determined in the laboratory

b) Generic name and quantities of the identified substance(s) or methods, the testosterone/epitestosterone ratio, the caffeine concentration according to the thresholds indicated in the current reference list.

The laboratory should also be prepared to supply the following information for the benefit of the athlete involved and the appropriate organisation, delegation or international federation in connection with the identification of the substance(s) or anomalies recorded in 5.2.2 (b) above:

– summary of the analytical procedures performed in the screening and in the identification stages;
– copies of the analytical data relevant to establishing the presence of banned substances or anomalies.

5.3 The report should be sent to:

– The authority that conducted the doping control
– The relevant sports federation or organisation
– The national anti-doping body (if applicable)

6. Procedures guaranteeing the confidentiality of such reports

6.1 The drug-testing laboratory shall perform all work with its own personnel and equipment and within its premises, unless otherwise authorised by the supervising body (National Anti-Doping Commission or other, according to the relevant regulations).

6.2 The report and other relevant data should be protected according to the national or/and international regulations and the general principles of data protection.

6.3 The laboratory should take every step to ensure that only the authorised persons are informed of the result; such authorised persons must not inform unauthorised persons.

7. Minor irregularities

7.1 Minor irregularities, which cannot reasonably be considered to have affected the results of otherwise valid tests, shall have no effect on such results. Minor irregularities do not include the chain of custody of the sample, improper sealing of the container(s) in which the sample is stored, failure to request the signature of the athlete or failure to provide the athlete with an opportunity to be present or be represented at the opening and analysis of the "B" sample.

8.17. Recommendation on basic principles for disciplinary phases of doping control (98/2)

The Monitoring Group of the Anti-Doping Convention, under the terms of Article 11.1.d of the Convention,

Considering that under Article 3 of the Anti-Doping Convention the Parties undertake to co-ordinate the policies and actions of their government departments and other public agencies concerned with combating doping in sport;

Considering that under Article 7 of the Convention the Parties undertake to encourage their sports organisations to harmonise their doping control procedures and notably, in Article 7.2.d; their:

"disciplinary procedures, applying agreed international principles of natural justice and ensuring respect for the fundamental rights of suspected sportsmen and sportswomen; these principles will include:
– the reporting and disciplinary bodies to be distinct from one another;
– the right of such persons to a fair hearing and to be assisted or represented;
– clear and enforceable provisions for appealing against any judgement made";
Being of the opinion that these principles could also provide a reliable and solid basis for the conclusion of bilateral and multilateral agreements in the fight against doping between organisations, agencies and countries Party to the Convention;
Being of the opinion that this would also encourage other countries and sports organisations to seek common standards;
Convinced of the need to establish common principles for disciplinary phases following doping control;
Being of the opinion that these common principles would ensure the fair and equitable treatment of athletes;
Recalling the Recommendation No. 1/95 of the Monitoring Group of the Anti-Doping Convention to Parties;
Recalling the Recommendation No. 1/97 of the Monitoring Group of the Anti-Doping Convention to Parties;
Having studied the International Olympic Committee's Medical Code and relevant disciplinary procedures adopted by the international sports federations;
Having examined this Recommendation with International and European sports organisations;
Recommends that Parties to the Anti-Doping Convention include, or where appropriate, strongly urge the national sports bodies concerned to include, in their Anti-Doping Regulations or other appropriate texts, Basic principles for disciplinary phases of doping control based on those appended to the present Recommendation.

Appendix
Basic principles for disciplinary phases of doping control

A. Anti-doping commission

A.1 Description of powers, competence and composition of the "Anti-Doping Commission" and similar bodies in national agencies

1.1 An independent body, either within the sport organisation or in national agencies, should be set up for the management of doping control results. This could be an "Anti-Doping Commission" or a similar body and responsible for organising all doping related matters except legal decisions which should be dealt with by a disciplinary panel. The members of the "Anti-Doping Commission" should be different from those who serve on the latter.

1.2 The Commission should be the body authorised to receive all laboratory results and athlete signature forms, and to review these on a confidential basis.

1.3 The decision to initiate disciplinary proceedings because of a breach of the anti-doping regulations – including a refusal to submit to an official control – should be taken by the Anti-Doping Commission.

1.4 The Commission should have members with competence in the following fields: law, medicine, pharmacology, analysis, as well as an experience in sports. Members should not be associated with the laboratory conducting the analyses.

A.2 Description of the role of Anti-Doping Commission when the A sample is positive

2.1 All A-sample test results confirmed at the laboratory as analytically positive should be sent confidentially to the Anti-Doping Commission and to the other national or international authorised body or persons. The Commission should review the results to ensure that the collection process, chain of custody and collection of the data were respected.

2.2 The athlete is notified by the Commission or relevant sport organisation and given a document describing the procedures that will be followed and his/her rights during these procedures, the possible sanctions, and information on the procedure for appeals.

2.3 The athlete has the right to submit an explanation for the presence of a banned substance or method. In the case of a control during competition, the Anti-Doping Commission, as well as the national anti-doping agency, may interview the athlete.

2.4 On the basis of the interview, the Commission may consider relevant facts and circumstances in deciding whether the positive sample constitutes a doping offence and may decide not to have the B sample analysed.

2.5 If the athlete admits his/her offence, disciplinary procedures may be taken on the basis of the A sample.

2.6 The athlete has the right to be present or to be represented during the analysis of the B sample.

2.7 The Commission and relevant sport organisation will make every effort to have sample B analysed as quickly as possible and in any event within 21 days after the athlete is notified.

2.8 Sample B is analysed in order to protect the athlete?s rights. This process allows the athlete to witness the opening of the B sample, to confirm both the coding and the integrity of the bottle, and for the duplication of the results from the A-analysis (in the case of a full analysis) or for confirmation (in the case of a screen).

2.9 On the basis of a report by the Anti-Doping Commission, the relevant sport organisation may provisionally or temporarily suspend the person concerned from competition until the B sample is analysed and/or disciplinary proceedings are initiated.

2.10 A result is declared positive only when both the A and B-samples are positive or when the A-sample is positive and the athlete concerned waives the requirement that the B-sample be analysed.

B. Disciplinary panel

B.1 Description of powers, competence and composition of Disciplinary Panel

1.1 An analytically positive result from sample B and/or a documented refusal to submit to an official control shall always lead to the initiation of appropriate disciplinary procedures.

1.2 A disciplinary panel should have the task of judging, as a court of first instance, all doping cases within the relevant sport organisation.

1.3 The name of the accused person should not be released until such a decision is taken (cf. B.2.7).

1.4 The disciplinary panel may impose such sanctions as are appropriate for the case. These sanctions should be clear and published beforehand. If the accused person appeals against the conviction and sanctions, the latter, including any suspension, should remain in force until the appeal body overturns them. The appeal proceedings, therefore, should be organised with due expedition to avoid any potential incorrect suspension.

1.5 The disciplinary panel should be a body independent from the Anti-Doping Commission. Its members should be different from those who serve on the Anti-Doping Commission. The panel should be composed of experts with medical, technical and legal knowledge in anti-doping questions.

B.2 Procedures ensuring a fair hearing

2.1 Following the provisions of the Convention for Protection of Human Rights and Fundamental Freedoms of the Council of Europe, in particular in Article 6.3, the possibility of a fair hearing and the defence of the rights of the individual suspected of an offence must be guaranteed. Every athlete shall have the right to a hearing before the relevant disciplinary body in advance any decision on sanctions is reached. This hearing should take place as soon as possible, and under normal circumstances, not later than three months after the final laboratory analysis.

2.2 The right to be heard includes the right to be acquainted with the charges and the right to appear personally, to be represented, to bring forward evidence, including witnesses, or to submit a defence in writing.

2.3 The accused person should be informed of the initiation of proceedings and the case against him or her in writing; the charge, and all other relevant documentary evidence and material which form the basis of the charge should be communicated to the accused person beforehand in good time.

2.4 The date of each stage of the disciplinary process should be duly determined. The accused person should be given reasonable time to prepare their defence.

2.5 The proceedings should be thorough and impartial.

2.6 Any measure or sanction shall be communicated in writing to the accused person or any other parties concerned.

2.7 The Disciplinary Panel and its members shall maintain in strict confidentiality the results of all testing and the identities of everyone involved in the doping control proceedings (cf. B.1.3). The violation of the professional secrecy should be sanctioned.

2.8 Disciplinary Panels should adopt rules of procedures, which are clear and enforceable, based on the principles set out in this chapter to ensure a fair hearing.

B.3 Guidelines for sanctions

3.1 Countries or sport bodies concerned should provide in their regulations for imposition of sanctions against doping offence. The sanctions should be sufficient for the offence proved, based on the severity of the infraction, and not encourage disregard for the regulations.

3.2 These sanctions should be consistent (i.e., having similar effects) both between different sports in one country and between International Federations.

3.3 Appropriate sanctions should also be planned and imposed to any refusal or failure to report or refusal to provide a sample.

3.4 Disciplinary panels should always investigate how the athlete concerned breached the regulations. They may take account of any mitigating factors.

3.5 Violations of anti-doping rules involving the supplying, administration and trafficking of doping substances should be regarded as serious offences. The sanctions levied for these actions should appropriately reflect even more severe sanctions than those provided for the cases of doping offences.

3.6 The sanctions applied to an individual found guilty of a doping infraction in one event or sport, should apply fully with regard to participation in all other events and sports and be respected by other authorities or sports for the length of the penalty period.

3.7 Appropriate sanctions should also be applied to any members of the athlete's entourage involved in the doping offence such as officials, doctors, veterinary doctors, coaches, physiotherapists and other officials or accessories associated with infringements of the anti-doping regulations. (Recommendation No. 1/97 on disciplinary measures to be taken with regard to members of the athlete's entourage and protection of minors, in application of Article 7.2.e of the Convention).

C. Appeals

C.1 Provisions for appeals

1.1 Sports organisations should ensure maximum respect for human rights and the principles of fair and impartial justice in the application of disciplinary procedures, particularly by respecting the distinction between the judicial and the executive power, and hence the independence of bodies concerned, so as to guarantee the right to defence, the right to be heard, and the right to appeal.

1.2 In accordance with this principle any person found guilty of a doping infraction should be informed of the judgement and of his/her right of appeal to a body empowered to hear such appeals, and the method for lodging such an appeal.
Such an independent body could be constituted within the sports system – at national and/or international level. This body may also be the arbitration body (cf. C.3).
The Appeal Board members should be different from those who serve on the Disciplinary Panel. These members are to be knowledgeable in anti-doping procedures and are to be experienced in the field of anti-doping in sports.

The Appeal Board should have the authority to review completely the decision taken by the Disciplinary Panel and to modify the sanctions imposed. This body should ensure that the original hearing and examination are in accordance with the principles of natural justice as set out in B.2.
The principles of a fair hearing as outlined at B.2 above should also apply to the proceedings within the appeal process.

C.2 Appeal Boards

2.1 The principles set out in B.1 and B.2 above should be adapted for Appeal Boards. As the Anti-Doping Commission is completely separate in powers and composition from the Disciplinary Panel, so the Appeal Board should be completely separate from the Disciplinary Panel as well.

C.3 Provisions encouraging the use of sports arbitration in cases of dispute

3.1 Sports organisations could provide the possibility to submit disputes concerning the application of their doping control rules to an independent sport arbitration body.

3.2 The arbitration body could be constituted within the sports system – at national and/or international level.

D. Other

D.1 Provisions under which the athlete accepts authority if it conforms to the above principles and common standards

1.1 Sports organisations should provide in their regulations the signature of a declaration by athletes showing that they are informed of the anti-doping regulations and that they agree to abide by them, that they will take part in any doping control activity organised by an appropriate body, including any authorised or official doping control at any time, and that they are aware of the possible consequence of any infraction.

D.2 Provisions enabling sports organisations and anti-doping agencies to adapt anti-doping regulations quickly in cases of necessity (e.g., adoption of new lists of banned substances and methods)

2.1 Sports organisations should adopt anti-doping regulations in conformity with the national anti-doping policy and with the principles of the relevant international sports organisations. These regulations should be regularly revised and updated to adapt them to current circumstances and knowledge.

8.18. Recommendation on blood sampling for doping medical controls (98/3)

The Monitoring Group of the Anti-Doping Convention, under the terms of Article 11.1.d of the Convention,
Whereas under Article 3 of the Anti-Doping Convention the Parties undertake to co-ordinate the policies and actions of their government departments and other public bodies concerned with combating doping in sport;
Whereas in Article 7 of the Convention the Parties undertake to encourage their sports organisations to harmonise their doping control procedures;
Considering that common principles for control procedures would ensure a fair and equitable system for athletes;
Being conscious that the procedures and techniques used in doping control should respect the individual rights of all sports persons;
Having studied the provisions of the Convention on Human Rights and Biomedicine of the Council of Europe;
Having discussed this Recommendation with international and European sports organisations;
Recalling that the principles of the Recommendation No. 1/95 of the Monitoring Group are relevant, mutatis mutandis, for blood sampling;
Being conscious that additional principles should be taken into account in view of the more intrusive character of blood sampling;
Recommends that Parties to the Anti-Doping Convention include, or where appropriate, strongly urge the national sports bodies concerned to include, in their Anti-Doping Regulations, the basic principles for blood testing for anti-doping control appended to the present Recommendation, for implementation if and when blood sampling is introduced.

Appendix
Basic principles for blood testing for anti-doping control

1. Introduction

1.1 The role of the Monitoring Group of the Anti-Doping Convention is to ensure for its part that the struggle against doping in sport is conducted as effectively as possible. However, the Monitoring Group, conscious of the need to protect the individual rights of all sports persons, maintains that there is an obligation upon the sports movement as a whole to ensure that the procedures and techniques used in doping control respect those rights.

1.2 Accordingly, it affirms that doping controls should always be as non-intrusive as the available technology permits, and that where blood-testing is concerned, this should only be resorted to when the use of urine as a control medium is incapable of procuring the desired effect.

1.3 For this purpose, the Monitoring Group states that, whilst the taking of capillary blood samples in quantities expressed in microlitres is in practical terms less intrusive than taking venous blood samples in quantities expressed in millilitres, the same ethical and legal considerations (and thus the present list of basic principles) apply to both categories of samples.

2. Necessity

The body or bodies wishing to take blood samples for the purpose of anti-doping control or related research must be able to show that there is a clear scientific need for blood samples in addition to urine samples.

3. Free and informed consent

3.1 Sports federations and other competent bodies, which intend to practice blood sampling for doping control, must ensure that:

- the authority to do so is enshrined in their anti-doping rules;
- sportsmen and women liable to be tested (or in the case of minors, their parent or guardian) explicitly acknowledge that authority when accepting the rules of the governing body or other agency;
- information, which is a prerequisite of consent, must be given in clear and accessible language, must mention the existence of blood sampling, the sampling method used, the frequency of samples allowed and, especially, the risks of intravenous tests.

3.2. Sports federations and other competent bodies have an obligation, before instituting controls, fully to inform sportsmen and women (or in the case of minors, their parent or guardian), when they accede to a level of competition at which they become liable to doping controls, concerning the implications of their consent. They should be able to furnish proof, in the case of a dispute, that this obligation has been discharged. If this obligation is satisfied, sports organisations may sanction refusal to submit for testing, but can in no other way enforce such testing.

3.3 Where sports federations or other competent bodies intend to use blood samples for purposes other than doping control (e.g. research), specific consent shall be obtained from the subject on each occasion. Neither refusal to give such consent nor positive results found in pursuance of research activities shall be recorded or attract any sanction.

4. Risk and responsibility

4.1 Sports federations and other competent bodies authorised under the terms of 3.1 and 3.2 above to take blood samples must take all appropriate measures to reduce medical risk to the athletes as far as possible.

4.2 Accordingly, all blood samples must be taken in a medically and scientifically satisfactory way and carried out by appropriately trained staff.

4.3 The procedures adopted for the taking of blood samples must clearly assign liability for any mishaps that may occur as a result of blood sampling.

4.4 The organisation to which such liability is assigned must be able to demonstrate that it is adequately covered by insurance related to all conceivable risks.

5. Others

5.1 Medical authorities should be consulted on the most appropriate time of testing not only during competition but also out of competition.

5.2 Multiple tests should be avoided.

5.3 A technical guide to procedures for the collection of blood samples, as in document T-DO (98)18, was also approved by the Monitoring Group at the 9th meeting, for the attention of those requiring such information and guidance.

8.19. Conclusions of the Monitoring Group of the Anti-Doping Convention (T-DO)
Extraordinary meeting of the Monitoring Group, Strasbourg, 5 November 1998

The Meeting was called:
to discuss the events of the summer and autumn and their implications for the work of the Monitoring Group;
to prepare the Monitoring Group's contribution to the World Conference on Doping convened by the International Olympic Committee in February 1999.
The fight against doping in sport has entered a new phase, and faces serious new challenges. All Parties and partners in sport need to find new ways of working – in their own sphere and together – and to establish more effective programmes to counter this scourge.

Part I
The Parties to the Convention agreed a number of priority issues for action by the Monitoring Group or at national level:

1. With regard to law:
   - to undertake a review of national laws affecting anti-doping work (anti-doping laws, laws on medical or banned substances, etc.) with a view to examining the scope for possible improvements and for greater consistency in the framework of the Anti-doping Convention;
   - to help provide information for national sports bodies on how the rule of law – including the Anti-doping Convention – affects sport.
2. With regard to medical care of sportsmen and sportswomen:
   - to improve the medical care and health protection of sportspeople, and to provide better information and education for those working – medically and otherwise – in their entourage, for example, through codes of professional conduct. National Medical Associations should be invited to draw up clear rules (with sanctions) on this matter. In this context, the Monitoring Group welcomes the co-operation of the IOC in the production of a CD-Rom and Internet versions of the Clean Sports Guide.
3. With regard to the availability of banned substances:
   - to seek, through the appropriate channels at national level, closer co-operation with police, customs and other relevant authorities with a view to reducing the supply of doping agents to sport and their use/demand within it. Research into the sociological aspects of the doping phenomenon could also help such reduction.

The Monitoring Group also stresses the need for national anti-doping agencies to increase the number of, and to reduce to a minimum the notice given for, out-of-competition controls. Another priority is to seek methods better to detect and to control the use of doping substances, EPO and other peptide hormones in particular. Regulations to prevent over production of these substances should also be introduced.

Part II

The Extraordinary Meeting also agreed to five proposals that would form the basis for the Monitoring Group's delegations' submissions to the IOC Conference with the aim of boosting the effectiveness of anti-doping work in general and of improving co-operation and harmonisation between the sports movement and that of the public authorities active in this field. Participation by the Monitoring Group in anti-doping during major international competitions could also help ensure consistency and transparency.

1. With regard to the proposed Olympic anti-doping agency
   The Monitoring Group supports the creation of such an agency, which should help to integrate the strategies and the activities already carried out by international sports federations and agencies. It could play an important role in inaugurating world-wide out-of-competition testing, especially in regions and countries without effective anti-doping programmes at the moment. Its activities would also need to complement those of existing national anti-doping agencies which presently carry out approximately 85% of anti-doping work. The agency should be authoritative, independent, international, transparent and non-profit making. It should have a research component. The Monitoring Group, which consistently seeks a better harmonisation and co-ordination of anti-doping work at international and national levels, would wish to play an active part in it, and will make proposals for its work in due course.
2. With regard to medical supervision
   The Monitoring Group will encourage the IOC, the IFs and NOCs to supervise more closely the entourage (medical and other) of athletes and teams.
3. With regard to eligibility and sanctions
   The Monitoring Group will ask the IOC to ensure that only those international federations adopting and effectively applying the common Medical Code proposed by the IOC, (including in particular the application of recommended sanctions in case of infractions, and the protection of the rights of sportsmen and sportswomen), can participate in the programmes of the Olympic Games.
4. With regard to the list of prohibited classes of substances and prohibited methods
   The Monitoring Group – which, as a contribution to harmonisation, adopts the same list of prohibited classes of substances and prohibited methods as the IOC's list – will ask the IOC to make concrete proposals on ways in which it can be associated with the drawing up this list.
5. With regard to the anti-doping laboratories
   In accordance with Article 11.1.b of the Convention, and as most accredited laboratories are financed by public funds in the country concerned, the Monitoring Group would like to be associated with the IOC in establishing quality systems and standards for anti-doping laboratories.

8.20. Declaration on the International protocol for doping control (ISO/PAS 18873)

Adopted by the Monitoring Group at its 11th Meeting on 30 – 31 March 2000 in Strasbourg

The Monitoring Group of the Anti-Doping Convention, under the terms of Article 11.1.d of the Convention,

Whereas under Article 3.1 of the Anti-Doping Convention the Parties undertake to co-ordinate the policies and actions of their government departments and other public bodies concerned with combating doping in sport;

Whereas in Article 7.2.c of the Convention the Parties undertake to encourage their sports organisations to harmonise their doping control procedures;
Considering that this would also encourage other sports organisations and countries to seek high common standards;
Convinced of the need to establish high quality standards for doping control in order to ensure a fair and equitable system for athletes;
Recalling its Recommendations No. 1/95 on standard urine sampling procedures for doping control in and out of competition, No. 1/98 on standard operating procedures at doping control laboratories, and No. 2/98 on basic principles for disciplinary phases of doping control, all of which contribute to the harmonisation of high standards;
Noting that the decision by the International Organisation for Standard to adopt the Publicly Available Specification (ISO/PAS 18873) means that the International Standard for Doping Control (ISDC) is recognised as an operational quality protocol,

1. Acknowledges that the ISDC (ISO/PAS 18873) provides a robust doping control standard which countries, anti-doping organisations and international and national sports federations should draw on and endeavour to implement within their own anti-doping programmes;
2. Recommends the ISO/PAS 18873 to Parties as the reference protocol for quality assurance in national doping control process and systems;
3. Recommends that the World Anti-Doping Agency recognises the ISO/PAS 18873 norm as the reference protocol in anti-doping controls, and encourages international sport organisations to base their anti-doping programmes on this norm;
4. Expresses its firm support for the work by ISO and its expert group for the preparation and adoption of an ISO norm for doping control, and its desire that the Monitoring Group be consulted at appropriate stages in this work.

8.21. Declaration on the use of altitude rooms/hyperbaric chambers

Adopted by the Monitoring Group at its 11th Meeting on 30 – 31 March 2000 in Strasbourg

As forbidding these techniques is probably not the best solution, the Group suggests warning those concerned on the risks of these processes:
High-altitude training is permitted for athletes, and it cannot be banned for natural reasons: some nations/athletes are normally located at high altitudes. Artificial environments mimicking the main consequence of high altitude (lowering of the partial pressure of oxygen, that means the percentage of oxygen in the inspired air) could theoretically be banned, because they are unnatural, and they could be controlled.
Contrary to natural high altitude, artificial means (hypoxic chambers) are not limited to conditions corresponding to several thousand meters above sea level: their pressure or oxygen content can theoretically be expanded to quite unnatural, dangerous or even lethal measures.
On the other hand, the real benefit in performance enhancement will certainly depend on further conditions: while enhanced performances have been observed under specific circumstances, they may lack under other ones.
Different technical concepts play probably an additional role: hypobaric chambers similar to high geographical altitude provide low air pressure and lower oxygen content per inhaled volume simultaneously, whereas other chambers lower only the oxygen content (lower percentage than the normal 20%). The physiological consequences or risks of those different conditions as well as the influence on performance can differ.

In general, these considerations have to assume technical perfection. Serious risks would be introduced, if the predetermined, physiologically justified parameters could not be technically guarantized.

But the possibility to obtain similar effects by natural (although more expensive and more time-consuming) means should be discouraged for at least unreasonably extended use, but not to prohibit these methods for the time being.

8.22. Resolution on the fight against doping (1/2000)

Bratislava, 30-31 May 2000

The European Ministers responsible for Sport, meeting in Bratislava for their 9th Conference on 30 and 31 May 2000, and the representatives of the other States Parties to the Anti-Doping Convention:

Welcoming the active role played by the Council of Europe in setting up the World Anti-Doping Agency;

Noting with satisfaction the Committee of Ministers' decision authorising the Council of Europe and the Monitoring Group of the Anti-Doping Convention to participate in the WADA Board;

Emphasising, considering the experience and expertise of the T-DO, the need to establish an effective partnership between the Monitoring Group of the Anti-Doping Convention and the Agency;

Noting with satisfaction the signing of the Anti-Doping Convention by 42 countries (36 of which have ratified it) since it was opened for signature on 16 November 1989 and the participation, as observers, of a number of other States and international sports organisations in the T-DO;

Welcoming the fact that the participants in the Sydney Summit on doping (November 1999), Unesco's Third International Conference of Ministers and Senior Officials responsible for Physical Education and Sport (MINEPS III, December 1999), the Assembly of the Ibero-American Sports Council and the meeting of the International Intergovernmental Consultative Group on Anti-Doping in Sport (February 2000) have acknowledged the Anti-Doping Convention as an international reference instrument for co-ordinating national anti-doping policies and have invited countries all over the world to accede to the Convention;

Noting with satisfaction the adoption by the Parliamentary Assembly of Recommendation 1464 (2000) on Doping in Sport;

Thanking the Council of Europe for its essential contribution to helping governments in the fight against doping;

Eager to ensure that the provisions of the Convention are effectively implemented;

Considering that, in order to combat doping effectively, it is essential that action should be taken against traffickers of doping agents;

Aware that it is up to governments to enact laws and regulations to harmonise national anti-doping legislation, particularly regarding the possession and trafficking of banned doping agents;

Concerned by the growing non-sport use of doping agents and considering that the necessary measures should be taken to prevent further proliferation;

1. Affirm their commitment to participate actively in the work of the World Anti-Doping Agency; agree that the Agency should apply a consistent transparency in its activities and should develop a complete list of banned substances and methods as well as clear criteria for the accreditation of laboratories; stress the need for the Agency to be in a

position to act as an independent observer in the management of test results at the Sydney Olympic Games;

2. Undertake to recognise the authority of the World Anti-Doping Agency to carry out unannounced out-of-competition controls in accordance with the Agency Statutes on their territories;
3. Recommend the designation, in consultation with the members states of the European Union, of Minister Suvi Linden (Finland) as the representative of the European continent on the Executive Committee of the WADA;
4. Approve the proposals submitted by the Monitoring Group aimed at improving the implementation and effectiveness of the Convention in particular the setting up of a binding control mechanism based on the "Compliance with Commitments" project; support the development of a common database on anti-doping initiatives, in cooperation with other partners;
5. Consider that it would be desirable, in the light of changes since the adoption of the Anti-Doping Convention in 1989, and of present needs in the fight against doping, to study the need for possible amendments and/or draft protocols to the Anti-Doping Convention;
6. Undertake to mutually recognise the authority of the sports organisations and national anti-doping agencies from host countries to carry out unannounced anti-doping tests on sportsmen and women from States parties to the Convention who are in another State party to the Convention without the need for bilateral agreements, and to introduce the regulations and administrative measures necessary for this mutual recognition in accordance with the highest international standards, as recognised by the Monitoring Group;
7. Undertake to introduce into their national legislation legal provisions in keeping with the principles set out in the draft recommendation (see Appendix to this Resolution) and to implement them effectively in order to seek out the persons responsible, particularly those who have set up networks for producing and distributing doping agents;
8. Invite the Committee of Ministers of the Council of Europe to:

Continue to ensure the Council of Europe's and the Monitoring Group's participation in the World Anti-Doping Agency and to give the Monitoring Group support so that it may co-operate effectively with the Agency;
Approve the designation, after consultation with the members states of the European Union, of Minister Suvi Linden (Finland) as the representative of the European continent on the Executive Committee of the WADA;
Adopt the measures in order to improve the application and the efficiency of the Convention and provide the Monitoring Group with the necessary means for implementing those measures;
Request the Monitoring Group to draw up a draft amending protocol to the Convention aimed at setting up a binding control mechanism, and on the mutual recognition of controls on the territory of other Parties;
Adopt the text of the draft recommendation (as it appears in the Appendix to this Resolution) (See Recommendation CM Rec 2000/16 as adopted by the Committee of Ministers at the beginning of this document) on the common basic principles to be introduced into national legislation with a view to combating the trafficking of doping agents.

8.23. Resolution on "A clean and healthy Sport for the third Millennium" (6/2000)
The European Ministers responsible for Sport, meeting in Bratislava for their 9th Conference on 30 and 31 May 2000

Bearing in mind the Resolutions and texts adopted at this Conference,
Reaffirming their belief that "sport for all" is a phenomenon of major importance which can unite the peoples of Europe across ethnic, cultural, social and economic boundaries,
Emphasising the positive role sport can play in society in furthering social cohesion and drawing individuals into mainstream society, and fighting exclusion,
Mindful of the benefits to physical health and social well-being of a lifestyle which includes regular sports activity,
Conscious of the need for all those involved in sport today to co-operate in ensuring 'A clean and healthy sport for the 3rd millennium' and to recognise their part in transmitting to their successors a heritage of sport, combining high ideals and firm principles, based on individual fulfilment and social progress,
Realise that achieving this depends on a determined effort to counter those practices that sully the image of sport, for example, corruption, doping, violence and sexual harassment and abuse, especially of children, young people and women,
Acknowledge the need to continue to strengthen national efforts to combat doping in sport, and underline the roles of the Anti-Doping Convention and the World Anti-Doping Agency in the international aspects of this fight,
Accept, furthermore, the need to educate, encourage and assist the world of sport to implement the fundamental principles for the sustainable development of sport for future generations, while respecting a balanced management of the environment,
Thank the Parliamentary Assembly, the Committee for the Development of Sport, the Standing Committee of the European Convention on Spectator Violence and the Monitoring Group of the Anti-Doping Convention for the work they have carried out to strengthen, develop and enhance co-operation in sport and further the aims of the Council of Europe since their last Conference in Lisbon in 1995,
Acknowledge the importance of the policy-making role at the European level of the Committee for the Development of Sport and the prominence given in its programme to values and ethics, which are the foundation for a clean and healthy sport in a democratic society, based on the principles of tolerance and fair play,
Note the invitation of the Government of Hungary to hold the 10th Conference in Budapest in 2004,
Thank the Slovak authorities for the smooth organisation of the Conference and the generous hospitality offered during it.

8.24. Recommendation 1464 (2000) on Doping
Text adopted by the Standing Committee, acting on behalf of the Assembly on 17 May 2000

1. The Assembly is alarmed at the increase of doping scandals in sport (for example, during the 1998 World Swimming Championships in Australia, during the Tour de France, in Italian football and in the recent World Ice Skating Championship in Nice). Both the health of athletes and the moral and ethical foundations of sport are at stake.
2. The Council of Europe's 1989 Anti-Doping Convention proposes a number of measures for more effective anti-doping programmes and policies and continues to be the sole legal framework for European and international co-operation in this field, not only

between governments but also between governments and international sports organisations.

3. The Assembly welcomes the setting up of the World Anti-Doping Agency (WADA and the active role played by the Council of Europe in its creation. It notes with satisfaction that both the Council of Europe and the Monitoring Group of the Anti-Doping Convention participate in the WADA Board. It welcomes continuing partnership with the European Union in this field.
4. It recalls its Recommendation 1292 (1996) on young people in high level sport. Some sports can put a particularly dangerous pressure on young athletes and lead them to doping. These sports should be more carefully monitored than others.
5. The Assembly feels that more should be done at European and world level for the protection of the health of athletes, and in particular young athletes, and of the ethical foundations of sport.
6. Consequently it recommends that the Committee of Ministers:
   a. give greater consideration to how the harmonisation of national legislation, including legislation on medicinal products and dietary supplements, might help to reduce the incidence of doping in sport and promote such harmonisation;
   b. improve the exchange of information and co-operation in this field;
   c. take an active stand in the Board of the World Anti-Doping Agency in order to highlight the quality of the work done by the Council of Europe bodies concerned and their experience in international co-ordination in the fight against doping;
   d. increase the resources of the Monitoring Group set up under the Anti-Doping Convention to enhance its effectiveness:
   e. encourage those few member states that have not yet ratified the Convention to do so as soon as possible and invite all the other countries in the world to accede to it;
   f. ask member states, and where appropriate, sports organisations. to:
      – ensure that athletes, coaches and any other persons found guilty of doping-related offences (prescribing, supplying, offering, administering or applying prohibited doping agents to athletes, facilitating their use or encouraging athletes in any wav at all to use them), are effectively punished;
      – improve protection for young athletes in order to avoid them being tempted by doping, in particular by providing them with adequate information on the negative consequences of doping for their health;
      – regard trafficking in doping agents as equivalent to drug trafficking and take all measures to ensure that the international organisations that fight drug trafficking include the fight against doping in their remit.

8.25. Recommendation Rec(2000)16 of the Committee of Ministers to member states on common core principles to be introduced into national legislation to combat the traffic in doping agents

Adopted by the Committee of Ministers on 13 September 2000 at the 720th meeting of the Ministers' Deputies

The Committee of Ministers, under the terms of Article 15.b of the Statute of the Council of Europe,

Bearing in mind the Resolution on "the fight against doping" adopted at the 9th Conference of European Ministers responsible for Sport, in Bratislava in May 2000;
Recalling that Article 4 of the Anti-Doping Convention (ETS 135) stipulates that "the Parties shall adopt, where appropriate, legislation, regulations or administrative measures to restrict the availability (including provisions to control movement, possession, importation, distribution and sale) as well as the use in sport of banned doping agents and doping methods and in particular anabolic steroids";
Recalling that, with reference to this article, the Monitoring Group adopted Recommendation (No.2/94) on measures to restrict the availability of anabolic steroids, which has influenced several countries' legislation in this field;
Considering that events in recent years have shown that the traffic in and use of doping agents is not restricted to anabolic steroids but extends also to other substances, such as erythropoietin and growth hormones;
Considering that a decisive factor in the fight against doping is political will on the part of the authorities to adopt and enforce in practice suitable legislation on seeking and identifying those responsible, especially those in control of networks producing and distributing doping agents, and that this task, which goes beyond the sole jurisdiction of ministers of sport, also concerns the police, customs and other authorities;
Aware that it is incumbent upon governments to enact laws and regulations which will harmonise bodies of national legislation on doping and the possession of and traffic in doping agents;
Recognising that the legislative measures must be backed up by effective co-ordination;
Considering the Clearing House study on Legislation and Regulations on Doping in 42 countries;
Considering that the ineffectiveness of the fight against suppliers of banned substances is due in part to the lack of international co-ordination in this field;
Considering that the Anti-Doping Convention and its associated recommendations (in particular Recommendation No.2/94 on measures to restrict the availability of anabolic steroids) constitute a common framework for the adoption and standardisation of national legislation on the production, movement and possession of doping agents,

1. Recommends that the Governments of the member states:
   A. Sign and/or ratify the Anti-Doping Convention (ETS 135) if they have not already done so;
   B. In applying the Convention, adopt suitable legislation and/or effectively apply existing legislation to deter and punish (by means that may include imprisonment) individuals and legal persons involved in the production, manufacture, transport, import, export, storage, offer, supply or any other form of traffic in doping agents. Such legislation should be based on the principles stated in the appendix to this recommendation.
2. Instructs the Secretary General to bring the Recommendation to the attention of the States Parties to the Convention and the observers which are not member states of the Council of Europe.

Appendix to Recommendation Rec(2000)16
Common core principles

1. The approach is not fundamentally different from that of laws against hard drugs. Governments should ensure, within the bounds of each country's system of law and admin-

istration, that the most appropriate and effective national means are used to combat the production, manufacture, transport, import, export, storage, offer, supply or any other form of traffic in doping agents. To do so, countries should review their legislation in the relevant areas of government responsibility with respect for doping agents, such as:

- criminal laws;
- laws and regulations on pharmaceutical products and medicines;
- customs laws and regulations;
- legislation on the protection of public health, etc.;
- legislation for the protection of children;
- laws concerning professionals (esp. medical doctors, veterinary doctors, pharmacists and laboratory workers);
- any other relevant legal act…

2. Legislation should also target the act of prescribing, supplying, offering, administering or applying prohibited doping agents to athletes, that of facilitating their use and that of encouraging athletes in any way at all to use them. This can be achieved by national legislation for sport or by a suitable alternative regime for the governance of sport at a national level with binding anti-doping provisions.
3. There are a number of specific issues or problems which should be addressed by governments in the exercise of their responsibilities:
   a. In cases of doping or non-sport use involving minors, and in order to reinforce their protection, there is a need for tougher sanctions for those who prescribe, supply, offer, administer or apply doping agents to them.
   b. The adoption of such legislation would require a common definition of doping agents (and related substances). With a view to harmonising legislative measures in this field, all definitions should be based on those adopted by the Monitoring Group in the appendix to the Anti-Doping Convention.
   c. Another major concern is that of improving information about medicines, and their effects as doping agents. A standard warning should be printed on medicine labels. It is also necessary to provide in national legislation that all contents of food or dietary supplements or vitamins, should be indicated on the packaging of these substances. This information should in particular specify whether the so-called dietary supplement contains a doping substance or a precursor of doping substance (for ex. a steroid and/or its precursors). The implications of Internet trade should be catered for.
   d. Provision should be made in national legislation for the seizure and confiscation of illegal substances, and to address money laundering.
   e. It would be prudent to extend the scope of legislative and administrative measures on the laundering of drug money to earnings derived from the trade in doping agents.
   f. Additional legislative and administrative measures should be adopted to coordinate the activity of the police, customs and courts.
   g. A system should be set up for pooling information on trafficking and traffickers in doping agents. Such a system could operate between countries on a bilateral basis or by means of existing international machinery.
   h. In order to improve international effectiveness, measures should be taken as required to improve the compatibility of police and customs administrative procedures in countries party to the convention. International consciousness and

co-operation should also be encouraged in international police and customs, organisations such as the world Customs Organisation and Interpol.

i. As the chemical complexity of doping agents does not always permit their identification by the police or customs, members of both police forces and customs services should receive adequate training.

8.26. Recommendation 1/2005 on the use of the Model Guidelines for Core Information/ education Programmes to Prevent Doping in Sport

The Monitoring Group of the Anti-Doping Convention, under the terms of Article 11.1.d of the Convention,
Whereas under Article 6 of the Anti-Doping Convention the Parties undertake to devise and implement, where appropriate in co-operation with the sports organisations concerned, the anti-doping organisations and the mass media, educational programmes and information campaigns emphasising the dangers to health inherent in doping and its harm to the ethical values of sport;
Welcoming, in this regard, Article 18 of the World Anti-Doping Code on Education:

- Convinced that information and education programmes should be planned for the long term, designed systematically and evaluated;
- Convinced that the Model Guidelines for Core Information/Education Programmes to prevent Doping in Sport can be of great value for the development, implementation, delivery and evaluation of information and education programmes.
- Having discussed this Recommendation with international and European sports organisations;
- Expressing its gratitude to the World Anti-Doping Agency for the close co-operation in the development of the Model Guidelines;
- Taking note with satisfaction that the Model Guidelines have been integrated in the World Anti-Doping Programme;

Recommends that Parties to the Anti-Doping Convention:

- Adopt, or where appropriate, strongly urge the relevant organisations concerned to adopt, the Model Guidelines for Core Information/education Programmes to Prevent Doping in Sport, appended to the present Recommendation, as a methodological tool, for the development and implementation of information and education programmes.
- Designate a person in charge of the development and implementation of information/ education programmes.

Chapter 9
ECONOMIC CHANGES

9.1. Resolution on Economic Changes in Sport (84/4)
The European Minister responsible for Sport meeting in Malta for their 4th Conference from 15 to 16 May 1984

Considering the fact that the concept of Sport for All, as adopted in the European Sport for All Charter, has received considerable backing in all member states;
Noting that the relationship between work and leisure is continually changing, and that both are vital to every human being;
Convinced that sport has an important contribution to make to the worthwhile use of increased leisure time and is a good means of improving the quality of people's lives, physically, mentally and socially;
Realising that this concept has considerably increased governments' responsibility in the promotion, development and implementation of sport programmes;
Conscious of the present worldwide economic recession, unemployment and limited public funds, the ever increasing costs of sports participation, and the costs of possible changes in sport facilities which are imposing great strains on policies and structures already established;
Aware of the fact that commercial sponsorship and marketing in sport are already recognised and accepted as an additional means of financing sport, and at the same time realising that the increasing business interest in sport and sport sponsorship are presenting serious threats to the independence and autonomy of sport organisations and undermining the ethical values of sportsmanship;

Resolve:
1. to safeguard the gains in participation achieved in the last decade;
2. in association with the voluntary and the commercial sectors, to establish policies for recreational and competitive sport, both nationally and internationally aiming at:
   a. clearly defining the roles of each sector;
   b. co-ordinating their involvement in the running and the use of facilities;
   c. implementing programmes for sports promotion among groups with low participation;
   d. to investigate further the above guidelines and the economic importance of sport in relation to changing social trends;

Invite the Committee of Ministers of the Council of Europe to instruct the CDDS to examine the questions raised by this Resolution.

Chapter 10
EMPLOYMENT

10.1. Resolution on Employment in Sport (84/5)

The European Ministers responsible for Sport, meeting in Malta for their 4th Conference on 15 and 16 May 1984

Considering that unemployment is one of the most pressing social problems in Europe;
Considering that governments have a major responsibility to find solutions to this problem;
Noting that a prerequisite for the practice of sport is the availability of sufficient qualified staff at each level of administrative and technical management, leadership and training/coaching;
Considering that such staff can be both voluntary and professional, and that professional staff can also be deployed in support of voluntary staff;
Considering that, because of the contribution of such qualified staff to the quality and accessibility of sport and thus to the benefit of sport, the voluntary sports organisations themselves should make a financial contribution to the employment of professional staff;
Considering that in view of the contribution of sport to health, social development and integration and to a positive use of leisure time for young and old, governments too have a responsibility to allow for the employment of professional staff;
Noting that during the Papendal seminar in 1993 "Professional support of volunteers in sport" it appeared that several obstacles existed to the appointment of an adequate number of qualified staff both for the promotion of sport and in the technical, administrative and organisational fields at different levels;

Resolve:

1. to study ways in which national "employment in sport programmes" could be realised; such programmes could consider ways of:
   a. encouraging sports organisations to put forward proposals for permanent employment at the different levels;
   b. considering if and how regional and local authorities can be associated with the development of an "employment in sport programme";
   c. joint financing by sports organisations and public authorities;
   d. examining the question of whether social benefit funds can be used for the financing of an "employment in sport programme";
   e. examining if and to what extent the commercial sector could participate in the financing of such a programme;

Invite the Committee of Ministers of the Council of Europe to ask the CDDS to monitor the follow-up to this resolution and, if necessary, to make further proposals, for example, the setting up of a working group.

Chapter 11
ENVIRONMENT

11.1. Recommendation No. R (81)8 of the Committee of Ministers to Member States on Sport and Physical Recreation and Nature Conservation in Inland Water Areas

Adopted by the Committee of Ministers on 26 May 1981 at the 334th meeting of the Ministers' Deputies

The Committee of Ministers, under the terms of Article 15b of the Statute of the Council of Europe,
Recalling the European Water Charter of 1968, where it is stated that there is no life without water and that it is a treasure indispensable to all human activity;
Recalling its Resolution (76) 41 on the principles for a policy for sport for all (the European Sport for All Charter) in which it is stated that "measures, including legislation where appropriate, shall be introduced to ensure access to open country and water for the purposes of recreation";
Recognising the constraints on both nature conservation and sport and physical recreation;
Considering that it will not always be possible to satisfy the need to conserve nature and to promote sport and recreation at the same place;
Conscious that, in areas of multiple use, the reconciliation of the several interests will depend at least in part on a better understanding by all those concerned of all the factors involved;
Hoping that problems may be overcome in a spirit of tolerance and understanding;
Convinced that the growing requirement of all members of society calls for a careful, waste-free and optimal use of diminishing water resources,

Recommends the governments of member states:

1. That they should use the following measures as guidelines in the management of inland water areas:
   a. as far as the reconciliation of the several interests is concerned:
      i. to conserve inland water areas for the benefit of society as a whole;
      ii. to improve communication and co-operation between all the relevant decision-taking authorities in order to find solutions to possible difficulties and to produce more consensus than exists to date;
      iii. to consider the preparation of inventories of inland water areas showing their ecological condition, scientific value and physical recreational characteristics and potential;
      iv. to consider developing on the basis of any such inventories an overall policy for inland water areas which would include designating prime use areas at national, regional and local levels;
      v. to encourage the development of education and interpretation programmes which would be designed, on the one hand, for trainers and users of sport and physical recreation, and, on the other, for those responsible for the management and conservation of inland water areas, and which would include material relating to each other's problems;
      vi. to plan for meeting the requirements of both nature conservation and sport and physical recreation, allowing for their specific constraints

and for demands of all sorts on inland water areas, compatible with paragraph a.i above;

b. as far as the management of inland water areas is concerned:
   i. to ensure that any management plans and policies, bearing in mind any prime uses, endeavour to satisfy all parties involved as far as possible and ensure that these plans are duly publicised;
   ii. to encourage the adoption of the following practical measures (in addition to legislation, bye-laws and regulations):
      - space and/or time zoning according to the activities and to the environment;
      - registration of motor boats, within agreed limits in each country, and licensing of fishermen (in order to obtain statistics for medium to long-term management plans);
      - ecological reserve management (which will include work by voluntary organisations);
      - safety education in outdoor recreational activities and the joint preparation of codes of conduct by conservationists and the appropriate sporting and recreational associations for each inland water area;
      - interpretation for the casual visitor, explaining the site's significance and promoting greater environmental awareness, with due attention to sport and recreation interests;
      - designation of prime use areas;
      - provision of adequate public facilities, managed, if possible, with the help of voluntary organisations, catering as far as possible also for the specific requirements of the handicapped;
      - considering partly paying for these facilities with the income derived from charges levied on users for boating and fishing;

c. to consider where necessary setting up advisory bodies representing all parties which could fulfil a most useful function in harmonising the different interests and preparing the ground for policy and management decisions. They might also make available to the organisations catering for sport, recreation and nature conservation, information assembled in the different member states on some of the issues at stake, including information on the situation regarding access to inland water areas, rivers in particular;

2. That they should ensure that local and regional authorities, nature conservation bodies and sport and recreation organisations are informed of this recommendation and invited to consider in what way their policies, management plans and programmes need to be revised in order to implement, within their sphere of competence, the proposals in this recommendation;
3. That they should provide the Secretary General of the Council of Europe with documentation on national initiatives so that he may prepare an annotated European bibliography of relevant research in areas of common interest.

11.2. Resolution on Sport and the Environment (86/8)

The European Ministers responsible for Sport, meeting in Dublin for their 5th Conference from 30 September to 2 October 1986,

Recognising the importance of sport as an essential factor in human development, and its contribution to health and the quality of life;
Noting that sports are practised to an increasing extent (competition, Sport for All, leisure sports) and aware of the fact that the establishment and the use of sports facilities may also have disadvantages for man and the environment;
Convinced that the setting of sports facilities close to residential areas is essential to promoting participation, to preserving ecologically fragile environments, by helping to reduce environmental problems caused by excessive traffic;
Recognising the importance of reconciling sporting and environmental interests when and where these are in conflict;
Desiring to build upon the principles of Recommendation N° R (81) 8 of the Committee of Ministers of the Council of Europe on sport and recreation and nature conservation in inland water areas;

Invite member governments:

1. to ensure that the interests of sports are taken into account in regional plans and urban development planning, having regard to environmental considerations, and that appropriate areas for sports facilities are indicated following consultation with sports organisations;
2. to make efforts, together with the sports organisations and the environmental protection associations, to ensure that careful use is made of nature and landscapes in the practice of sport.

11.3. Resolution on the draft Code for sustainability in sport: A partnership between sport and the environment (5/2000)

The European Ministers responsible for Sport, meeting in Bratislava for their 9th Conference from 30-31 May 2000

Convinced of the need for a partnership between sport and the environment which takes into account the existing international and national programmes directed towards sustainability in sport, together with those examples of good practice described in the Clearing House publication 'Environment and Sport. Awareness raising, education, training'.
Mindful that a clean and healthy environment is essential for those taking part in recreational or competitive sport and that many sports organisations and participants contribute actively to environmental protection,
Aware that the responsibility for sustainable development lies with all those active in sport and that the sports policy sector, the sports practice sector and the scientific sector, together with individual sportsmen and sportswomen, must be involved if progress is to be made in this field,

I Resolve:
to give their full support to the Code for Sustainability in Sport: A partnership between sport and the environment, reproduced in the Appendix i

II Invite the Committee of Ministers of the Council of Europe:
to adopt the 'Code for Sustainability in sport: A partnership between sport and the environment' (see Appendix) as a Recommendation to Governments,
to ask the Committee for the Development of Sport (CDDS) to give appropriate follow-up to this Code, by setting up a working group.

III Resolve:
to distribute the Code, once adopted, in their own language, among national sports and environmental organisations and promote its dissemination to all the appropriate target groups,
to encourage the authorities responsible for sport and the environment to work together
to encourage regional, national and international sports organisations and federations to develop campaigns, literature and educational materials in this area.

11.4. Recommendation Rec(2000)17 of the Committee of Ministers to member states on the Code of sustainability in sport: a partnership between sport and the environment
Adopted by the Committee of Ministers on 13 September 2000 at the 720th meeting of the Ministers' Deputies

The Committee of Ministers, under the terms of Article 15.b of the Statute of the Council of Europe,
Bearing in mind Resolution No 5/2000 on the draft Code for sustainability in sport: a partnership between sport and the environment, adopted at the 9th Conference of European Ministers responsible for Sport, in Bratislava in May 2000,
Bearing in mind Article 10 (Sport and Sustainable Development) of the European Sports Charter (Recommendation N° R(92)13 of the Committee of Ministers),
Considering the contribution which the Code can make towards the implementation of the aims of the Pan-European Biological and Landscape Diversity Strategy (Council of Europe and UNEP),
Acknowledging the importance to the Code of the work of the Committee for the activities of the Council of Europe in the field of biological and landscape diversity (CO-DBP), in particular the Group of specialists on "Tourism and the environment",
Conscious of the links, which exist between the following Recommendations and sustainable sports tourism:
Recommendation No. R (94) 7 on a general policy for sustainable and environment- friendly tourism development;
Recommendation No. R (95) 10 on sustainable tourism development policy in protected areas;
Recommendation No. R (97) 9 on a policy for the development of sustainable environment-friendly tourism in coastal areas,
Convinced of the need for a partnership between sport and the environment which takes into account the existing international and national programmes directed towards sustainability in sport, together with those examples of good practice described in the Clearing House publication "Environment and Sport: Awareness raising, education, training",
Aware that a clean and healthy environment is essential for those taking part in recreational or competitive sport,
Realising that many sports organisations and participants contribute actively to environmental protection but that certain sporting activities, particularly those practised in the most sensitive environments, may cause serious damage to nature and landscapes,
Aware that the responsibility for sustainable development lies with all those active in sport and that the sports policy sector, the sports practice sector and the scientific sector, together with individual sportsmen and sportswomen, must be involved if progress is to be made in this field,
Recommends the governments of member states to base their appropriate national policies on the "Code for Sustainability in Sport: a partnership between sport and the environment" as set out in the Appendix to this Recommendation.

Appendix to Recommendation Rec(2000)17

Code for sustainability in sport: a partnership between sport and the environment

Aims and definition

This Code aims to set out guidelines for a working partnership between sport and the environment. It is important to ensure that sports can be enjoyed, both today and in the future, by as many people as possible in the most favourable conditions, by which is meant sport in a clean and healthy environment.

Sport in all its forms, practised at all levels, whether recreational or competitive sport, shares with the whole of human society the duty of nurturing and safeguarding the natural environment for both present and future generations. The adoption of the definition of sustainable development `as development that meets the needs of the present without compromising the ability of future generations to meet theirs` is a starting point for action now.

The concept of sustainability in sport has already been incorporated into Article 10 of the European Sports Charter of 1992. This Article emphasises the responsibility of everyone involved in sport to protect the environment and promotes the introduction of a model of environmentally friendly sport. However, measures are needed to address those trends and practices in sport that are currently endangering the environment. The Code indicates realistic ways to ensure environmental protection. In practical terms this entails national policies that ensure respect for sustainability in sport in urban, open country and water areas.

The International Olympic Committee has organised conferences on sport and the environment, emphasised the need to respect environmental concerns when planning the Olympic Games and adopted Agenda 21, which reflects concern for the relationship between sport, the natural environment and sustainable development.

Responsibility for sustainable sport

This code focuses on the three sectors that bear the major responsibility for action which are:

- the policy sector, which is composed of groups and people concerned with the strategic choices, legislation, values and the underlying issues behind these questions. This includes governments and international organisations;
- the sports practice sector which is made up of sports organisations and federations, those engaged in the planning and construction of sports facilities, the educational sector, those concerned with sports tourism and the sporting goods industry. This group covers the whole spectrum from the large international and national sporting federations to the sports clubs at the grassroots level to the individual sportsman and woman;
- the scientific sector which embraces institutions, groups and individuals carrying out research, collecting and evaluating data and disseminating information.

Co-ordination between these sectors should be assured. Moreover the similarity of aims and concerns provides an opportunity to create close partnerships between those working for sustainable development in sport and those working for environmental conservation and protection. Environmental organisations can provide useful expertise.

Activities common to all three sectors

While each sector and its composite groups have a distinctive role to play in the area of sustainable sport there are areas where co-operation on common activities is essential. These include:

- exchanging information on progress and activities in their sector;
- emphasising the importance of education in environmental issues in relation to sport. Such education can take place in the framework of physical education and sports programmes in schools and universities, in sports clubs at all levels, in the programmes of international and national sports federations and associations and in sports management programmes;

- co-operating closely in the drawing up and implementation of international and national codes;
- alerting the media to the relevance and importance of this area and the need for closer co-operation. All three sectors should make a determined effort to involve the media in giving information on the need for measures and the actions being undertaken to halt the damage to the environment from sports activities;
- consulting on a broad basis to ascertain how widespread sports participation as favoured by `Sport for All` can be made compatible with the environmental concerns for sports facilities, sports related traffic, access to the countryside and the control of the noise, waste and pollution which sport generates.

The policy sector

To guarantee the practice of sport in a way that will contribute to sustainable development, national, regional and local governments should, as appropriate to their respective competence:

a. examine the need for legislation and similar measures on:
   - the use of non-renewable natural resources e.g. land, water, fossil fuels and the promotion of eco-friendly materials in the planning, designing, constructing, operating and maintaining sports facilities;
   - transport provision in the sitting of sports facilities, both indoor and outdoor open air sport, as a way of reducing sports related traffic and keeping sports participants and spectators away from sensitive areas and protecting fauna and flora;
   - the control of forms of sport and associated technological practices and changes that carry potential harm for the environment;
b. study the possibility of introducing financial incentives:
   - to help modernise sports facilities to reduce consumption of non-renewable resources;
   - to subsidise the development of sports facilities and the holding of sports events in proportion to the concern shown for the environment in their planning, as is already often the case for the disabled;
c. review their sports policies from the viewpoint of environmental friendliness;
d. consult at the international level to ensure that national legislation is compatible with that of other countries. This would prevent a situation where practices are forbidden or regulated in one country but can be engaged in freely without restriction elsewhere;
e. support and encourage the introduction of a "green" label that could be awarded to products, facilities, events, organisations etc. which are taking environmental concerns seriously;
f. when hosting major sports events ascertain that environmental concerns are taken into account from the outset throughout the whole operation.

The sports practice sector

All the sports and sports related bodies (sports organisations and federations, those engaged in planning, designing, operating and constructing sports facilities, the educational sector, the sports media, those concerned with sports tourism and the sporting goods industry) should be involved in the drafting and implementation of policies and projects at the national level. They should take steps to remain abreast of the results and research coming from the scientific sector. These measures would indicate the desirability of mainstreaming environmental concerns into all their programmes and short and long term planning.

Possible measures include:

- the appointment of a person, at whatever level is appropriate to an organisation, with responsibility for environmental questions;

- the drawing up of curricula and provision of packs for environmental education at all levels;
- the involvement of well known national sportswomen and sportsmen to support sustainability in sport;
- liaison between the sporting goods industry and the sports organisations and federations to promote the use of products which respect environmental concerns, possibly by the institution of an award or a special label;
- active respect for environmental factors in the management of sports facilities;
- promotion of environmental sensitivity in sports tourism.

The scientific sector
This sector should co-operate closely with both the policy and sports practice sector to:
- undertake surveys and research to ascertain ways to limit damage to the environment through sport;
- investigate ways to measure environmental impact of sports, by for example evaluating a monitoring system of the costs and benefits of sport (for example sports events) in relation to potential damage resulting ;
- recommend new ways of sports involvement which can protect both the concept of "Sport for All" and promote sustainability in sport;
- collect and evaluate information on measures on both the international and national projects designed to encourage environmentally friendly sport;
- ensure the wide dissemination of information, research results and data on sport and sustainability to the sports community;
- provide advice and documentation to the various bodies that make up the policy and sports practice areas;
- analyse the various laws and codes for compatibility within Europe.

A common responsibility
Achieving sustainability in sport is a task for the whole world of sport. Taking active responsibility for the environment is a vital and important step towards the attainment of a clean and healthy sport in the 3rd millennium.
Everyone shares this responsibility and must ensure that their activities do not damage the environment, but rather safeguard and sustain it.

11.5. Code for sustainability in sport: a partnership between sport and the environment

Aims and definition
This Code aims to set out guidelines for a working partnership between sport and the environment. It is important to ensure that sports can be enjoyed, both today and in the future, by as many people as possible in the most favourable conditions, by which is meant sport in a clean and healthy environment.
Sport in all its forms, practised at all levels, whether recreational or competitive sport, shares with the whole of human society the duty of nurturing and safeguarding the natural environment for both present and future generations. The adoption of the definition of sustainable development `as development that meets the needs of the present without compromising the ability of future generations to meet theirs` is a starting point for action now.
The concept of sustainability in sport has already been incorporated into Article 10 of the European Sports Charter of 1992. This Article emphasises the responsibility of everyone involved

in sport to protect the environment and promotes the introduction of a model of environmentally friendly sport. However, measures are needed to address those trends and practices in sport that are currently endangering the environment. The Code indicates realistic ways to ensure environmental protection. In practical terms this entails national policies that ensure respect for sustainability in sport in urban, open country and water areas.
The International Olympic Committee has organised conferences on sport and the environment, emphasised the need to respect environmental concerns when planning the Olympic Games and adopted Agenda 21, which reflects concern for the relationship between sport, the natural environment and sustainable development.

Responsibility for sustainable sport
This code focuses on the three sectors that bear the major responsibility for action which are:
- the policy sector, which is composed of groups and people concerned with the strategic choices, legislation, values and the underlying issues behind these questions. This includes governments and international organisations;
- the sports practice sector which is made up of sports organisations and federations, those engaged in the planning and construction of sports facilities, the educational sector, those concerned with sports tourism and the sporting goods industry. This group covers the whole spectrum from the large international and national sporting federations to the sports clubs at the grassroots level to the individual sportsman and woman;
- the scientific sector which embraces institutions, groups and individuals carrying out research, collecting and evaluating data and disseminating information.

Co-ordination between these sectors should be assured. Moreover the similarity of aims and concerns provides an opportunity to create close partnerships between those working for sustainable development in sport and those working for environmental conservation and protection. Environmental organisations can provide useful expertise.

Activities common to all three sectors
While each sector and its composite groups have a distinctive role to play in the area of sustainable sport there are areas where co-operation on common activities is essential. These include:
- exchanging information on progress and activities in their sector;
- emphasising the importance of education in environmental issues in relation to sport. Such education can take place in the framework of physical education and sports programmes in schools and universities, in sports clubs at all levels, in the programmes of international and national sports federations and associations and in sports management programmes;
- co-operating closely in the drawing up and implementation of international and national codes;
- alerting the media to the relevance and importance of this area and the need for closer co-operation. All three sectors should make a determined effort to involve the media in giving information on the need for measures and the actions being undertaken to halt the damage to the environment from sports activities;
- consulting on a broad basis to ascertain how widespread sports participation as favoured by `Sport for All` can be made compatible with the environmental concerns for sports facilities, sports related traffic, access to the countryside and the control of the noise, waste and pollution which sport generates.

The policy sector
To guarantee the practice of sport in a way that will contribute to sustainable development, national, regional and local governments should, as appropriate to their respective competence:

a. examine the need for legislation and similar measures on:
- the use of non-renewable natural resources e.g. land, water, fossil fuels and the promotion of eco-friendly materials in the planning, designing, constructing, operating and maintaining sports facilities;
- transport provision in the sitting of sports facilities, both indoor and outdoor open air sport, as a way of reducing sports related traffic and keeping sports participants and spectators away from sensitive areas and protecting fauna and flora;
- the control of forms of sport and associated technological practices and changes that carry potential harm for the environment;

b. study the possibility of introducing financial incentives:
- to help modernise sports facilities to reduce consumption of non-renewable resources;
- to subsidise the development of sports facilities and the holding of sports events in proportion to the concern shown for the environment in their planning, as is already often the case for the disabled;

c. review their sports policies from the viewpoint of environmental friendliness;

d. consult at the international level to ensure that national legislation is compatible with that of other countries. This would prevent a situation where practices are forbidden or regulated in one country but can be engaged in freely without restriction elsewhere;

e. support and encourage the introduction of a "green" label that could be awarded to products, facilities, events, organisations etc. which are taking environmental concerns seriously;

f. when hosting major sports events ascertain that environmental concerns are taken into account from the outset throughout the whole operation.

The sports practice sector

All the sports and sports related bodies (sports organisations and federations, those engaged in planning, designing, operating and constructing sports facilities, the educational sector, the sports media, those concerned with sports tourism and the sporting goods industry) should be involved in the drafting and implementation of policies and projects at the national level. They should take steps to remain abreast of the results and research coming from the scientific sector. These measures would indicate the desirability of mainstreaming environmental concerns into all their programmes and short and long term planning.

Possible measures include:
- the appointment of a person, at whatever level is appropriate to an organisation, with responsibility for environmental questions;
- the drawing up of curricula and provision of packs for environmental education at all levels;
- the involvement of well known national sportswomen and sportsmen to support sustainability in sport;
- liaison between the sporting goods industry and the sports organisations and federations to promote the use of products which respect environmental concerns, possibly by the institution of an award or a special label;
- active respect for environmental factors in the management of sports facilities;
- promotion of environmental sensitivity in sports tourism.

The scientific sector

This sector should co-operate closely with both the policy and sports practice sector to:

- undertake surveys and research to ascertain ways to limit damage to the environment through sport;
- investigate ways to measure environmental impact of sports, by for example evaluating a monitoring system of the costs and benefits of sport (for example sports events) in relation to potential damage resulting ;
- recommend new ways of sports involvement which can protect both the concept of "Sport for All" and promote sustainability in sport;
- collect and evaluate information on measures on both the international and national projects designed to encourage environmentally friendly sport;
- ensure the wide dissemination of information, research results and data on sport and sustainability to the sports community;
- provide advice and documentation to the various bodies that make up the policy and sports practice areas;
- analyse the various laws and codes for compatibility within Europe.

A common responsibility

Achieving sustainability in sport is a task for the whole world of sport. Taking active responsibility for the environment is a vital and important step towards the attainment of a clean and healthy sport in the 3rd millennium.

Everyone shares this responsibility and must ensure that their activities do not damage the environment, but rather safeguard and sustain it.

Chapter 12
ETHICS

12.1. Resolution on Ethical and Human Problems in Sport (78/3)
(Theme III)

The European Ministers of Sport, meeting in London,
Reaffirming their attachment to the principles set out in the European Sport for All Charter, and concerned to safeguard sport and sportsmen from exploitation of whatever kind;
Considering that modern sport is beset by a number of practices which are jeopardising the ethical basis of sport, and that these are no longer restricted to international competitive sport, but are beginning to affect sport at national, regional and club level;
Express their hope and confidence that the sports federations will overcome the problems facing them and offer their support in the quest for solutions;
Bearing in mind that the mental and physical health of their peoples is their common concern;
Resolve as follows:
On doping and health:
Considering that since the adoption by the Committee of Ministers of the Council of Europe of Resolution (67) 12 on the doping of athletes, the member states, their national sports organisations, as well as governments and sports organisations of non-member states, have made real but as yet insufficient efforts to solve the problems raised by the taking of illicit substances for the purpose of improving athletic performances;
Affirming that the continual and necessary search for better performances must not lead to a situation in which the ethical and human basis of sport is neglected:

1. condemn any measures designed to influence performances which are detrimental to the health of athletes or the ethics of sport, and any athletes who take such measures;
2. emphasise the importance they attach to the speedy implementation of effective methods for the detection of the consumption of illicit substances, particularly anabolic steroids and other tissue-developing agents such as testosterone, and to the banning of such substances;
3. invite their respective governments:
    a. to co-ordinate the action of the Ministers responsible for Health and for Sport, to support the governing bodies of sport in these tasks, and to intensify the co-ordination of relevant international research at a European level;
    b. to support the testing of athletes for illicit substances at and between events and also to support an international programme for monitoring the results of tests at suitable laboratories in each country, to which the responsible sports and medicine authorities have guaranteed access, subject to the usual rules of medical confidentiality;
    c. to recommend regular health checks for sportsmen and progressively to provide the facilities for this;
    d. to invite national sports organisations to intensify their efforts to preclude the taking of illicit substances and suggest the following measures which might be carried out at national level by each country's most appropriate sports organisation:

i. a publicity campaign directed at athletes on the dangers to health of doping, using for example the information contained in the background paper prepared for this conference;

ii. encouraging the maintenance of respect for the ethics and practice of sport;

iii. compiling and publishing, in agreement with international directives, accurate and detailed lists of stimulating agents and means of testing for them;

iv. instituting and supporting practical and regular doping tests;

v. working towards a stricter control of the issue of medical prescriptions involving potential doping agents;

vi. instituting stricter sanctions for athletes found using stimulants, which should be applied also to trainers, doctors or managers who have encouraged their use.

On professionalism and commercialism:
Desirous of preserving sport from excessive commercial exploitation;
Recalling the resolution on "Public Authorities and Sport for All" adopted at the Brussels Conference which stated that "the use of advertising is only acceptable as long as it is in the interests of sport and those who practise it and provided that sportsmen should in no circumstances become a vehicle for advertising";
Considering that neither professionalism nor semi-professionalism is to be condemned in itself, but that both have or can have a harmful effect on the ethical and human values of sport and may arouse feelings of frustration in sportsmen in their private lives;
Invite the Committee of Ministers of the Council of Europe to instruct the Committee for the Development of Sport to study and define in close co-operation with the non-governmental organisations concerned, the problems of professionalism and the role of advertising in sport to obviate consequences incompatible with human dignity and to draw up a code of ethics for commercial sponsorship;
On violence associated with sport:
Considering the serious problem of violence in and around sports grounds;
Bearing in mind the resolution of the congress on "Violence in Sport" held in Brussels on 7 and 8 September 1977;
Taking note of the document previously distributed by the Belgian Minister of Dutch Culture;
Considering the general desire to tackle this problem effectively without delay;
Recommend to the Committee of Ministers of the Council of Europe to instruct the CDDS to elaborate, in co-operation with the international sports federations and organisations, the necessary measures to banish violence from the world of sport;
Ask the Belgian Minister of Dutch Culture to carry out this decision in close liaison with the chairman of the CDDS in order to set up an appropriate structure within the Council of Europe.

12.2. Resolution No. 6/89 on the Presentation of Ethical Values in Sport

The European Ministers responsible for Sport, meeting at Reykjavik from 30 May to 1 June 1989 for their 6th Conference

Welcome the ratification, by fifteen States, of the European Convention on Spectator Violence and Misbehaviour at Sports Events and in particular at Football Matches;

Welcome the signature of this same Convention by five other States;
Welcome, in addition, the progress made in the struggle against new forms of self-inflicted violence including doping, which has lcd to the preparation of the draft Anti-Doping Convention;
Reaffirm their support for the positive values of sport and physical education in accordance with the terms of the European Sport for All Charter;

Encourage member states:
1. to campaign in and out-of-school for the preservation and the promotion of the most positive ethical values which the practice of sport engenders;
2. to support with the greatest determination initiatives aimed at education and responsibility in club life;

Invite the Committee of Ministers to ask the Committee for the Development of Sport:
1. to help the DS-SR to begin in 1989 the co-ordinated research project on ethical values of young people in sport proposed at its 9th meeting (October 1988);
2. to study ways of preventing destructive forms of aggression in sport and recreation; Agree to discuss ethical values in sport at their 7th Conference.

12.3. Resolution on the Code of Sports Ethics (92/3)

The European Ministers responsible for Sport, meeting in Rhodes for their 7th Conference, from 13 to 15 May 1992

Wishing to see sport develop in the spirit of the European Sports Charter;
Aware of the pressures which modern society, marked amongst other things by the race for success, the need for stars, and exposure to the mass-media, brings to bear on sport;
Convinced of the need to provide sportsmen and women with a system of values which will enable them to make responsible choices when facing such pressures;
Convinced that the including of the principles set out in the Code in physical education curricula and in the policies of sports organisations will favourably influence the attitudes of athletes and the general public to sport;

Resolve:
1. to give their full support to the Code of Sports Ethics appended hereto;
2. to disseminate the Code in their own language(s) amongst their sports organisations and to promote its dissemination amongst all the appropriate target groups, especially those working with young people;
3. to co-operate at European level to help diffuse the Code widely;

Invite the Committee of Ministers of the Council of Europe:
1. to adopt the present Code of Sports Ethics as a Recommendation to Governments;
2. to encourage the authorities responsible for school and out-of-school education to include the principles set out in the Code in physical education curricula;
3. to encourage regional, national and international sports organisations in developing their own campaigns to strengthen sports ethics to take account of the principles set out in this Code.

12.4. Resolution No. 3/92 on the Code of Sports Ethics
The European Ministers responsible for Sport, meeting in Rhodes for their 7th Conference, from 13 – 15 May 1992

Wishing to see sport develop in the spirit of the European Sports Charter;
Aware of the pressures which modern society, marked amongst other things by the race for success, the need for stars, and exposure to the mass-media, brings to bear on sport;
Convinced of the need to provide sportsmen and women with a system of values which will enable them to make responsible choices when facing such pressures;
Convinced that the including of the principles set out in the Code in physical education curricula and in the policies of sports organisations will favourably influence the attitudes of athletes and the general public to sport;

Resolve:
1. to give their full support to the Code of Sports Ethics appended hereto;
2. to disseminate the Code in their own language(s) amongst their sports organisations and to promote its dissemination amongst all the appropriate target groups, especially those working with young people;
3. to co-operate at European level to help diffuse the Code widely;

Invite the Committee of Ministers of the Council of Europe:
1. to adopt the present Code of Sports Ethics as a Recommendation to Governments;
2. to encourage the authorities responsible for school and out-of-school education to include the principles set out in the Code in physical education curricula;
3. to encourage regional, national and international sports organisations in developing their own campaigns to strengthen sports ethics to take account of the principles set Out in this Code.

12.5. Resolution No. 4/92 "Code of Sports Ethics"
The European Ministers responsible for Sport, meeting in Rhodes for their 7th Conference, from 13 – 15 May 1992

Resolution No. 4/92 "Code of Sports Ethics" adopted as Recommendation No. R (92) 14 by the Committee of Ministers [...]

12.6. Recommendation No. R (92) 14 of the Committee of Ministers to member states on the Code of Sports Ethics
Adopted by the Committee of Ministers on 24 September 1992

The Committee of Ministers, under the terms of Article 15.b of the Statute of the Council of Europe,
Considering that the aim of the Council of Europe is to achieve a greater unity between its members for the purpose of safeguarding and realising the ideals and principles which are their common heritage and of facilitating their economic and social progress;
Wishing to see sport develop in the spirit of the European Sports Charter;
Aware of the pressures which modern society, marked amongst other things by the race for success, the need for stars, and the exposure to the mass-media, brings to bear on sport;

Convinced of the need to provide sportsmen and women with a system of values which will enable them to make responsible choices when facing such pressures;
Convinced that incorporating the principles set out in the Code of Sports Ethics in physical education curricula and in the policies of sports organisations will favourably influence the attitudes of athletes and the general public to sport;
Wishing to complement Recommendation No. R (92) 13 on the European Sports Charter with a statement of ethical principles in sport;
Considering that the European Ministers responsible for Sport, meeting in Rhodes for their 7th Conference (1992), adopted such a statement of principles under the title of the Code of Sports Ethics;

Recommends that the governments of member states:

- give their full support to the Code of Sport Ethics as set out in the Appendix to this recommendation;
- disseminate the Code in their own language(s) amongst their sports organisations and to promote its dissemination amongst all the appropriate target groups, especially those working with young people;
- encourage the authorities responsible for school and out-of-school education to include the principles set out in the Code in physical education curricula;
- encourage regional, national and international sports organisations in developing their own campaigns to strengthen sports ethics to take account of the principles set out in the Code.

Instructs the Secretary General to transmit this recommendation to:

- the governments of States party to the European Cultural Convention not member states of the Council of Europe;
- to international organisations and to international sports organisations.

Appendix
Code of Sports Ethics
Fair play – the winning way
(Qui joue loyalement est toujours gagnant)

Aims
The basic principle of the Code is that ethical considerations leading to fair play are integral, and not optional elements, of all sports activity, sports policy and management, and apply to all levels of ability and commitment, including recreational as well as competitive sport.
The code provides a sound ethical framework to combat the pressures in modern-day society which appear to be undermining the traditional foundations of sport – foundations built on fair play and sportsmanship, and on the voluntary movement.
The primary concern and focus is fair play for children and young people, in the recognition that children and young people of today are the adult participants and sporting stars of tomorrow. The code is aimed however at the institutions and adults who have a direct or indirect influence on young people's involvement and participation in sport.
The code embraces the concepts of the right of children and young people to participate and enjoy their involvement in sport, and the responsibilities of the institutions and adults to promote fair play and to ensure that these rights are respected.

Defining Fair Play

Fair play is defined as much more than playing within the rules. It incorporates the concepts of friendship, respect for others and always playing within the right spirit. Fair play is defined as a way of thinking, not just a way of behaving. It incorporates issues concerned with the elimination of cheating, gamesmanship, doping, violence (both physical and verbal), exploitation, unequal opportunities, excessive commercialisation and corruption.

Fair play is a positive concept. Sport is a cultural activity which, practised fairly, enriches society and the friendship between nations. Sport is also recognised as an activity which, played fairly, offers the individual the opportunity of self-knowledge, self-expression and fulfilment; personal achievement. skill acquisition and demonstration of ability; social interaction, enjoyment, good health and well-being. Sport promotes involvement and responsibility in society with its wide range of clubs and leaders working voluntarily. In addition. responsible involvement in some activities can help to promote sensitivity to the environment.

Responsibility for Fair Play

Involvement and participation in sport among children and young people takes place within a wider social environment. The potential benefits to society and to the individual from sport will only be maximised where fair play is moved from the peripheral position it currently occupies to centre stage. Fair play must be given the highest priority by all those who, directly or indirectly, influence and promote sporting experiences for children and young people. These include:

1. governments: at all levels, and including agencies working with governments. Those involved in formal education have a particular responsibility.
2. sports and sports-related organisations including sports federations and governing bodies; physical education associations, coaching agencies and institutes, medical and pharmacological professions and the media. The commercial sector, including sports goods manufacturers and retailers and marketing agencies, also has a responsibility to contribute to the promotion of fair play.
3. individuals including parents, teachers, coaches, referees, officials, sports leaders, administrators, journalists, doctors and pharmacists, role models who have achieved levels of sporting excellence and fame and those who work on a voluntary or professional basis. Individuals may also have responsibilities in their capacity as spectators.

Each of these institutions and individuals has a responsibility and a role to play. This Code of Sports Ethics is addressed to them. It will only be effective if all involved in sport are prepared to take on the responsibilities identified in the code.

Governments

Governments have the following responsibilities:

- to encourage the adoption of high ethical standards in all aspects of society within which sport operates.
- to stimulate and support those organisations and individuals who have demonstrated sound ethical principles in their work with sport.
- to encourage the education profession to include the promotion of sport and fair play as a central part of the physical education curriculum.
- to support all initiatives aimed at promoting fair play in sport, particularly amongst the young, and encouraging institutions to make fair play a centra! priority in their work.
- to encourage research both nationally and internationally which would improve our understanding of the complex issues surrounding young peoples involvement in sport and which identifies the extent of poor behaviour and the opportunities for promoting fair play.

Sports and Sports-related Organisations

Sports and sports related Organisations have the following responsibilities:

In setting a proper context for fair play

- to publish dear guidelines on what is considered to be ethical or unethical behaviour and ensure that, at all levels of participation and involvement, consistent and appropriate incentives and/or sanctions are applied;
- to ensure that all decisions are made in accordance with a code of ethics for their sport which reflects the European code;
- to raise the awareness of fair play within their sphere of influence through the use of campaigns, awards, educational material and training opportunities. They must also monitor and evaluate the impact of such initiatives;
- to establish systems which reward fair play and personal levels of achievement in addition to competitive success;
- to provide help and support to the media to promote good behaviour.

When working with young people

- to ensure that the structure of competition acknowledges the special requirements of the young and growing child and provides the opportunity for graded levels of involvement from the recreational to the highly competitive.
- to support the modification of rules to meet the special needs of the very young and immature, and to put the emphasis on fair play rather than competitive success.
- to ensure that safeguards are in place to prevent the exploitation of children, particularly those who demonstrate precocious ability.
- to ensure that all those within or associated with the organisation who have a responsibility for children and young people are qualified at an appropriate level to manage, train, educate and coach them, and in particular that they understand the biological and psychological changes associated with the development of the child.

Individuals

Individuals have the following responsibilities:

Personal Behaviour:

- to behave in a way which sets a good example and presents a positive role model for children and young people; not in any way to reward, to demonstrate personally, nor to condone in others unfair play, and to take appropriate sanctions against poor behaviour;
- to ensure that their own level of training and qualification is appropriate to the needs of the child as they move through different stages of sporting commitment.

When working with young people

- to put as a first priority the health, safety and welfare of the child or young athlete and to ensure that such considerations come before vicarious achievement, or the reputation of the school, club, coach or parent;
- to provide a sporting experience for children that encourages a life long commitment to health related physical activity;
- to avoid treating children as simply small adults but to be aware of the physical and psychological changes that occur during maturation and how these affect sporting performance;

- to avoid placing on a child expectations unrelated to his or her capacity to meet them;
- to make the enjoyment of the participant a priority and never place undue pressure which impinges on the rights of the chid to choose to participate;
- to take as much interest in the less talented as in the talented and emphasise and reward personal levels of achievement and skill acquisition in addition to more overt competitive success;
- to encourage young children to devise their own games with their own rules, to take on the roles of coach, official and referee in addition to participant; to devise their own incentives and sanctions for fair or unfair play; and to take personal responsibility for their actions;
- to provide the child and young person and childs family with as much information as possible to ensure awareness of the potential risks and attractions of reaching levels of high performance.

Summary
Fair play is an essential part of successful promotion, development and involvement in sport. Through fair play, the individual, the sports organisations and society as a whole all win. We all have a responsibility to promote Fair play – the winning way.

12.7. Recommendation No. R (92) 14 Rev of the Committee of Ministers to Member States on the Revised Code of Sports Ethics
Adopted by the Committee of Ministers on 24 September 1992 at the 480th meeting of the Ministers' Deputies and revised at their 752nd meeting on 16 May 2001

The Committee of Ministers, under the terms of Article 15.b of the Statute of the Council of Europe,
Considering that the aim of the Council of Europe is to achieve a greater unity between its members for the purpose of safeguarding and realising the ideals and principles which are their common heritage and of facilitating their economic and social progress;
Wishing to see sport develop in the spirit of the European Sports Charter,
Aware of the pressures which modern society, marked amongst other things by the race for success, the need for stars, and exposure to the mass-media, brings to bear on sport,
Convinced of the need to provide sportsmen and women with a system of values which will enable them to make responsible choices when facing such pressures,
Convinced that including the principles set out in the Code in physical education curricula and in the policies of sports organisations will favourably influence the attitudes of athletes and the general public to sport,
Wishing to complement Recommendation No R(92)13 on the European Sports Charter with a statement of ethical principles in sport,
Considering that the European Ministers responsible for Sport, meeting in Rhodes for their 7th Conference (1992), adopted such a statement of principles under the title of the "Code of Sports Ethics",

Recommends the governments of member States:
- to give their full support to the Code of Sports Ethics as set out in the Appendix to this Recommendation;
- to disseminate the Code in their own language(s) amongst their sports organisations and to promote its dissemination amongst all the appropriate target groups, especially those working with young people;

– to encourage the authorities responsible for school and out-of-school education to include the principles set out in the Code in physical education curricula;
– to encourage regional, national and international sports organisations in developing their own campaigns to strengthen sports ethics to take account of the principles set out in the Code.

Instructs the Secretary General to transmit this recommendation to:

– the governments of States party to the European Cultural Convention not member States of the Council of Europe;
– to international organisations and to international sports organisations.

Appendix to Recommendation No. R (92) 14 rev
Code of Sports Ethics
Fair Play – the Winning Way
(Qui joue loyalement est toujours gagnant)

Aims

The basic principle of the Code of Sports Ethics is that ethical considerations leading to fair play are integral, and not optional elements, of all sports activity, sports policy and management, and apply to all levels of ability and commitment, including recreational as well as competitive sport.

The Code provides a sound ethical framework to combat the pressures in modern day society which appear to be undermining the traditional foundations of sport – foundations built on fair play and sportsmanship, and on the voluntary movement.

The primary concern and focus is Fair Play for children and young people, in the recognition that children and young people of today are the adult participants and sporting stars of tomorrow. The Code is also aimed at the institutions and adults who have a direct or indirect influence on young people's involvement and participation in sport.

The Code embraces the concepts of the right of children and young people to participate and enjoy their involvement in sport, and the responsibilities of the institutions and adults to promote fair play and to ensure that these rights are respected.

Defining Fair Play

Fair play is defined as much more than playing with the rules. It incorporates the concepts of friendship, respect for others and always playing within the right spirit. Fair play is defined as a way of thinking, not just a way of behaving. It incorporates issues concerned with the elimination of cheating, gamesmanship, doping, violence (both physical and verbal), the sexual harassment and abuse of children, young people and women, exploitation, unequal opportunities, excessive commercialisation and corruption.

Fair play is a positive concept. Sport is a social and cultural activity which, practised fairly, enriches society and the friendship between nations. Sport is also recognised as an individual activity which, played fairly, offers the opportunity for self-knowledge, self-expression and fulfilment; personal achievement, skill acquisition and demonstration of ability; social interaction, enjoyment, good health and well-being. Sport promotes involvement and responsibility in society with its wide range of clubs and leaders working voluntarily. In addition, responsible involvement in some activities can help to promote sensitivity to the environment.

Responsibility for Fair Play

Involvement and participation in sport among children and young people takes place within a wider social environment. The potential benefits to society and to the individual from sport will only be maximised where fair play is moved from the peripheral position it currently occupies to centre stage. Fair play must be given the highest priority by all those who, directly or indirectly, influence and promote sporting experiences for children and young people. These include:

- Governments: at all levels, and including agencies working with Government. Those involved in formal education have a particular responsibility.
- Sports and Sports-Related Organisations including Sports Federations and Governing Bodies; Physical Education Associations, Coaching Agencies and Institutes, Medical and Pharmacological Professions and the Media. The commercial sector, including sports goods manufacturers and retailers and marketing agencies, also has a responsibility to contribute to the promotion of fair play.
- Individuals including Parents, Teachers, Coaches, Referees, Officials, Sports Leaders, Administrators, Journalists, Doctors and Pharmacists; and those role models who have achieved levels of sporting excellence and fame; those who work on a voluntary or on a professional basis. Individuals may also have responsibilities in their capacity as spectators.

Each of these institutions and individuals has a responsibility and a role to play. This Code of Sports Ethics is addressed to them. It will only be effective if all involved in sport are prepared to take on the responsibility identified in the Code.

Governments

Governments have the following responsibilities:

- To encourage the adoption of high ethical standards in all aspects of society within which sport operates.
- To stimulate and support those organisations and individuals who have demonstrated sound ethical principles in their work with sport.
- To encourage the education profession to include the promotion of sport and fair play as a central part of the physical education curriculum.
- To support initiatives aimed at promoting fair play in sport, particularly amongst the young, and encouraging institutions to place fair play as a central priority in their work.
- To encourage research both nationally and internationally which improves our understanding of the complex issues surrounding young people's involvement in sport and which identifies the extent of poor behaviour and the opportunities for promoting fair play.

Sports and Sports-related Organisations

Sports and sports related Organisations have the following responsibilities:

In setting a proper context for Fair Play

- To publish clear guidelines on what is considered to be ethical or unethical behaviour and ensure that, at all levels of participation and involvement, consistent and appropriate incentives and/or sanctions are applied.
- To ensure that all decisions are made in accordance with a Code of Ethics for their sport which reflects the European code.
- To raise the awareness of fair play within their sphere of influence through the use of campaigns, awards, educational material and training opportunities. They must also monitor and evaluate the impact of such initiatives.
- To establish systems which reward fair play and personal levels of achievement in addition to competitive success.

- To provide help and support to the media to promote good behaviour.

When working with Young People,

- To ensure that the structure of competition acknowledges the special requirements of the young and growing child and provides the opportunity for graded levels of involvement from the recreational to the highly competitive.
- To support the modification of rules to meet the special needs of the very young and immature, and put the emphasis on fair play rather than competitive success.
- To ensure that safeguards are in place within the context of an overall framework of support and protection for children, young people and women, both to protect the above groups from sexual harassment and abuse and to prevent the exploitation of children, particularly those who demonstrate precocious ability.
- To ensure that all those within or associated with the organisation who have a responsibility for children and young people are qualified at an appropriate level to manage, train, educate and coach them, and in particular that they understand the biological and psychological changes associated with children maturation.

Individuals

Individuals have the following responsibilities:

Personal Behaviour

- To behave in a way which sets a good example and presents a positive role model for children and young people; not in any way to reward, to demonstrate personally, nor to condone in others unfair play and to take appropriate sanctions against poor behaviour.
- To ensure that their own level of training and qualification is appropriate to the needs of the child as they move through different stages of sporting commitment.

  When working with Young People,
- To put as a first priority the health, safety and welfare of the child or young athlete and ensure that such considerations come before vicarious achievement, or the reputation of the school or club or coach or parent.
- To provide a sporting experience for children that encourages a life long commitment to health related physical activity.
- To avoid treating children as simply small adults but be aware of the physical and psychological changes that occur during maturation and how these affect sporting performance.
- To avoid placing expectations on a child unrelated to his or her capacity to meet them.
- To put the enjoyment of the participant as a priority and never place undue pressure which impinges on the rights of the child to choose to participate.
- To take equal interest in the less talented as in the talented and emphasise and reward personal levels of achievement and skill acquisition in addition to more overt competitive success.
- To encourage young children to devise their own games with their own rules, to take on the roles of coach, official and referee in addition to participant; to devise their own incentives and sanctions for fair or unfair play; and to take personal responsibility for their actions.
- To provide the child and young person and child's family with as much information as possible to ensure awareness of the potential risks and attractions of reaching levels of high performance.

Summary

Fair play is an essential and central part of successful promotion, development and involvement in sport. Through fair play, the individual, the sports organisations and society as a whole all win. We all have a responsibility to promote FAIR PLAY – THE WINNING WAY. (Qui joue loyalement est toujours gagnant.)

Chapter 13
EUROFIT

13.1. Recommendation No. R (87)9 of the Committee of Ministers to member states on the Eurofit Tests of Physical Fitness

Adopted by the Committee of Ministers on 19 May 1987

The Committee of Ministers, under the terms of Article 15b of the Statute of the Council of Europe,

Recalling that the aim of the Council of Europe is to achieve a greater unity between its members for the purpose, inter alia, of facilitating their social progress by agreements and common action in social, cultural and scientific matters;

Recalling its Resolution (70) 7 concerning the recommendations in relation to the medical aspects of sporting activities, in particular the section "Sports Curricula in Schools" and "Biological and Psychological assessment of aptitude for different sports";

Recalling its Resolution (73) 27 on the Establishment of Sports Medicine Centres, particularly point B.II.1 of Appendix C on equipment for diagnosis and assessment of aptitude for physical exertion;

Recalling its Resolution (76) 41 on the principles for a policy of sport for all (the "European Sport for All Charter"), particularly Article III of the appendix which states that "sport, being an aspect of socio-cultural development, shall be related at local, regional and national levels to other areas of policy-making and planning, such as education, health, social service

Considering that physical fitness is an important component, not only of sport and physical education, but also of health and health education, and is necessary for a state of general well-being;

Considering that precise and reliable measures of physical fitness are of great value to individuals, to educators and to policy-makers, all of whom need them as an essential basis for working Out any programme or policy aimed at improving individual or general levels of fitness;

Considering that the teaching of, and learning about, physical fitness can make an important contribution to each person's own self-knowledge and motivation to keep fit. and to the educative process generally;

Considering that the testing, under controlled conditions, of the physical fitness of children will provide important data to be used for the working Out of national policies connected with children, health, nutrition, physical education and sport;

Considering that Eurofit provides a simple and practical set of tests of physical fitness, suitable for widespread use amongst school-aged children. and that it is designed, inter alia, to realise the objectives set out above, by providing knowledge of the condition of physical fitness amongst a wide range of school-aged children in each state;

I. Recommends the governments of member states:
   - i. to adopt – or to take steps leading to the adoption of the Eurofit tests of physical fitness as set out in the appendix to this recommendation, for the purpose of measuring and assessing the physical fitness of school-aged children (in the range from 6/7 to 16/18 years old);
   - ii. to take whatever steps may prove to be appropriate in the light of the knowledge obtained from the application of Eurofit in order to:

a. maintain or improve the basic standard of physical fitness amongst children, paying particular attention to those children or groups of children who are shown to have a low average level of physical fitness;
b. obtain data which may be used for a better co-ordination of policies concerning physical education, sport, health and health education;
c. alert others besides physical education teachers, including the children themselves, parents, schools, sports clubs, etc., to their several and mutual responsibilities in maintaining a reasonable standard of physical fitness among those committed to their charge;

iii. to ensure proper co-ordination between all the bodies which may be concerned with the implementation of Eurofit at national, regional or local levels (for example ministries responsible for education and sport, school health authorities), and to encourage sports organisations to be associated with the implementation of Eurofit;

iv. to enable the appropriate authorities and schools to obtain the material required for the Eurofit tests;

v. to arrange, where appropriate in conjunction with other member states, for the initial training of physical education teachers to include physical fitness testing, and for an adequate in-service training of those persons who may carry out the Eurofit tests;

vi. to set up a sufficient number of research units capable of carrying out the entire range of tests for national survey purposes in order to obtain objective data and to establish national reference tables for use at national level;

vii. to make arrangements for the collection and interpretation of the data resulting from the Eurofit tests and for their dissemination, so that appropriate national reference values may be established and used for follow-up purposes;

viii. to aim for each child in school to be assessed regularly, and preferably at least once a year, through the Eurofit tests, and to consider increasing the allocation of time given to the physical education curriculum in order to achieve this:

ix. to take appropriate steps for the translation and distribution of the handbook describing the Eurofit tests and their administration among the appropriate authorities, physical educationists and sports organisations;

II. Instructs the Secretary General to transmit this recommendation to:

a. the governments of States Parties to the European Cultural Convention which are not members of the Council of Europe;
b. the Directors General of the United Nations Educational, Scientific and Cultural Organisation and of the World Health Organisation.

Chapter 14
EUROPE SPORTS FUND

14.1. Resolution on the Setting Up of the Council of Europe Sports Fund (78/75)

Adopted by the Committee of Ministers on 15 December 1978

The Committee of Ministers,
Having regard to Resolution (76) 3 on committee structures, terms of reference and working methods;
Having regard to the specific terms of reference of the Steering Committee for the Development of Sport;
Considering that a Council of Europe Sports Fund should be set up,
Resolves:

1. to set up a Council of Europe Sports Fund for an indefinite period as from 1 January 1978;
2. to adopt the statute of this Fund which is appended to the present resolution and which constitutes a delegation of powers as defined in the said statute.

Appendix – Statute of the Sports Fund
Article 1 – Setting up of the Fund

1. There is hereby established a Council of Europe Sports Fund (hereinafter referred to as the Sports Fund).
2. The Sports Fund shall be a distinct administrative entity within the Council of Europe and shall be governed by the provisions of this statute.

Article 2 – Purpose

1. The purpose of the Sports Fund is to promote and finance activities in the sports sector in accordance with the Statute of the Council of Europe.
2. This purpose shall be pursued within the framework of a programme of multilateral co-operation in sport drawn up under the terms of the European Cultural Convention signed in Paris on 19 December 1954 and of the medium-term plans instituted by Resolution (74) 33 of the Committee of Ministers.
3. To this end the Fund may inter alia:
    a. support and facilitate the establishment of European institutions working in the sports sector;
    b. support individual or collective activities of European interest in the same sector in so far as such activities extend beyond the national framework;
    c. introduce, when financial resources permit, a policy of mutual aid in the sports sector on behalf of any member countries which desire it.

Article 3 – Co-operation with other foundations
The Secretary General of the Council of Europe may, by decision of the Committee of Ministers or on the proposal of the Committee for the Development of Sport and, in that case, with the approval of the Committee of Ministers, enter into arrangements with funds or foundations concerned with European sports activities with, a view to ensuring the co-ordination of their tasks.

Article 4 – Resources

1. The resources of the Sports Fund shall be as follows:
   a. i. a minimum annual contribution by members of the Council of Europe whose amount shall be fixed by the Committee of Ministers and shared between them according to the scale for contributions to the ordinary budget of the Council of Europe. This contribution shall take the form of a grant entered in the Council's budget;
      ii. a minimum contribution by states not members of the Council of Europe or non-member states acceding to the European Cultural Convention fixed, mutatis mutandis, according to the scale for contributions to the ordinary budget of the Council of Europe;
   b. voluntary contributions from members of the Council of Europe or non-member states acceding to the European Cultural Convention;
   c. any other contribution, donation or legacy subject to the provisions of Article 5, paragraph 5, of this Statute.
2. Members of the Council of Europe and non-member states acceding to the European Cultural Convention shall, in so far as their laws permit, accord to the subsidies granted by the Sports Fund and to any donations or legacies that it may receive, the fiscal privileges and exemptions which apply in their respective countries to sports, charitable or other activities of a non-profit-making character.

Article 5 – Administration

1. The Sports Fund shall be administered by the Committee for the Development of Sport, constituted and exercising its functions in accordance with the terms of reference given it by the Committee of Ministers.
2. The Secretary General of the Council of Europe shall take part as of right in meetings of the Committee for the Development of Sport, on which he shall sit in an advisory capacity as administrator of the Fund. He may appoint a representative. He shall carry out the decisions taken in regard to the Fund's management within the limit of the administrative resources made available by the Committee of Ministers and in accordance with the regulations of the Organisation.
3. The Committee for the Development of Sport, taking into account Article 2, paragraph 3, of this Statute, shall adopt an annual programme which shall be financed by the Sports Fund. It shall allocate the corresponding resources as prescribed in Article 6, paragraph 3, of this Statute.
4. The Committee for the Development of Sport shall be responsible for the execution of the programme financed by the Fund.
5. The Committee for the Development of Sport may accept any contribution, donation or legacy, such as referred to in Article 4, paragraph 1 c., of this Statute, up to the amount of 50,000FF (by decision of the Committee of Ministers in 1994, this amount was increased to 500,000FF). Contributions, donations or legacies of greater amounts may be accepted only subject to the approval of the Committee of Ministers.
6. The functions exercised by the members of the Committee for the Development of Sport shall not be remunerated. Members shall receive travelling and subsistence allowances at the rates in force for Council of Europe committees of experts. These shall be charged to the Council of Europe budget.
7. Any member of the Council of Europe or the Secretary General may refer to the Committee of Ministers a decision of the Committee for the Development of Sport consid-

ered to be incompatible with the aims of the Council of Europe as defined in Chapter I of its Statute. In such cases, the decision shall be suspended until the Committee of Ministers has reached a decision thereon.

Article 6 – Finance

1. The assets and properties of the Sports Fund shall be acquired and owned in the name of the Council of Europe and shall accordingly enjoy the privileges and immunities conferred upon the assets of the Council by agreements in force.
2. The assets of the Sports Fund may not be merged in the other assets of the Council of Europe. The Secretary General shall be responsible for keeping the special accounts of the Fund, which shall be maintained in accordance with the financial regulations adopted by the Committee for the Development of Sport.
3. a. The programme to be financed by the Sports Fund shall be accompanied by estimates of the expenditure which it will entail. If certain items of expenditure are to be spread over several years, the estimates shall mention the relevant expenditure for each year.
   b. In no case may the estimated expenditure in any given year exceed the total income anticipated for that year; to this end, there shall be annexed to the estimates a detailed statement of existing assets and resources anticipated in the course of that year; an indication shall also be given as to how expenditure envisaged for subsequent years shall be covered.
   c. No commitment of any kind may be undertaken on behalf of the Sports Fund in excess of the sums inserted in the estimates of expenditure for the current year. If necessary, the Secretary General may nevertheless increase the estimates for specific activities by not more than 10% within a given year, provided that such increases are fully compensated by the reduction of expenditure for other activities. All such adjustments shall be submitted to the Committee for the Development of Sport for ratification.
4. a. The Fund's accounts shall be checked annually by the Council of Europe auditors, who shall draw up their report and certify the accounts no later than six months after the financial year to which the accounts refer. So that the Secretary General may comment on the Board's report if he so desires, the Board shall supply him with a copy.
   b. The accounts and auditors' report shall be transmitted by the Secretary General to the Committee for the Development of Sport. After approving the accounts, the Committee for the Development of Sport shall transmit them, together with the report and any comments it may wish to make, to the Committee of Ministers.
   c. After examining the auditors' report and any observations which the Secretary General and the Committee for the Development of Sport may have made thereon, the Committee of Ministers may discharge the Secretary General of responsibility for the financial year concerned.
5. The working expenses of the Sports Fund shall be borne by the Council of Europe budget. Nevertheless, the question of total or partial reimbursement of these expenses by the Fund to the budget of the Council of Europe may be reviewed by the Committee of Ministers from time to time in the light of the Fund's resources.

Article 7 – Revision of the Statute
The Committee of Ministers of the Council of Europe may at any time revise the present statute of the Sports Fund, either at the request of or in consultation with the Committee for the Development of Sport.

Chapter 15
EUROPEAN CO-OPERATION

15.1. Resolution No. 3/75 on Areas for Cooperation

The European Ministers responsible for Sport, meeting in Brussels on 20 and 21 March 1975

Having regard to their resolution on the role of public authorities regarding the development of Sport for All;
Whereas the resolution outlines the range of areas which might lend themselves to joint action;
Invite the ad hoc Consultative Meeting, pending its conversion into a Council for the Development of Sport, to:

1. investigate the possibility of undertaking concerted action in one or more of those areas, according to an order of priorities to by determined, in co-operation with the Council of Europe bodies dealing with education and culture, authorities, environment, town and country planning, public health, social affairs, etc.;
2. give particular attention to the following forms of co-operation:
   a. the exchange of information in which the member states are asked to collaborate closely and ensure the efficiency of the Clearing House, particularly through active participation by the liaison offices;
   b. the co-ordination of members states efforts in scientific research by means of:
      i. circulation of information on research programmes completed, in progress or planned, so as to foster collaboration between countries and between researchers and to avoid duplication;
      ii. encouragement of division of labour in the execution of research projects on priority subjects selected by the ad hoc Consultative Meeting pending its conversion into a Council for the Development of Sport;
   c. exchanges of persons, visits, twinning arrangements, etc.;
   d. the pooling of experiences in the construction and management of sports facilities;
   e. the joint study of legislative measures, regulations and financial arrangements designed both to promote Sport for All and to provide safeguards for sport and those who practice it;
   f. mutual assistance for countries which request it;
   g. development of a method of evaluation enabling the results of sports policies to be readily compared.

15.2. Resolution No. 4/75 on Machinery for Co-operation

The European Ministers responsible for Sport, meeting in Brussels on 20 and 21 March 1975

Believing that sport is a significant element in educational and cultural development;
Affirming their belief in the principles embodied in the European Sport for All Charter;
Recognising that the implementation of these principles depends on co-operation between member governments, including periodic informal meetings between Ministers with responsibility for Sport and the establishment of working groups of Ministers to consider special areas of policy;

Considering that such co-operation requires the establishment of appropriate structures;
Recommend that the Committee of Ministers of the Council of Europe transform the ad hoc Consultative Meeting into a Council for the Development of Sport (CDS) with a status which will confer upon it a maximum of prestige and authority within the framework of Council of Europe structures and ensure effective co-operation with other bodies of the Council of Europe;
Entrust to the Secretary General of the Council of Europe the task of determining the level and size of the administrative unit necessary for the efficient functioning of the Council for the Development of Sport and the preparation of future Ministerial conferences.

15.3. Resolution No. 5/75

The European Ministers responsible for Sport, meeting in Brussels on 20 and 21 March 1975

Welcome the Belgian Government's initiative in organising the first Conference of European Ministers responsible for Sport;
Convey their warmest thanks to the Belgian Government for their generous hospitality;
Thank the Parliamentary Assembly of the Council of Europe for the support it has given the efforts of the Council for Cultural Co-operation by adopting Recommendation 588 (1970) on the development of Sport for All and the creation of co-ordinating structures, and Recommendation 682 (1972) on a European Sport for All Charter;
Confirm their intention to continue and expand co-operation between them and, each in their own country, to study all measures, including legislation where necessary, to implement the resolutions adopted;
Express their gratitude to the United Kingdom Government for their offer, in principle, to organise a second Conference of European Ministers responsible for Sport in 1977 or 1978.

15.4. Resolution on Future European Co-operation (78/2)

(Theme II)
The European Ministers responsible for Sport, meeting in London, from 4 to 7 April 1978

Conscious that, for most of the States Signatory to the European Cultural Convention, the Brussels Conference has helped to promote the formulation of a sports policy based on the principles of the European Sport for All Charter;
Recognising that the initiatives taken in this area of European co-operation have progressed favourably since 1975;
Considering that the efficiency of this co-operation is, to a very large extent, dependent on simple structures provided with adequate resources and prestige;
as regards the organs for co-operation:
Welcome the fact that the question of the status of the Committee for the Development of Sport (CDDS), an eminently appropriate body for European co-operation in sport, has been finally resolved;
Consider that this new structure should be so organised as to allow the Conference of Ministers to concentrate on policy issues, while the CDDS concerns itself with working out and implementing the Council of Europe's sports programme;
Recommend that the Conference of European Ministers responsible for Sport meets every three years;

Decide to continue the practice of holding informal meetings of Ministers responsible for Sport, so that they can consider developments in sport arising in a European or world-wide context;

as regards areas of co-operation, priority themes and scientific research:

Note with satisfaction the progress made in the various sectors selected by the CDDS;

Remind those responsible for the themes that as practical conclusions as possible are expected, capable of being applied at both European and national levels;

Pay tribute to the NGOs responsible for organised sports, and in particular for the initiatives taken in recent years;

Consider that the right to Sport for All must be able to be exercised by all those who for various reasons have difficulty in doing so;

Ask the Committee of Ministers of the Council of Europe to invite the CDDS where its future programme is concerned:

1. to encourage the co-ordination of research in sports sciences;
2. to commission an analysis of the relations between the situation of socially under-privileged groups and the types and levels of sporting activities they normally engage in or could engage in successfully, and in particular of the role that sport can play in helping to promote the integration of immigrants into society;
3. to provide for the greater involvement of women in the promotion of Sport for All programmes;
4. to promote specific research projects in fields directly related to its objectives, notably:
5. identification and encouragement of sporting talent, in accordance with the Sport for All Charter;
6. provision and equipment of integrated sports and recreation facilities;
7. building of low-cost sports facilities;
8. methods for detecting the use of illegal means of improving performance;
9. causes of and means of preventing anti-social behaviour at sporting events, which is becoming increasingly widespread;
10. study, in co-operation with the non-governmental bodies concerned, of possible ways of keeping changes in technical standards in the construction of sports facilities to the minimum made necessary by developments in sport and building techniques and of the international harmonisation of technical standards in the construction of sports facilities;
11. access to sport for old people, people whose occupation makes the regular practice of a sport difficult (for example, shift workers), socially under-privileged groups in densely populated industrial towns, immigrants, the physically, mentally or socially handicapped;

as regards means of action:

Welcome the decision of the Ministers' Deputies to set up a Sports Fund but note that the appropriations made available for European co-operation by the Council of Europe are still so inadequate as to have necessitated voluntary contributions by member states to this Fund;

Draw attention to the situation which will arise at the end of 1978 when the voluntary contributions to the Sports Fund are exhausted;

Invite the Committee of Ministers to review the budgetary situation of the CDDS as from 1979 and to vote it sufficient funds to carry out its programme;

as regards the Clearing House:

Acknowledge the essential and effective role played by this body in European co-operation;
Recognise that each liaison office and relay centre should be given, at national level, the resources necessary for optimum co-operation with the Clearing House;
Request that an adequate share of the CDDS budgets be allocated to overcoming the difficulties of administering the Clearing House, in order to ensure its survival;
as regards the next conference:
Recommend that one of the themes for the third Conference of European Ministers responsible for Sport be: "The importance of sport for social groups suffering from deprivation and urban stress";
Warmly thank the United Kingdom Government for its hospitality during this conference and gratefully accept the invitation of the Spanish Government to meet in Spain in 1981.

15.5. Resolution on Progress in European Co-operation since the Second Conference in 1978 and Priorities for Future European Sports Co-operation (81/2)

The European Ministers responsible for Sport, meeting in Palma de Majorca from 8 to 10 April 1981 for their 3rd Conference

Recalling the resolutions adopted at their 2nd Conference (London, 1978);
Confirm their view that the Conference of European Ministers responsible for Sport should concern itself with broad policy issues and that the Committee for the Development of Sport (CDDS) should determine and implement, within the framework of the medium term plans of the Council of Europe, the details of the consequent sports programme;
Appreciate the value of an analysis of the work of the preceding triennium as the first theme of their conferences;
Note with satisfaction the progress made with the work programme adopted at the second conference as reported in Theme I, and particularly within the priority themes;
Congratulate the CDDS on this progress;
Acknowledge the importance of the contribution of the Clearing House and of national and international non-governmental sports organisations to this progress;
Welcome the evident growth of co-operation and enthusiasm among member states for these conferences and the work of the CDDS;
Take cognisance of the fact that the introduction of new technologies in industrial societies will lead to increased leisure time and thus to a greater demand for opportunities for sport and physical recreation;
Appreciate the influence member states can have on international sports co-operation when they act together on important issues;
Reaffirm their obligation as democratic friendly nations to work together to develop sports policies for the benefit of all their peoples and to support the development of Sport for All and physical education programmes throughout the world, in particular through Unesco;
Reaffirm that the Council of Europe, through the CDDS in particular, remains the most appropriate framework for sports co-operation among the Contracting Parties to the European Cultural Convention;
Hope that links between the Council of Europe and the European Sports Conference can lead to improved technical and expert contacts with the countries of Eastern Europe for the benefit of all, and for the wider diffusion of knowledge;
Mark, in this context, their support for the Family Health Programme of the European Regional Office of the World Health Organisation;
Recognise that such friendly co-operation can have implications for Europe which go beyond sport;

Warmly thank the Spanish Government for its hospitality during this Conference and gratefully accept the offer of the Maltese Government to meet in April or May 1984 in Malta for the 4th Conference;

Resolve:

1. that each Ministerial Conference should evaluate the work of the preceding three years;
2. that the dialogue with the IOC, GAISF, ANOC and other world and regional bodies concerned with sport and sports sciences and medicine should continue and develop, in order, in particular, to eradicate as far as possible the problems of doping in sport by encouraging the use of doping control laboratories and to continue the implementation of Recommendation(79)8 of the Committee of Ministers of the Council of Europe on doping in sport, and the resolution adopted at their 2nd Conference (London, 1978) on doping and health;

Invite the Committee of Ministers of the Council of Europe:

1. to ask the CDDS in the period up to the 4th Conference:
    a. to continue and intensify its efforts in those areas of the programme where progress has been less than requested at their 2nd Conference, such as the European Courses and Events and the co-ordination of bilateral sports aid programmes for the benefit of member countries of the CDDS;
    b. to continue to encourage and develop the work of the Clearing House and to make appropriate provision for this in its budget;
    c. to work out, in co-operation with the Foundation Rika De Backer – Van Ocken, and other specialist international bodies, as a matter of urgency, measures designed to reduce or abolish violence associated with sport;
    d. to study the effects of increasing leisure time on physical recreation and sport policies and their contribution to the solution of unemployment problems;
    e. to consider the advisability of adopting new methods of work in addition to those already in operation, such as courses for trainers, coaches and managers;
    f. to undertake a co-ordinated research project assessing the results and impact of national Sport for All policies and campaigns, the results of which should be submitted to the 4th Conference;
    g. to undertake a study of the effects of professionalisation in sport;
    h. to undertake the following new priority themes: sport for children, sport for the family, sport for elderly people and sport for the working population; and to study cost-effective sports facilities (in particular energy-saving measures and rational management);
    i. to study problems associated with undue early specialisation and overtraining of gifted young sportsmen and sportswomen;
    j. to study issues connected with participation in international sports events;
    k. to ensure that the results of work achieved in the programme are put in a form which will facilitate their implementation at national level;
2. to recommend to governments of member states that they:
    a. provide full support for their national liaison officers working with the Clearing House, so as to ensure a fuller European co-operation;
    b. assess the implications for, and impact on, national Sport for All policies of the results of the past priority themes of the CDDS;

3. to recognise the significant contribution of sport to promoting European co-operation, and its greater potential for the future through an expanded work programme of the CDDS, by increasing the resources available to the CDDS in future years from within the total budget of the Council of Europe.

15.6. Resolution on European Sports Co-operation (84/10)

The European Ministers responsible for Sport, meeting in Malta for their 4th Conference on 15 and 16 May 1984

Recalling the European Sport for All Charter (Resolution (76) 41);
Reaffirming that the Council of Europe and the CDDS are the most appropriate fora for European Sports Co-operation at the intergovernmental level;
Congratulating the CDDS on its work in directing the implementation of the Charter, in particular in the exchange of technical information and expertise;
Applauding the contribution of the NGOs to this work;
Noting the increasing need for frequent political co-operation between member states in the field of sport;
Noting that the decisions of the autonomous international sports organisations have an impact upon the policies and expenditure plans of central and local government authorities;
Reaffirming, therefore, the need, expressed at their 3rd Conference for an effective and systematic dialogue between international sports organisations and intergovernmental organisations;
Concerned that the CDDS as presently constituted is not easily able to represent their collective views;
Noting the provisions of Resolution (71) 44 and of Resolution (76) 3;
Bearing in mind the discussions at this conference;
Request the Committee of Ministers of the Council of Europe to:

1. make arrangements for the preparation of their next conference which take account of the autonomy of the conference;
2. to ask the CDDS to study possible modifications to its working methods and/or terms of reference to be examined at their next conference and subsequently by the Committee of Ministers.

15.7. Recommendation 993 (1984) on European Sports Co-operation

The Assembly,
Having noted the report of its Committee on Culture and Education on European Sports Co-operation (Doc. 5270);
Being informed of the results of the 4th Conference of European Ministers responsible for Sport (Malta, 15 and 16 May 1984);
Welcoming the political interest shown by the Ministers in sports co-operation at this level, and sharing their conviction that "the Council of Europe and the European Cultural Convention ...should remain the principal framework for European intergovernmental co-operation in sport";
Recognising the need to associate more fully in this co-operation the sporting bodies and non-governmental organisations in the sports field;
Supporting the wish for greater autonomy of the Conference of Sports Ministers, and recalling the parallel of the Standing Conference of European Ministers of Education which acts as an overview body of European education co-operation;

Welcoming Recommendation No. (84) 8 of the Committee of Ministers, on the reduction of spectator violence at sporting events, and the common concern for action in this field shown by the sports ministers and by the Assembly in its Recommendation No. 963 (1983), and recalling the importance of education for fairplay;
Drawing attention to the many other areas of sports co-operation, in particular to the problems of funding sporting activity other than high level competition events;
Recalling its Recommendation No. 900 (1980) and Resolution No. 738 (1980), on the Olympic Games and the outlook for their future. and reasserting its concern at the increasing commercialisation and politicisation of the Olympic movement.
Recommends that the Committee of Ministers:

1. give positive follow-up to the resolutions of the Malta conference, in particular by providing adequate resources for implementing, in the intergovernmental Steering Committee for the Development of Sport, the proposals made by the conference:
2. give consideration to the ministerial contribution to European sports co-operation as a model for European co-operation in other sectors of the cultural field.

15.8. Resolution on Progress in European Sports Co-operation (86/2)

The European Ministers responsible for Sport, meeting in Dublin for their 5th Conference from 30 September to 2 October 1986

1. General
   Considering that sport continues to occupy an ever-increasingly important place in society and public policy, both because of its positive contributions to the happiness of citizens and to the health of society, and because of some undesirable effects deriving from a phenomenon of such mass popularity;
   Noting that Sport for All, the concept first conceived within the Council of Europe and developed in the European Sport for All Charter (Resolution (76) 41), has now become recognised universally and that Sport for All programmes have been discussed within many international governmental and non-governmental sports organisations;
   Expressing the wish that the Council of Europe might develop or strengthen its links with such organisations, whether universal, regional or European, in order to contribute actively to the development of such programmes;
   Recalling the proposals which they have submitted to the Committee of Ministers for starting a dialogue with Sports Ministers from other regions of the world, including with those from other European countries;
   Reaffirming their attachment to the framework of the Council of Europe, and the European Cultural Convention, as the most suitable one for the discussion of common problems and for the elaboration of common policies in the field of sport, and welcoming the Parliamentary Assembly's support and co-operation;
   Noting that the draft 3rd Medium-Term Plan of the Council of Europe provides a sound framework for continued co-operation and the further development of sports policies for the 1990s;
2. Work Programme 1984 – 1986
   Thanking the CDDS for undertaking work on the instructions of the Committee of Ministers on those resolutions adopted at their last Conference (Malta, 15 to 16 May 1984) in which they asked for action, and approving the results of it;
   Noting that the changes introduced by the CDDS into its working methods since 1984 take account of the question they evoked in Resolution N° 10/84 adopted at their last Conference;

Considering that these changes provide a sound and useful basis for continuing intensive co-operation between the Sports Ministers, the Committee of Ministers and the CDDS;
Looking forward to strengthening such co-operation in the future;
Noting the results of other work carried out by the CDDS from 1984 to 1986, and particularly welcoming the clarification of its sports information policy and the redefinition of its links with the Clearing House, and the completion of work on the Eurofit project on testing physical fitness;
Thanking the Clearing House for its constructive role in adapting itself to the new sports information policy of the CDDS;
Considering that the increase and growing diversity of participation in sport and physical recreation are bound up with significant changes in the relationships between sport, industry, research, public authorities and the media;
Welcoming and supporting the twin projects begun by the CDDS on the study of the economic significance of sport and on new partnerships in sport, and agreeing, as appropriate, to provide for the co-operation of their experts in this work;
Noting the Parliamentary Assembly's Recommendation 1047 on boxing;
Warmly thanking the Irish government for its organisation of and hospitality during this Conference;

Resolve:

3. General
to accept, gratefully, the offer of the Icelandic government to meet in Iceland in 1989 for their 6th Conference;
to continue to meet informally in order to exchange views on matters of common concern as needs arise, and gratefully to accept the offer of the Greek government to meet in Greece for their 13th informal meeting in 1987;
to continue and strengthen their dialogue with the international sports organisations;

4. with regard to Spectator Violence associated with Sport:
to congratulate the CDDS on its prompt preparation of the draft European Convention on Spectator Violence and Misbehaviour at Sports Events and in particular at Football Matches;
to welcome the report prepared by the CDDS on its activities concerning spectator violence associated with sport from 1983 to 1986;
to continue co-operation with the Union des Associations Européennes de Football (UEFA) and to express their gratitude for past co-operation;
to urge the Standing Committee of the European Convention, to pursue energetically the task entrusted to it by the Convention, where necessary in liaison with the CDDS;
Invite the Committee of Ministers of the Council of Europe:
to provide adequate support for the development of appropriate contacts with other organisations concerned with the development of sport, within and beyond Europe, both by the Sports Ministers themselves and by the CDDS as the Committee of Ministers may decide;
to support the continuation of work on violence associated with sport in general, and in particular to study the reasons for this violence and to begin work on the educational aspects and long-term prevention;
to support the proposals made by the CDDS to strengthen its work on sports information exchange and analysis and its input to the Clearing House;

5. to ask the CDDS:
   a. to study in the period up to the 6th Conference the following subjects:
      i. the economic significance of sport, and to report to the Conference on the results of this project;
      ii. the status and protection of sports participants at all levels;
      iii. the interrelationships between sport and linked socio-economic activities (such as tourism, health, leisure, the media) and to make proposals for new joint strategies and programmes;
      iv. new developments in leisure oriented sports facilities.

15.9. Resolution on European Sports Co-operation (89/2)

The European Ministers responsible for Sport, meeting at Reykjavik for their 6th Conference, from 30 May to 1 June 1989

Reaffirming their belief that sport is an integral part of education and culture, contributes to human development, plays an irreplaceable role in the quality of life of citizens, and that successful policies for sport can contribute to personal and social well-being;

Conscious of their duty to encourage by all appropriate means friendly and healthy participation in sport, and peaceful spectatorship of sports events;

Considering that sport and cultural activities and events on an increasingly broad European level could have a very positive impact on cultural and social progress and contribute to European unity;

Noting with satisfaction the participation as observers at the 6th Conference of European Ministers responsible for Sport of the Ministers from Hungary and Poland;

Work of the Committee for the Development of Sport (CDDS):

1. Thank the CDDS, the Clearing House and the authorities of member states for the work accomplished since the 5th Conference at Dublin in 1986, for the substantial reports on priority themes presented to this Conference, and take note of the results of this work;
2. Note with satisfaction that the major co-ordinated research project on 'Sport for All: injuries and their prevention' has been completed by the CDDS, and look forward to the early completion of the project on the 'Economic significance of sport', and hope that these studies, and their future reviews, will be of help to those responsible for framing national policies in these areas;
3. Consider that it is desirable for as many States as possible to join in the work of such projects and to participate in them to the greatest extent possible;
4. Attach particular importance to the completion of current projects such as Sports Management Training, the Social Protection of Athletes, the cultural and sporting aspects of traditional games, the planning of sports policies, the study of young people's ethical values in sport, etc.;
5. Note that the growing demands of the commercial sector on sport, and the increasing requirement for professional management within sport will put new strains on the traditional voluntary management of sport and its clubs;
6. Express their determination that they will try to ensure that the virtues and benefits of the voluntary ethos remain intact while helping the voluntary sports movement to adapt to these changes;
7. Note that while levels of participation in sport are still increasing, the average levels of physical fitness in member states are a cause for concern for the public authorities;

Resolve:

1. to study, within the framework of the States Party to the European Cultural Convention, all matters of common interest concerning sport, including the implications for sport in Europe of the common internal market;
2. to promote actively the implementation on a wide scale and on the common basis set out in Recommendation N° R (87) 9 of the Committee of Ministers, the Eurofit tests of physical fitness for school-aged children;
3. to make further efforts to enable disabled persons to exercise their right to sport, including at an elite level, whenever possible on an equal footing with able-bodied people and to promote their involvement with sports decision-making, following the principles set out in Recommendation N° R (86) 18 of the Committee of Ministers (Resolution N° 1/86 of the Dublin Conference) and urge the relevant international and national sports organisations to accelerate their own reforms and progress in these respects;
4. to take all appropriate steps to enable mentally handicapped persons to participate adequately in adapted physical activities;
5. to undertake, in conjunction with their central sports organisations, preventative campaigns to reduce the incidence of injuries in sport, and to promote safety in exercise and sport, following the principles set out in the Conference paper presented by the Dutch Minister;
6. to take account of the benefits of sport to national economies, public revenue, industry and employment, in facilitating the duty, as set out in the European Sport for All Charter adopted at their first Conference, of public authorities to ensure that there is sufficient provision of opportunities and facilities to enable all citizens, residents and visitors, regardless of age, sex, national origin or economic circumstances, who so wish, to take part in sport or physical recreation activities;
7. to bear in mind the importance of traditional games in both national and the European cultural heritages, and to take steps to preserve them at first by preparing a catalogue of them and, where appropriate, to enable young people to contribute to their further development;

Invite the Committee of Ministers of the Council of Europe:

1. to bear in mind the possibilities offered by sports co-operation in the context of its general policy adopted on 5 May 1989;
2. to encourage participation by states not yet party to the European Cultural Convention on Council of Europe activities on sport, wherever this may be of potential mutual benefit, in particular when such participation may enable sport better to play its due part in encouraging a sense of European cultural identity and/or in promoting international understanding and practical harmonisation in sport;
3. to continue to extend this participation to other non-European states where appropriate and on a case-by-case basis;
4. to initiate contacts with other intergovernmental sports organisations with a view to discussing problems arising in international sport;
5. to instruct the CDDS to pay particular attention to the following subjects in the period leading up to the 7th Conference:
    a. the preparation of a study on ways of organising:
        i. new sport activities on a European level and under the guidance of the responsible sports organisations;
        ii. seminars concerning the practical implementation of integrated sport and cultural activities;

b. the development of fair-play campaigns for the purposes, inter alia, of reducing violence and injuries among players and promoting the positive benefits of regular sporting activity;
c. the preparation of a draft text on:
   i. the role of sport in the educational processes of young people;
   ii. measures to improve the quality and effectiveness of the links between physical education in schools, school sport and out-of-school sport, and the links between schools and clubs to ease the passage and transition by young people into the world of adult sport and recreation;
   iii. ways and means of encouraging appropriate public and non-governmental organisations to develop a programme of multilateral sport exchanges for school-aged children;
d. the preparation, bearing in mind any proposals of the Standing Committee on Resolution N° 4/89 on Safety, of a draft text on Spectator Safety at Sports Grounds and Events;
e. the preparation of suitable tests to monitor the physical fitness of adults, building upon the philosophy of Eurofit;
f. the preparation of a draft text outlining the principles which should underlie the desirable role of the various partners of the sports movement involved in the promotion and development of Sport for All, including the public authorities, the commercial sector and the mass media.

The Conference:
1. Thanks the CDDS for preparing draft guidelines for future informal meetings of Sports Ministers and agrees that:
   a. informal meetings play a valuable part in European sports co-operation;
   b. they should be held on an ad hoc basis, to discuss urgent or particular topics;
   c. the host government should play a preponderant role in preparing informal meetings, giving where possible emphasis to the discussion of new topics;
   d. the object of informal meetings, as distinct from the triennial Conferences, is not necessarily to reach formal agreements but to discuss topical issues;
   e. an official report of proceedings is not necessary but a press communiqué should be prepared, summarising the main items of discussion;
2. Express their sincere gratitude to the host government and to the Icelandic Minister of Culture and Education, Chairman of the Conference, for the perfect organisation of and their warm hospitality during the 6th Conference;
3. Resolves to meet, at the kind invitation of the government of the Hellenic Republic in 1992 for their 7th Conference, at Rhodes;
4. Resolves to meet in informal meetings, as often as pressing needs may dictate, in accordance with the guidelines agreed above.

15.10. Resolution on European Sports Co-operation (92/5)

The European Ministers responsible for Sport, meeting at Rhodes for their 7th Conference, from 13 to 15 May 1992

Welcoming the political developments which, since their last meeting at Reykjavik, had brought about historical changes in Europe, enabling all Europeans to decide democratically on their future destiny;

Reaffirming the important role which sport has to play in human development, as an essential element of progress through education, culture and personal and social well-being;
With a view to facilitating the practice of sport at all levels, and determined to encourage the traditional voluntary management of sport and its clubs and associations;
Noting with satisfaction the presence at the 7th Conference, as participants or observers, of sports Ministers from Central and Eastern European countries;
Welcoming the existing connections and co-operation in the field of sport between the Council of Europe and the European Communities on the one hand, and the European Sports Conference on the other;
Thanking the CDDS and the authorities of all States parties to the European Cultural Convention for the considerable work carried out since the 6th Conference at Reykjavik, and particularly the texts submitted to this Conference, and taking note of the results of this work;
Welcoming the setting up of the Mutual Assistance programmes, aimed primarily at developing sport in the countries of Central and Eastern Europe;

Resolve:
1. to cooperate within the framework of the European Cultural Convention on all matters concerning sport which are of common interest, including the role which sport can play in democratic development;
2. to make all efforts for the effective implementation, at all levels, of the principles laid down in the European Sports Charter and the Code of Ethics for Sport, adopted at the present Conference, and to widely promote those principles;
3. to operate so that adequate resources, facilities and opportunities are made available to the sport sector in order to enable all citizens, including disabled persons, to benefit from the practice of sport or physical recreational activities;
4. to ensure that the economic dimension of sport is appropriately analysed and borne in mind, including such aspects as financing, management and marketing;
5. to reinforce bilateral programmes (both by governments and by sports organisations) for mutual assistance and sports development, as a necessary complement to multilateral programmes;

Invite the Committee of Ministers of the Council of Europe:
1. to intensify sports co-operation, as an element of its general policy in the new European political framework, and as a means of forwarding the cause of international understanding, whilst respecting the principle of the independence of sport;
2. to encourage, where appropriate and mutually beneficial, participation in Council of Europe work on sport by other States not yet party to the European Cultural Convention, in particular those participating in the Conference on Security and Co-operation in Europe and contacts with other intergovernmental organisations;
3. to encourage the necessary continued close co-operation in the field of sport between the Council of Europe, the European Communities and appropriate European sports organisations, and, where suitable, other international ones;
4. to invite the CDDS to address with particular attention the following subjects, in the period leading up to the 8th Conference:
    a. the follow-up given at all levels to the European Sports Charter and the Code of Sports Ethics, contributing where needed to the study of the necessary reforms of national legal frameworks;
    b. the ways and means of encouraging the activities of the voluntary sports clubs and associations as an important element of democracy;

c. the further development of mutual assistance programmes, particularly in favour of the new member countries from Central and Eastern Europe and the preparation of a long-term plan for such programmes;
d. the economy of sport, including its financial, management and marketing aspects and the contribution of sport to economic development nationally and internationally;
e. the promotion of Sport for All in all countries party to the European Cultural Convention;

The Conference:
Expresses its sincere gratitude to the host government and the Greek Under Secretary of State for Sports, Chairman of the Conference, for the excellent organisation and the generous hospitality during the 7th Conference;
Resolves to meet, at the kind invitation of the government of Portugal in 1995 for the 8th Conference, in that country;
Resolves, at the invitation of the French government, to hold an Informal Meeting in France in 1993, on the theme of "Sport and Money";
Resolves to meet in Informal Meetings, as often as pressing needs may dictate, in accordance with the guidelines for informal meetings agreed at the 6th Conference;
Notes that the government of the Czech and Slovak Federative Republic intends to offer to host the 9th Conference in 1998.

15.11. Order No. 479 (1992) on European Sports Co-operation

The Assembly, Referring to its Recommendation No. 1190 (1992), decides to play an active part in assisting central and east European countries to review their sports policies and provisions.
To this effect the Committee on Culture and Education (Sub-committee on Youth and Sport) is asked to liase with the Committee for the Development of Sport (CDDS) and to hold consultative meetings on sports legislation with the responsible parliamentary committees in central and eastern Europe.

15.12. Recommendation 1190 (1992)[6] on European sports co-operation

1. The Assembly last debated European sports co-operation in 194 (see Recommendation 993 and Doc. 5270). It expressed its satisfaction with the approach of the Council of Europe which was based on the Committee for the Development of Sport (CDDS) and the Conference of European Ministers responsible for Sport.
2. It has followed the activity of the CDDS, the ministerial conferences held in Dublin 1986, Reykjavik 1989 and Rhodes 1992, as well as the informal ministerial conferences held in Lisbon 1985, Strasbourg 1985, Athens 1988 and Budapest 1991.

[6] Assembly debate on 30 September 1992 (11th Sitting) (see Doc 6664, report of the Committee on Culture and Education, Rapporteur: Mr Müller). Text adopted by the Assembly on 30 September 1992 (11th sitting).

3. Four major texts have resulted:
   i. European Convention on Spectator Violence and Misbehaviour at Sports Events and in particular at Football Matches (1985);
   ii. Anti-Doping Convention (1989);
   iii. European Sports Charter (1992);
   iv. Code of Sports Ethics (1992).
4. The Assembly has taken account of the implications for sport caused by the political changes in central and eastern Europe. It considers that action is urgently needed on the parliamentary level to assure sports provision.
5. The Assembly has also noted the European Communitys position on sport as set Out in the communication of the Commission of 31 July 1991 and the constitution of the Communitys European Sports Forum. It welcomes the understanding and co-operation that has been established between the Community and Council of Europe in this field.
6. Many problems, however, remain and amongst them:
   i. sports provision in central and eastern Europe (and related legislation);
   ii. access to the countryside for sport and other leisure activities;
   iii. the classification of sites associated with sport;
   iv. equal sporting opportunities;
   v. continuing violence associated with sport;
   vi. doping;
   vii. money in sport.
7. The Assembly welcomes the fact that the next informal meeting of European Sports Ministers will tackle the question of money in sport (France, 1993).
8. It calls on governments of member states that have not yet done so, to ratify the conventions on violence and anti-doping referred to above.
9. It recommends that the Committee of Ministers ask governments of member states to implement as effectively as possible the new European Sports Charter and Code of Sports Ethics (agreed by the European Ministers responsible for Sport in Rhodes, 1992).
10. The Assembly further recommends that the Committee of Ministers:
    i. extend work on the values of sport and their promotion;
    ii. continue its efforts to assist sports provision in central and eastern Europe (with particular attention to legislation, a field in which the Assembly might also be involved);
    iii. prepare an agreement on access to the countryside for sport and other leisure activities;
    iv. classify sites of significance for sport.

15.13. Resolution on European Sports Cooperation (95/3)
The European Ministers responsible for Sport, meeting in Lisbon at their 8th Conference from 17 to 18 May 1995

Thanking the Committee for the Development of Sport, the Standing Committee of the European Convention on Spectator Violence, and the Monitoring Group of the Anti-Doping Convention for their substantial contributions to the development of European Sports Cooperation and the aims of the Council of Europe since their last Conference in Rhodes in 1992,
Affirming that sport plays a fundamental role in modern society, and that it is therefore integral to the achievement of the social progress enshrined in the statute of the Council of Europe,

Invite the Committee of Ministers, in the light of the texts adopted at this Conference, to ask the CDDS:

1. to intensify its activities based on the European Sports Charter (Recommendation (92) 13) and the Code of Sports Ethics (Recommendation (92) 14);
2. to study appropriate ways of promoting voluntary work in sport and of helping everybody to have access to sports activities;
3. to study ways of protecting sport from the negative effects of over commercialisation and media hype in some sports;

Decide to give high priority to the efficient application of the European Convention on Spectator Violence and the Anti-Doping Convention;
Note the invitation of the Cypriot Government to organise an Informal Meeting of Sports Ministers in 1996 or 1997 on the theme: "Sport and the Law";
Agree to meet, at the invitation of the Government of Slovakia, for their 9th Conference in 1998 or 1999, with an agenda reflecting the concerns of this Resolution;
Thank the Portuguese authorities for the organisation of this Conference and for their kind hospitality during it.

15.14. Recommendation 1565 (2002) on European sports co-operation
Text adopted by the Standing Committee, acting on behalf of the Assembly, on 29 May 2002

1. The Parliamentary Assembly last debated European sports co-operation in 1992 (see Recommendation 1190 and Doc. 6664). It expressed satisfaction with the approach of the Council of Europe, which was the first intergovernmental organisation to work seriously on the place of sport in society, through the Committee for the Development of Sport (CDDS). Over the years it has set out the fundamental principles that should underlie all sports systems.
2. It is important to look again at the Council of Europe's reasons for working in sport, because the resources for the sports sector are now facing drastic cuts and its visibility within the Organisation is at risk. Sport has close links with a number of areas and interacts with many other facets of the Council of Europe's work such as democracy, tolerance and social cohesion. Because of this universality the Assembly believes that sport should be addressed separately by an independent body, which can track these links and interact, orchestrate, act and capitalise on them.
3. The programme and activities of the Council of Europe in the field of sport are anchored in the revised European Sports Charter and revised Code of Sports Ethics. Two conventions are aimed to combat the negative aspects of sport and to advance the search for responses to specific problems, such as violence and doping – problems that have affected sport for some years: the European Convention on Spectator Violence and Misbehaviour at Sports Events and in particular at Football Matches and the Anti-Doping Convention.
4. The Council of Europe has worked positively to promote sport for all. Pursuant to Order No. 479 (1992) the Assembly has actively co-operated with the CDDS in meeting the challenge of helping the new member states in central and eastern Europe to improve their sports systems under the SPRINT programme.
5. Throughout central and eastern Europe this programme has used sport to teach democratic citizenship, given training for employment in sport and advised on the implementation of the European Sports Charter and respect for commitments undertaken under the two sports conventions. Helped by the programme, countries have set up

democratic sports systems, concentrating on new legislation and the reorganisation of the former hierarchic and elitist sport systems to make way for recreational sport programmes, helping people to be fit for life.

6. The Assembly notes that sport is one of the largest, if not the largest area of voluntary non-governmental organisational activity throughout Europe and that the CDDS is a meeting point for both governmental and non-governmental organisations.

7. The Council of Europe, through its Sport Department and the Monitoring Group of the Anti-Doping Convention, has played a key role (together with the European Union) in setting up and developing the World Anti-Doping Agency (WADA). Co-operation with WADA is becoming increasingly important as the Council of Europe explores ways of setting up machinery to channel the contributions of the various European countries through a central point.

8. New programmes are emphasising the value of sport for refugees and displaced persons in camps and those affected or disabled as the result of war or grave industrial accidents. The awareness of the contribution that sport can bring to refugees has been reinforced by media reporting, which has shown how in refugee camps, once the basic necessities of life are met, there is too much enforced leisure.

9. The Council of Europe should continue to examine and defend the right of everybody to practise a sport at which they may never excel, but which brings such rewards as improved mental and physical health, mobility, enjoyment, participation and, for some, a way back into society. Economic reality and market forces do not allow these benefits to be accurately calculated.

10. The Assembly therefore recommends that the Committee of Ministers:
    - i. ensure that the Sport Department is provided with the adequate resources, both human and financial, to enable the Council of Europe to pursue its work and to respond to new challenges in the field of sport;
    - ii. continue, in co-operation with the Assembly, its systematic review of sport legislation in all members states;
    - iii. promote sport as a means of overcoming political tensions;
    - iv. promote sport for all as part of education programmes for refugees and displaced persons;
    - v. develop sport as one of its contributions to the Stability Pact for South Eastern Europe;
    - vi. co-operate actively with the European Union in projects related to the 2004 European Year of Education through Sport;
    - vii. ask governments of member states to implement as effectively as possible the revised European Sports Charter and revised Code of Sports Ethics.

15.15. Recommendation 1566 (2002) on European cultural co-operation and the future role of the Assembly

Text adopted by the Assembly on 24 June 2002

1. The Parliamentary Assembly has followed closely the development of European cultural co-operation from its start in the Council of Europe. The present recommendation follows on from others and most recently from Recommendation 1265 (1995) on enlargement and European cultural co-operation and Recommendation 1299 (1996) on European cultural co-operation: activities of the European Union and relations with the Council of Europe.

2. In this context culture is used in its broad sense to include the arts, heritage, media, science, education, youth and sport, but in no order of priority.

The new challenges

3. The Assembly wishes to recognise the central importance of European cultural co-operation and to reaffirm its own contribution to this co-operation in the Council of Europe at the present moment.

4. On the one hand the upsurge of international terrorism has led to a greater realisation of the political relevance of cultural values, intercultural dialogue, education and tolerance.

5. On the other hand globalisation, through for example mass tourism or the new information technologies, has placed new pressures on areas such as heritage or languages, or even on gastronomy, requiring new policies to integrate the cultural perspective into economic planning for sustainable development.

6. Furthermore, while the process of enlargement of the Council of Europe is nearing completion (and has already done so as regards the European Cultural Convention), the new process of enlargement of the European Union is only beginning, with the potential risk for culture of a new dividing line in Europe.

7. There is therefore a perceived need for improving cultural co-operation not only within Europe (within the greater Europe) but also between Europe and neighbouring countries, especially in geographical areas such as the Mediterranean that have historical cultural links with Europe.

8. Finally, internal changes in the Council of Europe itself, notably the dissolution this year of the Council for Cultural Co-operation (Steering Committee for Cultural Co-operation), call for a new stocktaking of European cultural co-operation in which the Assembly should play a part.

The way forward

9. Education and culture should continue to remain central to the long-term mission of the Council of Europe. The Assembly can therefore welcome the inclusion of the cultural dimension in several key declarations adopted recently by the highest authorities of the Council of Europe, notably in the two Council of Europe Summits (Vienna 1993 and Strasbourg 1997), and in the Budapest Declaration for a Greater Europe without dividing lines, adopted by the Committee of Ministers in 1999.

10. However the Assembly must regret that the importance of culture in the broad sense has not been reflected in the subsequent cuts in budget and personnel that have mainly affected those sectors of the Organisation's activity.

11. Culture re-emerges as the mainstay of multilateral co-operation, following readjustment with the emerging democracies in central and eastern Europe and despite the extent to which political conflict in certain areas continues to feed on cultural differences.

12. Much of proven value in the Council of Europe's earlier work should be restated and repeated. For example permanent education, language and history learning, integrated conservation, youth participation, freedom of expression, tolerance, Sport for All, etc. Quality of life should be a shared objective throughout Europe. Cultural co-operation is a means of tackling the problem of exclusion in all its forms and should be pursued to the fullest extent. Education (formal and non-formal) remains the long-term key to economic, social and political progress as well as the basis for the development of the individual.

13. Certain new priorities and new challenges have emerged. Values have to be constantly defined, whether this is to take into account new social, political and economic circum-

stances or resist them. Management mantras of change for the sake of change should however be avoided.

14. The impact of the work of the Organisation suffers chronically from lack of follow up. The general principles and the many related recommendations and other proposals that have been made must be more clearly articulated and presented so as to be effective locally and to be appreciated by the parliaments and governments of member states.

Activities of the Assembly within the Council of Europe

15. The Assembly believes that its own contribution to the work of the Council of Europe is essentially one of initiation, of complementarity and interactivity. It proposes:
    i. to establish (where they do not yet exist) and to maintain active, informal working relations at all levels in the Council of Europe structures (ministerial, specialised ministry representatives, Congress of Local and Regional Authorities of Europe, Ministers' Deputies' rapporteur groups, Secretariat);
    ii. to reduce in practice its own involvement in institutional activities (statutory meetings, etc.) and to replace this with regular and efficient briefing, with more politically relevant participation and with joint planning at all appropriate levels;
    iii. to concentrate its own activities on selected priorities that complement what is done elsewhere in the Organisation.

Assembly external activities

16. The Assembly has an external role to play. It will therefore aim:
    i. to promote co-operation in the cultural field between governmental and non-governmental organisations through national parliaments;
    ii. to provide a forum for parliamentary debate on the cultural activities of those governmental organisations that do not have such a forum (UNESCO and OECD);
    iii. to encourage the participation of civil society, and in particular of young people in the activities of the Council of Europe, without necessary recourse to formal structures.

Committee of Ministers and cultural co-operation activities

17. The Assembly recommends that the Committee of Ministers, at institutional level:
    i. review Assembly representation in steering committees and consider in particular whether it is appropriate to maintain full membership of committees set up on the basis of the European Cultural Convention;
    ii. reintroduce, where appropriate, the practice of colloquies between parliamentarians and ministers at European conferences of specialised ministers;
    iii. reconsider the Assembly's earlier suggestion that the Committee of Ministers meet occasionally at the level of specialised ministers;

    and, more generally:
    iv. give a higher priority to the promotion of European cultural co-operation throughout the many fields involved (including media) and to its integration in the main policy fields of the Organisation as a whole and provide the appropriate resources and governmental co-ordination;
    v. ensure that information on Council of Europe activities is made available for use nationally (in an appropriate form and language);
    vi. pursue actively co-operation with other governmental organisations (UNESCO, OECD, etc.) and with the European Union with a view to establishing effective partnerships and a better sharing of available resources;

vii. take the necessary steps so that the European Union becomes party to the European Cultural Convention (Council of Europe) and that the broader Europe is included in any arrangements for cultural co-operation envisaged by the European Convention (European Union);
viii. continue to associate civil society with these activities and in particular young people.

15.16. Reply to Parliamentary Assembly Recommendation 1565 (2002) on European Sports Co-operation

Adopted by the Committee of Ministers on 20 November 2002 at the 817th meeting of the Ministers' Deputies

1. The Committee of Ministers has considered with interest Recommendation 1565 (2002) of the Parliamentary Assembly on European Sports Cooperation and welcomes the interest and concern expressed by the Assembly in this important area.
2. It understands the need for the sport sector to have increased resources, both human and financial (paragraph 10. i of the recommendation), given the number of areas within the work of the Council of Europe where sport interacts or should interact. It would stress the need for sport to continue to have a firm identity and strong visible presence within the organisation, as set out in paragraph 2 of the recommendation, in order to maintain the co-operation built up over three decades with other sectors of the Organisation.
3. With regard to systematic review of sport legislation in all member states (paragraph 10 ii), the Committee of Ministers firmly believes that proper legislation is one of the key foundations for a democratic sport system. It has welcomed the ready co-operation of the Sub-Committee on Youth and Sport to participate in Parliamentary hearings organised under the SPRINT programme to help countries bring their legislation in line with the criteria linked to the European Sports Charter.
4. With regard to promoting sport as a means of overcoming political tensions, also as a contribution to the Stability Pact for South-Eastern Europe (paragraph 10 iii and v), it should be noted that the sport sector of the Council of Europe has already worked and is continuing to do so in South East Europe. The example of the CDDS Action Plan for Bosnia and Herzegovina on rehabilitation for the disabled through sport showed clearly that sports programmes can act as a means to integrate and build confidence between ethnic groups and ease political tensions. It is the Committee of Ministers' conviction that sport can play a useful role within the Stability Pact.
5. With regard to promoting sport as part of educational programmes for refugees and displaced persons (paragraph 10 iv), it is to be noted that throughout greater Europe today there are some seven million refugees and displaced people. While only a certain percentage live in camps or temporary accommodation, sport in these circumstances can play an important role in combating physical and mental distress and providing a structure to life. As mentioned in paragraph 8, new programmes are planned to make sport and games for children and young people a distinct part of aid programmes for these groups. The CDDS project "Ballons Rouges" is a starting point for this.
6. With regard to co-operation with the European Union (paragraph 10 vi), the Committee of Ministers is encouraging member countries to contribute to the 2004 European Year of Education through Sport, particularly in the light of the follow-up to the 16th Informal Meeting of Ministers responsible for Sport in Warsaw on 12 and 13 September 2002. The CDDS is also planning active co-operation in this field.

7. The Committee of Ministers would stress the growing importance of both the sports Conventions drafted under its auspices. There is increasing emphasis on the anti-doping work throughout Europe and the Council of Europe has been an involved partner in the setting-up, establishment and the first 30 months of the existence of the World Anti-Doping Agency (WADA).
8. Hooliganism at sports events is unfortunately a phenomenon that is extending to countries that have not previously experienced this problem. The competence of the Council of Europe in this area was recognised by both Korea and Japan who sent delegations to a meeting in Strasbourg, organised by the Sport Department, to discuss this question prior to this year's World Cup held in their countries.
9. Finally the Committee of Ministers would stress the importance and the success of its programme of monitoring activities, both evaluation and advisory visits, carried out on the European Sports Charter and the two Conventions. The "Compliance with Commitments" project has already been used by 15 countries to implement effectively one or more of the three texts. Nonetheless, the Committee of Ministers is obliged to recognise that, given budgetary restrictions, it will not be possible to meet the current 35 outstanding requests for visits within a reasonable timescale.?

15.17. Reply to Parliamentary Assembly Recommendation 1566 (2002) on European cultural co-operation and the future role of the Assembly
Adopted by the Committee of Ministers at their 804th meeting on 11 July 2002

The Deputies
concerning Recommendation 1566 (2002) on European cultural co-operation and the future role of the Assembly
1. decided to bring it to the attention of their governments;
2. decided to communicate it to the European Union, to UNESCO and to OECD for information;
3. decided to communicate it to the Committee for the Development of Sport (CDDS), to the European Steering Committee for Youth (CDEJ), and to the Steering Committee on the Mass Media (CDMM) for information;
4. decided to communicate it to the Steering Committee for Education (CD-ED), to the Steering Committee for Higher Education and Research (CD-ESR), to the Steering Committee for Culture (CDCULT) and to the Steering Committee for Cultural Heritage (CDPAT), so they can take account of it in their work.
5. invited their Rapporteur Group on Education, Culture, Sport, Youth and Environment (GR-C) to prepare a draft reply for adoption at one of their forthcoming meetings.

15.18. Resolution III on European Sports Cooperation during the period 2004-2008

The European Ministers responsible for Sport, meeting in Budapest for their 10th Conference from 14-15 October 2004:
Bearing in mind that this conference takes place during the 50th anniversary of the European Cultural Convention, on the basis of which, and over many years, the Council of Europe has provided the platform for intergovernmental co-operation on questions related to sport;
Recognising that this co-operation, covering the whole continent, has led to the adoption of key texts for national and international sports policies, including three treaties and the Euro-

pean Sports Charter, and numerous texts showing the contribution of sport to modern society;
Agreeing that this "acquis" provides a sound basis for developing future sports co-operation programmes in the Council of Europe;
Considering that the 3rd Summit of the Council of Europe would be a timely occasion to adopt such programmes;
Noting with pleasure the recent enlargement of the European Union and the adoption of the draft constitutional Treaty and, in particular, Article III-282 covering education, youth, sport and vocational training, which sets the framework for promoting sporting values and the education and social potential of sport in co-operation with the Council of Europe;
Reaffirming in this context the importance for the future of European sports co-operation of close ties between the European Union and the Council of Europe;
Stressing the importance and significance of sport in modern society, notably from the political, social, cultural and economic perspectives;
Welcoming the European Union and the Council of Europe's co-operation in the field of sport and, in particular, the "European Crossroads – Sport, Front Door to Democracy" – the project to mark the European Year of Education through Sport (EYES 2004);
Recalling the Final Declaration of the Second Summit of Heads of State and Government of the Council of Europe (Strasbourg, 10-11 October 1997) which specifically welcomes the development of co-operation with other European organisations, and in particular the European Union;
Stressing the importance of avoiding overlapping of activities between the work programmes of the European Union and the Council of Europe in the area of sport;
Convinced that there is a need to identify possible new ways of co-operation between the two institutions in the field of sport.

Chapter 16
FACILITIES

16.1. Recommendation No. R (83) 6 of the Committee of Ministers to member states on Energy-Saving Measures in Sports Facilities
Adopted by the Committee of Ministers on 21 June 1983

The Committee of Ministers, under the terms of Article 15b of the Statute of the Council of Europe,
Recalling its Resolution (76) 41 on the principles for a policy of sport for all ("The European Spc for All Charter");
Bearing in mind that all member states have felt the need to conduct energy-saving programmes;
Noting that energy consumption in sports facilities represents an appreciable part of the total nation energy consumption in the member states;
Considering that the requirement to reduce energy consumption must not have as a direct or indirect consequence a lessening of opportunities to participate in sport, nor imperil the achievements of "Sport for All" gained over the past fifteen years;
Convinced that energy-saving measures could contribute to reducing the running costs of each sports facility without having a detrimental effect on participation rates in sport, nor on the comfort of the users of these facilities;
Considering that the implementation of effective energy-saving measures will help to make it possible to maintain existing staffing levels in sports facilities, to the benefit of the public;
Bearing in mind the need to share experiences in the member states so that each may better ensure the implementation and application of specific energy-saving measures for sports facilities.
Recommends the governments of member states:

i. to take the action set forth in Part I.A of this Recommendation;
ii. bring to the attention of, and encourage the implementation by, local authorities the series of energy-saving measures set forth in Part I.B of this Recommendation;
iii. bring to the attention of, and encourage the implementation by, managers of sports facilities sports organisations and participants, and designers and architects of sports facilities the series of energy-saving measures set forth in Parts II.A, II.B and II.C respectively of this recommendation;
iv. ensure a wide dissemination among all interested parties of this recommendation and take all other steps that may be appropriate for encouraging its implementation;
v. provide the Secretary General of the Council of Europe with information on developments and results on energy-saving measures in sports facilities when such information may be considered to be of interest to other member states.

Part I
A. Central government
A.I. Policy Aspects
a. Finance
1. Governments should encourage the adoption of a step-by-step approach by those considering capital investment in energy-saving measures:

i. implementation first of measures requiring little or no capital expense;
ii. consideration of other measures only after examining their cost effectiveness;
iii. basing proposals on evidence of achievable savings.

2. Governmental consideration should be given to the means (central agencies, committees, etc.) and to the methods (grants, loans, etc.) of financing the installation in sports facilities of cost-effective energy-saving measures as set Out in the table at Appendix 1 to this recommendation. Loans might be repaid at the rate of the anticipated savings to be derived from the installation of such measures.

b. Publicity
Governments should promote a general awareness of energy-saving possibilities in sports facilities directed towards sports participants and sports organisations, local authorities, managers and architects and designers. A travelling exhibition on different kinds of public facilities, designed especially for local authorities, is advised.
The initiation of a national "good energy management award" competition should be considered.

c. Information
Governments should sponsor the creation of a comprehensive and objective source of information on special energy-saving measures and appliances. Independent testing of claims made for certain appliances should be arranged.

d. Research and experience
Governments should encourage future research and development, including by industry, into alternative sources of energy using to the greatest advantage each member states own natural environment, climate and alternative energy sources. An experimental and testing programme is advised.
Governments should also consider ways in which the experience gained by managers and local authorities in energy-saving measures may be transmitted to designers and architects so that acquired experience is not lost.

A.II. Technical Aspects

a. Standardised units of measurement
Governments should encourage the adoption in their countries of the standardised unit of measuring energy consumption in indoor and outdoor swimming pools. halls and gymnasia and ice-skating facilities mentioned in Appendix II to this recommendation (that is, kilowatt-hours per square metre of usable activity space per year). Guidelines for the use of this unit are also set out in Appendix II.
On the basis of this standardised unit, governments should encourage the establishing of energy-saving measures permitting comparisons, the working out of norms and the international exchange of experience.

b. Advice and counsel
Governments should envisage the creation of a central co-ordinating commission on energy saving in sports facilities to provide an advisory service to those who run sports facilities. Amongst the tasks of this commission should be the creation of diagnostic teams of independent experts to help local authorities take appropriate measures, to provide advice to managers and sports clubs, to compare local performances with national norms and to prepare draft building regulations for new sports facilities which take account of their specific charac-

ter and which incorporate energy-saving measures (for example double glazing, insulation index, etc.). It should also give advice on methods of financing the introduction of energy-saving measures.

A.III. Education for Managers

Training

Governments should aim at instituting an appropriate national programme of initial management training (at least one year) for managers of sports facilities containing elements on energy-saving principles reflecting their relative importance.

Governments should take steps so that adequate in-service and refresher training courses on energy-saving measures in sports facilities are provided, for example for leaders of such courses.

B. Local government

Local authorities should establish energy-saving measures in sports facilities so that, inter alia, the provision of an adequate number of sports facilities necessary to a good community life is not harmed.

B.I. Technical Aspects

a. New facilities

1. When planning for a new sports facility, local authorities should in particular consider the contribution to energy saving that may be made by natural resources, existing energy supplies (such as waste heat from industry), or by combining facilities such as swimming pools and ice rinks.
2. Local authorities should require that the design plans contain:
   - an estimate of the likely annual energy consumption;
   - a description of energy-saving measures incorporated in the design.

   The estimate should be based on the standardised unit of measurement referred to under Part A.II.a of this recommendation and, if too divergent from any relevant norm, consequent modifications made as appropriate.

b. Existing facilities.

Local authorities should make provision to include energy-saving measures in existing sports facilities The table at Appendix T may help in determining what measures are appropriate and rational for each type of facility. The following order of priority is recommended:

i. improving immediate operational efficiency without additional investment;

ii. making minor adaptations giving short-term savings (simple measures);

iii. renewing technical plant and improving equipment giving long-term savings (more costly measures).

B.II. Training of Managers and Other Staff

1. Local authorities should ensure that all managers of sports facilities in their employment are fully aware of energy-saving possibilities and measures and are competent to oversee their introduction. They should ensure that managers also train the staff of facilities in energy saving.

2. They should appoint managers on the basis of qualifications and experience, including an assessment of their training in energy saving.
3. They should ensure that managers have access to information, new techniques available and that experience and knowledge acquired is adequately disseminated.
4. They should aim to ensure that the costs of training programmes and courses are recouped in energy-saving economics realised.

Part II

A. Managers of sports facilities

Managers should undertake a comprehensive examination of how energy consumption in the facilities they run could be reduced. They should make appropriate proposals for energy saving to their local authorities.

In pursuing energy saving, managers should follow the guidelines set out below:

1. Make the best and most efficient use of the facility and the machinery installed there (for example control adjustments, proper servicing).
2. Prepare plans for preventive maintenance to avoid, as far as possible, unexpected costly repair or capital expenditure.
3. Analyse present energy costs in the facility (heating, lighting. ventilation, water treatment, other machinery, staff costs, material costs).
4. Analyse the real use made of the facility (for example peak hours. activity sequences, etc.).
5. Review energy needs and practices in the light of the real use. the appropriateness of the machinery to the use, and adapt or modify when necessary and possible (for example capacity of boilers).
6. Install low-cost, energy-saving services (such as time-clocks, simple pool blankets).
7. Review management and use of the sports facility from the energy-saving point of view (for example timetables, ventilation needs, keeping temperatures as low as possible in the light of the activity, avoiding unnecessary changes in temperature).
8. After implementing the above measures, arrange for cost-benefit studies of possible major improvements (such as insulation, heat pumps, etc.).
9. Keep informed and up to date on energy-saving measures and consider how they may be applied to the facility.

B. Sports organisations and participants

Sports organisations and participants should consider ways in which they can contribute to energy-saving measures, as a matter of mutual interest, for example and in particular:

- by co-operating in the operation of energy-saving measures;
- by re-examining and keeping as low as possible their specific sporting needs which entail energy consumption – such as ambient temperature requirements at various levels of ability and play.

C. Designers and architects

Designers and architects should seek the most rational design of sports facilities from an energy-saving point of view. In this respect. they should take into account the results of the research and the experience referred to in Part 1, A.1.d, of this recommendation.

Appendix I
Table of energy-saving measures for sports facilities and their cost effectiveness
[...]

Appendix II
Standardisation of units of measurement of energy consumption in sports facilities
Definition

1. The average energy consumption of indoor and outdoor pools. halls. gymnasia and other "dry" facilities, and ice-skating facilities should be established on the basis of kilowatt/hours per square metre of usable activity space per year.
2. This measure will allow the energy performance of different facilities to be compared, whether in one country or several countries. Obviously, for each country there will be a range of figures and an average figure. The average will vary according to the nature of the facility and the location of the country.

Reasons for Choosing this Unit

3. The unit must be international and so money units cannot be used because of the variation of fuel prices from one country to another. The best unit is a unit of energy because this can be converted into money for any fuel in any country. It will also be independent of changes in fuel prices and can be used with reference to energy-saving measures. The kilowatt/hour (kWh) is a well-understood international unit.
4. Second, the unit of energy use should be related to the area of usable activity space in a facility, that is the pool water area, the sports space area, or icepad area. The sports activity space determines the total size and volume of a sports facility according to standard guidelines which exist in each country. For example, the area of the pool water determines the number of changing spaces and showers, and the number of people who can use the pool at one time.
5. The total energy used in one year should be calculated. This allows for variation of weather throughout the year and should allow annual energy budgets to be estimated – and therefore annual fuel bills – at the design stage. There will be a slight problem with outdoor Pools which may only be open for four or five months per year, but for the sake of consistency an annual figure for outdoor Pools should be calculated as for all other facilities.

Calculation of Basic Figures

6. The total energy consumption per square metre of activity space per year for each type of facility will be the sum of 6a to 6.e, and the sum of 6f to 6.h.
   - 6.1 Fabric losses, that is energy lost through the walls. roof, and floor of the building.
   - 6.2 Spare heating and ventilation (fresh air inflow and exchange rate).
   - 6.3 Domestic hot water heating, that is hot water used directly by participants in showers and wash-hand basins.
   - 6.4 Electricity, for lighting and power (for pumps, fan motors, etc.).
   - 6.5 Other losses, for example in kitchens, offices, etc.
   - 6.6 Pool water heating.
   - 6.7 Refrigeration (for ice rinks).
   - 6.8 Saunas.
7. These consumptions should be calculated for facilities designed in accordance with the standard codes in each country with no incorporated energy-saving measures unless

these are mandatory (for example wall and roof insulation). In addition to these basic figures, the essential parameters on which the figures are based should be stated. They will be:

7.1 Designed indoor temperatures and outdoor average temperatures, in degrees Celsius, and temperature of pool water.

7.2 The amount of time for which the building is open for use, in hours per year (out of a standard total of 365 x 24 = 8760 hours maximum).

7.3 The designed relative humidity.

7.4 Procedures used when closed (complete stoppage, antifreeze, etc.).

Utilisation of the Basic Figures

8. The calculation of the basic figures will make plain the amount of energy used in different types of facility and the proportion of this total used in different ways. Therefore it will:

8.1 Show where effort should be concentrated in order to make the greatest savings of energy.

8.2 Allow the total consumption of energy in sports facilities in a country to be estimated if the total area of activity space is known.

8.3 Allow a basic target for energy use in new facilities to be established.

8.4 Allow comparison of different facilities of a similar type in one country or in several countries.

8.5 Provide basic information for the cost / benefit analysis of energy-saving measures and techniques.

Chapter 17
FREE FIGHTING

17.1. Recommendation No. R (99) 11 of the Committee of Ministers to Member States on the Prohibition of Free Fighting Contests, Such As Cage Fighting

Adopted by the Committee of Ministers on 22 April 1999, at the 669th meeting of the Ministers' Deputies

The Committee of Ministers, under the terms of Article 15.b of the Statute of the Council of Europe,

Considering that the aim of the Council of Europe is to achieve a greater unity among its members for the purpose of safeguarding and realising the ideals and principles which are their common heritage and facilitating their economic and social progress, and that this aim may be pursued, inter alia, through common action in cultural matters;

Having regard to the Convention for the Protection of Human Rights and Fundamental Freedoms, and in particular Article 3, which states that "no one shall be subjected to torture or inhuman or to degrading treatment or punishment", and Article 8, from which it follows that the Contracting Parties should protect the physical integrity of persons within their jurisdiction;

Recalling Recommendation 963 (1983) of the Parliamentary Assembly on cultural and educational means of reducing violence, and the European Convention on Spectator Violence and Misbehaviour at Sports Events and in particular at Football Matches (1985);

Having regard to the ethical values and the role of sport in social integration, reaffirmed by the European Ministers of Sport at their 15th informal meeting (Nicosia, 1998), and their desire to see free fighting contests banned;

Bearing in mind its previous Recommendation No. R (92) 13 on the European Sports Charter, and in particular Article 1.ii of the charter which aims to protect sport, sportsmen and sportswomen from the dangers of "practices that are abusive or debasing";

Considering that, if violence in society is to be curbed, it must be combated in all its forms;

Being convinced that the member States of the Council of Europe should be in the forefront of efforts to prevent such violence;

Concerned by the growth of the phenomenon of so-called "sporting" violence as entertainment, as for example in the case of free fights;

Noting that cage fighting is wrongly promoted by its instigators as a sport or as one of the martial arts, but that, in reality, unlike sport and the martial arts, it is not governed by proper rules;

Considering that fighting contests such as cage fighting cannot be regarded as a sport and that it constitutes a danger to spectators, jeopardises the health of the contestants and has connections with unlawful activities, particularly gambling;

Considering that violence and barbarous and savage acts perpetrated in the name of sport have no social value in a civilised society which respects human rights,

Recommends that governments of the member States undertake all necessary measures to prohibit and prevent free fighting contests such as cage fighting;

Instructs the Secretary General to bring this recommendation to the attention of the governments of those States Parties to the European Cultural Convention that are not members of the Council of Europe.

Chapter 18
GOOD GOVERNANCE

18.1. Good Governance in Sports NGOs – Strasbourg, 6-7 May 2003

Conclusions
By Margaret Talbot (UK), Rapporteur General
We are on the last lap now and thank you for your stamina. George Walker said that our programme was like a triathlon: this is the last straight for the running side of that. If we are running a little bit slowly it is because we have seen so much in the two days we have been here. I do not wish to spend a lot of time on conclusions but I do want to draw some threads together and to reinforce this recognition that sport is a significant sector of NGO activity in almost all European countries and quite often the largest NGO sector in a country.

- Sport recognised to be a significant sector of NGO activity in almost all European countries – often the largest
- Sport therefore an important means of engaging people in active citizenship, enacting democratic principles in everyday activities
- General commitment of sport NGOs at national level to principles of good governance – democratic participation, transparency, accountability

I was in Northern Ireland recently and they were very pleased because sport had just taken over from religion as the most important area of volunteering. That is an interesting trend in a country where the church is so powerful. Therefore sport is an interesting means of engaging people in this active citizenship which is important to democratic principles so that they actually enact democratic principles in everyday activities although most of them are probably not aware of it.

Then there is the general commitment of sports NGOs at the national level to these principles. At least that has been the rhetoric that we have heard during the last two days and most of us here do believe that democratic principles are important enough that we should enact them. Of course that means that in terms of umbrella organisations perhaps we should be showing by example that the federation should be doing this too.

- National umbrella sports organisations can play an important role in helping Sports Federations and their clubs build the understanding, knowledge and confidence to embrace principles of good governance
- The challenge varies, according to countries' situations – new democracies, culture/structures
- Most important factor the willingness or commitment of leadership to principles of good governance in practice. Barriers of vested interest

There was lots of discussion about how national umbrella sports organisations can play this important role in helping the national federations and their clubs to build up the understanding and the knowledge and the confidence to embrace these principles. Sometimes we forget this issue of confidence. It may be that people know in their heads of the process of building the principles into the practice of everyday club management and so forth.

Of course the other thing we have heard so many times and particularly yesterday in the group discussions is how much the challenge varies according to the situations of in the particular countries – one's own situation. The new democracies almost have an advantage because of them starting anew, whereas some of the countries with long-established sport systems are suffering from a somewhat old-fashioned way of putting together statutes, as Michael has just been discussing about some of our sports in the UK. Also one delegate yesterday, when talking about this point, said, “Yes, we have new structures, but we have the same people in the new structures who were in the old structures” – so the mindset is the same. So we have huge variations in cultures, structures, mindset and so on.

Of course the most important factor is the commitment or willingness of the leadership to these principles and many people have referred to the barriers of vested interests and the inherent conservatism of some of our NGOs. I would like to give you a little example of this.

I have worked virtually all my life to try to forward progress in sports equity and particularly gender equity. I worked for sixteen years in a Catholic college in northern England where the college priest ran the college cricket team. We had two very talented women players who were of country level, one of whom was a wicket keeper and they are very valuable people indeed. He would not let them play and I used to talk to him about this and he said to me one day, “Margaret, I am all for women in the priesthood, but this is sport”. That says so much about the conservatism of sport but the barriers of vested interest are very strong in some of our NGOs and the way in which they protect old practice because that is the way it has always been done. The Canadians have a really good way of asking a question about that place of women in organisations in particular. They just have a motto: “Ask why and change it”.

- Different kinds of NGO infrastructure are desirable, possible, practicable, in different countries
- Effectiveness depends on recognition of collective functions (many at national level)
- Funding (especially for Confederations) a crucial issue (less so for NOCs)
- Issues of independence when governments provide funding for sports NGOs

Again, as we have heard this morning, different kinds NGO infrastructure are desirable and practicable in different countries and we have to recognise that there is no one model but the principles do allow us a common framework which is seen as particularly problematic for federations but less so for NOCs. I think this an area that has been enriched by the presentations this morning and the ideas it may have given some of you on the whole issue of independence. Can federations and confederations be independent? Can they be autonomous when they receive government funding? I think this is a particular issue that we need to address and it would be very useful for NGOs and the CDDS to address it together.

- NGOs need to recognise / identify the value of their own assets, eg. collective power, membership databases, intellectual / technical capital
- NGOs consider how they can diversify and increase their sources of income
- NGOs can learn much from each other – need to share good practice, experiences
- Basic data very important – NGOs need to know how many people and organisations they represent – and how they communicate with them

Coming back to this issue of funding, NGOs need to recognise and identify the value of their own assets. Quite often they do not understand the value of their own database, for instance, their collective power and their intellectual and technical capital. We saw that at the Manchester Commonwealth Games last year in Britain where the 10,000 volunteers used showed how important that technical capital was for running the events and without it the Games would never have happened. NGOs need then to look at how they can diversify and increase their income and we have heard a lot about that at this morning's sessions.

I think we need to look at ways of helping each other with our ideas on that because we can learn a great deal from each other I often think if people were shut together in a room you would not need a seminar, you would just actually need people to talk together. Then going back to where we started with the basic data, it is very important that NGOs have this data or have access to the data. They need to know how many people and how many organisations they represent and how they communicate with them because if they are claiming to be representative of sport then they have to show that they really are.

Practical measures and recommendations

For the CDDS

- Publish list of definitions – "sport" (as in the European Sports Charter), national umbrella organisation, sports federation, sports club, etc.
- Work with ENGSO to agree on definitions and functions

What I have tried to do here is to make recommendations, first of all for the CDDS. I guess that for the CDDS the first thing is to recognise the value of what they already have. Several people have asked what we mean by sport anyway and, as John Scott has said, we do have a definition within the European Sports Charter. However, I think we do need some more precise definition of what a federation, confederation umbrella organisation, or sports club etc. are and maybe it would be useful to work with ENGSO to agree on these definitions, so that we have a common language as a base for these common ideas.

- Provide list of existing resources / guidance / frameworks

(Need better knowledge of these – no need to spend valuable time re-doing work which has been previously done)

- Need constant updates for new people in GOs and NGOs, eg. Charter, Code of Ethics

Secondly, the CDDS should produce a list of their existing resources and guidance and frameworks and make it more generally available. I think that some of the questions that have come up during discussions could have been pre-empted if there had been access to that kind of material. So that we do not keep re-doing what has already been done before. I know that John is particularly keen on raising the level of our discussion during his chairmanship rather than going back to basics each time. This means constant updating for new people in both government and non-governmental organisations so that they are aware of what is available.

- Discuss ways of sharing good practice, good ideas, between NGOs
- Find ways of alerting NGOs to governmental concern & potential intervention – work more pro-actively with ENGSO

The CDDS should also discuss ways of sharing good practice and good ideas between NGOs and ways of alerting NGOs to governmental concern and potential intervention. It is also possible that more proactive work with ENGSO would be useful, because we do have an umbrella organisation at European level, which is capable of working with CDDS.

- Consider the data which the questionnaire requested – number of federations, numbers of sports clubs and their members, sports leaders (volunteers?)
- Important for demonstrating value of NGOs
- What about yourselves as representatives of member countries? There are responsibilities here too

This is one problem area where we probably need a definition aswell. By volunteers does it mean volunteers or does it mean paid officers? What does it mean? Does it mean coaches? We need to know and then need to look to the value of that data for looking at the value of the NGOS themselves. If you are going to convince governments that NGOs merit support then you need to demonstrate what their value is.

- Consider the functions which national umbrella organisations could play – and whether your current structures allow this
- Is there a need for greater co-operation between them, or even mergers?

Member countries should also look at the functions which the national umbrella organisations could play and there is quite a long list of functions which were identified in the discussion groups yesterday which must be included in the final report on this seminar because they are actually quite varied but they illustrate the collective power of confederations and NOCs when they embrace this agenda of collective good of sport. Also we need to ask if your current structures allow those functions to be fulfilled.

Is there a need for greater co-operation between national structures or even a merger? André-Noël referred to the different States' model of structures and the way in which several countries had several organisations or structures with perhaps some confusion between them at times.

How can the whole range of federations be helped to become more effective and demonstrate and how can this democratic practice be shared at national level? So there is a cascade coming through so what can be done at European level and what can be done at national level.

For the 2004 Conference of Ministers

What about the 2004 Ministerial Conference? I think they need a session on the value of NGO Sport and that is another reason for collecting this data. If we could collect that data on the value of NGO Sport across European that could be a fairly useful session which would focus the questioning of Ministers, and therefore the need to support NGO Sport. We could give examples of good practice of good governance and value for money and particularly data on the values of volunteering.

- Session on the value of NGO Sport, and the need to support it. Examples of progress towards good governance, value for money
- Data on value of volunteering

My organisation in Britain has just commissioned a piece of research which is looking at the existing research on volunteering across seven sources. This means that we have quite robust data and have some wonderful pieces of information from that. For instance the total value of sports volunteers in the UK is worth 108,000 full-time workers, which are in turn worth about 1.6 billion pounds sterling every year. That is quite a nice piece of information. That is based on 1996 prices so it is already out of date and is worth 2 billion by current prices so these sorts of things do focus attention and they are quite useful for dealing with Ministers.

- Which aspects of "good governance" do Ministers particularly wish to see developing among sports NGOs?
- What measures will governments put into place to help NGOs implement them?

On the other hand, ask the Ministers which aspects of good governance do they wish to see developing among the sports NGOs and what are they going to do to help it happen. Is it simply a question of the NGOs just having these principles thrown at them and being expected to comply or are the Ministers going to try to put into place some machinery for helping and supporting that process? There is a particular interest in trying to focus Ministers' interest on that issue.

- Recognition of sports NGO autonomy, even when financial support provided
- Should Ministers appoint officers of federations/confederations when they provide funding?
- Do governments consult early enough?

Maybe we should focus on helping them recognise the autonomy of sports NGOs even when financial support is provided, and maybe a specific question to put is: "Should Ministers be appointing officers of federations and confederations even when they do provide funding?" – as some countries have indicated during the seminar or in their questionnaires.

- Do governments consult at all and enough and do they consult early enough with the NGO sector?

- What are the fiscal measures which governments can take to help confederations, federations & clubs become more viable and independent? (eg. tax benefits, local taxes, access to lottery income)
- What are the fiscal measures which governments can take to help confederations, federations and their clubs become more viable and financially independent?

For me it makes no sense to have money leaking out of the NGO system and then they have to apply for grants to get some money back. It would be much better if we could keep the money in the system in the first place so I was very interested to hear Michael talk about the French framework which would be very useful in Britain. So tax benefits, local taxes and access to lottery funding and the whole issue of VAT might be looked at.

- What measures can Ministers consider which would support volunteers?

eg. financial bonds to cover insurance costs / liability, central structures to provide free police checks (for child protection), expert help in fund-raising, use of federations' assets (eg. databases, intellectual capital).

Lastly what measures can the Ministers consider that would support volunteers? The whole basis of the NGO sector is based on the volunteer effort and if we can not retain it and adjust this effectively then it is going to make our organisations even more fragile than they are now. In Western Australia and Nova Scotia the provincial governments have offered financial bonds to cover insurance liability for volunteers, so that volunteers would never be threatened with criminal action unless it could be proven that there was intent. So, in the case of an accident, in terms of when one has taken all reasonable precautions and you are covered by your federations, codes of conduct and practice, you would not be taken to court and this is one of the volunteer's greatest fears.

Central police structures provide free police checks for child protection and these kinds of infrastructure measures can be taken to help volunteers.

Expert help in fund-raising was suggested several times yesterday and the use of federations' assets, to which I have already referred, can help in becoming more financially independent.

So those are the suggestions for recommendations across those three groups – yourselves the NGOs, the CDDS and the Ministerial Conference next year and I would be very interested to hear other suggestions which can be fed into those.

Summary of the Conclusions

- Sport is recognised to be a significant sector of NGO activity in almost all European countries – often the largest
- Sport is, therefore, an important means of engaging people in active citizenship, enacting democratic principles in everyday activities
- General commitment of sports NGOs at national level to principles of good governance – democratic participation, transparency, accountability, etc.
- National umbrella sports organisations can play an important role in helping Sports Federations and their clubs build the understanding, knowledge and confidence to embrace principles of good governance
- The challenge varies, according to countries' situations – new democracies, culture / structures
- Most important factor is the willingness or commitment of the leadership to principles of good governance in practice; barriers of vested interest
- Different kinds of NGO infrastructure are desirable, possible, practicable, in different countries
- Effectiveness depends on recognition of collective functions (many at national level)

- Funding (especially for confederations) is a crucial issue (less so for NOCs).
- Issues of independence arise when governments provide funding for sports NGOs
- NGOs need to recognise/identify the value of their own assets, e.g. collective power, membership databases, intellectual / technical capital
- NGOs should consider how they can diversify and increase their sources of income
- NGOs can learn much from each other – need to share good practice, experiences
- Basic data are very important – NGOs need to know how many people and organisations they represent – and how they communicate with them

Practical measures and recommendations

For the CDDS:

- Compile and publish list of definitions – "sport" (refer to ESC). Also definitions of national umbrella organisation, sports federation, sports club, etc.
- Work with ENGSO to agree on definitions and functions
- Provide list of existing resources / guidance / frameworks (Need better knowledge of these – no need to spend valuable time re-doing work which has been previously done)
- Need constant updates for new people in GOs and NGOs, eg. Charter, Code of Ethics
- Discuss ways of sharing good practice, good ideas, between NGOs; ways of alerting NGOs to governmental concern and potential intervention – work more proactively with ENGSO

For member countries:

- Consider the data which the questionnaire requested – number of federations, numbers of sports clubs and their members, sports leaders (=volunteers?) – important for demonstrating value of NGOs
- Consider the functions which national umbrella organisations could play – and whether your current structures allow this. Is there a need for greater co-operation between them, or even a merger?
- How can the whole range of federations be helped to become more effective and democratic? How can the best practice be shared?

For the Conference of European Ministers responsible for Sport in 2004:

- Session on the value of NGO sport, and the need to support it, examples of progress towards good governance, value for money, data on value of volunteering
- Which aspects of "good governance" do Ministers particularly wish to see developing among sports NGOs? What measures will governments put into place to help NGOs implement them?
- Recognition of sports NGO autonomy, even when financial support provided. Should Ministers appoint officers of federations / confederations when they provide funding? Do governments consult early enough?
- What are the fiscal measures which governments can take to help confederations, federations and clubs become more viable and independent? (eg. tax benefits, local taxes, access to lottery income)
- What measures can Ministers consider which would support volunteers? eg financial bonds to cover insurance costs / liability; central structures to provide free police checks (for child protection); expert help in fund-raising, use of federations' assets (eg databases, intellectual capital)

Additional pointers towards future work raised by participants during discussion
Legislation
This area had aroused considerable interest and one point that had been stressed was the need for NGOs to be aware of both national and local legislation that affected them. This could point towards a drive towards education in this area.
The seminar had underlined the importance of a second revised edition of the study on sports legislation by André-Noël Chaker, which was now underway.
Some countries had voiced a request for a model sports law but countries differed so much that this was neither readily possible nor particularly desirable. It was thought that the need was more for model policies and basic principles that could be identified no matter what type of system was adopted.
The European Sports Charter could provide a good resource when framing a sports law. However, new areas, not mentioned in the ESC such as dispute resolution, had arisen which legislation would have to take into account. There was also growing consciousness of policies needed to help elite athletes adapt to other careers.
As shown by Mr Chaker, some countries had sports laws and some did not. It was stressed that a law is a defence mechanism if relations between NGOs and government authorities are not good at some later date.

Other areas
The question arose as to whether the promotion of an autonomous sports system was a desirable aim and, if so, what means could be used to achieve this.
NGOs could be asked to include information on governance in their annual reports which would keep the area to the fore. They could also add this area to their international strategy if they have one.
There was also the suggestion that an international database could be set up on the large sports NGOs – their governance, financial resources, etc.

18.2. Resolution on the Principles of Good Governance in Sport
10th Conference of European Ministers responsible for Sport , Budapest, Hungary, 14-15 October 2004

Resolution I
On The Principles of Good Governance in Sport
The European Ministers responsible for Sport, meeting in Budapest for their 10th Conference from 14 to 15 October 2004:
Convinced that the need existed to identify the underlying principles, which should be incorporated into a comprehensive policy for sport and good governance;
Conscious of the substantial work done previously by the Committee for the Development of Sport in developing policies designed to promote the principles of good governance in sport;
Welcoming the publication of the study by A-N Chaker on Good Governance in Sport, a European Survey;
Considering that non-governmental sports organisations are an essential basis for the development and continued survival of democratic sport, and also make a unique contribution to the realisation of societies based on the rule of law, pluralist democracy and respect for human rights – which are the guiding principles of the Council of Europe;
Recalling that "The Fundamental Principles on the Status of Non-Governmental Organisations in Europe" of 13 November 2002 provide a sound basis for governing the status of non- governmental organisations in Europe;

Bearing in mind the European Non Governmental Sports Organisation's (ENGSO) recommendation on transparency and credibility in sports organisations;
Reaffirming their commitment to the principles of good governance in sport, and agreeing that the implementation of these principles such as democracy, accountability, fairness, solidarity and transparency are keys to widening popularity of sport and strengthening the position of sports NGOs in civil society;
Bearing in mind the opinion of the Council of Europe Group of States against Corruption (GRECO) on corruption in sport;
Also recalling the Final Declaration of the Second Summit of Heads of State and Government of the Council of Europe (Strasbourg, 10-11 October 1997) which expresses the standard setting role of the Council of Europe, in particular, to seek common responses to the challenges posed by the growth in corruption;
Stressing their belief that the consistent application of the principles of good governance in sport would be a significant factor in helping to eradicate corruption in sport;
Resolve to:
Encourage all institutions, non-governmental organisations and other groups concerned in sport to devise, implement, strengthen and support initiatives based on the principles of good governance in sport, which include as minimum:

- Democratic structures based on clear electoral procedures open to the membership;
- Professional organisation and management, with an appropriate code of ethics and procedures for dealing with conflicts of interest;
- Accountability and transparency in decision making and financial operations;
- Fairness in dealing with the membership and solidarity;
- A basis for setting an equitable partnership between the public authorities and the sports movement.

Ensure that these principles of good governance are integrated into sports policies and practices at national level and to ensure that they are effectively monitored;
Convinced that the successful implementation by sports NGOs of effective good governance policies in their organisations would help to strengthen their self governance and autonomy in matters concerning sport and would further strengthen their position in relation to public authorities based on mutual respect and trust;
Invite all sectors – non-governmental sports organisations, civil society groups and voluntary institutions – to co-operate closely with the national authorities in order to achieve and implement the principles of this Resolution;
Stress the benefits which good governance in sport can provide in promoting fair play, sport for all and its key role in preventing corruption;
Reaffirm that the nature of sport itself, based on fair play and equal competition, requires that all unethical practices and behaviours in sport should be forcefully and effectively countered;
Invite the Committee of Ministers of the Council of Europe to ask member states to address this problem at national level and to take concrete steps to reduce the possibilities of malpractices in sport.
Note that proceeds from lottery and gambling are a significant source of income for sport in most European countries, and underline the right of governments to decide national lottery and gambling policies.

Resolution II
on
a) A progress within UNESCO on preparing
a new international instrument against doping in sport;

b) Questions related to the World Anti-Doping Agency (WADA)

The European Ministers responsible for Sport, meeting in Budapest for their 10th Conference on 14 and 15 October 2004:

With regard to UNESCO:

Reaffirming their desire to realise quickly the important political commitments they have accepted by signing the Copenhagen Declaration on Anti-doping in Sport;

Thanking the Council of Europe for its essential contribution to helping governments to meet these commitments and other objectives in the fight against doping;

Noting with satisfaction the progress made by governments and sport organisations in anti-doping to date, in particular in relation to the recognition, governance and funding of the World Anti-Doping Agency, the acceptance of the World Anti-Doping Code, the development and implementation of the Council of Europe Anti-Doping Convention (ETS 135) and its Additional Protocol (ETS 188) and other intergovernmental co-operation on anti-doping;

Recognising the progress made within UNESCO on drafting a new international instrument against doping in sport and that this should enable many more governments worldwide to become involved in the anti-doping work in accordance with commonly agreed principles based on the World Anti-Doping Code;

Considering that the new international instrument against doping in sport should incorporate an effective monitoring system;

Stressing that the new international instrument should be in place before the Turin Winter Olympic Games in February 2006;

With regard to WADA:

Expressing their satisfaction with the way the World Anti-Doping Agency (WADA) has developed since its creation in late 1999;

Stressing the importance, in accordance with the partnership nature of WADA, of striking a balance between the representatives of public authorities and those of the Olympic Movement in positions of leadership within WADA;

Resolve:

1.1 To co-operate closely on the new draft international instrument against doping in sport at UNESCO MINEPS IV Conference in Athens (6-8 December);

1.2 To seek to ensure that the standards under the new draft international instrument conform to the purposes of the World Anti-Doping Code;

1.3 To seek to ensure that the commitments under the new draft international instrument are as close as possible to the commitments made in the existing instruments, in order to promote compatibility between the two sets of instruments and to honour the existing commitments;

1.4 To ensure that the Secretariat of the new draft instrument will be integrated in its parent organisation;

1.5 To support the implementation of an integrated solution for the monitoring of the commitments under the existing instruments and the future instrument;

1.6 To stress in this context the importance of good co-operation between the Council of Europe and Unesco;

1.7 To clarify the relationship between the draft instrument and its annexes and the World Anti-Doping Code and its International Standards.

2. To seek, in consultation and co-operation with other regions, to develop a policy for identifying the requirements that would enable the public authorities to put forward, at the right time, an agreed candidate for the Chair of the WADA Foundation Board;

Approve:

1. The designation of Minister B. Mikkelsen (Denmark) being a representative of the public authorities as a candidate for the position of interim Vice-Chair of the Foundation Board (and Executive Committee) of WADA;
2. The designation of Minister J.F. Lamour (France) as the representative of the European continent on the Executive Committee of WADA.

Take note of:
The designation of Minister B. Mikkelsen (Denmark) as representative of the European continent on the Foundation Board of WADA up until the end of 2005.
Resolution III
on European Sports Cooperation during the period 2004-2008
The European Ministers responsible for Sport, meeting in Budapest for their 10th Conference from 14-15 October 2004:
Bearing in mind that this conference takes place during the 50th anniversary of the European Cultural Convention, on the basis of which, and over many years, the Council of Europe has provided the platform for intergovernmental co-operation on questions related to sport;
Recognising that this co-operation, covering the whole continent, has led to the adoption of key texts for national and international sports policies, including three treaties and the European Sports Charter, and numerous texts showing the contribution of sport to modern society;
Agreeing that this "acquis" provides a sound basis for developing future sports co-operation programmes in the Council of Europe;
Considering that the 3rd Summit of the Council of Europe would be a timely occasion to adopt such programmes;
Noting with pleasure the recent enlargement of the European Union and the adoption of the draft constitutional Treaty and, in particular, Article III-282 covering education, youth, sport and vocational training, which sets the framework for promoting sporting values and the education and social potential of sport in co-operation with the Council of Europe;
Reaffirming in this context the importance for the future of European sports co-operation of close ties between the European Union and the Council of Europe;
Stressing the importance and significance of sport in modern society, notably from the political, social, cultural and economic perspectives;
Welcoming the European Union and the Council of Europe's co-operation in the field of sport and, in particular, the "European Crossroads – Sport, Front Door to Democracy" – the project to mark the European Year of Education through Sport (EYES 2004);
Recalling the Final Declaration of the Second Summit of Heads of State and Government of the Council of Europe (Strasbourg, 10-11 October 1997) which specifically welcomes the development of co-operation with other European organisations, and in particular the European Union;
Stressing the importance of avoiding overlapping of activities between the work programmes of the European Union and the Council of Europe in the area of sport;
Convinced that there is a need to identify possible new ways of co-operation between the two institutions in the field of sport.
Resolve to:
Ensure the promotion of complementary activities in the field of sport between the European Union and the Council of Europe;
Consider that the Council of Europe's particular role in pan-European sports co-operation is linked to the core values of the Council of Europe (Human Rights, Parliamentary Democracy and the Rule of Law) and that future work in sport should bring out this connection more

strongly; examples of such activities are combating racism, xenophobia, gender discrimination and also at promoting equal opportunity for disabled persons;

Invite the European Union and the Council of Europe to develop where appropriate partnership agreements in the field of sport;

Invite the Committee of Ministers in the context of the 3rd Summit and bearing in mind Article III-282 of the European Constitution, to ensure that the Council of Europe continues adequately to support and fund its work in sports questions, for the benefit of Europeans and of governments of member states in conformity with its own values and missions;

Accept the kind offer of the government of the Russian Federation to organise the 17th Informal Meeting of Sports Ministers at Moscow, possibly in late 2005 or 2006, in the light of international sports developments.

Congress of Local and Regional Authorities of the Council of Europe

Recommendation 144 (2004) on the prevention of violence in sport, in particular at football matches: the role of local and regional authorities

The Congress,

1. Thanks the municipality of Lisbon for its warm welcome and hospitality and the National Association of Portuguese Municipalities (ANMP) for its support in the organisation of the first conference on "the role of local and regional authorities in preventing violence at sports events, in particular football matches" (Lisbon, 23-24 June 2003);
2. Expresses satisfaction at the backing given to this conference by the Council of Europe's integrated project "Responses to violence in everyday life in a democratic society" and the close cooperation established on that occasion with the Council of Europe's Directorate of Youth and Sport (DG IV);
3. Reasserts the principles set out in its Recommendation 16 (1996) and Resolution 27 (1996) on sport and local authorities;
4. Points out that:
    a. sport fosters social integration and participation and, in this respect, makes a valuable contribution to the democratic process;
    b. sport plays an important role in promoting understanding between European citizens;
    c. sport has significant economic benefits at the local, regional and national levels;
    d. sport, an important activity in our societies, is an integral part of local community activities, and local and regional authorities should therefore endeavour to promote and support it;
5. Concerned at the violence and misbehaviour in and around stadiums and on the streets of cities hosting sports events, particularly football matches, considers that appropriate policies must be implemented to prevent such behaviour, often the result of the excessive abuse of alcohol and drugs;
6. Considers that:
    a. players and athletes contribute to the prevention of violence by their "fair play",
    b. coaches, trainers and managing directors of teams have an essential role to play in the prevention of violence;
7. Bearing in mind:
    a. the work of the Council of Europe, which for over twenty years has been promoting a global approach to the prevention of violence at sports events, and in particular;

b. the recent recommendations by the Standing Committee of the Council of Europe Convention on Spectator Violence (ETS No. 120), which highlight the greater role that should be played by local authorities in preventing violence at sports events, notably through socio-educational action and fan coaching measures;

c. the implications for local and regional authorities of the European Union's initiatives and decisions concerning police cooperation to improve safety and security at international football matches;

d. the measures devised by FIFA (the International Federation of Football Associations), UEFA (the European Union of Football Associations), national football associations and the FESU (European Forum for Urban Security);

8. Aware of the diversity of situations in the countries of Europe as regards the degree of centralisation of public policy-making (policing and prevention);

9. Underlines:

a. the major role that local and regional authorities can and must play in preventing violence at sports events, whether as regulators, coordinators of safety or security measures, owners of sports facilities, employers of the staff running those facilities, protagonists in policies for the promotion of amateur or school sport or instigators of prevention-oriented social and educational measures;

b. the importance of good cooperation between local/regional authorities and police and security services;

10. Invites the Committee of Ministers to take note of the following principles asserted at the Lisbon Conference and bring them to the attention of the Committee for the Development of Sport (CDDS), the Standing Committee of the Council of Europe Convention on Spectator Violence and the relevant ministries in the member states:

a. As regards all sports events, local and regional authorities have a fundamental role to play in preventing violence in sport:

i. preventing violence is not merely a matter for the police. It is not confined to security measures and logistics. Prevention of violence in general, and violence in sport in particular, has a significant social and educational dimension. In this connection, in view of the exclusion of certain young people, local and regional authorities can help to promote the social integration and participation of young people;

ii. before any sports competition it is essential to adopt an integrated approach whereby all the authorities and bodies involved in the smooth running of the event are encouraged to cooperate in applying a common strategy. Each party (public or private) must be made aware of its own responsibilities and those of its partners;

iii. local and regional authorities can assume the role of mediating between the diverging interests of competition and match organisers, stadium managers, football clubs, the police, fans and local inhabitants. In some countries this role has probably not been paid sufficient attention so far, and this state of affairs should now be remedied;

iv. spectators should be treated as visitors to be welcomed and entertained. Local and regional authorities should recognise fan embassies' useful role in providing spectators with assistance and information and the positive influence they can have on their behaviour;

v. measures should be taken to deal with the misbehaviour of a small minority of individuals. In some cases these measures may be very strict, but they must remain proportionate to the problem being tackled and be carefully targeted so as not to penalise the vast majority of law-abiding fans who merely wish to enjoy the sports event;

vi. local and regional authorities should strive to create a festive atmosphere not only for visitors but also for local inhabitants;

b. As regards major sports events and competitions, in particular big football matches:

i. local and regional authorities should plan the event carefully well in advance. They should, in particular, provide for appropriate means of transport to be made available at the proper time;

ii. a major competition affords local and regional authorities an opportunity to promote their city or region, to show a positive image at the national and international levels, to boost the local economy and, in the longer term, to endow themselves with new infrastructure and facilities;

11. Invites those members states which have not yet done so to ratify the Council of Europe Convention on Spectator Violence and Misbehaviour at Sports Events (ETS No. 120);

12. Invites the Committee of Ministers and the relevant ministries to continue their support for the work of the Standing Committee of the Council of Europe Convention on Spectator Violence and Misbehaviour.

18.3. Recommendation Rec(2005)8 of the Committee of Ministers to member states on the principles of good governance in sport

Adopted by the Committee of Ministers on 20 April 2005 the 924th meeting of the Ministers' Deputies

The Committee of Ministers, under the terms of Article 15.b of the Statute of the Council of Europe,

Considering that the aim of the Council of Europe is to achieve greater unity between its members for the purpose of safeguarding and realising the ideals and principles which are their common heritage, and of facilitating their economic and social progress;

Bearing in mind the Committee of Ministers' Declaration on compliance with commitments accepted by member states of the Council of Europe (Strasbourg, 10 November 1994);

Also bearing in mind the Final Declaration of the Second Summit of Heads of State and Government of the Council of Europe (Strasbourg, 10-11 October 1997) which underlines the standard setting role of the Council of Europe, in particular, to seek common responses to the challenges posed by the growth in corruption;

Bearing in mind the European Convention on the Recognition of the Legal Personality of International Non-Governmental Organisations (ETS No. 124);

Bearing in mind "The Fundamental Principles on the Status of Non-Governmental Organisations in Europe" of 13 November 2002, which provide a sound basis for governing the status of non-governmental organisations in Europe;

Bearing in mind the opinion of the Council of Europe Group of States against Corruption (GRECO) on corruption in sport (2004);

Bearing in mind the European Non-Governmental Sports Organisation's (ENGSO) Recommendation on transparency and credibility in sports organisations;

Aware of the need to identify the underlying principles which should be incorporated into a comprehensive policy for sport and good governance;

Taking into account in this respect Resolution No. 1 on the principles of good governance in sport adopted at the 10th Conference of European Ministers responsible for sport in Budapest in October 2004;

Considering that good governance in sport is a complex network of policy measures and private regulations used to promote integrity in the management of the core values of sport such as democratic, ethical, efficient and accountable sports activities; and that these measures apply equally to the public administration sector of sport and to the non-governmental sports sector;

Reaffirming that the nature of sport itself, based on fair play and equal competition, requires that all unethical practices and behaviours in sport should be forcefully and effectively countered;

Stressing their belief that the consistent application of the principles of good governance in sport would be a significant factor in helping to eradicate corruption and other malpractices in sport;

Agreeing that the implementation of the principles of good governance in sport is a key to widening popularity of sport and strengthening the position of non-governmental sports organisations in civil society; to the encouragement of sport as a vehicle for participatory, active, healthy citizens and for social and ethnic integration; and to the promotion of gender mainstreaming in sport;

Considering that non-governmental sports organisations are an essential basis for the development and continued survival of democratic sport, and also make a unique contribution to the realisation of societies based on the rule of law, pluralist democracy and respect for human rights – which are the guiding principles of the Council of Europe;

Convinced that the successful implementation by sports non-governmental organisations of effective good governance policies in their organisations would help to strengthen their self-governance and autonomy in matters concerning sport and would further strengthen their position in relation to public authorities based on mutual respect and trust,

Recommends that the governments of member states:

1. adopt effective policies and measures of good governance in sport, which include as a minimum requirement:
   - democratic structures for non-governmental sports organisations based on clear and regular electoral procedures open to the whole membership;
   - organisation and management of a professional standard, with an appropriate code of ethics and procedures for dealing with conflicts of interest;
   - accountability and transparency in decision-making and financial operations, including the open publication of yearly financial accounts duly audited;
   - fairness in dealing with membership, including gender equality and solidarity;
2. ensure that these principles of good governance are integrated into sports policies and practices at national level, both in governmental and in non-governmental structures;
3. use these principles as the basis for setting an equitable partnership between the public authorities and the sports movement;
4. call upon all national institutions, non-governmental organisations and other groups concerned in sport to devise, implement, strengthen and support initiatives based on the principles of good governance in sport;
5. invite all sectors – non-governmental sports organisations, civil society groups and voluntary institutions – to cooperate closely with the national authorities in order to achieve and implement the principles of this Recommendation;
6. set up mechanisms to monitor the implementation of good governance in sport principles, and put in place mechanisms to deal with inappropriate or unethical behaviours in sport, including prosecution where necessary.

Chapter 19
HUMANITARIAN DISASTERS

19.1. Recommendation Rec(2003)7 of the Committee of Ministers to member states on the contribution of sport to alleviating the consequences of humanitarian disasters: "Ballons rouges"
Adopted by the Committee of Ministers on 30 April 2003

The Committee of Ministers, under the terms of Article 15.b of the Statute of the Council of Europe,
Considering that the aim of the Council of Europe is to achieve a greater unity between its members, notably by means of common action in social and cultural matters;
Conscious that, at the beginning of the twenty-first century, within the member states of the Council of Europe there are more than 7 million refugees and displaced persons, including children and young people, many of whom have been living in camps or collective accommodation for long periods of time;
Realising the positive contribution that physical activities can make to the physical and psychological health and to the lifestyles of those living in difficult circumstances, for example refugees and/or displaced persons, whether inside camps, collective accommodation or in the community;
Mindful of Article 39 of the United Nations Convention on the Rights of the Child which obliges States Parties to "take all appropriate measures to promote physical and psychological recovery and social reintegration of a child victim of (...) armed conflicts";
Aware that an increasing number of humanitarian organisations working in crisis situations are now convinced that once the preliminary emergency situation has stabilised and basic necessities are assured, sporting activities and games play an important role, especially in helping children and young people cope with the trauma they have experienced and in rebuilding confidence between different groups;
Taking note of the mandated role of the United Nations High Commissioner for Refugees in providing protection and durable solutions to refugees, and in co-ordinating, together with the host governments, humanitarian responses to refugees' situations;
Noting that many humanitarian organisations and sports organisations, as well as Unesco and the European Union, have shown interest in co-operating with the Council of Europe in setting up a project to assess needs, decide on the correct help and to provide sports equipment and organise activities in situations where people, and in particular children, are suffering in the aftermath of conflicts or crises,
Recommend that the governments of member states co-operate in the setting up and functioning of this network, which has a unique role and can add positive value to relief work throughout Europe by providing recreational sport and physical activity, through the suggestions for action set out in the Appendix to this recommendation.

Instruct the Secretary General:

a. to bring this recommendation to the attention of the Parliamentary Assembly and the Congress of Local and Regional Authorities of Europe and to ask them to inform him of any follow-up;

b. to transmit this recommendation to humanitarian organisations, inviting them to co-operate with the Council of Europe in the "Ballons rouges" project for post-emergency situations in Europe, where the provision of sports activities, equipment and trainers can help refugees and/or displaced persons;

c. to ask the sports organisations already working in this area to work in partnership with the Council of Europe in setting up this project to implement the "Ballons rouges" network;

d. to invite the leading international sports associations and federations to co-operate with this network and project by offering help, be it with equipment, trainers or important related services, such as transport and distribution;

e. to request the hosting governments and their national sports associations to co-operate with the "Ballons rouges" project and network and be actively involved in the elaboration and implementation of this programme.

Appendix to Recommendation Rec (2003) 7

Target Group

The target group of the project is children and young people, living in a crisis or post-emergency situation, who would benefit from games and sporting activities to help them in coming to terms with the consequent disruption and trauma.

Aim of the Project

The aim of the project is to provide physical activities, such as sport and games, which can:

- help to recreate a structured lifestyle;
- act as a psychological aid in coping with trauma;
- rebuild confidence between different groups;
- be used as a vehicle for important education in such areas as safety (for example, avoiding land mines) and hygiene (for example, avoiding disease).

Implementation of the Project

The implementation of the project is through the creation of a network of organisations called "Ballons rouges". This network will be composed of intergovernmental and humanitarian organisations and international sports organisations and federations, and will work with the Council of Europe.

Procedure

The following procedure is foreseen either:

- at times of crisis where there are movements of refugees and displaced persons within a member state or states of the Committee for the Development of Sport;
- or when, in a post-emergency situation, there are a large number of refugees or displaced persons continuing to live in camps or collective accommodation.

At such times the humanitarian organisations that are caring for displaced persons and refugees, having assessed the situation and needs and prepared a programme which includes a target group, a blueprint for implementation and criteria for evaluation:

- shall consult with the appropriate national authorities and discuss the desirability of seeking help from the network;
- inform the Council of Europe of the resulting decision, and, if appropriate,
- ask the Council of Europe to handle the request.

The Council of Europe shall subsequently inform the "Ballons rouges" network of the need for sports equipment, trainers and transport. It will invite the national authorities of the country or countries concerned to co-operate with all parties – the intergovernmental and humanitarian organisations, the Council of Europe and the sports associations and federations by:

a. facilitating customs controls for importing sports equipment;
b. facilitating visa controls for those visiting to organise and help with sports and games programmes;
c. contacting and seeking involvement, co-operation or help in the programmes, from their own national, regional and local sports federations and associations.

The implementation of the programme will be decided and carried out under the authority of the "Ballons rouges" network.
On such an occasion other member states of the Committee for the Development of Sport are also invited to co-operate with the intergovernmental and humanitarian organisations, the Council of Europe and the sports associations and federations in offering help, whether through the offer of sports equipment, personnel such as sports trainers or financial resources.

Setting up of an emergency fund
Member states of the Committee for the Development of Sport are invited to make voluntary contributions to a special account that, under the authority of the Secretary General of the Council of Europe or his representative, can be used to:

a. provide general sports equipment;
b. arrange and pay for the transport, if necessary, of the aforesaid equipment;
c. contribute to the expenses of personnel, such as sports trainers working with refugees and/or displaced persons.

General measures
The governments of member states are invited:

a. to assist the Secretary General with information on national organisations and bodies, together with the names of individual people capable of helping this project, to be included on a contact list for the network;
b. to set aside resources in the national budget for action to be taken in such situations.

Other points
Organisations offering help may decide that their contributions and help should be made either to crisis situations or to long-term post-emergency situations.

19.2. Implementating the Ballons Rouges project
Document approved by the CDDS at its 27th Meeting, 3-4 March 2004

Introduction
Following the adoption of Recommendation Rec (2003) 7 of the Committee of Ministers to member states on the contribution of sports to alleviating the consequences of humanitarian disasters: "Ballons rouges" and the study prepared by the Secretary General's consultant, Mr Ger Wegener, the Bureau and a meeting of the Working Group on the "Ballons Rouges" project, which took place in December 2003, proposed that the Council of Europe and the CDDS should maintain and develop their direct involvement in the project. As a follow-up to those meetings, the Secretariat studied the possibility of setting up a special account for the "Ballons Rouges" for voluntary contributions and to prepare a conceptual document for consideration by the CDDS at its meeting on 3-4 March 2004.

This document reflects the discussions and decisions taken by the CDDS at that meeting.
Position of the CDDS on the implementation of the Ballons Rouges project
The CDDS:

- approved the "Ballons Rouges" project as a pilot project for three years;
- agreed to establish the "Ballons Rouges" project on the basis of a partnership agreement based on voluntary contributions and external partnerships;
- agreed to ask for the protection of the "Ballons Rouges" name as a registered trademark following the procedures recommended by the Council of Europe Legal Affairs Department;
- asked the Committee of Ministers to set up a special account for receiving the voluntary contributions for the "Ballons Rouges" project;
- subject to a favourable decision by the Committee of Ministers, agreed to set up a Management Committee represented by all the contributors to the project, to assess the progress of the "Ballons Rouges" project and decide on the future strategies and in particular to prepare for the network to function also as a rapid reaction force in case of emergency situations;
- agreed at the end of the three-year period to present a report to the Committee of Ministers, so that the Committee of Ministers can review the mandate of the "Ballons Rouges" project and decide on its future;
- agreed to encourage the governmental (and other) authorities of member countries to make voluntary contributions to the "Ballons Rouges" project;
- agreed to encourage their national sports organisations to provide the Council of Europe with the names and contact details of the potential sports leaders for "Ballons Rouges" activities.

Chapter 20
IMMIGRANTS

20.1. Resolution on Sport for Immigrants (81/4)

The European Ministers responsible for Sport, meeting from 8 to 10 April 1981 in Palma de Majorca for their 3rd Conference,

Convinced that sport is important as a means of bringing about greater participation in the life of the host society;
Anxious to see the principles of Sport for All applied to everybody, and in particular to the least privileged groups;
Having analysed and discussed means of facilitating immigrants' access to the practice of sport;
Considering that steps should be taken to make it easier for immigrants to join sports clubs as a means of contributing to their participation in sport, and thus help bring them out of their isolation;
Considering that it is the duty of all to combat, by every available means, including the mass media, schools and governmental and voluntary organisations, those factors that have an adverse effect on immigrants' participation in sport in the society where they have settled;
Considering that the mass media, immigrants' associations, self-help organisations and schools should collaborate in putting out information prepared jointly by immigrants' representatives and sports organisations in order to reflect and meet as well as possible immigrants' needs and wishes;
Considering that, for example, they should encourage the building of sports facilities in areas which have a high concentration of immigrants and are particularly deprived;
Invite non-governmental sports organisations at international, national, regional and local levels to make an effort, or to increase the efforts they are already making, to encourage participation by immigrants;
Invite all organisations in contact with immigrants – local authorities and clubs – to launch specific action programmes drawn up in collaboration with immigrants' representatives;
Request the Committee of Ministers of the Council of Europe to ask the Committee for the Development of Sport:

1. to draw up and co-ordinate an action programme for participation in sport by immigrants in conjunction with the international bodies concerned;
2. to urge national authorities which have not yet done so to set up a number of pilot schemes at local level;
3. to evaluate these pilot schemes and draw lessons from them in order to help them to spread and to strengthen their impact.

Chapter 21
INTER-CULTURAL DIALOGUE

21.1. Conference on the Contribution of Sport to Inter-Cultural Dialogue

Istanbul, Turkey, 9-10 September 2004

The Istanbul Declaration

- Bearing in mind the Council of Europe's Recommendation Rec(2001)6 on the prevention of racism, xenophobia and racial intolerance in sport;
- Recalling the Council of Europe's Recommendation on the revised Code of Ethics and the principles of the appended Code of Ethics No. R(92)14 rev;
- Considering the Declaration on Inter-Cultural Dialogue and Conflict Prevention adopted by the European Ministers of Culture in Opatija, Croatia (2003);
- Recalling the Resolution adopted by the General Assembly of the United Nations on "Sport as a means to promote education, health, development and peace";
- In view of the 3rd Summit of the Heads of States of the Council of Europe (May 2005), the 10th Conference of European Ministers responsible for Sport (October 2004) and the 50th Anniversary of the European Cultural Convention (2005);

The participants of the Council of Europe's Conference on the Contribution of Sport to Inter-Cultural Dialogue, held in Istanbul on 9 and 10 September 2004, recognise that:

- The promotion of inter-cultural dialogue should be geared towards a large part of the population in today's globalised world;
- The fundamental values of sport, such as fair play, mutual respect, peaceful co-existence, tolerance and the fight against racism, xenophobia and anti-Semitism, need to be upheld and furthered;
- Sport has the power to open borders since the language of sport is universal and uncontroversial;
- Sport can develop essential skills, such as mutual respect, team spirit, integration and social inclusion, which form the basis of our society;
- Sport is an appropriate means to reach a large part of the population, in particular the younger generations;
- Sport and physical education, as an integral part of culture, need to be recognised as such and should be included in the educational systems of all countries;
- Properly promoted and delivered, sport can constitute a first step in the efforts to achieve inter-cultural dialogue by bringing together different nationalities and cultures in a common game with common rules;
- Sport may, however, also be misused and lead to intolerance, nationalism and violence;
- Therefore, in order to allow a true inter-cultural dialogue, additional measures must be added to the usual practice of sport.

To this end, the participants of the Conference recommended the following measures:

Sport for all

1. NGOs and public authorities should promote regional, national and international groups of children and young people to practice sport for leisure and take part in inter-cultural sport exchange programmes;
2. Trainers and leaders in charge of such programmes should be fully qualified i.e. a holistic approach needs to be developed;
3. Such inter-cultural sports exchange programmes should include other cultural activities and promote understanding and appreciation of different cultures e.g. music, dance, artwork, etc.;
4. Public authorities, sports organisations and communities should develop programmes based on the needs of the communities that allow the integration of immigrants into national sporting life.

Elite sport

5. To encourage and enable athletes, former athletes and coaches to use their position of role models to further inter-cultural dialogue. Towards that end, they should:
   - get involved in inter-cultural projects;
   - be encouraged to use their position to facilitate dialogue between these cultures, particularly those familiar with different cultures;
   - share their experience in sport e.g. that inter-cultural learning formed a part of their training to achieve elite status.
6. To raise awareness of the philosophy and history of the Olympic Games as an example of how to promote the peaceful co-existence of human beings and facilitate the efforts of those extending the values of the Olympic Games on a general every-day basis;
7. In order to achieve the above, it is essential that all relevant organisations include, in their activities, experience of top-level competition and respect gained for others.

Spectators and fans

8. Organisers of sports events should develop fan coaching, including inter-cultural education e.g. underline the importance of the preparation of fans for large or major sports events;
9. The journeys of supporters to other cultural regions in order to attend a large or major sports event (whether inside or outside their country) should be used to organise, with their counterparts, exchanges and dialogue between different cultures and thereby aim to prevent cultural misunderstandings;
10. The cultural and animation programmes around large or major events should aim to promote inter-cultural dialogue and celebrate the diversity of the participants.

Chapter 22
INTERNATIONAL SPORT

22.1. Resolution on the Increasing Impact of International Tensions on International Sport (81/7)

The European Ministers responsible for Sport, meeting from 8 to 10 April 1981 in Palma de Majorca for their 3rd Conference

After thorough analysis and discussion of the increasing impact of international tensions upon sport;
Concerned that such tensions between nations might extend to sport and hamper or restrict free international sports contacts;
Convinced that the relationship between sport and politics can benefit from timely and permanent consultations between the parties concerned;
Anxious to uphold and preserve the unity and independence of the international sports organisations;
Reaffirm the views expressed at their previous conference and meetings that decisions concerning international sports events should be taken by the independent sports organisations and not by governments or intergovernmental organisations;
Take note of the report prepared by the Parliamentary Assembly on the Olympic Games and the outlook for their future, and of its Recommendation 738, and its Resolution 900;
Invite the international sports organisations:

1. to comply with the just demands of the sportsmen and sports organisations of the developing countries so that the structures and procedures of the international organisations better reflect their participation in sport;
2. to establish regulations on the conditions for granting and withdrawing permission to stage international sports events;
3. to consider the suggestion made by the Greek Government that a site to be chosen by the IOC (Near Olympia) should be the permanent venue of the Olympic Games;
4. to set down rules (where they do not already exist) which should be as harmonious and comprehensive as possible, regulating admission to, and exclusion from, international sports events of countries or sports organisations and in so doing to make clear that racial, religious or other discrimination against athletes is incompatible with participation in international sport;
5. to reduce the excessive use of national symbols (for example, flags and anthems) and the exploitation of international sports events for nationalistic purposes;
6. to recognise, bearing in mind the responsibilities of both parties, that the interest of international sport would be best served by more regular and systematic dialogue with governments and intergovernmental organisations;

Call upon all governments to respect and defend the freedom of sport as an important factor in the development of international co-operation and understanding, and to support the independent sports organisations in their efforts to provide a regulation that would be applicable to international sports contacts;
Resolve to continue their exchanges of views on possible solutions to political problems in sport, and in particular with the Ministers responsible for Sport of other regions, and with

sports organisations of the member states of the Council of Europe, in the framework of the meetings of their informal working party;
Ask the Committee of Ministers to continue to give their support to these meetings;
Request the Committee of Ministers of the Council of Europe to bring this resolution to the attention of governments and relevant sports organisations and to take all appropriate action with a view to furthering its implementation;

22.2. Resolution on Undesirable Developments in International Sport (81/8)
The European Ministers responsible for Sport, meeting from 8 to 10 April 1981 in Palma de Majorca for their 3rd Conference

Upon thorough analysis and discussion of certain undesirable developments in international sport, and in particular the growing inequality of chances in competitions, and the explosion of costs associated with these competitions;
Concerned that these developments endanger fair and free sports relations, that they counteract the efforts made by the governments in the field of health and education and that they unnecessarily and unjustifiably increase the burden on the budgets of public authorities;
Concerned that commercial interests might affect elite sport in particular in a damaging way;

Invite the international sports organisations:

1. to reduce the inequality of chances by assistance programmes for countries less developed in sport (education and counselling, intensification of sports exchanges, provision of know-how);
2. to consider how the costs of international sports events can be decreased, if necessary by an alteration of the organisations' rules as well as an appropriate limitation of facilities and equipment;
3. to preserve the integrity of sport and the personal integrity of sportsmen;

Call upon all governments, and in particular the contracting parties to the European Cultural Convention, to support the international sports organisations in the above tasks;
Request the Committee of Ministers of the Council of Europe to bring this resolution to the attention of governments and relevant sports organisations and to take all appropriate action with a view to furthering its implementation.

22.3. Resolution on International Sports Competitions (86/6)
The European Ministers responsible for Sport, meeting in Dublin for their 5th Conference from 30 September to 2 October 1986

Recalling Resolution (76) 41 of the Committee of Ministers of the Council of Europe on the Principles for a Policy of Sport for All, and especially Articles 2, 3, 5 and 8 of its Appendix;
Considering they share some responsibility for the general interest in relation to the staging of major sports events;
Stressing the important reinforcing role of major sports events on sports development and behaviour;
Noting the initiative of the Dutch Minister responsible for Sport in proposing a meeting of Ministers responsible for sport from those countries regularly hosting major international sports events;

Emphasise that the appropriate sports organisations should be invited to such a meeting and help with its preparation;
Agree that in the context of their next informal meeting they will discuss this proposal further with a view to holding the proposed meeting within the next three years.

Chapter 23
LESBIANS AND GAYS

23.1. Recommendation 1635 (2003)[7] on Lesbians and gays in sport

Parliamentary Assembly, 25 November 2003

1. The Parliamentary Assembly declared itself to be against discrimination in sport in Resolution 1092 (1996) on discrimination against women in sport and more particularly in the Olympic Games.
2. It recalls that the Olympic Charter states that "any form of discrimination with regard to a country or a person on grounds of race, religion, politics, sex or otherwise is incompatible with belonging to the Olympic Movement".
3. Discrimination based on sexual orientation goes against the European Convention on Human Rights and its Protocol No. 12, Article 1 on the general prohibition of discrimination, and is not acceptable in Council of Europe member states.
4. Sport is a key factor in social integration and the European Sports Charter states that participation in sport should be open to all.
5. Gays and lesbians complain that they are at a disadvantage when it comes to participation in sports activities both in regular sports organisations and at school.
6. The Assembly believes that homophobia in sport, both among participants and in their relations with spectators, should be combated on the same grounds as racism and other forms of discrimination.
7. The Assembly therefore calls on member states to:
   i. launch active campaigns against homophobia in sport and widen existing campaigns against xenophobia in sport to include homophobia;
   ii. include homophobia and abusive language directed at gays and lesbians as grounds for accusation of discrimination and harassment on the basis of sexual orientation;
   iii. make homophobic chanting at or around sports events a criminal offence, as is presently the case with racist chanting;
   iv. involve NGOs from the gay and lesbian community in their sports campaigns and in all other necessary confidence-building steps.
8. The Assembly also calls on European sports organisations to:
   i. make homophobic chanting and other homophobic abuse an offence against their constitutions, as is already the case for xenophobic and racist chanting and other abuse;
   ii. call upon UEFA to adapt its Ten Point Plan for Professional Football Clubs so as to include action against homophobia;
   iii. adopt or adapt practical guidelines for professional sports clubs to help them fight against all discrimination, including racism, xenophobia, gender discrimi-

[7] Text adopted by the Standing Committee, acting on behalf of the Parliamentary Assembly, on 25 November 2003 (see Doc. 9988, report of the Committee on Culture, Science and Education, rapporteur: Mr Banks; and Doc. 10001, opinion of the Committee on Equal Opportunities for Women and Men, rapporteur: Ms Kósá-Kovács).

nation and homophobia; launch active campaigns against homophobia in sport; and widen existing campaigns against xenophobia in sport to include homophobia.

9. The Assembly encourages the media to depict fairly and accurately the strength and competence of female and male athletes, whatever their sexual orientation, to refrain from using sexist language and gender stereotypes while covering sports events and to elaborate a code of conduct for sports commentators.

10. Finally, the Assembly recommends that the Committee of Ministers:
    i. extend the grounds listed in Article 4 of the European Sports Charter to discrimination on the grounds of sexual orientation;
    ii. address the issue of homophobia and discrimination in sport and education in the preparation of the 10th Conference of European Sports Ministers in 2004;
    iii. call upon the National Ambassadors for Sport, Tolerance and Fair Play to include this element in their mission;
    iv. consider including the issue of homophobia in the European Convention on Spectator Violence and Misbehaviour at Sport Events and in particular at Football Matches.

23.2. Lesbians and gays in sport – Parliamentary Assembly Recommendation 1635 (2003)

Reply adopted by the Committee of Ministers on 17 November 2004 at the 904th meeting of the Ministers' Deputies

1. The Committee of Ministers has considered Parliamentary Assembly Recommendation 1635 (2003) on lesbians and gays in sport, and welcomes the Assembly's interest and engagement in the issue of discrimination on the basis of sexual orientation. The Recommendation was forwarded to the governments of its member states. It was also sent to its Steering Committee for the Development of Sport (CDDS).

2. The Committee of Ministers shares the Assembly's view that homophobia in sport should be combated in the same way as racism and other forms of discrimination. It recognises that the issue of homophobia in sport is a matter of concern for sports policy makers and sports organisations as a means of promoting tolerance and of ensuring non-discrimination in sport (see Article 4.1 of the European Sports Charter, R (92) 13 revised). The Charter states that the access to sport facilities or to sport activities should be open to all without discrimination.

3. The Committee of Ministers shares the Assembly's view that sport is a key factor in social cohesion as set out in Recommendation No. R (99) 9 on the role of sport in fostering social cohesion. The Committee of Ministers considers that the main platform for further action in this area is at national level.

4. With regard to the Assembly's view regarding possible amendment of Article 4 of the European Sports Charter (paragraph 10.i.), the Committee of Ministers does not consider it necessary to amend the European Sports Charter, as all points raised in the Recommendation are covered by the revised Charter.2

Note

5. With regard to the Assembly's proposal to address the issue of homophobia and discrimination in the preparation of the 10th Conference of European Ministers responsible for Sport (Budapest, 14-15 October 2004), the main subject of this Conference was

"Good Governance in Sport". The conclusions of the Conference on this subject are also applicable to this issue.

6. As regards the proposal to call upon National Ambassadors for Sport, Tolerance and Fair Play (paragraph 10.iii.) to include this element in their mission, the Committee of Ministers points out that this network, set up by the CDDS and currently under the Standing Committee of the Convention on Spectator Violence, has organised a series of Round Tables on Sport, Tolerance and Fair Play to which the European Gay and Lesbian Sport Federation has been invited as an observer. Thus, the network of National Ambassadors for Sport Tolerance and Fair Play considers that its activities to promote tolerance include the fight against homophobia. The Committee of Ministers notes that this is the first step taken towards this end within the mission of the National Ambassadors.

7. As regards paragraph 10.iv. of the Recommendation, it was brought to the attention of the Standing Committee of the Convention on Spectator Violence at its 24th meeting at Porto on 10-11 June 2004, which has confirmed that all spectators, irrespective of age, gender, race, religion, disability or sexual orientation should be able to attend sporting events in safety, security and comfort without discrimination. The same principles of non-discrimination, in all its forms, including sexual orientation, apply also to players. As regards the proposals at paragraph 10.iv. of the Recommendation, the Standing Committee has considered that this issue is included in its programme on fighting discrimination, for example in its work on sport, tolerance and fair play.

Chapter 24
LOCAL AUTHORITIES

24.1. Recommendation 16 (1996) on Sport and Local Authorities

The Congress, on a proposal from the Chamber of Local Authorities,

1. Having taken note of the report on the European Conference on Sport and Local Authorities held in Gödöllo (Hungary) from 1 to 3 February 1996, presented by Mr Meintz, Rapporteur on behalf of the Working Group on Sport;
2. Considering that sport, being a school for democratic ideals, social participation and integration, plays an important role in promoting international understanding;
3. Considering that sport shall be related at local, regional and national levels to other areas of policy-making and planning such as education, health, social services, town and country planning, conservation, the arts and leisure services;
4. Considering that an effective sports policy can only be determined and put into operation through co-operation by all private and public agencies concerned either directly or indirectly with sport, both voluntary and compulsory;
5. Considering that sport is an integral part of society which provides significant positive economic effects, and that the economic stimulus generated by sport contributes to local, regional and national economic development;
6. Recommends that the governments of member states
   a. acknowledge the vital role played by local authorities in the promotion of sports;
   b. foster permanent and effective co-operation between public authorities, voluntary and private organisations active in the field of sports;
   c. provide advice and assistance to local authorities with regard to the construction and management of their sports facilities;
   d. adapt their financial contributions to the "grass roots" dialogue between consumers and local public sports financiers;
   e. promote the participation of low income or needy groups through targeted subsidies;
   f. set aside public funds to ensure that public sports facilities are accessible to and usable by disabled persons;
   g. encourage mixed public and private financial support for sport;
   h. pay attention to the specific needs and difficulties faced by the sports organisations of the new member countries in Central and Eastern Europe in obtaining public and private financing for their activities;
   i. support the medical use of physical activities in order to gain, conserve and improve health at the level of "Sport for All" and to guard against possible hazards;
7. Recommends that the Committee of Ministers of the Council of Europe
   a. transmit the Final Declaration of the Gödöllo Conference to the CDDS asking it to take account of the views and proposals contained therein;
   b. instruct the CDDS to continue and deepen the dialogue with the CLRAE on matters of mutual interest and to invite it to take part in its activities, in particular in its specialised conferences.

24.2. Resolution 27 (1996) 1 on Sport and Local Authorities

The Congress, on a proposal from the Chamber of Local Authorities.

1. Having taken note of the report on the European Conference on Sport and Local Authorities held in Gödöllo (Hungary) from 1 to 3 February 1996. presented by Mr Meintz, Rapporteur on behalf of the Working Group on Sport;
2. Considering the important role played by local and regional authorities in improving living standards, economic progress and cultural development;
3. Considering that sport forms an integral part of local cultural activities, it is therefore vital that local authorities have an active, conscious attitude and approach as to how involvement in sport can be integrated into local policies in general;
4. Considering that sports and physical activities must not be the exclusive preserve of certain age groups and special categories of persons but should be accessible to the general public in the framework of the "Sport for All" concept;
5. Calls on local and regional authorities
   a. to make available appropriate support and resources from public funds for the development of sport;
   b. to co-operate with the commercial and the voluntary sectors and to encourage mixed public and private support for sport;
   c. to diminish the financial inequalities with regard to the needs of top-level sport and those of sport for all;
   d. to promote the health and well-being of all groups and individuals wishing to undertake sporting activities;
   e. to encourage and support a greater participation by older persons in appropriate sporting and other physical activities;
   f. to provide opportunities for all young people to become involved in sport, and to emphasise the value of physical activity rather than the technical or competitive element;
   g. to take all appropriate policy measures to encourage greater involvement of women in sport;
   h. to facilitate the access of the least privileged groups to the practice of sport and physical activity;
   i. to create a welcoming climate for disabled people, recognising their right to be helped and improving their position in society;
   j. to promote measures in the fields of physical, health and safety education to advertise sports and other suitable physical activities for their beneficial effects on health;
6. Invites the Bureau of the Congress
   a. to regularly examine the role and responsibilities of local and regional authorities in relation to sport, and to re-establish the Working Group on Sport in due course;
   b. to support concrete action aimed at providing sport for all;
   c. to reinforce European co-operation in this field between local and regional authorities;
   d. to deepen the dialogue with other bodies of the Council of Europe having responsibilities in the area of sport.

24.3. European Conference on Sport and Local Authorities
Gödöllo, Hungary, 1-3 February 1996

Final Declaration
The participants the European Conference on Sport and Local Authorities, held in Gödöllo (Hungary) from 1 to 3 February 1996,

1. Thanking the Council of Europe and in particular its Congress of Local and Regional Authorities of Europe for taking the initiative of organising this conference;
2. Thanking the Mayor and the Municipality of Gödöllo for their warm welcome and hospitality;
3. Underlining the important role played by local and regional authorities iii improving living standards, economic progress and cultural development;
4. Emphasising that sport forms an integral part of local cultural activities, and therefore it is vital that local authorities have an active. conscious attitude and approach to how involvement in sport can be integrated into local policies in general;
5. Stressing that sport, being a school for democratic ideals, social participation and integration, plays an important role in promoting international understanding;
6. Considering that sports activities are beneficial not only for the development of personality but also for the attainment of good health, the improvement of physical qualities, greater personal fulfilment. a better and more wholesome use of leisure and the improvement of the quality of life;
7. Considering also that sports and physical activities must not be the exclusive preserve of certain age groups and special categories of persons but should be accessible to the general public in the framework of the "Sport for All" concept;
8. Acknowledging the vital role played by the Council of Europe in the promotion of sport as an important factor in human development, in particular by setting international standards through such instruments as the European Sports Charter and Code of Sports Ethics;
9. Call on the Congress of Local and Regional Authorities of Europe to regularly examine the role and responsibilities of local and regional authorities in relation to sport, to support concrete action aimed at providing sport for all, and to reinforce European co-operation in this field between local and regional authorities. and between the Congress and other bodies of the Council of Europe;
10. Adopt and commend to the favourable consideration of the Congress the Final Declaration of the Gödöllo Conference as follows:

Sport for All: the Roll and Responsibilities of Local Authorities

11. Sport shall be acknowledged as an important factor in human development and appropriate support shall be made available out of public funds. Encouragement of physical and sports activities should be the task of every local and regional authority;
12. Sport, being an aspect of socio-cultural development, shall be related at local, regional and national levels to other areas of policy-making and planning such as education, health, social service, town and country planning, conservation, the arts and leisure services;
13. Art effective sports policy can only be determined and put into operation through co-operation by all private and public agencies concerned either directly or indirectly with sport, both voluntary and compulsory;
14. Local and regional authorities should foster permanent and effective co-operation between public authorities and voluntary organisations active in the field of sports;

15. Since the scale of participation in sports depends on the extent, the variety and the accessibility of facilities, public authorities shall take account of local, regional and national requirements, and incorporate measures designed to ensure full use of both new and existing facilities;
16. Public authorities should provide sufficient sports grounds and installations for the needs of the people, readily available to all at affordable prices;
17. The construction of local sports facilities should be based on present and future needs in various sports activities. taking into account population and socio-economic trends. The facilities should be easily accessible for users of all ages, irrespective of their state of health, e.g. the disabled or the elderly;
18. Encouragement must be given to the provision of facilities which can be used for both school sport and voluntary sport and, whenever possible, to the combination of cultural and sports facilities, without compromising on the interests of sport;
19. As far as possible, local sports facilities should be adapted to the needs of special groups, such as the very young, adolescents, school leavers, isolated and elderly people, and the disabled.
20. Local authorities should aim at promoting the health and well-being of all groups and individuals wishing to undertake sporting activities;
21. Local authorities should encourage and support efforts to promote a greater participation by older persons in appropriate sporting and other physical activities;
22. In particular, they should stimulate the development of a policy on sport for older persons and to encourage a wider knowledge and awareness of the beneficial effects of regular exercise. They should also develop an adequate range and variety of programmes designed to preserve fitness and to improve health through regular sporting activity, paying attention to the social needs, motivation and physical potential of different age groups;
23. Appropriate and well-balanced programmes should be made available to provide opportunities for all young people to become involved in sport and physical activity. Local authorities, together with the sports organisations concerned, are responsible for providing the necessary leadership in the development and promotion of a sports policy for young people;
24. Physical education should be a part of every school curriculum, placing emphasis on the physical and mental health of pupils. Stress should be laid on the value of physical activity rather than on the technical or competitive element;
25. Local authorities should take all appropriate policy measures in their countries to encourage greater involvement of women in sport. Iii particular, they should encourage sport federations and other parties involved to recognise and accept their individual responsibilities in facilitating a fundamental attitude towards women participation in sport;
26. They should promote a greater use by women of the existing opportunities available to them to take part in sport. The position of women in the promotion and administration of sport as a public service should be reviewed. The organisation of programmes and facilities to enable all members of families to participate in sport together should be encouraged;
27. The principles of sport as an important means of bringing about greater participation in the life of the host society should apply to everyone, and, in particular, to the least privileged groups. Immigrantș access to the practice of sport should be facilitated. They should be able to join sport clubs to help bring them out of their isolation;

28. Local authorities should encourage the building of sports facilities in areas which have a high concentration of immigrants and which are particularly deprived. They should increase their efforts to launch specific action programmes to foster participation by immigrants and other socially marginalised groups;
29. Sport and physical recreation has an important role in helping alleviate poor living conditions. Local authorities should carry out comprehensive policies with special emphasis on the needs of those living in areas of deprivation.

The Financing and Management of Sport

30. Sport is an integral part of society which provides significant positive economic effects. The economic stimulus generated by sport contributes to consumption, income and employment, as well as to local, regional and national economic development;
31. Sports facilities and amenities have wider effects in terms of job creation. There has been a manifold increase in the number of employment opportunities opened up by sport and allied sectors;
32. The growth and increased variety of sources of funding for sport are helpful to its development. There are considerable differences existing between the countries of Europe regarding the proportion of sport funding coming from the public sector, consumers and private sources, the role of central, regional and local authorities;
33. Sports activities are largely financed by private households, local and regional authorities, private sponsors and contributions from the voluntary sector. In the vast majority of European countries local authorities are the biggest public financial partner of sport, far ahead of central governments;
34. Appropriate support and resources from public funds (at local, regional and central levels) shall be made available for the development of sport. Local authorities should facilitate the direct and indirect public financing for sport in general and sport for all in particular, both in current and capital expenditure;
35. A financial balance should be maintained between public and private (including household and commercial) expenditure in sport. Mixed public and private financial support for sport should be encouraged, including the generation by the sports sector itself of resources necessary for its further development;
36. Sports financing and management should be increasingly based on direct and ever closer relations between participants and local public decision-makers. The financial contributions of the state and enterprises, comparatively minor, should increasingly adapt to this "grass roots" dialogue between consumers and local public sports financiers;
37. Local authorities, in association with central authorities, the voluntary and the commercial sectors, should establish policies for recreational and competitive sport, aiming at co-ordinating their involvement in the running and the use of facilities;
38. Commercial sponsorship and marketing in sport are already recognised and accepted as an additional means of financing sport. Well-managed sponsorship agreements benefit both sport and the sponsor, therefore it should be encouraged and promoted by local authorities;
39. The voluntary sector plays a decisive role in sport and thus contributes in a major way to the balanced development of society in general and of sport in particular. Local policies supporting voluntary groups and volunteers (for example through tax measures) should be encouraged, thereby providing even more efficient support for sport;
40. Whilst taking due consideration of the importance of voluntary work, the creation of new jobs and further development of training for current and future employees in the sports sector should be encouraged;

41. Finance for sport is differently distributed between components of the sports sector. Local authorities should aim at diminishing the financial inequalities with regard to the needs of top-level sport and those of sport for all. In the interest of solidarity between sports, sports with less media appeal, which are thus unable to attract major funding, should be helped;
42. All taxpayers contribute to the financing of sports facilities. Nevertheless, consumers of sport can be called upon to contribute more through charges, commensurate with the type of activity pursued. Subsidies from public authorities may promote participation and benefit low income or needy groups, simultaneously achieving redistributive goals and healthier lifestyles;
43. Local authorities should understand the specific needs and difficulties faced by the sports organisations of the new member countries in Central and Eastern Europe in obtaining public and private financing for their activities;

Sport and Health

44. Sport has a vital role in contributing to the adjustment and rehabilitation of the physically and mentally handicapped;
45. The promotion and development of sport and physical recreation for all disabled persons is an important means of improving the quality of their life, as well as contributing to their rehabilitation and integration in society. Local authorities should aim at creating a welcoming climate for disabled people, recognising their right to be helped and improving their position in society;
46. They should ensure that public sports facilities are accessible to and usable by disabled persons. In particular. public money should be set aside to help with the conversion of existing facilities and to familiarise architects and managers of sports facilities with the requirements of disabled people:
47. Local authorities should encourage and work closely with the sport organisations concerned in order to develop appropriate activities at all levels of sport for disabled persons and to ensure in particular that recreational participation in sport is adequately provided for;
48. They should consider ways in which disabled persons may be offered opportunities for integrating into traditional sport clubs and organisations. They should also encourage disabled persons to contribute directly to the development of sports policies which concern them;
49. Local authorities should develop policies designed to give the general public more information on sport for disabled people. They should do their utmost to introduce physical activities and sport in the education, rehabilitation and preventive treatment of the handicapped, and to better integrate handicapped persons into sports activities primarily aimed at the non-handicapped;
50. They should take measures to make sports facilities more easily accessible. encourage the training of specialist staff and support the setting-up of independent bodies responsible for the organisation of sports adapted to different kinds of handicap;
51. Local and regional authorities should encourage practice, teaching and research in the field of sports medicine. They should also promote measures in the fields of physical. health and safety education to advertise sports and other suitable physical activities for their beneficial effects en health;
52. The medical use of physical activities should be supported in order to gain. conserve and improve health at the level of "Sport for All" and to guard against possible hazards;

53. Local authorities should take an active part in educational campaigns to point out the risks involved in using or advocating the use of doping agents, in particular that many such agents present serious long-term dangers to health;

54. Local authorities should closely co-operate with bodies responsible for health education to advertise sport as a means of acquiring, conserving and improving physical and mental health and improving the quality of life in general.

Chapter 25
MEDICAL AND HEALTH ASPECTS

25.1. Resolution on the Medical Aspects of Sport (70/7)
Adopted by the Ministers' Deputies on 7 March 1970

The Committee of Ministers,
Considering that the aim of the Council of Europe is to bring about a closer union between its Members by means, inter alia, of the adoption of common regulations in the social field;
Considering that the World Health Organisation defines health as a state of complete physical, mental and social well-being and aims at the attainment by all people of the highest possible level of health;
Considering that sports activities are beneficial not only for the development of personality but also for the attainment of good health as defined above;
Addresses the following recommendations to the governments of member states;
Invites the governments of the member states to inform it at the end of five years of action taken in application of this resolution.

Sports curricula in schools

1. Physical education should be a part of every school curriculum.
2. Physical education should be given two or three times a week with a minimum of three hours per week. Where possible an hour a day of physical education could be given in primary and secondary schools.
3. After consultation where necessary with the family doctor, school doctors should see that the physical education of each child is adapted to his condition. It is important that pupils with a permanent or mental handicap and delicate children take part in as many physical activities as possible.
4. School doctors should co-operate as far as possible with physical education instructors in order to advise the pupils under their supervision on any health problems connected with their participation in all sport activities.
5. In out-of-school competitive sports, primary emphasis should be placed on the physical and mental health of the pupil, including the development of his character, rather than on his performance or on the interest of the sports club.
   With a view to avoiding the possible detrimental effects of over-training it is desirable that the headmaster be informed of students' participation in out-of-school competitive sports.

Participation in competitive sport and medical examinations

6. a. Younger age groups.
   Too intensive strenuous training should be avoided for younger age groups until their bones are fully grown, for example, eighteen to twenty years.
   Competitive sports which cause overloading of the respiratory, cardiovascular and neuro-muscular systems should be excluded, in the case of girls, before the ages of eleven to thirteen and, in the case of boys, before the ages of twelve to fourteen.

b. Older age groups.
Stress should be laid on the value of physical activity rather than on competitive sport. At older ages strenuous competitive sport should be avoided, especially if there has been no great physical activity in the preceding years.

7. The load of the training programme and of the competition should be adapted to the age of the very young and older sportsman.
8. Whenever possible, it would be advisable to have for the very young age groups specially educated teachers for sports in school and specially educated trainers and coaches for competitive sport out of school.
9. There should be adequate medical instruction in the training courses for coaches and trainers.
10. Every boy or girl who takes part in competitive sport may have a medical examination as frequently as parents, doctors, trainers or coaches think it is necessary. The frequency depends also on the kind of sport and the intensity of the competition or training programme.
11. Where a school child is engaged in competitive sports there should be a special medical card introduced for him and kept as long as he continues with competitive sports activities.
12. Facilities need to be provided whereby medical examinations can be arranged for persons engaged in strenuous competitive sports activities.

Biological and psychological assessment of aptitude for different sports

13. It is desirable that government support is given to establish laboratory and sports medical units which are necessary in order to carry out the modern functional tests related to sport.
14. These units should be supplied with adequate equipment and trained personnel.
15. Research related to the application of biological and psychological tests for sports purposes should be encouraged.

Training of experts in sports medicine and establishment of sports medicine centres

16. Encouragement of physical and sports activities should be the task of every government. Planning and execution of this task demands expert medical say in these matters.
17. There is a need for physicians with special training in sports medicine and the qualifications of the experts in this field, both full-time and part-time, should be specified and their training established, with courses leading to a recognised diploma.
18. Consideration should be given to the possibility of establishing a national sports centre for research, training and reference in countries where they do not exist.
19. Co-operation between national centres should be encouraged.

Health and hygiene problems affecting sports activities

20. Anti-doping measures envisaged by Resolution (67) 12 should not only be enforced, but should also be reinforced through health education.
21. Sports activities call for a discipline of life which provides an excellent opportunity for health education. Such education should be directed not only at all people active in sport, but also at instructors, trainers, sport organisers and parents and should include personal hygiene and its behavioural components.
22. The authorities should provide sufficient sports grounds and installations for the needs of the people, readily available to all at low prices. The health control of such establishments should be placed under the competent health authorities.

23. An exchange of doctors and other personnel between countries should be encouraged in order to increase their knowledge of sports medicine. Medical fellowships in this field should be made available by governments and the various international organisations concerned, as is already the case within the framework of the Medical Fellowships Programme of the Council of Europe.

25.2. Resolution on Hygiene of Sports Installations (72/30)
Adopted by the Committee of Ministers on 19 September 1972

The Committee of Ministers,
Considering that the aim of the Council of Europe is to achieve a greater unity between its members by means, inter alia, of common action in the field of public health;
Considering that the World Health Organisation defines health as a state of complete physical, mental and social well-being and aims at the attainment by all people of the highest possible level of health;
Considering that sports activities are beneficial not only for the development of personality and for the attainment of good health as defined above but also for the improvement of physical qualities and for personal fulfilment;
Considering also that benefits from such activities are more effectively derived by the provision of well-designed and easily maintained sports installations (indoor and outdoor installations and swimming pools), and sports activities carried out under unfavourable conditions may cause harm and injury;
Recommends governments of member states to implement as fully as possible the principles concerning the hygiene of sports installations given in Appendix A to the present resolution and to take into account the possible sources of dangers listed in Appendix B;
Invites the governments of member states to inform the Secretary General of the Council of Europe every five years of the action taken by them in respect of the present resolution.

Appendix A
Hygiene of sports installations

General requirements
1. Construction plans should be drawn up in agreement with designers, engineers, architects, doctors and sports authorities (medical and local).
Construction plans should be based on present and future needs in various sports activities including the long-term operational requirements of the installation, taking into account population and socio-economic trends.
   a. Location.
   Gymnasia, sports fields and swimming pools should be easily accessible for users of all ages, irrespective of their state of health, e.g. the disabled or the elderly, and available for all seasons and be situated in areas conducive to health improvement.
   b. Building material and design.
   Material should be harmless to the users, sound, easy to clean, non-inflammable and durable.
   Minimum requirements of artistic design should be met to increase the well-being of the users, spectators and staff members.

c. Equipment, furniture and furnishings.
Equipment should not be dangerous, and be easy to maintain and kept in a constant state of good repair. Furniture and furnishings should be capable of withstanding hard wear and tear.
Special fittings for different sports, such as fire alarm bells, life-saving equipment etc., should be carefully considered and be easily accessible and of maximum efficiency.

2. Sanitation and heating.
a. The health authorities responsible for the area should ensure that a plentiful supply of water is available for both drinking and washing purposes. Drinking water should be readily available in sufficient quantity cooler than the surrounding temperature and easily accessible.
b. Proper drainage systems should be laid down to secure proper sewage disposal.
c. Heating of water should be effectively and safely installed for washing purposes. Heating of the building and rooms should be kept under constant supervision.

3. Maintenance, repair and cleanliness.
The health authorities and other bodies concerned should ensure that all building materials, equipment and apparatus are easily disinfected, cleaned and maintained in perfect working conditions.
There should be no overcrowding in any part of the building. Storage and changing rooms should be kept properly aired and used according to the purposes for which they were initially intended. Any change in their use should not cause any interference with other sections of the installation.

4. Medical facilities.
Every sports gymnasium, sports field and swimming pool should have appropriate medical facilities for emergencies.

5. Personnel.
Responsibilities should be clearly defined. Administrative, technical and auxiliary staff should be well trained to carry out their duties efficiently. All personnel engaged in training and instruction in sports activities should have the necessary physique, intelligence and psychological knowledge to deal with people undertaking sports activities.

6. Fire fighting.
Fire fighting equipment should be provided and placed in easily accessible positions.

7. Health control.
Health authorities should exercise the necessary health control of all three types of sports installations, e.g. indoor installations, outdoor installations and swimming pools.

Special requirements.

In addition to the general requirements stated above, the following principles should be taken into account with particular reference to all three types of sports installations.

Indoor Installations

These should aim at promoting the health and well-being of all groups and individuals wishing to undertake sporting activities.

8. Location, design, material and use.
The needs of special groups, such as the very young, adolescents, elderly people, the disabled, those who are exposed to the dangers of harmful effects of environment (i.e.

industry) and the needs of the highly trained athlete should be given due consideration in selecting the site and building indoor installations by adapting these as far as possible to one or to several of the groups.

Long-term requirements concerning use (wear and tear), upkeep and maintenance should be given due consideration in building indoor installations, taking into account future needs of various groups and individuals.

a. Floors.
Construction of floors should be undertaken according to expert knowledge. In regard to floor construction and floor covering, special attention should be given to various types of floors which should be designed to meet the needs of the different age groups for the various types of sports activities that they practice. The floor should not be too cold or with too hard a surface, too wet or too damp. It should be easy to clean, quickly reparable and usable for bare feet.
Certain types of synthetic material should be avoided, especially those which do not provide sufficient protection, in particular to children of all ages, against friction, rebounds, slipping (bumps and injuries). The use of proper footwear should also be stressed and controlled.

b. Selective use of facilities.
Provision should be made for multipurpose halls to meet the needs of special groups of activities, taking into account all possible risk factors.

9. Safety.
Each country's safety regulations should be strictly applied in respect of all sports activities.

10. First-aid, life-saving, medical care.

a. There should be first-aid boxes located in strategic places in indoor installations. These should be checked and refilled periodically. The keys for them should be kept by the supervisory staff on duty (including teachers).
Every indoor sports hall should be provided with at least one first-aid room, easily reached from activity areas. The way to the first-aid room should be clearly marked and not obstructed. In the first-aid room, there should be a telephone with the list of doctors and special hospitals and ambulance services for immediate use.

b. In major sports events there should be a physician in attendance. Furthermore, a physician should be appointed to supervise and inspect periodically the hygienic and safety measures and there should always be a doctor on call in case of accidents.

c. Rooms for medical examinations and other medical purposes should be provided.

d. Rest rooms for athletes should also be provided.

e. Sports supervisors and attendants in indoor installations should be instructed in basic first-aid.

f. Emergency exits in sufficient number and capacity should be clearly indicated and kept in workable condition.

11. Changing, cleaning, shelter.

a. An adequate number of changing rooms should be provided.

b. The direction of participants' and spectators' flow (from the entrance to changing and cleaning places to sports halls or vice-versa) should be clearly indicated and separated from each other.

12. Air supply, heating, air conditioning and lighting.
Maximum use should be made of daylight. Air supply, heating, air conditioning and lighting for the different sports installations should be installed in accordance with the specifications existing in the different countries and be compatible with the cubic capacity of the hall, with the number of participants and/or with the number of spectators. Air conditioning should satisfy minimal requirements.
Smoking should be prohibited.
13. Noise control.
Acoustic requirements and effects of different sporting activities should be taken into consideration in the planning and construction of sports installations and in timing the different sporting events.
14. Rest rooms, recreation and refreshments.
    a. There should be sufficient provision of these for the general public as well as for participants in sports activities, taking into account group activities in competitive sports events.
    b. Wherever necessary, there should be suitable rooms for special purposes, such as physiotherapy, sauna etc.
    c. Separate rest rooms should be provided for use by staff only.
15. Facilities for disabled persons.
For disabled persons there should be slopes for wheelchairs, handrails, facilities for privacy in changing, cleaning and toilet facilities.
16. Accommodation for staff members.
Proper accommodation should be provided for maintenance and supervisory staff.

Outdoor Installations

17. Location, size and lay-out of the grounds.
    a. The site should be selected, taking into account the present and anticipated needs in various sports activities.
    b. The size of the grounds should meet the required standards for each sport, leaving enough space for safety between players and spectators.
    c. For the safety of the players and the spectators, space between pitches should be fixed with a minimum distance separating the outside limits of the pitches at the edge of the stadia.
    d. Seats should be provided for spectators.
    e. Arrangements of grounds and material.
    In comprehensive sports complexes attention should be given to:
        i. laying down specific rules for use of sports grounds;
        ii. arranging the equipment with a view to reducing the causes of accidents;
        iii. providing the athletes with sufficient training and warming up areas;
        iv. providing proper and adequate training for children of school age by classes in physical training;
        v. new methods of treating the soil so that maintenance is improved and muscle and joint damage is prevented;
        vi. the use of resilient and very thick material on jump-landing areas and in the construction of their borders;
        vii. providing a reception area for those taking part in sport, including adequate and hygienic cloakrooms and rest rooms (see paragraph 7 under Indoor installations).

18. Use and maintenance of the grounds and equipment.
    a. Those engaging in sports activities should be informed of the indispensable safety precautions regarding the use of the grounds and equipment.
    b. Maintenance of the grounds and equipment should be undertaken periodically, the sockets and fittings being tested and the grounds inspected.
    c. All dangerous and defective equipment should be replaced immediately.
    d. Education in the hygiene and safety of sports installations should be a part of the programme of the training courses.
19. First-aid, life-saving, medical care.
    In addition to the provisions laid down under paragraph 3 above regarding indoor installations, the first-aid centre should open on to the grounds and have an emergency exit providing isolation, quick first-aid and urgent removal.
    There should be a proper ambulance access point.
    It would be desirable that athletes be vaccinated against tetanus.

Swimming pools

20. Planning and layout.
    a. Planning should take into account local preferences regarding recreational and performance needs.
    b. Spectators and participants should be separated.
    c. Pools should be divided into sections for swimming, diving and for beginners.
    d. Large competitive pools should have a gymnasium.
    e. Facilities should include:
        i. quick drying rooms;
        ii. warm rest benches;
        iii. foot and body showers;
        iv. clothes storage.
    f. Special emphasis should be laid on hygienic measures such as:
        i. temperature of water and building;
        ii. ventilation;
        iii. methods of cleaning and disinfection and technical advice on these matters should be sought from engineering services.
21. Use.
    a. Special attention should be given to the methods of cleansing pools prior to their use with particular reference to the prevention of the spreading of skin, eye, ear and other infections.
    b. Excessive window glazing, which creates problems for those responsible for the safety and welfare of bathers, should be prevented because of its blinding effects.
22. Material.
    The floor should be of a good gripping material with a quick-drying surface. It should be kept hygienic and safe.
23. First-aid, life-saving, medical care.
    a. Adequate first-aid and essential life-saving should be undertaken by trained personnel. Life savers should be present at all times when the pools are in use.
    b. Adequate life-saving and resuscitation equipment should be readily available and kept in good working order.
    c. Telephone numbers of the nearest doctor and hospital should be listed in a prominent place in the first-aid room.

d. Directional signs should be placed in prominent positions indicating the way to:
   i. the first-aid room;
   ii. toilets;
   iii. canteen.

24. Special groups of users.
Special arrangements should be made for the disabled and should include:
   a. entrance for wheelchairs to pools, changing rooms, toilets, cleansing areas and to water for drinking and washing purposes;
   b. equipment and aids to pools such as handrails etc.

25. Staff.
Lockers and sitting-rooms should be provided for staff.

Appendix B

Examples of possible sources of danger with respect to hygiene and safety for athletes and spectators at sports installations.

Dangers arising from an insufficient preparation of design and building

1. Inadequate briefing of architects and others responsible for the planning and building in modern design and material.
2. Insufficient or lack of medical consultation for the preparation of hygiene and safety devices and measures.
3. Failure to consult expert athletes on the planning of sports installations.
4. Failure to plan adequately for long-term upkeep, maintenance and repair.

Dangers arising out of structural faults

5. Mistakes in the allotment of rooms for activities:
   a. location of first-aid room not clearly indicated, not easily accessible, not easily connected with ambulance or parking areas;
   b. lack of provision of space for all age groups and not only for the competitive sportsmen;
   c. lack of sufficient boundary space especially in outdoor installations;
   d. insufficient segregation of activities and spectator areas;
   e. lack of rest and recreational facilities.
6. Lack of emergency exits.
7. Disturbances and interference due to noise.
8. Disturbances due to overglazing of windows, insufficient or other illumination (stairs) or blinding effect.

Missing or faulty technical installation and equipment

9. Slippery floors.
10. Use of floor materials unsuited for the sports activity or age group.
11. Hanging wires.
12. Insufficient air supply, air turnover, over-heating or insufficient heating, draughts.
13. Fatal accidents due to failure or absence of life-saving equipment (or adequately trained personnel).
14. Insecure or wrongly-placed barriers.
15. Lack of special provisions for the disabled:
   a. proper entrances and doors;
   b. lifts and slopes;

c. proper handrails;
d. special provisions in toilets, changing and washing facilities.

16. Insecure temporary stands for spectators.
17. Risk of falling from heights due to insufficient guards.
18. Accidents caused by falling objects.

Danger caused through lack of sanitary facilities

19. Failure to secure sufficient and appropriate sanitary equipment, including toilets, wash-basins and showers. Lack of towels (one-way towels or warm air electrical equipment) for hand-drying and lack of toilet paper.
20. Bad odours due to insufficient cleaning, (for example inaccessible corners or insufficiently ventilated lockers and locker rooms).
21. Infections caused by coli or other bacterial or virus sources due to insufficient or faulty changing of water in swimming pools.

Special danger points in swimming pools (not covered elsewhere)

22. No segregation of swimming and diving pools.
23. Lack of adequate pre-cleansing methods (e.g. to prevent infections).
24. Insufficient attention to the daily control of the acceptable chlorine content of the water.
25. Lack of playpens for small children who are likely to wander about.
26. Lack of life-saving equipment being placed in appropriate places where immediate use can be made of it at any time.

Dangers arising from insufficient control and maintenance

27. Lack of maintenance staff.
28. Accidents due to deteriorated grounds (especially in outdoor installations).
29. Burns due to acid cleansing materials.
30. Slipping on wet or slippery floors, due to faulty or indiscriminate use of polish or cleansing methods (detergents).
31. Injuries from wood (splinters) or broken glass (old bottles).
32. Danger of infection due to insufficient dirt or water removal.
33. Inadequate first-aid due to lack of knowledge by teachers, coaches, supervisory and maintenance staff.
34. Inadequate first-aid due to insufficiently equipped first-aid box or first-aid rooms.
35. Using rooms for purposes for which they are not intended, e.g. first-aid room for storage etc.
36. Lack of sufficient ground control (control of spectators).

Dangers due to recklessness or negligence on the part of athletes

37. Insufficient knowledge or disregard of rules and safety regulations of the specific kind of sport.
38. General negligence in hygiene and disregard of physiological or mechanical laws.
39. Accidents due to the ignorance or disregard of existing diseases or weaknesses.
40. Spread of infection caused by unknown or a disregard of existing infectious conditions.
41. Accidents due to fatigue or exhaustion.
42. Accidents due to overstrain, over-training and psychological stress.
43. Handling unknown or dangerous equipment.

44. Increased personal danger due to activating existing predispositions (e.g. rheumatism, allergies).
45. Ignorance or disregard on the part of trainers and coaches of the minimum requirements of hygiene and safety.

25.3. Resolution on the establishment of sports medicine centres (73/27)
Adopted by the Committee of Ministers on 26 October 1973

The Committee of Ministers,
Considering that the aim of the Council of Europe is to achieve a greater unity between its Members and that this aim may be pursued, inter alia, by the adoption of common regulations in the social field and particularly in the public health field;
Noting that the World Health Organisation defines health as a state of complete physical, mental and social well-being and aims at the attainment by all people of the highest possible level of health;
Considering that sports activities are beneficial not only for the development of personality but also for the attainment of good health as defined above, the improvement of physical qualities, greater personal fulfilment, a better and more wholesome use of leisure and the improvement of the quality of life;
Considering also that sports and physical activities must not be the exclusive preserve of certain age groups and special categories of persons such as selected athletes, and that they should be available not only as physical education as part of every school curriculum but also, and particularly, to the general public in the framework of the "Sport for All" concept;
Considering also that, if they are to be fully beneficial, these activities require medical supervision and well-equipped sports installations, since sporting activities carried out in poor conditions may have harmful consequences;
Recognising the need to provide medical supervision for individuals and the general public, in order to ensure maximum benefit for the health of all persons engaging or wishing to engage in competitive or recreational sports

Recommends that the governments of member states:
1. encourage practice, teaching and research in the field of sports medicine;
2. encourage or propose measures in the fields of physical, health and safety education to advertise sports and other suitable physical activities for their beneficial effects on health, and in educational measures take account of the advisability of undergoing a medical examination before engaging in such activities, especially in the case of "Sport for All" movements and veteran athletes who wish to resume competitive sport after a period of inactivity;
3. encourage the inclusion in the curricula of physical education and sports training centres of instruction in sports medicine, especially with regard to developmental and exercise physiology and first-aid treatment for sports injuries;
4. encourage the establishment of sports medicine centres where the need exists, and the resources are available, according to the individual conditions in member states, taking into account the definitions given in Appendix A and the principles set out in Appendix B and Appendix C;
5. make use, in establishing such centres, of the existing means for the exchange of personnel and information between the member states of the Council of Europe;

Invites the governments of member states to inform the Secretary General of the Council of Europe every five years of the action taken by them in respect of this resolution.

Appendix A

Definitions

The definitions below were drawn up for the purposes of this resolution.

1. Sports medicine.
   Application of the art and science of medicine from a preventive and therapeutic point of view to the practice of sports and physical activities in order to utilise the opportunities afforded by sport for maintaining or improving health and to avoid possible dangers.
2. Sports medicine centre.
   A unit (not necessarily geographical but rather functional) to provide medical supervision in all branches of sport.
3. Aims and objectives of sports medicine centres.
   The best possible health of all persons taking part in sports or physical activities, making the best possible use of sport and promoting the adoption of healthy attitudes which afford effective prevention of the diseases of modern civilisation.

Appendix B

Functions of sports medicine centres

Sports medicine centres should be staffed and equipped in order to discharge:

1. Preventive medical functions:
   a. in assessing the state of health of the individual in order to establish his capacity and be directed to suitable activities (sports for the more gifted, courses of appropriate instruction or treatment for the others);
   b. in medical supervision and training of people engaged in sports or other physical activities, particularly children and those taking part in high-level competitive sport, to enable them to attain the desired performance without endangering their health;
   c. in medical use of physical activities to gain, conserve and improve health at the level of "Sport for All" and to guard against possible hazards;
   d. in participating in the planning and control of hygiene and safety precautions for all types of sports installations, these functions being performed in conjunction with other experts and responsible authorities.
2. Therapeutic functions:
   a. by employing techniques in the field of traumatology and internal and physical medicine for the treatment and functional rehabilitation of athletes to enable them to resume training as soon as appropriate;
   b. by contributing to the adjustment and rehabilitation of the physically and mentally handicapped.
3. Instruction and health education functions:
   a. through the training of sports doctors;
   b. through the information of doctors in general;
   c. through contributions to the training and information of sports instructors and coaches;
   d. through the health education of the public by:
      i. lectures arranged for particular age groups or categories of persons explaining how to derive full benefit from the exercise of a sport and how to avoid the risks of specific kinds of sports;

ii. advice and guidance to teachers, coaches etc. in matters of health education pertaining to the various kinds of sports and related problems such as nutrition, medication, use of leisure time etc.;

iii. close collaboration with bodies responsible for health education to advertise sport as a means of acquiring, conserving and improving physical and mental health and improving the quality of life in general.

4. Basic and applied sports medicine research:

a. particularly directed to studying the effects of sports and other physical activities on the health and well-being of different age and population groups and to studying the most suitable means of practising and supervising sports and physical activities in order to obtain the best results. Special emphasis should be laid on the standardisation of tests and measurements, and on the collection and processing of data at national and international level.

Appendix C

Organisation and equipment of sports medicine centres

In regard to this resolution and those adopted previously, Resolution (70) 7 on the Medical Aspects of Sport, and Resolution (72) 30 on Hygiene of Sports Installations, sports medicine services should be made available to individuals and associations by the medical profession, the public health and school health services, and by sports medicine centres.

There should be at least one (national) sports medicine centre in every member state.

In organising national and/or regional sports medicine centres, consideration should be given to attaching new institutions to colleges and universities where there will be access to laboratories, specialists and hospital facilities.

Likewise, in using and regrouping existing resources, functional units working as sports medicine centres could be envisaged.

National sports medicine centres

1. The functions of national sports medicine centres could be seen as:

a. the provision of medical services in the broadest sense for the purposes of sport;

b. teaching;

c. research.

Suggested requirements for a national sports medicine centre:

2. Accommodation: waiting rooms, reception, secretariat with the necessary equipment and facilities, changing rooms and examination rooms.

These premises should be designed in such a way that several doctors can work together easily as a team.

3. Medical services.

The premises should be designed for rational operation to provide for:

a. diagnosis and assessment of aptitude for physical performance;

b. treatment of disorders and injuries caused by sports;

c. rehabilitation.

a. Diagnosis

i. Heart, lung, circulatory and pulmonary functions laboratory: spiro-ergometer with small testing station for continuous recording of pulse, blood pressure and electrocardiograph readings under strain. Single, triple and sextuple direct tracers should be available to record these figures, so that further heart and circulation factors, such as heartbeat, arterial pulse etc., may be recorded simultaneously. Telemetric equipment, especially for training control.

ii. Radiographic and radioscopic laboratory: suitable equipment for general and special X-ray examinations, for example determination of heart volume, tele-radiography, large X-ray kymograph, for example, for observation of circulation. Radiographic and radioscopic equipment for at least minor casualties, for example, portable X-ray apparatus with universal stand, mainly for first-aid purposes.

iii. Clinical and biochemical laboratory: equipped to conduct not only routine urine and blood tests but also modern enzyme testing, also including electrophoresis and gas chromatography apparatus (doping tests).

iv. Anthropometric, dynamometric, audiometric and optometric equipment.

b. Treatment

i. Equipment and facilities for first-aid and traumatological treatment of sports injuries, to be provided in a special department.

ii. Mobile and portable emergency instrumentation and apparatus.

iii. Transportation facilities.

iv. Equipment for the treatment of various other minor disorders.

v. Equipment and facilities for physio-, kinesi-, electro- and hydrotherapy.

c. Rehabilitation

i. Equipment such as:

- bicycle ergometer for exercise therapy;
- rowing apparatus with sliding seat;
- wall pulleys adjustable for height and tension;
- several sets of mobile exercise apparatus with variable pushing and pulling tension;
- special sport gyroscope, special rollers for foot exercises, and miscellaneous apparatus for gymnastics and play therapy such as hoops, balls, staffs, rings etc.

4. Teaching

Proper training facilities with modern equipment and teaching aids, including well-equipped classrooms and lecture rooms:

a. suitable wall charts, skeletons, anatomical models;

b. slides and educational films;

c. dressings;

d. dummies, automatic recording etc., for demonstrating and practising various types of medical procedures, cardiac massage and artificial respiration.

Instruction should be directed primarily to the training of sports doctors, medical students, paramedical personnel, coaches and physical training and sports teachers. A national sports medicine centre could play a key part in the biomedical side of physical education and further training courses. This could be coupled with sports medicine training for medical students during their studies (lectures or practical work on sports medicine and the physiology of sporting performance), refresher training for sports doctors, as well as appropriate lectures on the training of coaches.

5. Research

a. Equipment should be geared to the specific branch of research (for instance, research in biomechanics calls for special apparatus for measuring forces, pressures, acceleration and velocity, partly with telemetric and cinematographic equipment).

b. Documentation, information and statistics for sports medicine. Documentation section with sports literature, magazine collections, collections of offprints and possibly a file on sports facilities; access to electronic data processing devices.
c. Translation service.
d. Sports medicine library.
e. Technical services with the following equipment:
    i. universal reproduction equipment in conjunction with a miniature (35 mm) camera;
    ii. microfilming equipment;
    iii. microfilm reader, equipped with projection facilities for a large group of readers, and for the reproduction of readable large-size prints;
    iv. universal enlarger;
    v. photocopying equipment;
    vi. paper and film cutting devices;
    vii. equipment for binding notebooks, periodicals and books.
f. Workshop
Other sports medicine centres.
Other sports medicine centres may be established on the basis of regional or local demands as regional and/or local sports medicine centres.

The functions of those centres may be seen on three operational levels:
1. the original function of preventive sports medicine (that is, to establish that the practice of competitive sports is not contra-indicated) and medical supervision of training;
2. therapeutic and emergency measures;
3. health education functions.

All these functions (1 to 3) are listed in Appendix B.
At all events, minimum equipment should always be provided for the purpose of medical aptitude tests.
It should be stressed that the value of check-ups for those who undergo them lies in the information and safeguards they thereby acquire, including a better knowledge of themselves. The relationship between physical condition and training is of direct concern to the athlete, and opens up a dialogue with the athlete and trainer which goes beyond the preventive stage into the realm of health education.

If local and regional sports medicine centres are established, the local centres should concentrate their efforts mainly on:
1. preventive medicine in all its aspects (covered under 1a. and b. in Appendix B);
2. diagnosis of the commonest disorders;
3. possibility of consulting specialists and laboratories;
4. co-operation of sports physicians, physicians in general practice, coaches, physical education instructors and teachers, for the mutual exchange of information on basic health education.

The regional centres should concern themselves in addition with:
1. basic therapy and rehabilitation methods;
2. training and information for doctors, teachers, trainers, coaches and the general public;
3. (where possible) research activities.

Regional sports medicine centres might either:

1. comprise all the services and specialised equipment needed or,
2. be more rudimentary in structure but have links with laboratories or specialised hospital departments, so that all types of sports medicine, preventive sports medicine, training supervision and treatment could be carried out in these centres.

Suggested requirements for sports medicine centres other than national centres.
In addition to the usual offices, waiting room, changing room, WC and examination room, there should be a first-aid and resuscitation room.

In premises for routine sports medicine and special check-ups, an X-ray room is indispensable, and a small laboratory an asset.

1. Equipment for diagnosis and assessment of aptitude for physical exertion:
   a. equipment for routine biological checks;
   b. radiographic and radioscopic apparatus;
   c. electrocardiograph (whether or not transistorised) single, triple or sextuple tracing and phonocardiography;
   d. telemeter;
   e. spiroergometer suited to the size and requirements of the institute and, if possible, equipment for blood gas analysis;
   f. clinical laboratory for urine and blood tests and, if possible, also for enzyme analyses;
   g. audiometric and optometric equipment.
2. Treatment facilities and equipment.
   One or two medium-sized rooms with changing cabins should be enough for treatment purposes:
   a. equipment for first-aid and resuscitation;
   b. sets of instruments for traumatology;
   c. portable sets of surgical instruments;
   d. well-equipped first-aid outfits for emergencies.

Provision should also be made for extremely rapid transport facilities.
Likewise, there should be a library with a selection of reference works appropriate to the requirements and special purposes of the centre.

Chapter 26
NEW PARTNERSHIPS

26.1. Resolution on New Partnerships in Sport (86/7)
The European Ministers responsible for Sport, meeting in Dublin for their 5th Conference from 30 September to 2 October 1986

Recalling the European Sport for All Charter, approved at their first Conference and adopted by the Committee of Ministers of the Council of Europe as Resolution (76) 41 on the Principles for a Policy of Sport for All;
Taking note of the "European Sports Sponsorship Code" of which the 3rd Conference at Palma de Majorca (1981), "took note with satisfaction";
Having considered the results of the seminar "New partnerships in sport", Papendal, April 1986, concerning the contributions of government, sport, commerce and media to the development of sport;
Recognising that interest by the media and the commercial sector in sport has increased considerably during the last decade;
Are of the opinion that the impact of the media and the commercial sector on sport and on sports policy has on the whole contributed positively to the development of sport;
Considering that these interests will continue to increase in the years to come;
Recognising that for the development of the aims of governmental policies for sport and their means of action there is a need for a continuous exchange of information and development of practical co-operation, leading, in many cases, to consultation and if possible, co-ordination of the aims and means of action between the other parties involved;
Recommend that such exchange, consultation and co-ordination should where necessary, take place in meetings between the four parties involved;
Invite the Committee of Ministers of the Council of Europe to ask the CDDS to consider ways of organising a similar exchange and consultation at European level.

Chapter 27
OLDER PERSONS

27.1. Recommendation No. R (88) 8 of the Committee of Ministers to Member States on Sport for All: Older Persons

Adopted by the Committee of Ministers on 18 April 1988 at the 416th meeting of the Ministers' Deputies

The Committee of Ministers, under the terms of Article 15.b of the Statute of the Council of Europe,
Recalling its Resolution (74) 31 on health care and social work for old people living at home, and in particular Section VI on leisure, physical exercise and part-time activities;
Having regard to the Resolution adopted by the European Ministers responsible for Sport at their 3rd Conference at Palma de Majorca in 1981 on priorities for future European sports co-operation;
Recognising the fact that both the number of older persons and, more particularly, their proportion of the total population are growing steadily in many member states of the Council of Europe, and that the implementation of the European Sport for All Charter since 1975 has bypassed many of the present generation of older people, and that they therefore need, in many cases, special measures taken on their behalf;
Anxious to enable people to take part in physical activities throughout their lives, and that the principles of the European Sport for All Charter should apply to every social group regardless of age;
Convinced that sport greatly contributes to the preservation of physical mobility, of the health and fitness of older persons, promotes social contact and independence, and adds a zest and motivation to their lives,

I. Recommends the governments of member states:
   1. to take the necessary steps to encourage and support efforts to promote a greater participation by older persons in appropriate sporting and other physical activities;
   2. to co-operate with sports organisations, local authorities and other relevant institutions in their task and, in particular, to follow the guidelines set out in the appendix to the present recommendation;

II. Instructs the Secretary General to transmit this recommendation to the governments of non-member states, party to the European Cultural Convention;

III. Instructs the Secretary General to transmit this recommendation to the Directors General of the World Health Organisation and of the United Nations Educational, Scientific and Cultural Organisation.

Appendix to Recommendation No. R (88) 8
Guidelines for "Sport for all: older persons"

1. To set out, considering the physical, mental and social benefits to be expected, objectives for the promotion of sport of older persons.
2. To analyse existing needs and possibilities in order to determine which gerontological and socio-economic factors and what forms of organisation may encourage or discour-

age older persons to participate in physical activities in each member state, and to encourage the spread of successful pilot projects which overcome obstacles, difficulties or prejudices.

3. To stimulate the development of a policy on sport for older persons and to encourage a wider knowledge and awareness amongst public bodies, sports organisations, organisations working with older persons and older persons themselves of the beneficial effects, both social and physical, of regular and appropriate exercise, and to overcome prejudices with regard to the scale and range of activities suitable for older persons, including the very old.
4. To encourage, where appropriate, the development of basic and applied research aimed at improving the provision of "Sport for all: older persons", and the dissemination of such research results; such research should also study the prevention of injuries, the need for special medical care and supervision, and the promotion of the independence, responsibility and autonomy of older people for their own activities, in which sport may play a part.
5. To encourage the development of physical activities based on the physical state of the potential participant, rather than on his or her chronological age, and particularly for those older persons who may not have previous experience of such activities.
6. To develop an adequate range and variety of programmes and facilities designed to improve social communication, to preserve fitness and to improve health through regular sporting activity, paying attention to the social needs, motivation and physical potential of different age groups, to involve older persons in the elaboration of such programmes and to incorporate appropriate medical support and supervision.
7. To encourage the development of sport programmes and structures that will enable the present generation of middle-aged participants to continue to practise sport as they attain a higher age group.
8. To increase, intensify and improve the initial, refresher and further training of leaders of sports and physical activities for older persons, to encourage older people themselves to participate in such training courses and to encourage other potential leaders, such as physiotherapists, to acquire training in the organisation and conduct of appropriate physical activities.
9. To pay particular attention to the development of programmes for those older persons living permanently in institutions or homes, particularly those lacking any form of physical activities.
10. To recognise that older persons may wish to aspire to take part in competitive sports, either in age-based classes of ordinary sports or in specially organised events with adapted disciplines, and to make due provision for this in the overall programmes of "Sport for all: older persons".
11. To ensure that, when sports policies are being decided, the interests and views of older persons are given due consideration.
12. To encourage the preparation and diffusion of information about opportunities in "Sport for all: older persons"; this information should be designed to reach the various kinds of older persons and use media to which they are likely to respond.
13. To encourage existing frameworks providing "Sport for all: older persons" to develop their policies and programmes in accordance with the recommendation and to use these frameworks as the basis of their own policies as far as possible and appropriate.

Chapter 28
OLYMPIC GAMES

28.1. Resolution 719 (1980) on the Moscow Olympic Games

The Assembly,
Recalling its Recommendation 889 on the crisis in Afghanistan and Resolution 718 on the arrest and forced exile of Dr Andrei Sakharov;
Bearing in mind the unchanging moral values underlying democracy and sport, draws to the attention of the National Olympic Committees of member states and the athletes of Europe the seriousness of the events which have taken place in Afghanistan during the last month, together with the treatment accorded to Professor Sakharov, and urges them to take these events into account in making their decisions as to whether to participate in the Olympic Games in Moscow or in the ceremonies associated with them;
Calls on European governments, in the light of their contacts with their National Olympic Committees and through them with the International Olympic Committee, to endeavour to concert in the framework of the Conference of European Ministers responsible for sport a common position with regard to the Olympic Games in Moscow.

28.2. Resolution 738 (1980) on the Olympic Games and the Outlook for their Future

The Assembly,
Noting with regret that the Olympic Games are moving further and further away from the ancient ideal which it sought to revive at the close of the last century;
Noting that they no longer comply strictly with their purpose, namely participation in competitive sport for the honour and the physical and moral development of the individual;
Deploring the fact that they have also, indeed mainly, become a political and commercial competition between major states and large cities, and that economic, industrial, financial, nationalist and ideological interests interfere with their competitive spirit;
Deploring the impossibility, given the immense investments required for providing the facilities and organisation connected with an Olympiad, for medium-sized and small countries to take their turn in organising the Games;
Deploring the fact that, instead of contributing towards peace, the Games are a source of discord in international relations;
Recalling that the Games were in ancient times the occasion of a sacred truce, that no athlete from a nation at war could participate, and that warring cities were obliged to lay down their arms, at least temporarily, if they wished their champions to be allowed to compete;
Hopeful that this aspect of the Olympic spirit too can be restored, and that encouragement will be given to any arrangements making it possible throughout the duration of the Games for hostilities between nations or peoples engaged in armed conflict to be broken off;
Bearing in mind that in antiquity the Games were always held in the same place, at a site specially dedicated to that effect:
Recalling the proposals made by the Government of the Republic of Greece in 1976, and repeated in 1980, for the permanent establishment of the Games in Greece;
Recalling the Resolution on Sport in Society adopted by the Conference of European Ministers responsible for Sport in London in 1978;

Welcoming the interest shown by the Conference of Local and Regional Authorities of Europe which has recently indicated its intention of supporting this resolution;
Having taken note of the report by its Committee on Culture and Education (Doe. 4585), which includes reference to studies and talks conducted in Greece, requests:

1. that all competent public authorities. international and national organisations and bodies unite their efforts to prevent the Olympic Games from being dominated by politics and tainted by sheer scale, commercialisation, professionalism or any other kind of abuse threatening their survival;
2. that, in order to achieve this, the summer Olympic Games should henceforth be regularly and definitely be held on the same site, namely in the neighbourhood of Olympia where they originated;
3. that this place, to be known as "Nea Olympia", should be granted the appropriate international status and placed under the authority of the International Olympic Committee;
4. that the Greek Government and the International Olympic Committee define the international status of Nea Olympia;
5. that arrangements be made to enable the facilities of Nea Olympia to be financed by an international fund;
6. that Nea Olympia may become a place where nations are brought closer together, and sports and cultural activities permanently organised, in particular by the construction of treasuries for art and athletes hostels;
7. that the organisation and running of Olympic competition my conform as closely as possible to the idea of individual fulfilment, international fraternity and the promotion of peace, which is their raison d'être;
8. that the winter Olympic Games be organised according to the same principles;
9. that the governments of member states provide the International Olympic Committee with all possible support and all necessary assistance as a contribution towards the achievement of these aims.

28.3. Recommendation 900 (1980) on the Olympic Games and the Outlook for their Future

The Assembly,
Recalling the Resolution on Sport in Society adopted by the Conference of European Ministers responsible for Sport in London in 1978;
Referring to its Resolution 738 on the Olympic Games and the outlook for their future, in which it supported the idea of the return of the Games to their country of origin;
Considering the proposals to this effect made by the Government of the Republic of Greece in 1976, and repeated in 1980;
Recommends that the Committee of Ministers invite the governments of member states, in consultation with the International Olympic Committee. to do everything in their power. as rapidly as possible, so that the aims set out in Resolution 738 may be put into effect.

28.4. Resolution on the Olympic Games (84/3)

The European Ministers responsible for Sport, meeting in Malta for their 4th Conference, from 15 to 16 May 1984, express their complete and wholehearted support for the Olympic Games, both now and in the future. They wish the International Olympic Committee well in their current efforts to maintain and enhance the success of the Olympic movement.

28.5. Written Declaration No. 109 (1984) on the Olympic Games

The undersigned, members of the Assembly,

1. Noting that the Olympic Games are on the point of extinction; the Soviet Union has announced that it will boycott the summer Olympic Games in Los Angeles, and other countries from the Eastern bloc will doubtless do the same. which would again mean that there will be only limited participation in the Los Angeles Games;
2. Pointing out that in 1980 the United States and other Western countries boycotted the Olympic Games in Moscow, that in 1976 the majority of African countries took no part in the Montreal Games and that the Olympic Games are, therefore, now likely to fail foul of international political conflict for a third time; and that the future of the Games is thus seriously put in doubt;
3. Consider that boycotts of the Olympic Games have never helped to improve the political situation but, on the contrary, have always had detrimental effects on sport and those who take part in it, and that, although sport as a major social movement can certainly not remain cut off from political events, it will always come off worst when caught up in conflicts which cannot be resolved politically;
4. Declare that the member states of the Council of Europe must not stand idly by, and accordingly ask the Committee of Ministers and the governments of all member countries to take political steps to overcome the serious crisis threatening the Olympic Games.

28.6. Resolution on the Games of the XXIV Olympiad in 1988 (86/10)

The European Ministers responsible for Sport, meeting in Dublin for their 5th Conference from 30 September to 2 October 1986,

Conscious of the international significance of the Olympic Games;
Taking note of the efforts of the IOC effectively to deal with the many difficult issues facing the Olympic movement;
Express their full support for the Olympic Games now and in the future; and for the work of the IOC to secure this continued development of the Olympic movement and their desire to ensure the greatest possible participation in the 1988 Olympic Games and beyond.

28.7. Resolution on the 1992 Olympic Games: Albertville and Barcelona (89/7)

The European Ministers responsible for Sport, meeting in Reykjavik from 30 May to 1 June 1989 for their 6th Conference,

Taking note of the holding of the Winter Olympics and the Summer Olympics in the same year, in two European countries, France and Spain;
Reaffirming the international significance of the Olympic Games as a fundamental element of communication between peoples and of the development of sport;
Express their full support for the Olympic Games at Albertville and Barcelona, and for the work of the countries organising these two events.

28.8. Written Declaration No. 206 (1991) on South Africa and the Olympic Games

The undersigned, members of the Assembly,
Recall that South Africa was excluded from the International Olympic Committee (IOC) in 1970 as a result of its policy of racial segregation in sport;
Note that the Head of the South African State, Mr Frederik de Klerk, announced that the last laws on apartheid would be abolished in his country in the next few weeks;
Wish that the new Interim National Olympic Committee of South Africa (INOCSA) be recognised by the IOC and that South Africa be allowed to participate in the 1992 Olympic Games in Barcelona, if the following conditions are satisfied:

1. abolition of apartheid;
2. conformity with the Olympic Charter;
3. INOCSA becomes a full Olympic Committee:
4. normalisation of relations with the international sports federation and the continuation of efforts to unify South African sports on a non-racial basis;
5. normalisation of relations with the African confederations.

Chapter 29
PHYSICAL EDUCATION

29.1. Resolution (66) 38 on Physical Education, Sport and Outdoor Pursuits

Adopted by the Ministers' Deputies on 24 September 1966

The Committee of Ministers,

Having regard to the Recommendation on Physical Education, Sport and Outdoor Pursuits submitted by its Council for Cultural Cooperation at the instigation of its Committee for Out-of-School Education;

Considering that physical activities and sport have a specific contribution to make for the development of the individual;

Considering that the reduced physical demands made by modern working conditions and the constant increase in leisure have created urgent additional needs for outdoor activities and sport to compensate for the widespread industrialisation and urbanisation of our society;

Considering that the practice of sport gives opportunities for the individual to exercise his capacity for leadership and acceptance of responsibility in a democratic society;

Invites member Governments,

a. to give wide publicity to these considerations among bodies which have an influence on public opinion, emphasising the value for coming generations of the proper use of leisure;

b. to secure recognition at all stages of the educational process (primary, secondary and higher) of the value of physical education, sport and outdoor pursuits as an integral part of that process. This implies an atmosphere of freedom where the young can exercise a spirit of initiative by having responsibilities in the organisation of their activities and clubs. An introduction should be given to a wide range of activities appropriate to adult life;

c. to ensure that courses adequate in scale and quantity are available to train full and part-time teachers and leaders, paid and voluntary. These suitably qualified staff should be encouraged to work not only in educational establishments but also in sports centres of various types including industrial sports clubs; joint appointments between schools and such centres can help to bridge the gap between school and out-of-school activities. Appropriate financial provision will be necessary for this purpose and for provision of facilities;

d. to ensure that provision is made for the combined planning and joint use of facilities, coordination of public, private, school and out-of-school activities is needed at all levels. This is particularly necessary in the case of the instalment and use of facilities.

Chapter 30
PRISONERS

30.1. Resolution Sport for Prisoners and Young Delinquents (86/3)

The European Ministers responsible for Sport, meeting in Dublin for their 5th Conference from 30 September to 2 October 1986;

Considering the importance of not neglecting humanitarian factors recognised by human rights;
Taking account of each country's domestic law;
Pointing out that the European Sport for All Charter makes no distinction of social category;

Invite the member governments of the Council of Europe to:

1. recognise the value and benefits of physical education and sports activates in prisons and other custodial centres;
2. encourage and, where necessary, offer support, including financial, to sports organisations so that they offer their aid and experience in developing with prison authorities sports programmes – be they competitive or not – especially for particular categories of detainees;
3. prepare for detainees' release and social reintegration through the organisation of sports meetings inside and if possible outside establishments, one means of so doing being to allow inmates to join sports clubs;
4. encourage, where necessary, prison departments to provide animators to help detainees develop and organise their own sport and recreation as an exercise in independence;
5. assist the deployment and training of an adequate number of motivated and qualified staff (from prison services, sports associations, voluntary organisations or other sources, as appropriate to needs and circumstances) to carry out the aforementioned programmes;
6. provide opportunities for prison and detention centre staff to take basic or further training for a sports or physical educational qualification;
7. encourage sports authorities and prison services to run common training schemes so that qualifications are mutually recognised;
8. enable teachers of sport and physical education who wish to work in prisons or detention centres to gain experience of them;
9. provide prison establishments with sports facilities and enable those without their own facilities to have access to suitable local facilities where security considerations permit;
10. encourage the development of research strategies, where necessary, to assess the effects of regular sport and recreation on detainees' physical and mental well-being and on former detainees;
11. encourage the development of sports programmes for potential young offenders (that is, those at risk of custodial sentences should they further offend) via co-operation between sports organisations, municipalities, police, probation services and voluntary organisations;

Invite the Committee of Ministers to ask the CDDS to ensure that the work begun on this project is properly pursued.

Chapter 31
PROFESSIONAL SPORT

31.1. Resolution 1204 (1999) on Europe and professional sport

1. The Assembly recalls the judgement of the European Court of Justice in the Bosman case of December 1995 which declared illegal in the countries of the European Economic Area the transfer rules and the nationality clause applied by UEFA (Union of European Football Associations) in respect of professional football in Europe.
2. While being fully aware that this judgement ensures that professional footballers are able to exercise the right to the free movement of workers, the Assembly nevertheless draws attention to the appreciable repercussions for professional sport in general (and particularly team sports). the financial survival of small clubs, and the training and employment of young sportsmen and women in Europe as a whole.
3. The Assembly shares the desire, voiced first of all by UEFA, to find a way of reducing the negative impact of these implications in a way compatible not only with European law and other recognised legal texts, but also with the satisfactory development of sport throughout Europe.
4. Accordingly, the Assembly points out that the impact on developments in professional sport in Europe, and team sports in particular. of the liberalisation and technological development of television, resulting from the remarkable increase in demand for sports broadcasts and the prices paid for these broadcasts, has been at least as important as that of the Bosman judgement.
5. The Assembly is particularly concerned about the implications of the transformation of high-level football from a sport in its own right to a television event and the widening financial gap between high-level professional clubs and the rest of the football community.
6. It is concerned about the possible malfunctions of the procedures for the licensing of sports equipment (in particular with regard to exclusive agreements).
7. There is a danger that the conversion of sports clubs into joint stock or other corporate forms may result in the same economic group controlling several teams participating in the same competition. This would give rise to concern about the genuine nature of a match between two teams controlled by the same economic group, especially when major financial incentives are at stake.
8. It is also concerned about the veiled threats from some major European clubs to create their own European championship. While welcoming UEFA's efforts to overcome these threats by adapting the rules of the Champions' League, the Assembly notes that unless sufficient funds are spread throughout the game there is a danger of widening disparities between "rich" and "poor" clubs, thereby having an adverse effect on the competitiveness of national championships.
9. The Assembly asserts the specific, social, unifying, educational and cultural role of sport. It recalls, in this connection, the European Sports Charter and the European Code of Sports Ethics adopted by the Council of Europe in 1992. Sport is much more than a mere business matter: the opponents depend on each other, unlike in industry and the service sectors.

10. Consequently, the Assembly calls on the competent authorities in the member states of the Council of Europe:
   i. to authorise the centralised marketing, for example by federations, of sports events broadcasting rights insofar as this would ensure a fair distribution of income among the participants;
   ii. to include the main sports competitions on the list of events of major significance provided for in the European Convention on Transfrontier Television;
   iii. to support non-governmental sports organisations and the millions working for sport on a voluntary and unpaid basis throughout Europe.
11. The Assembly also calls on European sports federations and in particular on UEFA:
   i. to implement or continue implementing the centralised marketing of television rights for competitions coming under its competence and to ensure the fair distribution of income among participants so as to maintain financial balance and a spirit of solidarity in European sport;
   ii. to ensure that the new rules of the Champions' League do not have any adverse effect on the competitiveness of national championships;
   iii. to propose, as a means of remunerating clubs for their activities in the training of young players, a non-discriminatory "training fee" which could be limited to the first transfer of a player as a professional, or to transfers of players under a given age;
   iv. to prohibit the participation in the same competition of more than one club belonging to the same owner;
   v. to ensure that the rules applied by the European Union to the European Economic Area are compatible, from the standpoint of sporting equity, with those in force within each state and outside the European Economic Area.
12. Finally, the Assembly calls on the European Union:
   i. to recognise the specific nature of sport whose social, unifying, educational and cultural role should not be undermined by commercial activities;
   ii. to accept the principle of remunerating clubs for their activities in the training of young players through non-discriminatory training fees;
   iii. to accept the legality of the centralised marketing of sports events broadcasting rights with a view to the fair distribution of income among participating clubs and to the grass roots of the sport;
   iv. to accept the continued organisation of sporting competition in Europe along national territorial lines;
   v. to apply in the European Economic Area rules that are compatible, from the standpoint of sporting equity, with those in force within each state and outside the European Economic Area.

Chapter 32
SOCIAL COHESION

32.1. Recommendation No. R (99) 9 of the Committee of Ministers to Member States on the Role of Sport in Furthering Social Cohesion

Adopted by the Committee of Ministers on 22 April 1999, at the 669th meeting of the Ministers' Deputies

The Committee of Ministers, under the terms of Article 15.b of the Statute of the Council of Europe,

Following up the Final Declaration of the second summit of the Council of Europe, 10 and 11 October 1997, where the heads of state and government stated that "social cohesion is one of the foremost needs of the wider Europe and should be pursued as an essential complement to the promotion of human rights and dignity", and recognised "the role of sport in promoting social integration, particularly among young people";

Acting in response to the Action Plan resulting from the summit, where the heads of state and government instructed the Committee of Ministers to "define a social strategy to respond to the challenges of society" and "to establish a programme for the promotion of the interests of children in partnership with the international and non-governmental organisations concerned";

Acknowledging that while sport is not the answer to all societal ills it can play a distinctive part in fighting marginalisation and can act as a valid tool in working for social cohesion across the whole spectrum of society, not only among young people;

Having regard to the discussions of the 15th Informal Meeting of Ministers Responsible for Sport held in Cyprus on May 14 and 15, 1998 where a central theme for debate was the role of sport in achieving social cohesion;

Conscious of earlier texts in the same area, such as:

- the European Sports Charter, No. R (92) 13, which underlines the right of everyone to participate in sport and insists that sport be kept free of any kind of discrimination on the grounds of religion, race, sex, political or social status;
- Recommendation No. R (95) 17 on the significance of sport for society, which relates to the place of sport in social development;
- those adopted by the Congress of Local and Regional Authorities of Europe, including Recommendation (96) 16 on sport and local authorities and the chapter in the European Urban Charter, 1993, which states that "sport provides the means of interaction for individuals and communities, bringing them closer together. It can help, particularly with young people, in giving them a sense of direction and avoid social alienation. It can help in the fight against drug abuse and exclusion";

Aware that participation in institutional and community life in Europe today is undergoing a genuine crisis, especially with regard to the democratic participation of certain groups of citizens in civil and leisure activities;

Directing the attention of governments to the unique role which sport can play in this context, as an activity that already involves a significant percentage of the population, either as participants or spectators;

Bearing in mind the practical programmes and concrete results set out in the Clearing House publication on Social cohesion and sport which gives examples of the best current practice,

Recommends that the governments of member States:

1. while adopting global and integrated sports policies at national level to facilitate the participation of all people in sport, particularly target groups of disadvantaged or excluded people and:
   a. with regard to the disabled:
      – adapt sporting facilities and facilitate access and transport to these facilities and recreation areas as set out in Recommendation No. R (86) 18 on the European Charter for Sport for All: disabled persons;
      – set up projects designed for the disabled to stimulate self-confidence in their own physical abilities, together with programmes which make them aware of the potential physical, psychological and social benefits of sport;
      – encourage mainstream sporting bodies to make provision for, and contact with, disabled sporting bodies and to take measures towards eliminating the distinction between disabled and mainstream sport in order to provide acceptance and integration for the disabled in the world of sport;
   b. with regard to the unemployed:
      – use sports programmes at low cost to provide regular activities for this group. Such programmes should include contact with a wide sector of the population, encourage feelings of achievement and self-worth and envisage using the unemployed in positions of responsibility;
      – develop job creation programmes and projects in the field of sport;
   c. with regard to migrants, ethnic groups and refugees:
      – promote sport both as an aid to integrating people in the society in which they currently live and to break down the barriers between different groups;
      – increase the number of, and publicise knowledge about, sports facilities and activities in areas where these groups live;
      – provide specific programmes for groups which might suffer from a double disadvantage, for example, being a woman or girl and a migrant;
      – use sport as a means to tackle the possible isolation of women and girls in these groups and link it with educational programmes in other areas, such as nutrition and fitness sports;
      – ensure that no sports club practises discrimination;
      – develop projects where the various groups – such as national minorities – are encouraged to bring fresh impetus or enthusiasm to certain sports and introduce new sports and traditional games into the society where they live;
   d. with regard to children:
      – use sports programmes to help children appreciate the sensation of being both an individual and a valued member of a functioning effective group, which is part of education for democratic citizenship;
      – ensure that physical education remains compulsory in schools and that sufficient time is given to it to allow teachers to take into account the social dimension of sport;
      – take measures to guarantee that physical education classes are carried out by qualified teachers aiming to provide high quality experiences;
      – support out-of-school sports programmes to extend the scope and range of physical education in schools and to make good any possible deficiencies;

e. with regard to young people:
   - develop policies and programmes to encourage the personal development and involvement in society of young people through sport;
   - ensure measures to co-ordinate in-school and out-of-school physical education, sport and recreational activities to give follow-on programmes for young people before they leave school, so that they remain involved in life-long sport;

f. with regard to women:
   - take measures to encourage women to make time in their lives for sporting activities and fight prejudices about sport being seen as a male domain;
   - ensure that opportunities for everyday recreational sport are available for all women;
   - make better provision at sports facilities for mothers, such as crèches for small children;
   - make specific provision for those who have special needs which might arise because of their social background, lack of access to facilities, or the fact that they are not in paid employment;

g. with regard to senior citizens:
   - ensure that older people can enjoy the benefits of suitable sports activities, which can help prevent social isolation and preserve functional (physical and mental) capacities, as set out in Recommendation No. R(88) 8;
   - take measures to draw on the wealth of experience that this group can offer as volunteers in the sports movement;

2. associate local and regional authorities and non-governmental sports associations with the development and implementation of these policies.

Further information on these groups and examples of means for achieving these objectives are set out in the explanatory memorandum to this recommendation.

32.2. Resolution on principles for policies using sport to promote social cohesion (2/2000)

The European Ministers responsible for Sport, meeting in Bratislava for their 9th Conference from 30-31 May 2000

Conscious of the substantial work done previously by the Committee for the Development of Sport in developing policies designed to promote the social inclusion of various specific minority groups through sport,
Convinced that the need existed to identify the underlying principles, which should be incorporated into a comprehensive policy for sport and social cohesion,
Remembering the Declaration issued at the close of the Second Summit of the Heads of State and governments of member States of the Council of Europe (Strasbourg, 10-11 October 1997), which recognised 'the role of sport in promoting social integration, particularly among young people',
Aware that programmes which have social cohesion as one of their aims should respect both the principles underlying such a comprehensive policy and the provisions of the European Sports Charter (R (92)13) and the Code of Sports Ethics (R (92)14),

Bearing in mind the Recommendation No. R (99) 9 of the Committee of Ministers to member States on the role of sport in furthering social cohesion, which recommends that governments in adopting sports policies should especially target particular groups of disadvantaged or excluded people,
Stressing their belief that sport is a significant social right that should be available and accessible to all people,
Recalling that research has shown that sport does make a contribution to social development, and when based on the correct principles can help counter some problems in society as recognised in both R. (95) 17 on 'The Social Significance of Sport for Society' (Section 2 of the Appendix), and the Declaration on this subject adopted at their 8th Conference,
Resolve to:
Ensure that the principles, as submitted to the Conference in the document 'Towards a comprehensive policy on sport and social cohesion' and reproduced in the Appendix to this Resolution, are built into global and integrated sports policies at national level and incorporated into subsequent programmes, to facilitate the participation of all people in sport,
Further ensure that programmes which use the potential of sport to further social cohesion are rooted in these policies,
Take into account the potential of sport in national programmes designed for the different groups of unemployed people, recognising that besides the acknowledged benefits for mental and physical health, training and education in sport can lead to employment,
Acknowledge the benefits which sport can provide for refugees and displaced people and welcome and support the work of the CDDS in this area,
Recognise the positive contribution made to sport by the inclusion of ethnic and cultural minorities, and people with disabilities which helps promote a tolerant and diverse society,
Invite all sectors ' non-governmental sports organisations, civil society groups and voluntary institutions ' to co-operate closely with the national authorities, in view of the range and complexity of issues to be tackled, in order to achieve and implement a policy which harnesses the potential of sport to further social cohesion.

Appendix
Principles for policies using sport to promote social cohesion
The articles of the European Sports Charter commit the governments of member States to taking the necessary steps to enable every individual to participate in sport'. Sport is defined as meaning 'all forms of physical activity 'aimed at expressing or improving physical fitness and mental well-being, forming social relationships'.' As already mentioned the policy adopted to further social cohesion should agree with the spirit and the Articles of the Charter.
Programmes using sport to further social cohesion may be designed and implemented at the central, regional or local government levels or entrusted to the voluntary sports sector. Given the range of issues that need to be tackled there are good reasons for all sectors to be involved. Some problems leading to social exclusion need to be tackled at national level, whereas others may best be dealt with at the local level.
There are good grounds for inviting non-governmental sports organisations, civil society groups and voluntary institutions to take a leading role in combating social exclusion through the use of sport. However, when the voluntary sector is made responsible for running such programmes it is essential to ensure that there is both close co-operation and adequate government funding.
Sources of new funding should be investigated. It may be that large sports federations and associations could be encouraged to fund and/or run programmes on social cohesion. The use of

European funds for urban regeneration or unemployment programmes could also be explored in the context of programmes on unemployment, sport and social cohesion.
Any policy that is designed to use sport to further social cohesion, whether on an international, national or local level should be established according to the following guidelines. The policy should:

a) respect the provisions of the European Sports Charter and its foundation principle of 'Sport for All';
b) accord with the ethical principles outlined in the Code of Sports Ethics and Fair Play;
c) should start, if at all possible, from a basis of hard data and systematised information. If this is not available planners should use existing evidence;
d) have clear output and outcome goals which are recognised and shared by those framing and implementing the policy;
e) have built-in evaluation criteria and sufficient flexibility to respond quickly to the findings of any evaluation; The policy should be designed to bear in mind that society is dynamic and always in the process of change;
f) should pay scrupulous attention to all types of diversity, in accordance with Article 4 of the European Sports Charter;
g) be co-active with other areas (synergy). Links with the areas of education, tolerance and fair play in sport are particularly important as a tolerant society is a pre-condition for social cohesion;
h) avoid using sport as a palliative measure, but instead identify the real needs and see how sport can contribute towards meeting them;
i) consider the need for follow-up activities after the conclusion of the initial programme, which may be linked into sports;
j) recognise the potential of both organised and unorganised sport. Unorganised sport taking place outside of federations, sports associations and clubs, like street football, also creates groups and links between players.

Incorporating the principles into programmes
Programmes set up under a policy of using sport as a tool to encourage social cohesion should:

a) respect the factors outlined in points a-j above;
b) include a message on social cohesion;
c) define the common objectives according to the local or specific needs of the target group. The starting point for any specific programme has to be the position of people who make up the target group and their potential resources;
d) embody the concept of local ownership and control with a firm commitment to democracy. Direction and decisions should, whenever possible, take place at the local level, not 'somewhere up there';
e) welcome and incorporate the ideas and suggestions of participants;
f) encourage and provide the opportunities for participants to have real responsibilities and involvement;
g) pursue quality across the spectrum. Projects should offer opportunities for good training, both to participants and leaders;
h) stress the role and importance of partnership. Any group that is set up should be open to newcomers, who on joining can identify readily with the club and its aims and feel that it is 'their' group;
i) adopt a wide conception of sport when designing programmes (e.g. avoid thinking that all sport is team sport, that all sport takes place in clubs).

Chapter 33
SOCIALLY UNDERPRIVILEGED

33.1. Resolution on Sport for Socially Underprivileged and Marginal groups (84/8)
The European Ministers responsible for Sport, meeting in Malta for their 4th Conference on 15 and 16 May 1984,

Convinced that sport is an important way of helping the social reintegration of all kinds of socially underprivileged and marginal groups;
Anxious to see that the principles of Sport for All should apply to everybody, and in particular to these groups;
Considering that steps should be taken to ease their access to the practice of sport;
Considering that it is the duty of all governmental authorities to encourage by all available means the building of sports facilities for these groups;

Request the Committee of Ministers of the Council of Europe to ask the CDDS:
1. to draw up an action programme for participation in sport for these vulnerable groups, in conjunction with the governmental sports authorities;
2. to develop an action programme for the spreading of Sport for All for these target groups.

Chapter 34
SPONSORSHIP

34.1. Resolution on the European Sports Sponsorship Code (81/1)

The European Ministers responsible for Sport, meeting from 8 to 10 April 1981 in Palma de Majorca for their 3rd Conference,

Bearing in mind the European Sport for All Charter, adopted at their 1st Conference at Brussels in 1975, and in particular Article 5 according to which "Methods shall be sought to safeguard sport and sportsmen from exploitation for political, commercial or financial gain ...";
Recalling the resolution adopted at their 2nd Conference at London 1978 on professionalism and commercialism;
Noting that several international sports federations and national confederations have already adopted their own sports sponsorship regulations;
Convinced that it would be to the benefit of sport and the general public to set out in a generally accepted and supplementary voluntary code regulations for sponsorship in sport;
Take note with satisfaction of the European Sports Sponsorship Code (guiding principles and explanatory memorandum) prepared by the CDDS;
Request the Committee of Ministers to ask the Committee for the Development of Sport to study with the non-governmental organisations concerned the implications of a European television satellite network and marketing of video-cassette programmes for sports sponsorship;
Ask the Secretary General of the Council of Europe to transmit these guidelines to the non-governmental sports organisations for information.

Chapter 35
SPORT AS A MEANS OF PEACE

35.1. Declaration on Sport as a means of Peace
The European Ministers responsible for Sport, meeting in Malta for their 4th Conference on 15 and 16 May 1984

Considering that the Olympic Games and the Olympic ideal have always been – both at the time of the original Games and today – an invitation to peace and mutual understanding;
Declare today that this invitation would only be an empty gesture if it is not accompanied by common efforts by all countries to find ways for dialogue which would facilitate participation by everybody in the great four-yearly festival of youth to proclaim the unshakeable desire of the people of the world to live in peace.

Chapter 36
SPORT FOR ALL CHARTER / EUROPEAN SPORTS CHARTER

36.1. Recommendation 588 (1970) on the Development of Sport for All and the Creation of Co-ordinating Structures

The Assembly,
Noting that the transformations of modern society and their corollaries such as industrialisation, automation and urbanisation tend:
1. to eliminate the minimum regular physical exercise essential to man's physical equilibrium;
2. to accentuate man's psychological solitude and dependence on his environment;

Considering that, in such a society, sport has to fulfil two vital functions, namely:
1. a biological function of preserving and developing the physical capacity of present and future generations;
2. a socio-cultural function of helping man, in the context of permanent education and cultural development, to triumph over certain living and working conditions which threaten his development and balance, by giving him means of satisfying his needs of communication, expression and creativeness;

Believing that these considerations warrant, and indeed demand, immediate and extensive measures designed to place sport as a socio-cultural activity within the reach of an ever-widening range of the population, in accordance with the concept "Sport for All" defined by the Council for Cultural Co-operation;
Considering moreover that by its very nature such action requires at both national and European level a concerted and co-ordinated effort by very diverse institutions: ministerial departments, local authorities, sports organisations, permanent educational bodies, industrial and financial circles, trade unions and other professional organisations etc.;
Observing that both on a European level and in most of the member countries the structures that would make such concerted and co-ordinated effort possible are lacking;
Recommends that the Committee of Ministers invite the member governments of the Council of Europe:
1. to launch or support, at national level, "Sport for All" campaigns such as already exist in some member countries:
2. to encourage, if they do not already exist, the creation of national co-ordinating structures for that purpose;
3. to provide the Council of Europe with co-ordinating machinery to promote "Sport for all" on a European scale.

36.2. Recommendation 682 (1972)[8] on a European "Sport for All" Charter
Text adopted by the Assembly on 20 October 1972 (13th Sitting).

The Assembly,

1. Recalling its Recommendation 588 (1970) on the development of Sport for All and the creation of co-ordinating structures;
2. Reaffirming that, in a society increasingly dominated by machines, man needs a certain amount of physical exercise for both his physical and his mental well-being;
3. Observing that a policy for the development of Sport for All, the aim of which is to bring sport as a socio-cultural activity within the reach of as many people as possible, raises problems which cannot be satisfactorily solved within a purely national framework;
4. Believing in this context that the adoption of common principles would enable national policies to be progressively harmonised;
5. Welcoming the fact that the work done by the Council for Cultural Co-operation and various other international bodies has already enabled several common principles to be established;
6. Emphasising, however, that a systematic and comprehensive approach to the problems connected with Sport for All would in particular make it possible to identify objectives and means in regard to a European policy for the development of Sport for All;
7. Conscious that the adoption by the Committee of Ministers of a European "Sport for All" Charter, defining the principles that might serve as a common framework for the actions of governments and the various other authorities concerned, would provide a sound and coherent basis for the drawing up of various agreements applicable to particular sectors, even of a European Convention on Sport for All;
8. Recommends that the Committee of Ministers:
   (a) adopt a European "Sport for All" Charter on the principles set out in the report of its Committee on Culture and Education (Doc. 3186);
   (b) invite the Council for Cultural Cooperation and its subsidiary organs:
      (i) to see that the charter is implemented;
      (ii) to direct their work towards the preparation of a European convention in the light of the European "Sport for All" Charter.

36.3. Resolution No. 1/75 on Sport for All
1st Conference of European Ministers responsible for Sport, Brussels, 20-21 March 1975

Resolution No. 1/75 on Sport for All [...] having been incorporated into Resolution (76)41 adopted by the Committee of Ministers is therefore superseded.

36.4. Resolution No. 2/75 on the role of public authorities as regards the development of Sport for All
1st Conference of European Ministers responsible for Sport, Brussels, 20-21 March 1975

The European Ministers responsible for Sport, meeting in Brussels on 20 and 21 March 1975,

---

8 Assembly debate on 20 October 1972 (13th Sitting) (see Doc. 3186, report of the Committee on Culture and Education).

Recalling the principles of the Sport for All Charter;
Considering that public authorities play a major role in the promotion of sport for the benefit and welfare of the community as a whole;
Adopt the following resolution:

1. The responsibilities of public authorities:
   a. Without prejudice to their right of initiative, the public authorities' role is primarily complementary and should take the form of support for private action to the benefit of everyone and the provision of conditions encouraging the greatest possible number of people to practise sport;
   b. Sport should form an integral part of cultural, educational, social and health development programmes;
   c. As effective sports policy can only be determined and put into operation through co-operation by all private and public agencies concerned either directly or indirectly with sport, both voluntary and compulsory;
   d. Encouragement should be given to the training and further training of qualified personnel;
2. Participation by different social groups.
   a. From the point of view of permanent education, closer links should be formed between school sport and physical education, and voluntary sport.
   b. The public authorities should, wherever possible, encourage the following to practise sport:
      i. young workers and apprentices, as well as school pupils and students;
      ii. persons with special occupational and family obligations;
      iii. physically, mentally, and socially handicapped persons;
      iv. elderly people;
      v. migrants.
3. Practical conditions for engaging in sport
   a. Regiona l development plans should contain planning outlines for the provision of sports facilities.
   b. Legislation should secure access to nature to as great an extent as is compatible with i protection and the provision of adequate playing space in housing areas and whenever urban renewal operations are taking place.
   c. Encouragement must be given to the provision of facilities that can be used for both school sport and voluntary sport and, whenever possible, to the combination of cultural and sports facilities.
4. Finance
   a. The public authorities have a duty to provide voluntary sport with a wide range of aid.
   b. The use of advertising is only acceptable as long as it is in the interests of sport and tho~ who practice it and provided that sportsmen should in no circumstances become a vehicle for advertising.
   c. The local authorities bear as great a financial responsibility as the central and regional authorities.
5. Safeguards for the integrity of sport and sportsmen
   a. Every effort should be made to ensure that sport never gives rise to excessive behaviour nor becomes an instrument of political propaganda, a factor of personal and social alienation, or a means of diverting attention from important economic and social problems.

b. National legislation should afford those who practise sport the maximum degree of freedom compatible with permanence in the organisation of sport.

36.5. Resolution on the role of public authorities as regards the development of Sport for All (75/2)

Principles for a policy of sport for all
(Defined by the Conference of European Ministers responsible for Sport in Brussels (1975) under the title "European Sport for All Charter")

Article 1
Every individual shall have the right to participate in sport.

Article 2
Sport shall be encouraged as an important factor in human development and appropriate support shall be made available out of public funds.

Article 3
Sport, being an aspect of socio-cultural development, shall be related at local, regional and national levels to other areas of policy-making and planning such as education, health, social service, town and country planning, conservation, the arts and leisure services.

Article 4
Each government shall foster permanent and effective co-operation between public authorities and voluntary organisations and shall encourage the establishment of national machinery for the development and co-ordination of sport for all.

Article 5
Methods shall be sought to safeguard sport and sportsmen from exploitation for political, commercial or financial gain, and from practices that are abusive and debasing, including the unfair use of drugs.

Article 6
Since the scale of participation in sport is dependent, among other things, on the extent, the variety and the accessibility of facilities, the overall planning of facilities shall be accepted as a matter for public authorities, shall take account of local, regional and national requirements, and shall incorporate measures designed to ensure full use of both new and existing facilities.

Article 7
Measures, including legislation where appropriate, shall be introduced to ensure access to open country and water for the purpose of recreation.

Article 8
In any programme of sports development, the need for qualified personnel at all levels of administrative and technical management, leadership and coaching shall be recognised.

36.6. Resolution (76) 41 on the Principles for a Policy of Sport For All
Adopted by the Committee of Ministers on 24 September 1976

The Committee of Ministers.
Recognising that the aim of the Council of Europe is the achievement of greater unity between its members for the purpose of safeguarding and realising the ideals and principles which are their common heritage and of facilitating their economic and social progress, in particular by pursuing common objectives designed to protect and promote European culture;
Recalling Recommendation 588 (1970) of the Consultative Assembly on the Development of Sport for All and the creation of co-ordinating structures, and Recommendation 682 (1972) on a European Sport for All Charter;
Aware of the diverse contributions which sport can make to personal and social development through creative activities and recreational pursuits and of mans need for physical exercise for both his physical and his mental well-being;
Acknowledging the universal appeal of sport and its particular value in a rapidly changing world which is characterised on the one hand by increasing leisure and on the other by urbanisation and technological development that tend to isolate man from his natural environment;
Emphasising that the concept of sport for all, first formulated by the Council of Europe in 1966 to promote cultural development, relates to policies which seek to extend the benefits of sport to as many people as possible;
Stressing the comprehensive nature of this concept which embraces sport in many different forms, from recreational physical activity to high level competition;
Realising that sport for all raises problems which cannot be satisfactorily solved within a purely national framework;
Maintaining in this context that the formulation of common principles would enable national policies to be progressively harmonised;
Welcoming the work already done by the Council for Cultural Co-operation and various other international bodies in establishing common principles;
Recalling the Conference of European Ministers responsible for Sport held in Brussels (1975);
Considering that a text defining these principles, as retained by that Conference of European Ministers responsible for Sport under the title of the "European Sport for All Charter", might provide a common basis for the actions of governments and other authorities concerned,
Recommends to member governments:

1. to base their national policies as far as possible on the principles contained in the "European Sport for All Charter" appended to this resolution;
2. to distribute the "Charter" as widely as possible among interested persons and bodies within their territory.

Appendix
Principles for a policy of sport for all
(Defined by the Conference of European Ministers responsible for Sport in Brussels (1975) under the title "European Sport for All Charter")

Article 1
Every individual shall have the right to participate in sport.

Article 2
Sport shall be encouraged as an important factor in human development and appropriate support shall be made available out of public funds.

Article 3
Sport, being an aspect of socio-cultural development, shall be related at local, regional and national levels to other areas of policy-making and planning such as education, health, social service, town and country planning, conservation, the arts and leisure services.

Article 4
Each government shall foster permanent and effective co-operation between public authorities and voluntary organisations and shall encourage the establishment of national machinery for the development and co-ordination of sport for all.

Article 5
Methods shall be sought to safeguard sport and sportsmen from exploitation for political, commercial or financial gain, and from practices that are abusive and debasing. including the unfair use of drugs.

Article 6
Since the scale of participation in sport is dependent, among other things, on the extent. the variety and the accessibility of facilities, the overall planning of facilities shall be accepted as a matter for public authorities, shall take account of local, regional and national requirements, and shall incorporate measures designed to ensure full use of both new and existing facilities.

Article 7
Measures, including legislation where appropriate, shall be introduced to ensure access to open country and water for the purpose of recreation.

Article 8
In any programme of sports development, the need for qualified personnel at all levels of administrative and technical management, leadership and coaching shall be recognised.

36.7. Resolution on the Impact of Sport for All Policies and Programmes (84/2)
The European Ministers responsible for Sport, meeting in Malta for their 4th Conference, on 15 and 16 May 1984

Recalling:
1. the principles of the European Sport for All Charter;
2. the work of the CDDS, and in particular the rationalisation project and evaluation study of the impact of Sport for All policies and programmes;
3. the cultural and social values of Sport for All, and its benefits for health, self-realisation, and the quality of life;

Considering:
1. that there is a positive relationship between the existence of a specific Sport for All policy and the level of participation;
2. that although the aims, objectives, values, and the means for realising a Sport for All philosophy do not significantly differ, a Sport for All strategy allows for many different approaches depending on the economic, socio-cultural and geographical circumstances of member states;

3. that the needs of the communities for sports opportunities are best assessed at the local level and that they are best provided at an economic cost through co-operation between local and national authorities and organisations, both public and private;

Declare:

1. that the policies of Ministries responsible for sport and of the national sports bodies should as far as possible aim to ensure the continued provision of high quality opportunities for the whole population to take part in physical activities and of aid and support for all participants in sport at any level or ability, of all ages and origins so that a sports policy can meet the needs and demands of modern society;

Resolve:

1. to improve the impact of national Sport for All policies by implementing more fully at national level the work of the Council of Europe in sport;
2. that Sport for All requires adequate, multi-purpose, low energy-cost facilities, which are well managed and provide for recreational needs, and that full use should be made of all existing facilities, including municipal, club and educational facilities;
3. to encourage the media, and especially television, while recognising their independence, to promote, where possible, Sport for All;
4. to encourage the use of full-time or part-time voluntary or professional workers in Sport for All and to foster the training of specialists in marketing and management, organisation and promotion;
5. to make full use of all possibilities of financing Sport for All;
6. to foster an awareness among the international sports organisations of the desirability of making available some of the money coming from international sports events for Sport for All programmes launched by competent organisations, especially in developing countries;
7. to encourage the most cost-effective use of modern information technology in the field of Sport for All;

Invite the Committee of Ministers of the Council of Europe to instruct the CDDS:

1. to prepare proposals for improving the effective implementation of the work of the Council of Europe on promoting Sport for All within member states, with particular reference to the points agreed in this resolution;
2. to provide for more efficient bilateral and multilateral co-operation and co-ordination of aid in Sport for All development for some member states, and in particular the exchange of information;
3. to explore, where necessary, ways of increasing the importance of physical education in schools as a means of promoting Sport for All.

36.8. Resolution on Sport for All: Injuries and their Prevention (86/5)

The European Ministers responsible for Sport, meeting in Dublin for their 5th Conference from 30 September to 2 October 1986

Recognising that sport has an overall beneficial impact on physical, social and psychological well-being;
Convinced of the health protection and health promotion potentials of sport;
Aware of the medical and health care problems related to mass participation in sport;

Convinced that the costs of these problems can be reduced by adequate prevention measures;
Aware of the lack of sufficient scientific information on the mechanisms of injury occurrence;
Holding the view that European co-operative action in the field of the prevention of sports injuries is both necessary and desirable;
Invite the Committee of Ministers of the Council of Europe to ask the Committee for the Development of Sport (CDDS):

1. to ensure the proper execution of the co-ordinated research project "Sport for All: injuries and their prevention" which should include study of the problems concerning education and information, training, medical checks and guidance, facilities and equipment, and to evaluate the effects of different national prevention programmes;
2. in the light of the results from this project, to consider ways in which healthy participation in sport and recreation might be promoted in a co-ordinated European programme.

36.9. Resolution on the new European Sports Charter (92/1)
Adopted by the European Ministers responsible for Sport, 7th Conference, Rhodes, 13-15 May 1992

Political Declaration
Recent developments in the countries of Central and Eastern Europe, and the resulting revolutions, have made it essential for the Council of Europe to devise and implement a strategic plan covering the major aims in the field of sport but nevertheless leaving sufficient room for flexibility in the choice of activities.
Such a plan should define the future activity of the Committee for the Development of Sport and provide not only a medium-term programme, but also guidelines for the Committee's organisation and decision-making procedures.
By stating the Committee's purpose and aim and by identifying where the necessary resources are to come from and how they are to be used, this plan will allow the Council of Europe to pursue a coherent set of sports policies designed to achieve the goals it has set itself, including – by virtue of its voluntary and club basis – the role of sport as a school for and in democracy.
The present situation of sport in Europe has prompted us to confirm the rightfully important position of this sector in society today. It has led us to stress the role which should be given to it in today's society, and request the means to succeed in this.
The mixed public and private nature of financial support for sport should be encouraged, including the generation by the sports sector itself of the resources necessary for its further development. This could apply in particular to those countries the economies of which are in transition, and where the level of available resources may therefore be subject to fluctuations.
The physical fitness of many Europeans has not reached a satisfactory level, notwithstanding the growth of sport's economic and media impact. It is indispensable to give physical education in schools its appropriate place and importance, public authorities' sports budgets should be set at an adequate level, and the sports movement helped to maintain its long-standing tradition of voluntary work.
These concerns, among others, have convinced us of the need to revise the 1975 European "Sport for All" Charter.
This instrument, whose key ideas remain valid, was felt to be in need of overhauling and updating so as to meet the challenge of integration and rapprochement, and the necessary co-operation between all the CDDS member states, with a view to the "greater unity" between its

members which remains the fundamental purpose of the Council of Europe's action.
These then were the considerations that led us to draw up the new European Sports Charter.

36.10. Resolution No. 2/92 "The European Sports Charter"
7th Conference of European Ministers responsible for Sport, Rhodes, 13-15 May 1992

Resolution No. 2/92 "The European Sports Charter" adopted as Recommendation No. R(92)13 by the Committee of Ministers [...]

36.11. Recommendation No. R (92) 13 Rev of the Committee of Ministers to Member States on the Revised European Sports Charter
Adopted by the Committee of Ministers on 24 September 1992 at the 480th meeting of the Ministers' Deputies and revised at their 752nd meeting on 16 May 2001

1. The Committee of Ministers, under the terms of Article 15.b of the Statute of the Council of Europe,
2. Considering that the aim of the Council of Europe is to achieve a greater unity between its members for the purpose of safeguarding and realising the ideals and principles which are their common heritage and of facilitating their economic and social progress;
3. Bearing in mind the European Convention for the protection of human rights and fundamental freedoms and notably the "right to freedom of peaceful assembly and to freedom of association with others", and the enjoyments of rights "without discrimination on any ground such as sex, race, colour, language, religion, political or other opinion, national or social origin, association with a national minority, property, birth or other status";
4. Bearing in mind its Resolution (76)41 on the Principles for a Policy for Sport for All, as defined by the European Ministers responsible for Sport at their first Conference in 1975 under the title of the "European Sport for All Charter", and that this Charter has provided an essential basis for governmental policies in the field of sport and enabled many individuals to exercise their "right to participate in sport";
5. Bearing in mind its Recommendations No R(80)1, on Sport and Television; No R(81)8 on Sport and Physical Recreation and Nature Conservation in Inland Water Areas; No R(83)6 on Energy-Saving Measures in Sports Facilities; No R(86)18 on Sport for All: Disabled Persons; No R(87)9 on the Eurofit Tests of Physical Fitness; No R(88)8 on Sport for All: Older Persons; which have contributed to the implementation of Sport for All policies;
6. Considering that sport is a social and cultural activity based on voluntary choice which encourages contacts between European countries and citizens, and plays a fundamental role in the realisation of the aim of the Council of Europe by reinforcing the bonds between peoples and developing awareness of a European cultural identity;
7. Wishing to promote the diverse contributions which sport can make to personal and social development through creative activities, recreational pursuits and the continuous search for improving sporting performance and bearing in mind that physical exercise helps promote both the physical and the mental well-being of individuals;
8. Bearing in mind the political, economic, social and other changes in Europe since 1976, the rapid pace of such changes, and their impact upon sport, and that a new

European Sports Charter is necessary to reflect these changes and to face up to future challenges;

9. Bearing in mind the close interrelationship between sound environmental conditions and sporting activities as well as the need to integrate environmental considerations and the principle of sustainable development in sport;

10. Bearing in mind the need to accompany, on a wider basis, the European Convention on Spectator Violence and Misbehaviour at Sports Events and in Particular at Football Matches and the Anti-Doping Convention, which have already contributed to the safeguarding of the values of sport;

11. Acknowledging that public authorities should develop reciprocal co-operation with the sports movement as the essential basis of sport, in order to promote the values and benefits of sport, and that in many European States, governmental action in sport is taken in order to be complementary to and support the work of this movement (subsidiarity);

12. Considering that it is necessary to agree on a common European framework for sports development in Europe, based on the notions of pluralist democracy, the rule of law and human rights, and the ethical principles set out in Recommendation No R(92)14 on the Code of Sports Ethics;

13. Considering that the European Ministers responsible for Sport, meeting at Rhodes for their 7th Conference (1992), the first occasion on which Sports Ministers from all European countries had participated in the work of the Conference, adopted a resolution defining such principles for sport policies under the title of the "European Sports Charter" and undertook to follow and implement them as far as their authority permits,

I. Recommends the governments of member States:
   1. To base their national policies for sport, and, when appropriate any relevant legislation, on the 'European Sports Charter' as set out in the Appendix to this Recommendation;
   2. To invite their national sports organisations to take account of principles set out in the European Sports Charter in the elaboration of their policies;
   3. To take steps to ensure a wide dissemination of the European Sports Charter;

II. Instructs the Secretary General to transmit this Recommendation to:
   a. the governments of States party to the European Cultural Convention not member States of the Council of Europe;
   b. to international organisations and to international sports organisations.

Appendix to Recommendation No. R(92)13 rev
EUROPEAN SPORTS CHARTER

Article 1 – Aim of the Charter

Governments, with a view to the promotion of sport as an important factor in human development, shall take the steps necessary to apply the provisions of this Charter in accordance with the principles set out in the Code of Sports Ethics in order:

i. to enable every individual to participate in sport and notably:
   a. to ensure that all young people should have the opportunity to receive physical education instruction and the opportunity to acquire basic sports skills,
   b. to ensure that everyone should have the opportunity to take part in sport and physical recreation in a safe and healthy environment,

   and, in co-operation with the appropriate sports organisations,

c. to ensure that everyone with the interest and ability should have the opportunity to improve their standard of performance in sport and reach levels of personal achievement and/or publicly recognised levels of excellence,

ii. to protect and develop the moral and ethical bases of sport and the human dignity and safety of those involved in sport, by safeguarding sport, sportsmen and women from exploitation for political, commercial and financial gain and from practices that are abusive or debasing including the abuse of drugs and the sexual harassment and abuse, particularly of children, young people and women.

Article 2 – Definition and Scope of the Charter

1. For the purpose of this Charter:
   a. "Sport" means all forms of physical activity which, through casual or organised participation, aim at expressing or improving physical fitness and mental well-being, forming social relationships or obtaining results in competition at all levels.
   b. This Charter complements the ethical principles and policy guidelines set out in:
      i. the European Convention on Spectator Violence and Misbehaviour at Sports Events and in Particular at Football Matches,
      ii. the Anti-Doping Convention.

Article 3 – The Sports Movement

1. The role of the public authorities is primarily complementary to the action of the sports movement. Therefore, close co-operation with non-governmental sports organisations is essential in order to ensure the fulfilment of the aims of this Charter, including where necessary the establishment of machinery for the development and co-ordination of sport.
2. The development of the voluntary ethos and movement in sport shall be encouraged, particularly through support for the work of voluntary sports organisations.
3. Voluntary sports organisations have the right to establish autonomous decision-making processes within the law. Both governments and sports organisations shall recognise the need for a mutual respect of their decisions.
4. The implementation of some of the provisions of this Charter may be entrusted to governmental or non-governmental sports authorities or sports organisations.
5. Sports organisations should be encouraged to establish mutually beneficial arrangements with each other and with potential partners, such as the commercial sector, the media, etc., while ensuring that exploitation of sport or sportspeople is avoided.

Article 4 – Facilities and Activities

1. No discrimination on the grounds of sex, race, colour, language, religion, political or other opinion, national or social origin, association with a national minority, property, birth or other status, shall be permitted in the access to sports facilities or to sports activities.
2. Measures shall be taken to ensure that all citizens have opportunities to take part in sport and, where necessary, additional measures shall be taken aimed at enabling both young gifted people, as well as disadvantaged or disabled individuals or groups to be able to exercise such opportunities effectively.
3. Since the scale of participation in sport is dependent in part on the extent, the variety and the accessibility of facilities, their overall planning shall be accepted as a matter for

public authorities. The range of facilities to be provided shall take account of public, private, commercial and other facilities which are available. Those responsible shall take account of national, regional and local requirements, and incorporate measures designed to ensure good management and their safe and full use.

4. Appropriate steps should be taken by the owners of sports facilities to enable disadvantaged persons including those with physical or mental disabilities to have access to such facilities.

Article 5 – Building the Foundation

Appropriate steps shall be taken to develop physical fitness and the acquisition of basic sports skills and to encourage the practice of sport by young people, notably:

i. by ensuring that programmes of and, facilities for sport, recreation and physical education are made available to all pupils and that appropriate time is set aside for this;
ii. by ensuring the training of qualified teachers in this area at all schools;
iii. by ensuring that appropriate opportunities exist for continuing the practice of sport after compulsory education;
iv. by encouraging the development of appropriate links between schools or other educational establishments, school sports clubs and local sports clubs;
v. by facilitating and developing the use of sports facilities by schools and by the local community;
vi. by encouraging a climate of opinion in which parents, teachers, coaches and leaders stimulate young people to take regular physical exercise;
vii. by providing education in sports ethics for pupils from primary school onwards.

Article 6 – Developing Participation

1. The practice of sport, whether it be for the purpose of leisure and recreation, of health promotion, or of improving performance, shall be promoted for all parts of the population through the provision of appropriate facilities and programmes of all kinds and of qualified instructors, leaders or "animateurs".
2. Encouraging the provision of opportunities to participate in sport at work places shall be regarded as an integral part of a balanced sports policy.

Article 7 – Improving Performance

The practice of sport at higher levels shall be supported and encouraged in appropriate and specific ways, in co-operation with the relevant sports organisations. The support will cover such areas as talent identification and counselling; the provision of suitable facilities; developing care and support with sports medicine and sports science; encouraging scientific coaching and coach education and other leadership functions; helping clubs to provide appropriate structures and competitive outlets.

Article 8 – Supporting Top level and Professional Sport

1. Methods of providing appropriate direct or indirect support for sportsmen and women who reveal exceptional sporting qualities shall be devised in co-operation with sports organisations, in order to give them opportunities to develop fully their sporting and human capacities, in the full respect of their individual personality and physical and moral integrity. Such support will include aspects related to the identification of talent, to balanced education while in training institutes, and to a smooth integration into society through development of career prospects during and after sporting excellence.
2. The organisation and management of professionally organised sport shall be promoted through appropriate competent bodies. Practitioners engaging professionally in sport

should be provided with appropriate social status and protection and with ethical safeguards against all forms of exploitation.

Article 9 – Human Resources

1. The development of training courses by appropriate bodies, leading to diplomas and qualifications to cover all aspects of sports promotion shall be encouraged. Such courses should be appropriate to the needs of participants in different kinds and levels of sport and recreation and designed for both those working voluntarily or professionally (leaders, coaches, managers, officials, doctors, architects, engineers, etc.).
2. Those involved in the leadership or supervision of sports activities should have appropriate qualifications paying particular attention to the protection of the safety and health of the people in their charge.

Article 10 – Sport and Sustainable Development

Ensuring and improving people's physical, social and mental well-being from one generation to the next requires that sporting activities including those in urban, open country and water areas be adjusted to the planet's limited resources and be carried out in accordance with the principles of sustainable development and balanced management of the environment. These include:

– taking account of nature and environmental values in the physical planning and building of sport facilities;
– supporting and stimulating sports organisations in their efforts to conserve nature and the environment;
– increasing people's knowledge and awareness of the relations between sport and sustainable development and their understanding of nature.

Article 11 – Information and Research

Suitable structures and means for the collection and dissemination of pertinent information on sport at local, national and international levels shall be developed. Scientific research into all aspects of sport shall be promoted. Arrangements shall be made for diffusing and exchanging such information and the results of such research at the most appropriate level, locally, regionally, nationally or internationally.

Article 12 – Finance

Appropriate support and resources from public funds (i.e. at central, regional and local levels) shall be made available for the fulfilment of the aims and purposes of this Charter. Mixed public and private financial support for sport should be encouraged, including the generation by the sports sector itself of resources necessary for its further development.

Article 13 – Domestic and International Co-operation

1. Appropriate structures for the proper co-ordination of the development and promotion of sport, both between the various public administrations and agencies concerned by sports questions, and between the public and voluntary sectors, shall be developed when they do not already exist at central, regional and local levels in order to achieve the aims of this Charter. Such co-ordination will take account of other areas of policy making and planning such as education, health, social service, town and country planning, environment, the arts and other leisure services, and ensure that sport is an integral part of socio-cultural development.
2. Co-operation at European and international level is also necessary for the fulfilment of the aims of this Charter.

Chapter 37
SPORT IN SOCIETY

37.1. Resolution on Sport in Society (78/1)
(Theme I)

The European Ministers responsible for Sport, meeting in London, from 4 to 7 April 1978,
Recalling the resolutions adopted at their first conference and particularly their recommendation on the "European Sport for All Charter";
Affirm their belief in the importance of sport as a means of promoting international understanding, mutual respect and friendly social contacts between and within communities;
Support the international governing bodies of sport in their efforts to develop the moral and physical qualities, as expressed in the Olympic ideal, which are the basis of true sport;
Deplore the improper intrusion of political considerations unconnected with sport into international sport;
Recognise that international politics have become involved in sport, and that some countries' sports policies render them ineligible to take part in international sports events;
Emphasise their opposition to discrimination in sport which is based on race, religion, politics or any other criterion in contradiction to the Olympic Charter, and draw the attention of the governing bodies of sport to the International Declaration against Apartheid in Sports, adopted by the General Assembly of the United Nations;
Assert the importance of maintaining the independence of the national and international sports bodies in all matters concerning the conduct of their affairs and the organisation of international sporting events, as well as their responsibility for ensuring that the principles set out in this resolution are upheld in their own sports;
Remind these bodies that governments also have a duty to encourage the practice of sport and of the need to work with governments in the accomplishment of this task;
Conscious of the increasing costs of preparing for, staging and participating in international sports competitions, but nevertheless determined to extend the principle and the reality of Sport for All throughout the world;
Urge international non-governmental sports bodies to consider what action should be taken where, in their opinion, a national sports body is not justified in suddenly withdrawing its athletes from an event for non-sporting reasons;

Invite the Committee of Ministers of the Council of Europe to recommend governments of member states:

1. to take steps, in consultation and co-operation with national and international sports bodies, to protect international competitions from detrimental influences;
2. to support the attempts of developing countries to introduce programmes of physical education, provide sports facilities and offer wider opportunities for their citizens to practise and enjoy sport;
3. to co-ordinate activities in the field of sport and to co-operate as far as possible in the implementation of practical programmes of aid;

Invite non-governmental organisations to work towards an early restriction on external signs liable to engender confusion between nationalism and sport, such as the excessive use of anthems, flags, and similar symbols.

37.2. Declaration on the Significance of Sport for Society: Health, Socialisation, Economy

Investment in Sport is a Sound Investment
We, Ministers responsible for sport in Europe, meeting in Lisbon from 17 to 18 May 1995,
Having considered the scientific evidence concerning the Significance of Sport for Society;

Declare that sport:
1. promotes good health and well-being in society;
2. provides an important environment for education and socialisation for everyone: girls and boys, women and men as well as valuable opportunities for personal enjoyment, social contacts and integration;
3. contributes fundamentally, as the most popular of all voluntary associative activities, to the development and maintenance of democratic societies with active citizens;
4. plays a major and increasing role in the economies of European countries and offers potential for economic development;
5. contributes to the implementation of the principles proclaimed in the Vienna Declaration adopted by the Heads of State and Government of the members States of the Council of Europe in October 1993, particularly in relation to tolerance;
6. is a full partner in society and thus should be considered as an essential element in policymaking, most particularly in the health. social and economic fields.

We therefore intend acting in co-operation with different public authorities and autonomous sports organisations, to draw up, in accordance with the European Sports Charter, national policies and strategies to promote the development of sport, increase regular physical activity among people of all ages and strengthen sport as a factor for social development. These strategies and policies will:
1. promote co-operation amongst sports planners, decision-makers and other partners in the public, voluntary and private sectors as well as between them and their opposite numbers in other fields such as education, health, economic, social and environmental policies;
2. pay increased attention to the economic dimension of sport, to the importance of voluntary work in this sector and to the financing of the various components of sport taking account of their differing popularity and media appeal;
3. take into account the needs, desires and priorities of individuals and groups, as well as sporting traditions and popularity of different sports, and the principles set out in the Brighton Declaration on Women in Sport;

PRINCIPLES
In relation to each of the following three fields, we shall be guided by the principles set out below:

1. Health
The widest health benefits of regular physical activity by the population are achieved by enhancing motivation and by expanding opportunities for physical activities from early childhood to old age which can be practised by the largest numbers of people as part of their daily activities:
a. such activities, for instance walking or cycling, should in any ease involve moderately intensive exercise for at least half an hour every day;

b. the order of priority for support of different activities aiming at health benefits should be based on their efficacy, safety, equality of opportunities for participation and cost effectiveness.

Higher priority should be given to finding and offering opportunities to motivated but sedentary or irregularly active people. They can be found and should be sought especially among people with limited opportunities or with restricted independence and freedom of choice.

A longer term goal should be to motivate those at present lacking the will to exercise.

Measures should be taken to reduce the risk of injuries including, where appropriate, changes in the rules and practices of individual sports, improvements in the environment, education of all parties involved and dissemination of information on effective prevention programmes and on measures leading to rapid recovery from injuries.

2. Socialisation

Higher priority should be given to providing possibilities for physical activities and sport for children and young people both at school and in leisure-time, in conditions enabling them to enjoy sport, to learn cooperative skills, to create a positive approach towards movement as an appropriate form of recreation and to get involved in decisions concerning their own activities The European Manifesto on Young People and Sport, adopted at the present Conference, is a means to this end.

Due account should be taken of the capacity of playing games to encourage children to engage in various social roles and thus develop their ethical and social consciousness.

Special emphasis should be given to creating possibilities for more girls to participate in and remain involved in sport.

The level and intensity of training and competition should be appropriate to the age and physical and mental development of the child. Those responsible for guiding children participating in top-level competition at an early age must ensure that the stress of achievement and overspecialisation is minimised and ensure that they do not harm their physical, psychological or moral integrity.

Ethical values and fair play as embodied in the Code of Sports Ethics should be included in the development of all activities.

Training of teachers, coaches, trainers, instructors and leaders, should emphasise the cooperative skills and spontaneous activity of children and the development of a lifelong interest in sport.

Possibilities for valuable social contact through sports for the adult population at large as well as for groups with special needs should be promoted as emphasised in the Resolution on Tolerance and Sport adopted at the present Conference.

The irreplaceable role played by voluntary sports organisations for society in general and as a means of promoting democracy should be recognised.

The strengthening of international contacts at grass-roots level should be encouraged to contribute to social co-operation, integration and peace.

3. Economy

Public authorities should ensure that they continue to hold primary responsibility for creating and maintaining the conditions for the development of sport as defined in the European Sports Charter. The economic impact of public investment in sport should be recognised and promoted.

The private sector should be encouraged to participate in creating these conditions.

In order to ensure that there are opportunities for all, a complementarity in public as well as private (including consumer and commercial) financing of sport should be maintained. Sports sponsorship has an important role to play in this.

Help should be available to sports with less media appeal, and thus unable to attract funding, in the interests of solidarity between sports.
Measures (such as tax relief) encouraging the voluntary involvement of individuals or groups have proven to be a cost-effective support for sport and should be promoted.
Whilst taking due consideration of the importance of voluntary work, the creation of new jobs and further development of training for current and future employees in the sports sector should also be encouraged.

We invite the Committee of Ministers:

1. to consider adopting the above principles in the form of a Recommendation to member states;
2. to assign responsibility to the CDDS for the follow-up thereto, assuming an active role:
   a. in promoting co-operation with the European and international organisations which contribute to the promotion of sport in order to make the best possible use of European resources;
   b. by extending the project on the Significance of Sport for Society to include, for instance, environmental aspects;

   in carrying out the following priority action:

1. Health

The CDDS should draft European strategies and promotional programmes to provide support services in close cooperation with other relevant international bodies in order to increase people's interest and participation in exercise and sport in a health-enhancing and safe way. It should in particular:

a. promote the collection of comparable information on motivation, preferences, and activity habits of people in different countries and their various population groups with regard to regular physical activity and on opportunities for, and barriers to, participation in sport.
b. continue to base its activities in this field on scientific data and to stimulate research to gain better, more reliable and more detailed knowledge of the health effects of physical activity, including sports and exercise injuries and their prevention.
c. promote the implementation of the new health-related fitness assessment battery, Eurofit for Adults, in order to provide the needed support services such as dissemination of information, training of testers. organisation of cooperative meetings, etc. and to monitor the status of health-related fitness of populations among the member countries, and to promote comparative research.

2. Socialisation

The CDDS should strengthen cooperation with the European sports organisations with the aim of supporting versatile voluntary activities and developing European cooperation for young sport leaders.
It should promote, at European level, the implementation of the Brighton Declaration on Women and Sport with the aim of developing a sporting environment that enables and values the full involvement of girls and women in every aspect of sport.
It should encourage the promotion of practical pilot projects implementing the principles of the Vienna Declaration and the Resolution No. 2/95 on Tolerance through Sport.

3. Economy

In close co-operation with sports organisations, the CDDS should promote good practices to improve the recruitment, training and retention of volunteers in sport in all member countries.

It should pursue, through co-ordination or promotion, further work on the economic benefits of sport and structures of sports financing in Europe, paying attention to the needs of new member countries.

The above principles are inspired by:

1. the Vienna Declaration adopted by the Heads of State and Government of the member states of the Council of Europe in October 1993;
2. the Framework Convention on the Protection of National Minorities;
3. the European Sports Charter, the Code of Sports Ethics and the Manifesto on Young People and Sport;
4. the European Convention on Spectator Violence and the Anti-Doping Convention;
5. the Final Communiqué of the 14th Informal Meeting of European Sports Ministers in Strasbourg in April 1994 on Sport and Money and to the Ministers' decision to discuss these questions further at this Conference at Lisbon;
6. previous CDDS work related to the requirements of a safe and healthy sport, to the promotion of sport for groups with special needs, to the economic importance of sport and to the role of voluntary work.

The Ministers also note with satisfaction that the Final Ten of the United Nations Social Summit at Copenhagen, in March 1995, and in particular paragraphs 72(h) and 74 (e), recognise the role of sport in promoting equality and social integration.

They are based on the collection and critical analysis of existing scientific evidence conducted by experts in each of the three fields examined. These analyses have been published in the form of scientific reviews.

The reviews were examined by groups of scientific specialists designated by delegations to the CDDS and position papers were drawn up together with members of the CDDS. The essence of the position papers is summarised in the considerations and arguments set out below:

1. Health

Recent scientific evidence shows convincingly the importance of sport and physical activity to health and in particular:

Sport and regular physical activity are fundamental to good health and well-being at all stages of life.

The benefits of regular physical activity are unique and available for people of all ages, and those least active can gain the most.

There is a common need for health-enhancing physical activity, but in different societies the degree of need, the traditions. the willingness to participate, and the opportunities vary considerably.

Achieving an increase in participation in regular physical activities requires thorough planning, intensive promotion and careful implementation by alliances of national and local government, and voluntary and commercial agencies.

The provision of opportunities for health-enhancing physical activity and Sport for All citizens is one of the important responsibilities of government at all levels.

Current knowledge and relevant experience gained in previous national and international campaigns provide an ample basis for immediate action to create opportunities for people to benefit from the health-enhancing effects of regular physical activity.

Although injuries do occur in sport and physical activity, they are for the most part of relatively minor severity and their health consequences are far outweighed by health-enhancing outcomes of physical activity which is suitable for the persons practising it.

2. Socialisation

Socialisation is a life-long and complex process by which individuals learn the skills, attitudes, values and behaviours that enable them to participate in society;

Because of its popularity, sport provides an important environment for socialisation and gives participants lots of fun and enjoyable experiences which contribute to self-development.

Sport, whether practised formally or informally, offers a good framework for, and nourishment of, social contacts, cooperation and relations. It is a most effective medium for the integration of groups with special needs, for improving international understanding, for learning democracy, and for harmony.

The crucial factors for socialisation are cooperation between individuals, the quality of leadership, the level of, and importance given to, competition and individual spontaneous activity, free choice and decision-making versus over-formal organisation.

Acquisition of ethical values and principles of fair play in sport is an inseparable part of socialisation, creating possibilities for learning individual responsibility, consideration of common rules and respect for others.

Despite these advantages, in some countries many young people, and especially girls, do not have adequate scope for participating in sport activities.

Sport is too often seen only as an achievement-oriented activity which easily rejects the less gifted and may cause damage to self-esteem.

Games are very important since they form a bridge between spontaneous play and formal sport.

3. Economy

Sport is an integral part of society which provides significant positive economic effects. The economic stimulus generated by sport contributes to consumption, income, and employment, as well as to local, regional and national economic development. Increased investment in sport contributes to economic wealth.

Sports activities are largely financed by private households, national and public authorities and private sponsors and, in particular, the contributions from public and voluntary sectors. This provides a basic guarantee of wide-ranging sports opportunities.

Sports facilities and amenities make a significant economic contribution and have wider spin-offs in terms of job creation – in both the short and long terms.

Finance in sport flows differently between the components of the sports sector.

The mass media industries have an ever-increasing influence on the development of sport.

Well-managed sponsorship agreements benefit both sport and the sponsor.

37.3. Recommendation on the Significance of Sport for Society (95/17)

Adopted by Ministers' Deputies the on 12 October 1995

The Committee of Ministers, in application of Article 15.b of the Statute of the Council of Europe,

Considering the importance of sport in fostering good health and well-being in society;

Considering that sport provides girls and boys, and men and women with an environment conducive to education and the social development of the individual;

Aware of the growing role played by sport in the economies of European countries, to which it makes a substantial contribution;
Convinced that sport contributes to the implementation of the principles set forth in the Vienna Declaration adopted by the Heads of State and Government of the member States of the Council of Europe on 9 October 1993, notably with regard to tolerance;
Stressing that sport is a fully fledged partner in the social framework and therefore a key factor in public policy-making, particularly in the social, economic and health fields;
Having noted the Declaration on the significance of sport for society adopted by the 8th Conference of European Ministers responsible for Sport (Lisbon, 17-18 May 1995);
Anxious to follow up the principles set out in the above mentioned Declaration;
Recommends that the Governments of member States, in conjunction with the competent public authorities and autonomous sports associations, and in accordance with the European Sports Charter, frame national policies and strategies which foster the development of sport, encourage people of all ages to take up a regular physical activity and reinforce sport as a factor in social development, in compliance with the principles set out in the Appendix to the present Recommendation.

Appendix
Principles

1. Health

   The widest health benefits of regular physical activity by the population are achieved by enhancing motivation and by expanding opportunities for physical activities at any age which can be practised by the largest numbers of people as part of their daily activities:

   a. in any case, moderately intensive exercise for at least half an hour every day seems desirable for everyone;
   b. the order of priority for support of different activities aiming at health benefits should be based on their efficacy, safety, equality of opportunities for participation and cost-effectiveness.

   Higher priority should be given to finding and offering opportunities to motivated but sedentary or irregularly active people. They can be found and should be sought especially among people with limited opportunities or with restricted independence and freedom of choice. A longer term goal should be to motivate those at present lacking the will to exercise.

   Measures should be taken to reduce the risk of injuries including, where appropriate, changes in the rules and practices of individual sports, improvements in the environment, education of all parties involved and better dissemination of information on effective prevention programmes and on measures leading to rapid recovery from injuries.

2. Socialisation

   Higher priority should be given to providing possibilities for physical activities and sport for children and young people both at school and in leisure-time, in conditions enabling them to enjoy sport, to learn cooperative skills, to create a positive approach towards movement as an appropriate form of recreation and to get involved in decisions concerning their own activities The European Manifesto on Young People and Sport, adopted at the 8th Conference of European Ministers responsible for Sport (Lisbon, 17-18 May 1995), is a means to this end.

   Due account should be taken of the potential of team games to encourage children to engage in various social roles and thus develop their ethical and social consciousness and their sense of responsibility in social relations.

Girls should have more opportunities to participate in and remain involved in sport.

The level and intensity of training and competition should be appropriate to the age and physical and mental development of the child. Those responsible for guiding children participating in top-level competition at an early age must make a point of ensuring that the stress of achievement and over-specialisation is minimised and ensure that they do not harm their physical, psychological or moral integrity.

Ethical values and fair play as embodied in the Code of Sports Ethics should be included in the development of all activities.

Training of teachers, coaches, trainers, instructors and leaders, should emphasise the cooperative skills and spontaneous activity of children and the development of a lifelong interest in sport.

Possibilities for valuable social contact through sports for the adult population at large as well as for groups with special needs should be promoted as emphasised in the Resolution on Tolerance and Sport adopted at the 8th Conference of European Ministers responsible for Sport (Lisbon, 17-18 May 1995). In this context, the irreplaceable role played by voluntary sports organisations should be recognised.

The strengthening of international sporting contacts at grass-roots level is an essential contribution to social co-operation and integration and peace.

3. Economy

Public authorities should ensure that they continue to hold primary responsibility for creating and maintaining the conditions for the development of sport as defined in the European Sports Charter. The economic impact of public investment in sport should be recognised and promoted.

The private sector should be encouraged to participate in creating these conditions.

In order to ensure that there are opportunities for all, a complementarity in public as well as private (including consumer and commercial) financing of sport should be maintained. Sports sponsorship has an important role to play in this.

Help should be available to sports with less media appeal, and thus unable to attract funding, in the interests of solidarity between sports.

Measures (such as tax relief) encouraging the voluntary involvement of individuals or groups have proven to be a cost-effective support for sport and should be promoted.

Whilst taking due consideration of the importance of voluntary work, the creation of new jobs and further development of training for current and future employees in the sports sector should also be encouraged.

Chapter 38
TELEVISION

38.1. Recommendation No. R (80) 1 of the Committee of Ministers to Member States on Sport and Television[9]

Adopted by the Committee of Ministers on 24 January 1980 at the 313th meeting of the Ministers' Deputies)

The Committee of Ministers, under the terms of Article 15.b of the Statute of the Council of Europe,

Recalling its Resolution (76) 41 on the "Principles for a policy for sport for all";

Bearing in mind the responsibility of governments to encourage the provision of appropriate opportunities for the practice of sport at all levels of experience and for the benefit of all citizens;

Convinced that television constitutes an important medium for the attainment of these objectives and welcoming the fact that most television organisations already devote a significant proportion of their broadcasts to programmes dealing with various aspects of sport and recreation;

Bearing in mind the diverse ways in which sport is organised in the member states and that, in many of them, protection of the independence of sports organisations is guaranteed either by the Constitution or by government policy;

Underlining the principle prevailing in the member states whereby broadcasting organisations are autonomous and independent of government as regards the content of programmes and their daily management,

Recommends the governments of member states to take the necessary steps in the light of their structures and traditions to encourage the national sport and television organisations to establish, where necessary, by creating suitable arrangements, consultation and co-operation between them in order to:

1. discuss matters of general principle and any other questions affecting both parties, as well as ways and means whereby television could further stimulate the practice of sport;
2. promote the development of a range of television programmes designed to foster the practice of sport; investigate and experiment with new kinds of programme (including methods and times of presentation) with that objective; consider the role of entertainment in the televised broadcasting of sport; study ways in which both parties might work together in order to help overcome some of the problems connected with sport faced by both television and sports organisations (such as the popularisation of new or minority sports, the treatment of violent episodes associated with sporting events both on and off the field of play, undue commercial intrusion into amateur sport); and consider all other appropriate and cognate measures;

[9] When the Recommendation was adopted, the Representatives of Ireland and Switzerland, referring to Article 10.2.c of the Rules of Procedure for the meetings of the Ministers' Deputies, reserved the right of their governments to comply with it or not.

3. stimulate and where possible co-ordinate national research efforts (with particular emphasis on audience surveys) into various aspects of sport and television and, by means of suitable scientific research projects, assess and monitor the initiatives, experiments and projects which it has encouraged and developed; Requests the governments of member states to provide the Secretary General of the Council of Europe, by the first day of January 1981, with a report indicating what steps and measures they have taken to follow up this recommendation and illustrating the effects such steps and measures have had.

Chapter 39
TOLERANCE AND FAIR PLAY

39.1. Resolution on Tolerance and Sport (95/2)

The European Ministers responsible for Sport, meeting in Lisbon at their 8th Conference from 17 to 18 May 1995

Recalling the past work of the Council of Europe on the universality of sport and the need to keep sport free of discrimination in all its forms, and in particular:

1. Committee of Ministers' Resolution (76) 41 on the principles for a Policy on Sport for All, and particularly Article 1 of the Appendix which states that "every individual shall have the right to participate in sport";
2. Their own Resolution on Sport in Society, adopted at their 2nd Conference (London, 1978), in which they emphasised "their opposition to discrimination in sport based on race, religion, politics or any other criterion ...";
3. Their Resolution on Sport for Immigrants, adopted at their 3rd Conference (Palma de Majorca, 1981), in which they expressed their conviction "that sport is important as a means of bringing about greater participation in the life of the host country", and their concern "to see the principles of Sport for All applied to everybody, in particular to the least privileged groups", and considered "that it is the duty of all to combat, by every available means ... those factors that have an adverse effect on immigrants' participation in sport in the society where they have settled";
4. Their Resolution on Sport for socially under-privileged and marginal groups, adopted at their 4th Conference (Malta, 1984);
5. Their Resolutions on apartheid in sport, adopted at their 5th and 6th Conferences (Dublin, 1986 and Reykjavik, 1989) and whilst expressing their profound satisfaction that apartheid is no longer practised in South Africa, maintaining that the principles should apply wherever discrimination of any kind is imposed;
6. The European Sports Charter and Code of Sports Ethics (Committee of Ministers' Recommendations Nos. R(92)13 and R(92)14; and in particular Article 4 of the European Sports Charter;
7. The work of the Standing Committee of the European Convention on Spectator Violence and Misbehaviour at Sports Events and in particular at Football Matches on racial and xenophobic abuse and discrimination at football matches;
8. The considerable work of the Committee for the Development of Sport on ways in which sport can give disadvantaged groups more opportunities to participate in and integrate with society;

Referring to the Plan of Action against racism, xenophobia, antisemitism and intolerance adopted by the Summit of Heads of State and Government of the member States of the Council of Europe (Vienna, October 1993), which requires all sectors of the Organisation to be mobilised in the struggle against these unacceptable phenomena;

Deploring the fact that some forms of sport have so often provided a pretext for outbreaks of intolerance and violence, sometimes racist or xenophobic in character;

Confident nonetheless of the vast potential sport offers as a ground for intercultural encounters and understanding, as a workshop for socialisation and integration – particularly for disadvantaged groups – and as a school for democracy;

Considering that for this reason the Committee for the Development of Sport and the Standing Committee of the European Convention on Spectator Violence and Misbehaviour at Sports events and in particular at Football Matches can, in their respective spheres, contribute significantly to the implementation of the Action Plan by reinforcing the main axes of their work:

1. non-discrimination in sport, and access to it for all;
2. the repudiation of, and fight against, violence and the climate that engenders it;
3. sport as a factor in socialisation and integration;
4. sport as a school of democracy and civic values;

Taking account of sport's potential, in particular through the intense media coverage which brings it to a broad and enthusiastic public, to project the image of team spirit and solidarity and to promote mutual understanding and respect;

Emphasising that well-known teams and sports stars have a particular responsibility because they represent role-models, especially for the young:

1. Declare their support for the Plan of Action and the European Youth Campaign against racism, xenophobia, antisemitism and intolerance, and in this context welcome the proposal by the Netherlands Minister to organise a major meeting/manifestation with the participation of young sports people, sporting personalities, the mass media, and those with public responsibilities, to demonstrate the commitment of those involved in sport to the fight against intolerance;
2. Undertake, at national level:
   a. to participate in the European Youth Campaign against racism, xenophobia, antisemitism and intolerance by stepping up the contribution of the sports sector, in particular through campaigns aimed at raising awareness and changing behaviour;
   b. to develop even further the practice of sport by improving sports facilities, particularly in districts where intolerance poses a particular problem, in co-operation, where appropriate, with the competent sport organisations;
   c. to encourage training for sports teachers, trainers and organisers on the fight against racism and intolerance;
3. Invite the Committee of Ministers:
   a. to ask the CDDS, in furtherance of its commitment to tolerance in and through sport:
      i. to encourage the development of activities concerning sport as a school for democratic ideals and to intensify its work on sport as a medium for social participation and integration as shown in the European Manifesto on Young People and Sport and the Declaration on the Significance of Sport for Society also adopted at the present Conference;
      ii. to study, in co-operation with the Steering Committee on the Mass Media (CDMM), the potential contribution of the media in helping to promote tolerance through sport;
      iii. to support the meeting on tolerance through sport to be organised by the Netherlands government;
4. Ask the Standing Committee of the European Convention on Spectator Violence:
   a. to intensify that part of its work which is devoted to the struggle against all forms of discrimination and intolerance in sport and to draw up a plan of action to this end;
   b. to develop means of monitoring, in cooperation with the other partners concerned, the implementation of measures designed to combat discrimination and incitement to hatred and violence associated with some sport events;

c. to study what other means may be opportune to ensure that sports events take place peacefully and in a sporting spirit based on mutual respect by all concerned.

39.2. Declaration on Sport, Tolerance and Fair Play

We, participants at the Round Table on Sport, Tolerance, and Fair Play, meeting in Amsterdam on 11th April 1996,
Having in mind
- the Vienna Declaration and the Plan of Action against racism, xenophobia, antisemitism and intolerance adopted by the Heads of State and Government of the Council of Europe in Vienna in October 1993;
- the Resolution on Tolerance and Sport adopted by the European Ministers responsible for Sport at their 8th Conference in Lisbon in May 1995;
- the European Sports Charter adopted by the European Ministers responsible for Sport at their 7th Conference in Rhodes in May 1992 and subsequently adopted by the Committee of Ministers of the Council of Europe as Recommendation No. R (92) 13,

declare as follows:

I. We are confident that sport offers a vast potential to society as a ground for intercultural encounters and understanding, as a workshop for socialisation and integration – not least for disadvantaged groups – and as a school for democracy. We fully agree in this respect with the Declaration on the Significance of Sport for Society adopted at the Lisbon Conference of Sport Ministers. Sport is a vital area of education, particularly for young people.

II. We also believe in sport's ability, notably through the intense media coverage which brings it to a broad and enthusiastic public, to project an image of fair play, team spirit and solidarity and to promote mutual understanding and respect. Major sporting events, at world and European level, with very large television audiences, provide a rich opportunity to bring home the message of tolerance. In addition, hundreds of thousands of smaller but no less important competitions for all ages, all levels and all sports are organised each year throughout Europe and the world. Each represents an opportunity for implementing new initiatives with regard to tolerance and fair play.

III. We emphasise the important responsibility borne by well-known teams and sports stars as role-models – especially for the young – and consider that it is very important that every individual and organisation involved in sport, whether governmental or non-governmental, amateur or professional, should combat intolerance and violence at sporting events by all appropriate means.

IV. We welcome the very valuable work that has been done by individuals, by the sports movement, by governments and by European institutions concerning the universality of sport and the need to keep it free of discrimination in all its forms, and express our support for all those national and international sports organisations which have drawn up and implemented plans of action to promote tolerance and fair play in sport.

V. We regret the fact that some forms of sport have too often provided a pretext for outbreaks of intolerance and violence, sometimes racist or xenophobic in character, as well as for showing those tendencies, such as the incidence of foul play, lack of discipline, doping and corruption which are in contradiction with the fundamental values of sport and undermine its effectiveness as a positive influence in society.

VI. We believe that the following are the most important ways of creating a climate of tolerance:

Education
Just as intolerance is born of ignorance and misunderstanding, tolerance is engendered by knowledge and understanding. It follows that everything begins amongst the young: at home, in classrooms, on playing fields and in sports clubs.
Awareness
No opportunity should be missed to ensure that all sporting events, and any media coverage associated with them, raise awareness of the message of tolerance.
Participation
One of the most basic guarantees of fair play and tolerance is to ensure that as many people as possible practise sport regularly within a sound ethical framework.
Incentives
Rewards for outstanding examples of fair and tolerant behaviour are one way of helping people to understand the importance of positive attitudes to the success of their sport as well as of harmony and justice in society.
Sanctions
In the last resort, dispositions must exist in law and in the rules of sport to sanction unacceptable discrimination and incitement to racial hatred by appropriate means.
Communication
Most of these elements depend for their effectiveness on communication of clear and unambiguous information amongst all individuals and organisations concerned.

In this context, we recommend to all potential partners the guidelines set out in the Appendix to this Declaration.
With this in mind, we

1. encourage all countries to find ways, at national level:
   - to ensure that sport plays its full role in campaigns to promote tolerance in society as a whole;
   - to devise national plans of action on sport, tolerance and fair play using the guidelines in the Appendix to this Declaration;
   - to consider organising joint sports projects with neighbouring countries and/or countries of origin of minority groups to promote tolerance and help dispel prejudice between different groups;
2. invite all governmental and non-governmental organisations to share their experience through exchanges of information concerning their efforts to promote tolerance and fair play;
3. invite all sports organisations which have not yet done so to adopt action plans on tolerance and fair play;
4. invite the media to give their support to the promotion of tolerance and fair play and to consider ways of giving more prominence to the subject, as well as to events and campaigns organised to promote it;
5. invite the organisers of forthcoming major international sports events to work out initiatives for promoting tolerance and fair play through these events;
6. invite sponsors of sporting events and sport organisations to include clauses in sponsorship agreements whereby the sponsored organisations or persons undertake to support the aims of tolerance and fair play to the best of their ability;
7. appeal to sports stars to use their influence to help promote tolerance and fair play;
8. invite the Council of Europe to give appropriate follow-up to this Declaration;
9. invite all national and international organisations, both governmental and non-governmental, which have influence in the domains of activity covered by this Declaration, including:

- The European Union (Parliament, Commission and Committee of the Regions)
- Unesco
- The International Olympic Committee
- National and international sports organisations

to bear the aims of this Declaration in mind in the conduct of their activities and, if they have not already done so, to take appropriate action.

Appendix

Guidelines for action programmes on Sport, Tolerance and Fair Play

The following guidelines are divided into two parts, each having its own aims and needs:

1. Encouraging national programmes to promote Tolerance and Fair Play and eliminate discrimination and racism
2. Encouraging international programmes aimed at strengthening the positive values of each sport, and promoting the principles of tolerance and fair play at major international events

Aims

With the support and close co-operation of all concerned:

- to promote tolerance and fair play in and through sport using concrete measures and activities;
- to create and consolidate, in and around sport, a morality which maintains and strengthens the positive values of sport for individuals and society.

1. National programmes to promote Tolerance and Fair Play and eliminate discrimination and racism.

   Governments, regional and local authorities, national, regional and local sports organisations should support, in their respective fields of competence, action to promote tolerance and fair play, each country stressing the aspects relevant to its national situation.

   National campaigns against discrimination and in favour of tolerance could make use of sport in their efforts to raise awareness and modify behaviour.

   All programmes aimed at promoting tolerance and fairness in sport or society should embody, as a basic prerequisite, equitable treatment for and participation by women at all levels in the organisation and practice of sport.

   1.1 Children and young people

   Priority could be given to encouraging training for sports administrators and trainers and others involved in the fight against discrimination and intolerance. For this purpose, training and information material should be prepared for parents, coaches and teachers on tolerance and fair play in sport as proposed in the Council of Europe's Code of Sports Ethics.

   1.1.1 Schools could be encouraged to educate pupils in sports ethics from an early age, and teachers, including physical education teachers, could be helped to draw up appropriate course material.

   1.1.2 Sports clubs, especially those who work with schools, could be encouraged to consider education in tolerance and fair play as part of their role.

   1.1.3 Activities could be devised to raise parents' awareness of the importance of fairness and tolerance in their children's sporting lives.

   1.1.4 Rules could be re-examined to see whether they sufficiently reflect the principles of Fair Play and Tolerance, make games and sport more attractive, particularly for young people, and encourage the practice of sport on a social level.

1.2 Sport for All and amateur sport in general

More effort is needed to remove obstacles to participation in sport on all levels for all groups in society, most particularly for women, and for those groups which are not equally represented in sport, or excluded by custom or practice. The aim should be to promote conditions in which everyone can, within reason, participate or be involved fully in the sport of their choice on an equal basis.

The practice of sport can be encouraged and developed by improving the availability and attractiveness of sports facilities, particularly in districts where intolerance poses a particular problem.

1.3 Spectator sport and professional sport

Sport can be a focus for tensions, but it can also be the means of creating a climate of tolerance for the benefit of society as a whole (projects in professional and spectator sport such as "Fairständnis" (Germany), "Discrimination offside" (Netherlands), "Kick racism out of football (United Kingdom) have already proved their worth, as have other, more general fair play promotion experiments such as "Schools without racism" (Belgium), the "Blue Card" (France) or the "Green Card" (Finland and others)).

1.3.1 National federations, clubs, organisers and the media could work together, with the support of public authorities, to draw up and implement action plans in favour of tolerance and fair play as part of countries' national sporting life. These plans could involve coaches, trainers, sports participants and players, teams and clubs, schools, young people, and parents.

1.3.2 Players and athletes have great potential influence on spectators, especially young people, and this influence could be used to support actions in the field of tolerance and fair play.

1.3.3 Stress should be laid on encouraging positive behaviour rather than merely repressing unacceptable conduct. Nevertheless, plans can only be credible if they are backed up by appropriate, effective sanctions.

1.3.4 Sports organisations, sports clubs and their officials could consider adopting policies for treating all sportsmen/women equally in recruitment and selection for positions at all levels in their clubs.

1.3.5 One board or committee member could be given responsibility for matters of Tolerance and Fair Play in his or her club. He or she would then be the person to whom people could turn to for all activities in this field.

1.3.6 In order to prevent unacceptable behaviour in the long term, sports organisations could develop an approach geared to the needs of their "customers" – i.e members / supporters. In larger clubs or associations, an extensive network of stewards could be part of this approach.

1.4 Sports organisations are recommended to consider the following as part of their plans of action for tolerance:

1.4.1 examining the wording of their codes of conduct and ethics;

1.4.2 preparing guidelines and plans for competitions and major events which stimulate fair and tolerant attitudes amongst spectators and supporters;

1.4.3 ensuring that spectators are fully informed about the rules of games and sports as well as the regulations applicable in stadia and the law concerning discrimination and racist behaviour;

1.4.4 providing appropriate sanctions for unacceptable behaviour;

1.4.5 creating and publicising schemes to reward fair play and proper behaviour by sportspeople, clubs, teams and spectators;

1.4.6 educating spectators and the media to respect the decisions of officials, and examining the potential of technological means to provide umpires, judges and referees with more objective data. The transparency of decisions is a major factor in maintaining a sporting atmosphere.

2. Encouraging international programmes aimed at strengthening the positive values of each sport, and promoting the principles of tolerance and fair play at major international events

2.1 Introduction

Many international sports organisations have acknowledged their great responsibility in the fight against intolerance and violence in sport and for the promotion of Tolerance and Fair Play. They can guide and support their member organisations in tackling the problems by drawing up comprehensive rules which include positive and negative sanctions.

2.2 Promotion of Tolerance and Fair Play

2.2.1 International sports organisations could examine the rules of their game or sport and their competitions, including the role and powers of referees, umpires and officials to see what more can be done to promote the principles of tolerance and fair play, particularly with regard to disciplinary codes and the terms of reference of disciplinary commissions.

2.2.2 They could, where possible and useful, ensure co-ordination between tolerance initiatives undertaken by their members.

2.2.3 They could also encourage their member associations to adapt their own rules to exclude any unacceptable discrimination.

2.2.3 Clubs and officials could be helped to be more aware of, and to know how to deal with discrimination and intolerance amongst spectators and/or players.

2.2.4 Rules could ensure that, where sanctions are imposed on clubs or individuals, they should be applied rapidly and effectively.

2.2.5 The media could consider ways in which the impact of the portrayal of outbreaks of unacceptable behaviour can be reduced, and more prominence given to examples of good practice.

2.3 Organisers of sports events could make use of the measures laid down in the European Convention on Spectator Violence and the recommendations of its Standing Committee.

2.4 Special characteristics of major international events

Major events, such as the 1996 European Football Championships in England and the Olympic Games in Atlanta, USA and the 1998 Football World Cup in France and Winter Olympics in Japan can be used to reinforce the promotion of Tolerance and Fair Play and to fight intolerance and violence. The same applies to other international events extensively covered by the media, such as tennis, volley-ball, golf, skiing, cycling, motor-racing and football.

The relevant international sports organisations, participating countries and all participants, officials and spectators are encouraged to become actively involved in this action.

2.4.1 Every means of information (television and press advertising, hoardings, display screens, public address systems, leaflets, etc.) can be used to raise awareness of the values of tolerance and fair play and the existence, and the aims and the mechanics of tolerance and fair play programmes.

2.4.2 All participants could make a declaration on tolerance and fair play before or at the start of the event, either before leaving their countries or at the opening; media coverage could increase impact.

2.4.3 Schemes to reward good, fair and tolerant behaviour could be further developed.

2.4.4 The regulations governing participation in international sport events could provide for a Fair Play clause (anti-violence/anti-discrimination). Sanctions for intolerant or discriminatory behaviour by players, officials or supporters could be incorporated in contracts (where appropriate) or rules.

2.4.5 Following the example of UEFA, Fair Play competitions could be extended to cover spectators' behaviour and plans drawn up to avoid unacceptable behaviour in sports venues. Spectators and clubs, etc. should then be well informed about the consequences of any shortcomings in this respect.

2.4.6 Spectators could take part in selecting winners of Tolerance and Fair Play prizes for participants.

39.3. Final Statement
2nd Round Table on Sport, Tolerance and Fair Play
Lisbon, 20 November 1998

We, the participants at the 2nd Round Table on Sport, Tolerance and Fair-Play, held at Lisbon on 20 November 1998,

Recalling

the Declaration adopted at the first Round Table, held in Amsterdam on 11 April 1996,

the Declaration adopted at the Second Summit of the Council of Europe in Strasbourg on 10 October 1997, in which the Heads of State and Governments of the 40 member States recognised the "role of sport in promoting social integration, particularly among young people",

that at their 15th Informal Meeting at Nicosia on 14-15 May 1998, the Sports Ministers unanimously endorsed the role of sport in promoting social cohesion,

Conscious of the work on tolerance of the United Nations, UNESCO and the Council of Europe,

Having taken note of the several national and European initiatives, including the European Union's Year Against Racism in 1997, to promote fair play, tolerance and social cohesion taken since the Amsterdam Round Table, together with the positive results which are emerging from the interim reports on these projects, as seen from the report submitted by the Clearing House,

Respecting the fair play campaigns and initiatives taken by the national and international Olympic organisations, based on the fundamental principles of the Olympic Charter, by UEFA in the European Football Championships and by the FIFA in the World Cup, certain regrettable incidents during the latter event in 1998 having reinforced in the minds of sports leaders, policy makers and educationalists the continuing need for programmes to promote tolerance and fair play amongst both spectators and players,

Welcoming the role of ENGSO in encouraging its national member sports organisations to make tolerance and fair play campaigns part of their habitual work, and taking note of the results of the Seminar on Sport against Racism (Stockholm, December 1997),
Viewing with pleasure the appointment by many member countries of the CDDS of National Ambassadors for Sport, Tolerance and Fair Play, and expressing thanks to these ambassadors for the many practical suggestions and proposals they have made for promoting fair play and tolerance in and through sport (see Appendix 1),
Acknowledging the work of the European Fair Play Movement, its member organisations and the value of its databank (see Appendix II),
Bearing in mind that the Committee for the Development of Sport might wish to ask the Ministers' Deputies of the Council of Europe to submit to the special 50th anniversary meeting of the Committee of Ministers a report on sport and social cohesion,
Agreeing that while the goal of social cohesion is one of paramount importance, the work on tolerance and fair play throughout Europe must continue and intensify by means of exchanging information, facilitating, negotiating on the European level and the dissemination of knowledge in this area,
Affirming, in this respect, the indisputable link which exists between tolerance and social cohesion, as tolerance is a "sine qua non" and a necessary seed bed for social cohesion, so that minority groups are offered acceptance,
Stressing that the shared interests and values generated through sports participation are important factors in moving towards social integration, by teaching social skills and the abilities necessary in other areas of life besides sport, thus opening the way to active democratic citizenship;
Reaffirming the potential of sport to bring together all kinds of people and thus to act as a way of encouraging tolerance and understanding between different groups of people;
Recognising, however, that sport alone cannot solve all the problems of society in the fields of social exclusion and human dignity, nor prove a cure for the forms in which those problems may be expressed including intolerant behaviour, and hooliganism;
Considering that appropriately targeted sponsorship can also play a role in promoting sport, tolerance and fair play;
Requesting policy makers at all levels – national, regional and local – to consider this potential more carefully when making plans for strengthening tolerance, social integration and cohesion in their countries and localities;

Suggest that such policies and plans should be based on the following strategies and seven point plan:

I Identifying the aims and improving tolerance by continually keeping in mind the many links between social exclusion and intolerant behaviour;
- stressing the potential and outreach possibilities of sport as a way of improving self-respect and creating those sentiments of self worth and belonging, which may militate against intolerant behaviour;
exploring the possibilities inherent in sport to counter social exclusion amongst children and young people and to avert anti-social behaviour, including expressions of intolerance;

II Carrying out appropriate policies and
- giving priority to sports projects which promote the integration of children and young people, especially those who find themselves confronted by economic, social and cultural differences, for example, migrant children and those from different social and cultural backgrounds;

– developing specific activities for those who are excluded because of age or disability or for other identifiable reasons.

III Dismantling the barriers by

– developing all activities and initiatives which are liable to effectively combat the negative practices found in contemporary sport (doping, violence, discrimination of all types) so that in all cases the search to perform well will be linked with respect for human dignity, tolerance and fair play;

– envisioning and developing sports policies which are tools to fight all forms of exclusion (economic, social, cultural, disability, etc.) and which recognise equality between women and men.

IV Advertising the opportunities by

– discovering ways to ensure that voluntary workers in the field of social exclusion and those running programmes to combat intolerance are encouraged to familiarise themselves with the possibilities offered by and through sport, particularly specific local sports programmes;

– making known and developing the employment possibilities offered through sport and recreation, whether on a full-time or part-time basis, which will promote integration into working life, still seen as the main touchstone in the general sense of integration;

– developing educational programmes to help create positive perceptions of sport for those who may feel that sport is yet another of the opportunities reserved for those who already “have”.

V Beginning at the grass roots by

– encouraging all types of local schemes directed towards sport, tolerance, fair play and thus social cohesion and promoting co-operation between the various providers, both in the public, voluntary and private sectors;

– making local sports facilities more welcoming and more attractive for casual and ad hoc participants;

– encouraging different groups to be involved in planning and organising their own activities;

– stimulating the sports organisations and local clubs to make yet further efforts to develop activities which are socially inclusive, and to seek out leaders or representatives from among those who are excluded to work together in various pilot schemes;

– reserving an appropriate place in school programmes, for sport as a way of promoting tolerance and fair play.

VI Using the information by

– exploiting the data contained in the publications of the Clearing House on “Valuable Initiatives in the Field of Tolerance and Fair Play” and the databank of the European Fair Play Movement, both of which contains many examples of good practice;

– promoting initiatives such as the national campaigns “Fair Play, Different Colours, One Game”, “Starting the wave”, “Fair Play 2000”, “A Podium for All” and “Fair Comes First” as a means of intercultural exchange and dialogue;

– preparing national contributions for the “Testament on Tolerance 2000” which will set out in written or visual form the effectiveness of the programmes which have been undertaken to foster sport, tolerance, social cohesion and fair play, to be presented to the 3rd Round Table;

– finding ways and financial means for the practice of fair play and tolerance, in the context of initiatives which cross borders.

VII Following up these initiatives

– at the 9th Conference of European Ministers responsible for Sport, due to be held in Bratislava in Spring 2000;

– at the 3rd and final Round Table on Sport, Tolerance and Fair Play, which the Cyprus Sports Organisation has kindly offered to host.

Appendix I

Proposals by the National Ambassadors

Practical measures for encouraging fair play and tolerance in sport

The national ambassadors for Sport, Tolerance and Fair Play, meeting in Lisbon on 19-20 November, discussed the following recommendations and fields for action, some of which were first proposed at their first meeting in December 1997. They further deliberated on the role of sport in teaching tolerance and encouraging social cohesion, in line with the Statement of the Second Round Table.

Having appreciated at first hand all the benefits and privileges that participation in sport can bring, together with some of the negative aspects such as expressions of intolerance, cases of doping and demonstrations of bad behaviour on the sports field, and desirous of seeing a return to a world of sport characterised by fair play, tolerance and ethics, the national ambassadors would commend action in the areas outlined in this paper.

The national ambassadors, furthermore, express their willingness to make a contribution to national programmes, where appropriate, and to bear in mind the importance of the link between sport, tolerance, fair play and social cohesion.

The following points detail measures for activities to encourage fair play and tolerance and to put the subject high on the sporting agenda.

A DEVELOPMENT OF MEASURES TO ENCOURAGE FAIR PLAY AND TOLERANCE

In this area there would appear to be five major initiatives which could be taken.

i Increasing attention should be placed on the educational sphere and projects on tolerance and fair play introduced into sports clubs and schools. Efforts should be made to recreate the concepts of fair play and tolerance in sport as attainable objectives. Particular attention should be paid to the 10-14 year age group, because experience has shown that this is a particularly receptive group in this area. Where these programmes exist national ambassadors could visit children's sports clubs and schools.

ii A compendium of the various programmes on teaching tolerance and fair play should be published by the Council of Europe in co-operation with the Clearing House. The compendium should take account of programmes that the European Commission have developed in this area.

iii Ambassadors should encourage the holding of a national Fair Play and Tolerance Day in their respective countries, and actively associate themselves with international days on tolerance.

iv. Where appropriate governments might be asked to consider legislation to promote tolerance and fair play in sport.

A European prize awarded for tolerance in sport should be set up. Although there are many prizes for fair play, the exercise of tolerance goes one step further and could, perhaps, be seen as fair play in the face of provocation. A prize for tolerance differs from a prize for fair play in that a sportsman or woman may theoretically play a sport fairly without encountering prejudice or discrimination. A prize for tolerance, however, might be awarded to a sports person who has suffered discriminatory practices etc. but has refused to retaliate.

B GETTING THE MESSAGE ACROSS

i The establishment of a strong network between the national ambassadors is to be encouraged, with the exchange of expertise, ideas etc. Efforts should also be made to establish contacts in countries which have not appointed a national ambassador.

ii. There is support for the adoption of a tune to be played throughout Europe before sporting events. This tune will, it is hoped, come to be a signature tune for fair play and tolerance in sport. Countries could add words in their national language to the tune.

iii. National sports federations can play a key role in any initiatives and should be kept closely informed, be involved in all campaigns in this area and accepted as full partners. They have extensive "know how" at the national level and can, for example, offer advice and help in the area of educational programmes and hold joint campaigns.

iv. A necessary measure related to activities on tolerance and fair play is to acknowledge the importance of sport for children and their rights in this area. The Code of Ethics of the Council of Europe already covers a number of points. It must to be recognised that the rights of children in sport, include the right of a child to play as a child, to be treated with dignity, to receive appropriate training from competent and responsible people, to practise sport in security and the right NOT to be a champion.

v. The national ambassadors should encourage the media and press in their respective countries to take a broader view of sport coverage and sports news so that other aspects of the sports scene, for example the problems in sport are adequately covered. Currently the emphasis seems to lie on the results of games.

vi. As a long-term project one might envisage the setting up of a working group of national ambassadors to travel throughout Europe advocating fair play and tolerance programmes and appearing at high profile sports events. A project of this kind would need sponsors, and serious financing.

Appendix II

Contribution of the Non-governmental Sports Organisations

In all activities to encourage sport, tolerance and fair play, the non-governmental organisations are aware that they have an important role to fulfil which they willingly undertake.

In recent years, an increase in undesirable behaviour in sport, a growth in discrimination, have shown the need for both reflection and action by the non-governmental sports organisations. These problems are also a result of what happens in society surrounding the sport.

The growth of the new Europe has resulted in a call for co-operation and an exchange of experience between those organisations which have a rich and long experience in the area of fair play and tolerance in sport and new movements, doted with enthusiasm and fresh dynamism.

While maintaining that fairness and tolerance in sport should be considered the norm ‘ and not a quality calling for reward ‘ the non-governmental organisations nevertheless agree that awards in this area can help, both to emphasise the importance of fair play and call the attention of the society to these problems. In this context the possibility of an European award might be considered.

All possible ways should be explored to build and strengthen co-operation between governments, intergovernmental organisations, particularly the Council of Europe, the non-governmental organisations in this field, particularly European Fair Play Movement (EFPM), European Non-Governmental Sport Organisation (ENGSO), European Olympic Committees (EOC) and international sports federations. This should include regular contact between the various bodies in the framework of conferences, sports events etc. and co-operation in action plans or campaigns. Although all parties have a unique role to exercise they can but benefit from a sharing of tasks. The national ambassadors for sport, tolerance and fair play could act as points of reference and might undertake a bridge-building role.

Moves to promote co-operation between different non-governmental organisations, working in whole or in part in the same areas, should also be welcomed. Closer interaction could well result in a wider promotion of the values of fair play and tolerance in sport throughout Europe.

39.4. Resolution on preventing racism, xenophobia and intolerance in sport (No. 4/2000)

The European Ministers responsible for Sport, meeting in Bratislava for their 9th Conference on 30 and 31 May 2000:

Noting the Declaration adopted at the European Conference on the Social Dimension of Football (Strasbourg, 22-23 November 1999);

Reaffirming strongly their commitment to the defence of the ethical values in sport and to the role sport plays in education for mutual respect, tolerance, fair-play, and against discrimination;

Welcoming the growing role of sport, especially football, in the development of communities but also concerned by recent outbreaks of racist behaviour at sports events;

Determined to offer all the support possible to host countries and the organisers of EURO 2000 to prevent outbreaks of spectator violence and misbehaviour during the Championships;

Agree to take at national level all necessary measures effectively to prevent and to combat racist behaviour, xenophobia and intolerance in all sports, in particular in relation to football matches;

Invite the Committee of Ministers to ask the Committee for the Development of Sport (CDDS) and the Standing Committee of the European Convention on Spectator Violence and Misbehaviour at Sports Events and in particular at Football Matches (T-RV) to prepare a draft text on the legislative, statutory, administrative, educative, legal and police measures to eliminate racist and xenophobic propaganda and behaviour of all kinds at sports events. This text should bring to the fore the respective and joint responsibilities which are incumbent upon both governments and non-governmental organisations (sport clubs, sport events organisers, stadium owners, etc.) to counter such behaviour.

39.5. Recommendation Rec(2001)6 of the Committee of Ministers to member states on the prevention of racism, xenophobia and racial intolerance in sport

(Adopted by the Committee of Ministers on 18 July 2001 at the 761st meeting of the Ministers' Deputies)

The Committee of Ministers, under the terms of Article 15.b of the Statute of the Council of Europe,

Bearing in mind the Declaration adopted by the Heads of State and Government of the member states of the Council of Europe at the Vienna Summit (1993) and, in particular, the Declaration and Plan of Action for combating racism, xenophobia, anti-semitism and intolerance;

Bearing in mind the European Convention on Human Rights and its protocols, in particular Protocol No. 12;

Bearing in mind the European Convention on Spectator Violence and Misbehaviour at Sports Events and in particular at Football Matches;

Bearing in mind Recommendation No. R (97) 20 of the Committee of Ministers to member states on 'hate speech';

Bearing in mind Resolution No. 4 on preventing racism, xenophobia and intolerance in sport adopted at the 9th Conference of European Ministers responsible for Sport in Bratislava in May 2000;
Bearing in mind the measures advocated by the European Commission against Racism and Intolerance (ECRI);
Bearing in mind the Political Declaration and the General Conclusions adopted by the European Conference against Racism and Intolerance (13 October 2000);
Recognising the growing role played by sport in socialisation and community development;
Aware of the role of sport in educating young people in particular, in mutual respect, tolerance, fair-play and against discrimination;
Considering that racism, racial discrimination, xenophobia and intolerance constitute a serious threat to sport and its ethical values;
Taking note of the initiatives taken by several international sport organisations, and in particular those taken by FIFA and UEFA;
Aware that hooliganism, violence in sport and racist/neo-nazi/extreme right-wing movements may be bound up with each other;
Considering that a number of further specific measures are needed in order to eradicate racism, xenophobia and racial intolerance from sport;
Considering that the promotion of a democratic and tolerant society, free from racism and discrimination of all kinds requires an effort by the whole population,
Recommends the governments of member states adopt effective policies and measures aimed at preventing and combating racist, xenophobic, discriminatory and intolerant behaviour in all sports and in particular football, drawing inspiration from the guidelines in the appendix to this Recommendation;
Transmits this Recommendation to the European Commission against Racism and Intolerance;
Calls upon all sport organisations, such as FIFA, UEFA and national football associations, to assist in these aims with all the means available to them.

Appendix to Recommendation Rec(2001)6
Guidelines

A. Definition

1. In this document, racism is used in the broad sense, covering xenophobia, anti-Semitism, discrimination and all related forms of racial and ethnic intolerance.
2. Racism in sport is not a phenomenon confined to football grounds. Nor is it confined just to players of colour. It can affect all sports and can manifest itself at several levels, in amateur sport and at institutional and international levels, as well as in the media. It can occur at local level particularly, but not exclusively, in the interaction (for real or imagined reasons of colour, religion, nationality or ethnic origin) between or against players, teams, coaches and spectators and also against referees. It can include the abuse of teams or even whole groups.

B. Sharing responsibilities and co-ordination

1. The responsibility for combating racism in sport falls to public authorities (the legislative authority, the courts, the police, governmental bodies responsible for sport and local authorities) and non-governmental organisations (professional and amateur national sports associations, clubs, local sports associations, supporters' clubs, players' organisations, anti-racist associations and so on).

2. In designing a policy and action to effectively combat racism, an overall approach involving all the partners should be adopted. At national level, the tasks and responsibilities of all those involved should be set out in a framework agreement.
3. As well as their prerogatives in relation to law making, the courts and the police, government bodies should also act as co-ordinators. The co-ordination framework should include a means of consultation between the parties concerned.
4. Governments should also support non-governmental organisations, particularly national sports organisations, clubs and anti-racist associations, upon whom falls the principal task of implementing awareness-raising, educational and information programmes on racism in sport. The payment of grants to sports organisations and clubs could be made conditional on a firm commitment and effective action by them to combat racism.
5. At international non-governmental level, particular leadership and disciplinary responsibilities lie with sports governing bodies (in the case of football, FIFA and UEFA) and their affiliated national organisations.

C. Legislative measures

1. Although constitutional and legal rules prohibiting all sorts of discrimination exist in most of the Council of Europe member states, special legislative measures should be taken to deal with the issue of racism in sport.
2. Every government should ensure that its legal and administrative systems are given the most appropriate and effective national legal means of combating racism in sport. To give an example, legal measures on combating racism in sport could be introduced into the existing body of legislation, in, for example, the penal code. Such measures could also be adopted as part of a specific sports law, or the law concerning the fight against violence in sport or the law relating to a particular sport, for example football.
3. Legislation should proscribe as criminal offences all types of act (flaunting of banners or symbols) or words (insults or chanting), committed or uttered at sporting events such as to incite violence or other discriminatory behaviour against racial, ethnic or religious groups or members of those groups on the grounds that they belong to such a group.
4. Legislation should provide for strict penalties for racist acts committed in sports arenas. In addition, other non-penal sanctions such as exclusion or banning from stadiums should be provided for.
5. In order to make criminal penalties more effective and increase their deterrent character, proceedings should automatically be brought for all racist acts.
6. Legislative measures should not be limited to repressive provisions. Existing laws should also be reviewed in order to eliminate any provisions that create or encourage any discriminatory situation, particularly in laws on various sports (cf. those on football) or laws on the status of sporting organisations: for example, immigrants or migrants legally resident in a given country should not be counted in the quotas applied to players transferred direct from a foreign country. In certain European countries, the quotas imposed on sportspersons of non-European Union nationality prevent young people from immigrant families from playing in official (professional or amateur) leagues there.

D. Implementation of legislative measures

1. In the fight against racism, co-operation and joint strategies between the police, the courts, event organisers, stadium/club managers, stewards, supporters and non-governmental organisations are essential to identify the guilty persons and gather evidence of the offence.

2. Video cameras and CCTV systems installed in stadiums for public safety and public order reasons should also be used to assist in the identification of racist offenders.
3. Police officers and stewards should intervene effectively to show that racist acts or chanting are not harmless activities and that their perpetrators will not go unpunished.
4. Police officers and stewards should be made aware of the problem of racism, informed of the laws and regulations and trained to act on and deal with the problem of racism. To help in the identification of perpetrators of racist offences, specially trained police officers should be assigned to each major club/stadium.
5. An information system should be developed which includes data on racist offences and their perpetrators and a means of communicating information between the police and organisers of sports events. Information systems on hooliganism, where they already exist, could be used to this end.
6. Actions that have been taken against those who have engaged in racist behaviour should be given appropriate publicity.

E. Measures to be taken in sports grounds

1. As part of an integrated approach, legislative measures should be supplemented with regulations and educational and social measures. To this end, governments should urge sports organisations and clubs:
   a. to recognise that racism and all other forms of discrimination are a major problem in sport, especially in football;
   b. to adopt and publicise firm and unequivocal anti-racist policies;
   c. to include clauses in their rules and regulations valid at all level of competition which enable referees, umpires or other match officials to impose effective sporting sanctions on participants who perpetrate racist acts (gestures, insults, etc.) either immediately during the competition or as a consequent disciplinary measure;
   d. to take effective measures to instil in players, coaches and other individuals a moral spirit of fair play especially with regard to their attitude towards others of differing ethnic groups;
   e. to state clearly in their regulations and those of the stadium that racist slogans, symbols, gestures and chanting are strictly prohibited in and around stadiums and indicate the penalties that will be incurred for any breach of these regulations (expulsion from the stadium, cancellation of any season tickets and ban on future access, stadium bans and events played behind closed doors, etc.): provisions should also be provided to discontinue the sports events during which supporters display placards bearing racist and/or xenophobic slogans or incitements to violence;
   f. to include in the conditions of sale for season-tickets and other tickets that the holders undertake not to engage in racist acts;
   g. to take practical measures inside and in the vicinity of stadiums, for example: public announcements condemning racism should be made during matches; the sale or distribution of handouts, posters, stickers or any other form of racist publication should be forbidden and actively prevented; racist graffiti should immediately be removed, and so on.

F. Measures to be taken at local level

1. Governments, at national and local levels, and with the impulse of locally elected representatives, should implement, and encourage local sporting organisations and clubs

to devise programmes adapted to the local situation in order to exploit to the full the potential which sport offers for social and cultural integration. To this end, they should establish dialogue and partnership with organisations involved in combating racism in sport, in particular with supporters' clubs, migrants' associations and ethnic minority groups.

2. Ethnic minority communities' organisations should be involved in the fight against racism in sport in the context of a wider struggle for migrants' rights, against racist attacks and to encourage inclusion.
3. Governments should support and take necessary measures to facilitate the participation of members of different ethnic minorities in sport activities. In this respect, co-operation of amateur and school clubs with professional teams should be encouraged.
4. Event organisers should be encouraged to foster more inclusive stadium and sport venue culture and atmosphere, to attract members of different ethnic groups as spectators and supporters by, for example, offering them cut-price or free tickets.
5. Governments should urge local authorities and sports governing bodies to encourage and support movements and initiatives to promote sportsmanship and tolerance, and educational and social projects: the adoption and publication of a code of ethics (based, for example on the Code of Sports Ethics in Recommendation R (92) 14) and sportsmanship, meetings with schoolchildren, messages from famous sportspersons (such as the national Ambassadors for Sport, Tolerance and Fair Play), matches with amateur community-group clubs and supporters' embassies at professional matches, and so on.

G. Measures to be taken at institutional level

1. Equal opportunities policies, including training to raise awareness on cultural and ethnic diversity, should be developed and applied in sporting organisations and clubs.
2. Education and awareness campaigns on the elimination of racism in sport should be introduced at all levels, involving international sports federations, European sport organisations, national federations and clubs, and young people and children.
3. Governments should urge sporting organisations to review their regulations and delete any rule which might give rise to or foster discrimination between different national and ethnic groups (cf. C.6).
4. Governments should urge sports federations and clubs to set an example by making sure that community groups are represented among their managers, staff, trainers, officials and so on. This would not necessarily mean introducing quotas, but it does mean making room for ethnic minority groups.
5. Governments should help sporting federations and clubs with appropriate anti-racism initiatives, if necessary through making grants.
6. Governments should support other non-governmental organisations and campaigns to combat racism and xenophobia in sport, if necessary through making grants.

H. International co-operation within the Standing Committee

1. Racist offences committed at international matches and other international sports events in Europe should be dealt with in the framework of international police co-operation and be included in the system for exchanging information. The forms for exchanging information contained in the Appendix to T-RV Recommendation No. 1 (97), and the list of national correspondents for bilateral contacts on matters connected with football hooliganism drawn up by the Standing Committee of the European Convention on Spectator Violence (T-RV) could be used for this purpose.
2. Exchange of information on good practice in combating racism in sport should be encouraged within the Standing Committee (T-RV).

3. The measures taken to combat racism in sport should be regularly assessed in each country. National reports on the implementation of this recommendation should be submitted to the Standing Committee as part of the procedure for monitoring the application of the convention. Such reports would include information on the activities of national and international non governmental organisations involved in this work.

Chapter 40
VIOLENCE

40.1. Resolution on Violence Associated with Sport
London, April 1978

Considering the serious problem of violence in and around sports grounds;
Bearing in mind the resolution of the congress on "Violence in Sport" held in Brussels on 7 and 8 September 1977;
Taking note of the document previously distributed by the Belgian Minister of Dutch Culture;
Considering the general desire to tackle this problem effectively without delay,
Recommend to the Committee of Ministers of the Council of Europe to instruct the CDDS to elaborate, in co-operation with the international sports federations and organisations, the necessary measures to banish violence from the world of sport;
Ask the Belgian Minister of Dutch Culture to carry out this decision in close liaison with the Chairman of the CDDS in order to set up all appropriate structure within the Council of Europe.

40.2. Recommendation 963 (1983)[10] on cultural and educational means of reducing violence
Parliamentary Assembly of the Council of Europe, Thirty-fourth Ordinary Session, 28 January 1983

The Assembly,

A. Introduction
1. Having noted the report of its Committee on Culture and Education (Doc. 5013)
2. Taking note of the Hearing on violence held by that Committee in Assisi from 1 to 3 September 1982 on the occasion of the 800th anniversary of the birth of St. Francis;
3. Gravely concerned at the occurrence of violence in modern society, in particular terrorism, but also delinquency, vandalism and rape;
4. Suspicious in principle of some of the justifications advanced for direct physical violence, but recognising that those in authority on certain occasions have to use varying acceptable degrees of force for the protection of society, of lives and of property;
5. Believing that violence in modern society is related to the stresses exercised on human nature by external factors of a social, economic and cultural character;
6. Recalling the report of its Committee on Culture and Education on war toys (Doc. 4742) and the resolution adopted on this subject by the European Parliament on 13 September 1982;

[10] Assembly debate on 28 January 1983 (28th Sitting) (see Doc. 5013, report of the Committee on Culture and Education). Text adopted by the Assembly on 28 January 1983 (28th Sitting).

B. Regarding terrorism

7. Recalling its Recommendations 916 (1981) and 941 (1982) on the defence of democracy against terrorism in Europe;
8. Considering that terrorism is a permanent challenge to fundamental democratic values, and may well prompt states to take legislative, judicial or administrative measures (such as keeping records on individuals for the purposes of prevention, restrictions on personal freedoms, etc.) that may pervert the very character of democracy;
9. Aware of the fact that combating terrorism may, because of the growth of politically motivated crimes and offences, create imbalances in the arsenal of penalties, and disrupt prison systems;
10. Convinced that the symbolic, spectacular or revolting nature of terrorism and the exaggerated reflection sometimes given of it by the media helps it achieve a social impact out of all proportion to the resources it deploys and even to its ultimate goal, something which distinguishes it from ordinary violence;
11. Noting that terrorism imitates the methods, means and language of warfare without triggering off the usual collective defence mechanisms;
12. Conscious that terrorism is moreover a factor of major cultural destabilisation and can undermine the individual's confidence in the values, interests or institutions under attack;
13. Considering that measures to suppress terrorism must be based on an analysis of its causes.
14. Recommends that the Committee of Ministers invite member governments:
    a. to take the necessary steps to alert communities in which terrorism is breeding to the serious threat it presents to democracy and freedoms;
    b. to make available in all member countries a "White Paper on democracy and terrorism", a work which would be prepared by the Council of Europe and based on the European Convention on Human Rights, international agreements and Member states' constitutions, and whose purpose would be to demonstrate the fact that terrorism is a major European problem imperilling democracy and to proclaim Europe's determination to combat political violence;
    c. to foster studies of the cultural and social causes of the growth of terrorism by giving thought to the selling up of an independent European Foundation for the study of terrorism;

C. Regarding the media

15. Concerned at the increasing tendency towards emphasis on violence in the media, and in particular on its portrayal in the visual media (television, video, film, advertising, comics, or still photography);
16. Conscious that prolonged exposure to such media violence can have a direct cumulative effect on young children and a minority of adults, and a growing effect on the accepted values of society;
17. Welcoming the recent Declaration by the Committee of Ministers on freedom of expression (1982), and recalling Article 10 of the European Convention on Human Rights (1950) and the United Nations Convention for the Repression of Obscene Publications (1947);
18. Concerned that artistic freedom should not be used as an alibi for purely commercial interests;
19. Believing that national legislative or voluntary restrictions are becoming increasingty impracticable in the light of direct broadcasting by satellite and other technological

developments, and drawing attention to the fact that the production, distribution and sale of media software kas already progressed beyond the control of individual states;

20. Stressing the urgency of co-ordinated action involving European states, broadcasting institutions and commercial audio-visual concerns;

21. Recommends that the Committee of Ministers
    - a. request the broadcasting organisations to co-operate on the elaboration of codes of conduct or guidelines covering the portrayal of violence, including terrorism, that can apply to as broad an area in Europe as possible, and where necessary provide autonomous supplementary structures to enable the effective elaboration of such common codes;
    - b. encourage the elaboration of similar guidelines for other media such as films, written material, video and new forms of visual media that may be developed;
    - c. encourage the establishment in each member state of a. independent monitoring of broadcast and other visual media through viewer associations and other bodies, b. closer consultation between the public and the programme makers, and c. public accountability for media content whether to parliament, to the courts or to public opinion, and envisage at a subsequent stage closer co-ordination between member States on these aspects;
    - d. arrange for the regular publication of an up-to-date survey of existing guidelines, legislation and administrative structures regarding the media in all member states;
    - e. ask member governments:
        - i. to sponsor further independent research into the effects of the media;
        - ii. to consider introducing legislation to ensure that media violence involving individuals is condemned alongside incitement to racial hatred or obscenity;
        - iii. to take the appropriate measures to ensure that broadcasting companies give particular attention to means of protecting sensitive people, especially children, from prolonged exposure to media violence;
        - iv. to make clear to the press and to the audio-visual media their special responsibility as regards the dissemination of models of political violence, and therefore make proper understanding of the effects of the media a necessary part of the qualification of all personnel employed in the media field;

D. Regarding sport

22. Concerned with the continued presence of violence in sport and with the growth of violence associated with sport on local, national and international levels;

23. Welcoming the action already taken by the sports federations to reduce violence in sport by modifying the rules of individual and team games, with special reference to violent sports such as boxing, and by increasing the authority of refereeing;

24. Questioning, however, the efficacity of existing sanctions, in particular in top-level professional sport, and believing that responsibility lies as much with trainers and management as with individual players;

25. Believing that concerted action by the public authorities and the sporting bodies is necessary to control violence associated with sport, and that the media could help in this action, and stressing the positive role to be played by responsible supporters' clubs

26. Welcoming the activity of the International Alliance for Non-Violent Sport and for Fair Play, and noting the results of the symposium organised by the Alliance in Monte-Carlo on 16 and 17 November 1982;

27. Recalling the Council of Europe's European Sport for All Charter, and reaffirming its belief in the ideals and values of sport, especially Olympic sport as expressed in its Resolution 738 (1980), on the Olympic Games and the outlook for their future;
28. Believing that it is necessary to reaffirm and re-establish these positive values of sport and fair play as a direct contribution to solving the problem of violence in modern society;
29. Recalling the resolution on violence associated with sport, adopted by the Conference of European Ministers responsible for Sport in London 1978, and hoping that the ministers concerned will reconsider urgently the question of violence and sport;
30. Recommends that the Committee of Ministers:
    a. ask the Steering Committee for the Development of Sport to give consideration to effective European Intergovernmental co-operation on violence and sport, including the elaboration of a European convention, or other forms of European agreement on the introduction of specific legislation in member states;
    b. co-ordinate such activity with other sectors through the steering committees responsible for mass media, culture and education, and criminal matters;
    c. support the Campaign of the International Alliance for Non-Violent Sport and for Fair Play;

E. Positive approaches, and in particular education

31. Stressing the power of example of parent, teacher or state, and noting also the role played by the churches, youth organisations and other disinterested institutions in encouraging young people to participate in social goals;
32. Underlining the need for schools constantly to readjust to the changing patterns of modern society, and noting the conclusions reached by the Council for Cultural Co-operation project on "Preparation for life";
33. Insisting on the importance of the proper preparation of children to understand the messages put across by the media, and noting the positive contribution of the media in presenting society as condemning and rejecting violence;
34. Wishing to ensure that the systematic teaching of non-violent behaviour is an integral part of all compulsory education, and welcoming the proposal by the Quaker Council for European Affairs to conduct a study on existing models in Europe of such education;
35. Hoping that the Standing Conference of European Ministers of Education will pay close attention to the contribution education can make to encouraging constructive, non-violent behaviour;
36. Recommends that the Committee of Ministers:
    a. associate the Council for Cultural Cooperation with study of models of education for non-violent behaviour and co-operation;
    b. invite member governments or, through them, the local or regional authorities responsible for education:
        i. to review the content of existing school and university curricula in order to avoid thoughtless glorification of conflict and violence, and to introduce in schools the systematic teaching of non-violent behaviour;
        ii. to encourage the introduction in certain European universities of the study of terrorism;
        iii. to make available for use in schools, for example in the context of history lessons, material highlighting the odious and regressive nature of political violence and denouncing the ideologies that provoke and manipulate such violence;

iv. to make it possible for young people to opt out of experiments involving violence to living animals should they object to these on grounds of conscience, without prejudice to their subsequent careers;
v. to ensure that schools adhere to non-violent approaches with regard to their own internal problems and that they avoid any recourse to violent punishment;
vi. to encourage real participation in school life by allowing the gradual development of pupil responsibility and the continued involvement of parents, and by permitting the school and its community to fulfil its indispensable educational role;
vii. to introduce into the school curriculum the critical understanding of the media, and to provide the necessary in-service and preparatory training of teachers;
viii. to ensure a proper place for sport (both individual and team sports) in schools, with particular stress on the principles of fair play.

40.3. Declaration on Spectator Violence at Football Matches and other Sports Events

Rotterdam, November 1983

European Ministers for Sport meeting in Rotterdam for their 10th informal meeting recall their discussions at their ninth meeting in Paris of the problems of violence and sport and the resolutions on violence associated with sport adopted at their conferences in London and Palma de Majorca. They take account also of the concern of the Parliamentary Assembly of the Council of Europe as set out in Recommendation No. 963 (1983) on cultural and educational means of reducing violence.

They reaffirm their particular concern about violence and misbehaviour among spectators at football matches and at other sporting events which represent a serious problem at national and international levels for sport and for society generally, not least the cost of policing. They acknowledge the long-term value of fostering better appreciation of the sporting ideal and the importance of fair play among players and spectators alike: but they are convinced that immediate priority should be given to the formulation and implementation of practical measures to discourage and curb violent behaviour by spectators.

They welcome the decision by the Committee for the Development of Sport of the Council of Europe to study the problem and note with satisfaction that the Working Group set up for this purpose has prepared proposals. The European Ministers support the principles underlying the Group's recommendations, which respect the autonomy of national and international sports federations but emphasise that public and sporting authorities must act together to counteract the problems of spectator violence.

In particular, the Ministers generally welcome and agree the recommendations for governments. They also stress the value of the practical measures identified in the Working Group's proposals, for example, segregation of rival supporters, the close control of ticket sales in support of this and the overall importance of coordinated pre-match planning by all concerned.

The European Ministers also note that these proposals endorse the importance of deterring spectators from violence, for example, through ensuring that the courts are able to impose deterrent penalties on those convicted of offences related to spectator violence, and that visiting foreign spectators face the prospect of trial, and appropriate punishment if convicted, if they are arrested in connection with acts of violence at sports events.

The Ministers agree to seek, with the appropriate sporting and public authorities, the immediate implementation of the Working Group's proposals not only within their own countries but also by developing bilateral cooperation on the occasion of forthcoming matches between their countries and their clubs. They recommend the proposals for formal adoption by the Council of Europe with possible drafting changes to reflect the different legal and administrative conditions in member countries and concerning the positive role of the media.

40.4. Recommendation of the Committee of Ministers to Member States on the Reduction of Spectator Violence at Sporting Events and in particular at Football Matches (84/8)
Adopted by the Committee of Ministers on 19 March 1984

The Committee of Ministers, under the terms of Article 15b of the Statute of the Council of Europe,
Recalling its Resolution (76) 41 on the "Principles for a policy of Sport for All";
Bearing in mind the resolution adopted by the European Ministers responsible for Sport on "violence associated with sport" at their 2nd Conference (London, 1978), and their declaration on spectator violence at football matches and other sports events, adopted at their 10th informal meeting in Rotterdam, in 1983;
Having regard to Recommendation 963 (1983) of the Parliamentary Assembly on cultural and educational means of reducing violence;
Respecting the established independence of sports federations, including the international football authorities and the national football authorities in member states;
Emphasising the important contribution made by sport and, especially, because of their frequency, football matches between national and club teams from member states, to international understanding and European co-operation;
Supporting the principle of fair play in sport and recognising the value of a thorough appreciation of this sporting ideal among spectators;
Considering that, in order to reduce violence in society generally, action must be taken against all forms of violence;
Concerned by the growth of violence associated with sport, and in particular by misbehaviour and violence among spectators at football matches, which damages sport by tarnishing its public image, by deterring spectators and which may also discourage participation at the level of the sports so affected;
Concerned that violence and misbehaviour impose greater social and economic costs on the communities of member states, including those arising from injury to third parties, policing and damage to property;
Considering that the governments of member states and the sports organisations have separate but complementary responsibilities in combating spectator violence and that the two should work together to this end;
Commending the actions already taken by member states and by the responsible national and international football authorities to reduce or contain this problem;
Convinced that member states of the Council of Europe should take a lead in seeking solutions to the problem, and that their first priority should be the implementation by governments and by football authorities of practical measures which will have an immediate impact,

Recommends that the governments of member states:

1. Should, as far as football matches are concerned, and within applicable constitutional limits:

a. acknowledge their responsibility, complementing that of regional and local government and of other public agencies, and that of the football authorities, to curb violence amongst spectators;

b. co-ordinate at national level the policies and actions of government departments and other public agencies against spectator violence, and foster similar co-operation to this end at other levels;

c. attach immediate priority to the formulation and implementation of practical measures designed to reduce spectator violence in the short term, including:

   i. appropriate steps to provide that adequate police resources are available to counter anticipated outbreaks of violence, both within the immediate vicinity of and inside the stadiums and along the transit routes used by spectators and also to encourage co-operation including the exchange of information between the police forces of the different localities involved;

   ii. the consistent employment of, or where such does not exist the consideration of the adoption of, appropriate legislation, with a view to ensuring that those found guilty of offences related to spectator violence receive appropriate penalties, taking into account the serious nature of violent offences, which penalties may also deter others from similar acts;

2. That they co-operate fully with and take all possible steps to encourage their national football associations to:

a. ensure that effective measures are taken at and within stadiums to reduce spectator violence at football matches and in particular:

   i. to ensure that the design and physical fabric of football stadiums provide for the safety of spectators, do not readily facilitate violence between spectators, allow effective crowd control by police and contain appropriate barriers or fencing so as to protect the playing field and to control the movement of spectators around it;

   ii. to segregate rival supporters, with one or more terraces reserved for visiting supporters only;

   iii. to ensure this segregation by controlling the sale of tickets for matches, and to avoid the casual sale of tickets that might undermine such segregation;

   iv. to ensure insofar as it is legally possible the exclusion of known troublemakers;

   v. to ensure the provision of an effective public address system and that full use is made of this, of the match programme brochure and of other publicity outlets to encourage good behaviour by spectators;

   vi. to restrict, if not ban, the sale of alcoholic drinks, including beer, and, if the sale of such beverages is permitted, to ensure that they are not available in potentially dangerous containers;

   vii. to take all practicable steps to ensure that spectators do not bring in any objects that might be used in acts of violence;

   viii. to consider appointing liaison officers to discuss before matches arrangements for crowd control with all appropriate public authorities so as to ensure that any relevant rules are enforced through concerted action;

   ix. to encourage the establishment of official supporters' clubs and the appointment of stewards from within their membership to help manage and inform spectators at matches and to accompany parties of supporters travelling to away fixtures;

b. ensure that the rules and guidelines of the Union des associations européennes de football (UEFA) for the avoidance of crowd disturbances are implemented as a minimum standard at all relevant matches and to consider adapting and extending them as appropriate to national circumstances so as to have a clear set of rules applicable to domestic matches;

3. That they work closely with their respective national football authorities to:

a. seek arrangements to assist with the financing of alterations to the physical fabric of stadiums or other measures necessary to improve safety and to curb spectator violence;

b. consider the possibility of introducing a system of stadium licensing to promote the safety and orderly behaviour of spectators especially for those stadiums used for matches likely to attract large or unruly crowds;

c. invite the media – whilst supporting their editorial independence and recognising their responsibility to report acts of violence – to highlight example of fair play and sporting behaviour by participants or spectators, in order to give publicity to the authors of such acts and encourage their peers to emulate them;

d. foster co-operation among relevant public authorities, football clubs and stadium owners to ensure good spectator access to stadiums (including bus and car parking facilities), unnecessary obstacles to spectator access being a possible stimulus to aggression among spectators;

e. consider the introduction of procedures and studies to monitor the impact of measures to alleviate violence and misbehaviour by football spectators;

4. That, in addition, on the occasion of international club and representative matches or tournaments they should:

a. co-operate closely and encourage similar close bilateral and multilateral co-operation as appropriate both among the relevant national football authorities involved and among the respective national public authorities (for example, police forces) including those of countries which may be crossed by visiting spectators;

b. seek to ensure, bearing in mind each member state's legal procedures and the independence of the judiciary, that visiting spectators apprehended in connection with acts of spectator violence are tried under procedures which are in accordance with the principles set out in paragraph 3.b above, or, where appropriate, take advantage of the possibility of transferring proceedings against such persons to the country of residence;

5. That, as far as other sports events are concerned where violence and misbehaviour among spectators may be a problem, they apply the same principles and ideas as are embodied in this recommendation, with respect both to governmental action and to action in co-operation with the national sports organisations concerned;

6. That, so far as the general causes of violence among players and spectators are concerned, they take additional long-term measures to prevent the growth of violence in sport by promoting the sporting ideal through educational and other campaigns and by giving support to the notion of fair play, especially among young people, so as to enhance friendship among sports players and spectators;

Instructs the Secretary General to transmit this recommendation to the governments of those states party to the European Cultural Convention which are not members of the Council of Europe.

40.5. Resolution on Spectator Violence Associated with Sport (84/6)

The European Ministers responsible for sport, meeting in Malta for their 4th Conference, on 15 and 16 May 1984

Confirming their continuing disquiet about incidents of violence among spectators attending sporting events and especially at international club and representative football matches between teams from their countries;
Deploring especially the incidents which have occurred throughout the current football season in several member countries;
Confirming their determination to do what they can to reduce, if not eliminate, such anti-social behaviour;
Acknowledging especially the initiatives taken by UEFA in preparing regulations and guidelines for national football federations on measures to be taken at matches staged under its auspices;
Convinced that efforts to defeat this problem need the co-operation of all involved in the organisation and staging of sports events, governmental and non-governmental organisations alike;
Take note, with pleasure, of the adoption by the Committee of Ministers of the Recommendation N° (84) 8, on the reduction of spectator violence at sporting events and in particular at football matches;
Appreciate that the provisions of this recommendation would do much to reduce the violence associated with football;
Resolve to do all within their competence to ensure full implementation and resolve to draw it to the attention of their respective national football authorities;
Ask the Secretary General of the Council of Europe to bring this Recommendation to the attention of UEFA;
Invite the Committee of Ministers of the Council of Europe to ask the CDDS, in the period up to the 5th Conference, to monitor the operation of the provisions of this recommendation, to review its effectiveness and to consider what steps could be taken in the future to further the objective of stopping spectator violence;
Recommend that UEFA and other specialist bodies should be consulted, as appropriate, on any further measures.

40.6. Resolution No. 1/85 on a European Convention on Spectator Violence and Misbehaviour at Sports Events and in particular at Football Matches

The European Ministers responsible for Sport, meeting for their 12th Informal Meeting at the Council of Europe on 27 June 1985, have resolved:

1. to agree on a European Convention on Spectator Violence and Misbehaviour at Sports Events and in particular at Football Matches;
2. to invite the Committee of Ministers to adopt and open for signature the Convention (See Recommendation No. R (84) 8 [...] at the earliest opportunity in order that it may come into force in time for the next football season;
3. to request all governments entitled to do so to become Parties to the Convention as soon possible.

40.7. Resolution No. 2/85 on a Dialogue with UEFA

The European Ministers responsible for Sport, meeting for their 12th Informal Meeting at the Council of Europe on 27 June 1985.
Expressing the will to take rapid and effective measures aimed at preventing spectator violence and countering increasing violence at sports events in general;
Considering the responsibility of governments and sports organisations respectively for maintaining public safety and order at sports events;
Recognising the prime responsibility of UEFA for laying down the conditions at matches organised under their auspices;
Agree to propose to UEFA:

1. to introduce binding requirements for the use of stadia for matches under the auspices of UEFA, which take account of national conditions and the level of the various matches and the threat of possible spectator violence, paying particular regard to:
   a. the design, physical fabric, and condition of the stadium;
   b. the size of spectator sections;
   c. the separation of spectator sections;
   d. access, exit and escape routes;
   e. technical control, monitoring and operational facilities;
2. to introduce binding requirements, bearing in mind the provisions in the proposed European Convention, for matches under the auspices of UEFA with regard to:
   a. ticket sales;
   b. segregation;
   c. admission controls;
   d. bans on carrying weapons and dangerous objects;
   e. forces to maintain safety and order on stadium premises;
   f. sales of beverages.
3. to involve national football associations and governments in laying down these requirements;
4. to identify matches where spectator violence may be anticipated and to initiate suitable consultations and preparations to prevent and control spectator violence.

Ask the Committee of Ministers to instruct the CDDS, pending the creation of the standing committee foreseen in the proposed Convention, to hold initial discussions with UEFA and prepare a draft memorandum of understanding which would give effect to the above proposals and to provide for this work; and to report back as soon as possible to a future meeting of Sports Ministers.

40.8. European Convention on Spectator Violence and Misbehaviour at Sports Events and in particular at Football Matches

Strasbourg, 19 August 1985

The member States of the Council of Europe and the other States party to the European Cultural Convention, signatory hereto,
Considering that the aim of the Council of Europe is to achieve a greater unity between its members;
Concerned by violence and misbehaviour amongst spectators at sports events, and in particular at football matches, and the consequences thereof;
Aware that this problem is likely to put at risk the principles embodied in Resolution (76) 41 of the Committee of Ministers of the Council of Europe known as the "European Sport for All Charter";

Emphasising the important contribution made to international understanding by sport, and especially, because of their frequency, by football matches between national and club teams from European states;
Considering that both public authorities and the independent sports organisations have separate but complementary responsibilities to combat violence and misbehaviour by spectators, bearing in mind that the sports organisations also have responsibilities in matters of safety and that more generally they should ensure the orderly conduct of the events they organise; considering moreover that these authorities and organisations should work together for this purpose at all appropriate levels;
Considering that violence is a current social phenomenon with wide repercussions, whose origins lie mainly outside sport, and that sport is often the scene for outbreaks of violence;
Being resolved to take common and co-operative action to prevent and control the problem of violence and misbehaviour by spectators at sports events,
Have agreed as follows:

Article 1 – Aim of the Convention

1. The Parties, with a view to preventing and controlling violence and misbehaviour by spectators at football matches, undertake, within the limits of their respective constitutional provisions, to take the necessary steps to give effect to the provisions of this Convention.
2. The Parties shall apply the provisions of this Convention to other sports and sports events in which violence or misbehaviour by spectators is to be feared, as appropriate to the specific requirements of such sports and sports events.

Article 2 – Domestic co-ordination

The Parties shall co-ordinate the policies and actions of their government departments and other public agencies against violence and misbehaviour by spectators, where appropriate through setting up co-ordinating bodies.

Article 3 – Measures

1. The Parties undertake to ensure the formulation and implementation of measures designed to prevent and control violence and misbehaviour by spectators, including in particular:
    1. to secure that adequate public order resources are employed to counter outbreaks of violence and misbehaviour, both within the immediate vicinity of and inside stadia and along the transit routes used by spectators;
    2. to facilitate close co-operation and exchange of appropriate information between the police forces of the different localities involved or likely to be involved;
    3. to apply or, if need be, to adopt legislation which provides for those found guilty of offences related to violence or misbehaviour by spectators to receive appropriate penalties or, as the case may be, appropriate administrative measures.
2. The Parties undertake to encourage the responsible organisation and good conduct of supporters' clubs and the appointment of stewards from within their membership to help manage and inform spectators at matches and to accompany parties of supporters travelling to away fixtures.
3. The Parties shall encourage the co-ordination, insofar as legally possible, of the organisation of travel arrangements from the place of departure, with the co-operation of

clubs, organised supporters, and travel agencies, so as to inhibit potential trouble- makers from leaving to attend matches.

4. The Parties shall seek to ensure, where necessary by introducing appropriate legislation which contains sanctions for non-compliance or by any other appropriate means, that, where outbreaks of violence and misbehaviour by spectators are to be feared, sports organisations and clubs, together with, where appropriate, stadium owners and public authorities, in accordance with responsibilities defined in domestic law, take practical measures at and within stadia to prevent or control such violence or misbehaviour, including:
   1. to secure that the design and physical fabric of stadia provide for the safety of spectators, do not readily facilitate violence between spectators, allow effective crowd control, contain appropriate barriers or fencing, and allow security and police forces to operate;
   2. to segregate effectively groups of rival supporters, by allocating to groups of visiting supporters, when they are admitted, specific terraces;
   3. to ensure this segregation by strictly controlling the sale of tickets and to take particular precautions in the period immediately preceding the match;
   4. to exclude from or forbid access to matches and stadia, insofar as it is legally possible, known or potential trouble-makers, or people who are under the influence of alcohol or drugs;
   5. to provide stadia with an effective public address system and to see that full use is made of this, of the match programme and of other publicity outlets to encourage spectators to behave correctly;
   6. to prohibit the introduction of alcoholic drinks by spectators into stadia; to restrict, and preferably ban, the sale and any distribution of alcoholic drinks at stadia, and to ensure that all beverages available are in safe containers;
   7. to provide controls so as to ensure that spectators do not bring into stadia objects that are likely to be used in acts of violence, or fireworks or similar devices;
   8. to ensure that liaison officers co-operate with the authorities concerned before matches on arrangements to be taken for crowd control so that the relevant rules are enforced through concerted action.
5. The Parties shall take appropriate social and educational measures, bearing in mind the potential importance of the mass media, to prevent violence in and associated with sport, in particular by promoting the sporting ideal through educational and other campaigns, by giving support to the notion of fair play, especially among young people, so as to enhance mutual respect both amongst spectators and between sports players and also by encouraging increased active participation in sport.

Article 4 – International co-operation

1. The Parties shall co-operate closely on the matters covered by this Convention and encourage similar co-operation as appropriate between national sports authorities involved.
2. In advance of international club and representative matches or tournaments, the Parties concerned shall invite their competent authorities, especially the sports organisations, to identify those matches at which violence or misbehaviour by spectators is to be feared. Where such a match is identified, the competent authorities of the host country shall arrange consultations between those concerned. Such consultations shall take place as soon as possible and should not be later than two weeks before the match is due to take place, and shall encompass arrangements, measures and precautions to be

taken before, during and after the match, including, where necessary, measures additional to those included in this Convention.

Article 5 – Identification and treatment of offenders

1. The Parties, respecting existing legal procedures and the principle of the independence of the judiciary, shall seek to ensure that spectators committing acts of violence or other criminal behaviour are identified and prosecuted in accordance with the due process of the law.
2. Where appropriate, particularly in the case of visiting spectators, and in accordance with the applicable international agreements, the Parties shall consider:
    1. transferring proceedings against persons apprehended in connection with violence or other criminal behaviour committed at sports events to their country of residence;
    2. seeking the extradition of persons suspected of violence or other criminal behaviour committed at sports events;
    3. transferring persons convicted of offences of violence or other criminal behaviour committed at sports events to serve their sentences in the relevant country.

Article 6 – Additional measures

1. The Parties undertake to co-operate closely with their appropriate national sports organisations and clubs and where appropriate, stadium owners, on arrangements regarding the planning and execution of alterations to the physical fabric of stadia or other alterations, including access to and egress from stadia, necessary to improve safety and to prevent violence.
2. The Parties undertake to promote, where necessary and in appropriate cases, a system laying down requirements for the selection of stadia which take into account the safety of spectators and the prevention of violence amongst them, especially for those stadia used for matches likely to attract large or unruly crowds.
3. The Parties undertake to encourage their national sports organisations to review their regulations continuously in order to control factors which may lead to outbreaks of violence by players or spectators.

Article 7 – Provision of information

Each Party shall forward to the Secretary General of the Council of Europe, in one of the official languages of the Council of Europe, all relevant information concerning legislative and other measures taken by it for the purpose of complying with the terms of this Convention, whether with regard to football or other sports.

Article 8 – Standing Committee

1. For the purposes of this Convention, a Standing Committee is hereby established.
2. Any Party may be represented on the Standing Committee by one or more delegates. Each Party shall have one vote.
3. Any member State of the Council of Europe or other State party to the European Cultural Convention which is not a Party to this Convention may be represented on the Committee as an observer.
4. The Standing Committee may, by unanimous decision, invite any non-member State of the Council of Europe which is not a Party to the Convention and any sports organisation concerned to be represented by an observer at one or more of its meetings.

5. The Standing Committee shall be convened by the Secretary General of the Council of Europe. Its first meeting shall be held within one year of the date of the entry into force of the Convention. It shall subsequently meet at least every year. In addition it shall meet whenever a majority of the Parties so request.
6. A majority of the Parties shall constitute a quorum for holding a meeting of the Standing Committee.
7. Subject to the provisions of this Convention, the Standing Committee shall draw up and adopt by consensus its own Rules of Procedure.

Article 9

1. The Standing Committee shall be responsible for monitoring the application of this Convention. It may in particular:
    1. keep under review the provisions of this Convention and examine any modifications necessary;
    2. hold consultations with relevant sports organisations;
    3. make recommendations to the Parties concerning measures to be taken for the purposes of this Convention;
    4. recommend the appropriate measures to keep the public informed about the activities undertaken within the framework of this Convention;
    5. make recommendations to the Committee of Ministers concerning non-member States of the Council of Europe to be invited to accede to this Convention;
    6. make any proposal for improving the effectiveness of this Convention.
2. In order to discharge its functions, the Standing Committee may, on its own initiative, arrange for meetings of groups of experts.

Article 10

After each meeting, the Standing Committee shall forward to the Committee of Ministers of the Council of Europe a report on its work and on the functioning of the Convention.

Article 11 – Amendments

1. Amendments to this Convention may be proposed by a Party, the Committee of Ministers of the Council of Europe or the Standing Committee.
2. Any proposal for amendment shall be communicated by the Secretary General of the Council of Europe to the member States of the Council of Europe, to the other States party to the European Cultural Convention, and to every non-member State which has acceded to or has been invited to accede to this Convention in accordance with the provisions of Article 14.
3. Any amendment proposed by a Party or the Committee of Ministers shall be communicated to the Standing Committee at least two months before the meeting at which it is to be considered. The Standing Committee shall submit to the Committee of Ministers its opinion on the proposed amendment, where appropriate after consultation with the relevant sports organisations.
4. The Committee of Ministers shall consider the proposed amendment and any opinion submitted by the Standing Committee and may adopt the amendment.
5. The text of any amendment adopted by the Committee of Ministers in accordance with paragraph 4 of this article shall be forwarded to the Parties for acceptance.
6. Any amendment adopted in accordance with paragraph 4 of this article shall come into force on the first day of the month following the expiration of a period of one month after all Parties have informed the Secretary General of their acceptance thereof.

Final clauses

Article 12

1. This Convention shall be open for signature by member States of the Council of Europe and other States party to the European Cultural Convention, which may express their consent to be bound by:
    1. signature without reservation as to ratification, acceptance or approval, or
    2. signature subject to ratification, acceptance or approval, followed by ratification, acceptance or approval.
2. Instruments of ratification, acceptance or approval shall be deposited with the Secretary General of the Council of Europe.

Article 13

1. The Convention shall enter into force on the first day of the month following the expiration of a period of one month after the date on which three member States of the Council of Europe have expressed their consent to be bound by the Convention in accordance with the provisions of Article 12.
2. In respect of any signatory State which subsequently expresses its consent to be bound by it, the Convention shall enter into force on the first day of the month following the expiration of a period of one month after the date of signature or of the deposit of the instrument of ratification, acceptance or approval.

Article 14

1. After the entry into force of this Convention, the Committee of Ministers of the Council of Europe, after consulting the Parties, may invite to accede to the Convention any non-member State of the Council of Europe by a decision taken by the majority provided for in Article 20.d of the Statute of the Council of Europe and by the unanimous vote of the representatives of the Contracting States entitled to sit on the Committee of Ministers.
2. In respect of any acceding State, the Convention shall enter into force on the first day of the month following the expiration of a period of one month after the date of the deposit of the instrument of accession with the Secretary General of the Council of Europe.

Article 15

1. Any State may, at the time of signature or when depositing its instrument of ratification, acceptance, approval or accession, specify the territory or territories to which this Convention shall apply.
2. Any Party may, at any later date, by declaration addressed to the Secretary General of the Council of Europe, extend the application of this Convention to any other territory specified in the declaration. In respect of such territory the Convention shall enter into force on the first day of the month following the expiration of a period of one month after the date of receipt of such declaration by the Secretary General.
3. Any declaration made under the two preceding paragraphs may, in respect of any territory mentioned in such declaration, be withdrawn by a notification addressed to the Secretary General. Such withdrawal shall become effective on the first day of the month following the expiration of a period of six months after the date of receipt of the notification by the Secretary General.

Article 16

1. Any Party may, at any time, denounce this Convention by means of a notification addressed to the Secretary General of the Council of Europe.
2. Such denunciation shall become effective on the first day of the month following the expiration of a period of six months after the date of receipt of the notification by the Secretary General.

Article 17

The Secretary General of the Council of Europe shall notify the member States of the Council of Europe, the other States party to the European Cultural Convention and any State which has acceded to this Convention, of:

1. any signature in accordance with Article 12;
2. the deposit of any instrument of ratification, acceptance, approval or accession in accordance with Article 12 or 14;
3. any date of entry into force of this Convention in accordance with Articles 13 and 14;
4. any information forwarded under the provisions of Article 7;
5. any report established in pursuance of the provisions of Article 10;
6. any proposal for amendment or any amendment adopted in accordance with Article 11 and the date on which the amendment comes into force;
7. any declaration made under the provisions of Article 15;
8. any notification made under the provisions of Article 16 and the date on which the denunciation takes effect.

In witness whereof the undersigned, being duly authorised thereto, have signed this Convention.

Done at Strasbourg, this 19th day of August 1985, in English and French, both texts being equally authentic, in a single copy which shall be deposited in the archives of the Council of Europe. The Secretary General of the Council of Europe shall transmit certified copies to each member State of the Council of Europe, to each State party to the European Cultural Convention, and any State invited to accede to this Convention.

40.9. Recommendation on alcohol sales and consumption (87/1)

Adopted by the Standing Committee of the European Convention on Spectator Violence and Misbehaviour at Sports Events and in Particular at Football Matches during their 2nd meeting, 1987

The Standing Committee,

Stresses the importance of applying the provisions of Article 3.4.f, which are believed to have been very effective in contributing to the reduction of spectator violence;

Recommends the Contracting Parties to implement, in so far as it is legally possible, two additional measures, where high-risk matches are to be expected:

a. to extend the provisions of Article 3.4.f to include the travel arrangements of groups of supporters visiting matches;
b. to encourage the use of powers that may be vested in local authorities to restrict, or to ban, the sale of alcohol in the neighbourhood of stadia, for a predetermined period, before, during and after such matches.

40.10. Recommendation on crowd searches (87/2)
Adopted by the Standing Committee of the European Convention on Spectator Violence and Misbehaviour at Sports Events and in Particular at Football Matches during their 2nd meeting, 1987

The Standing Committee,
Recognises the importance of crowd searches to the achievement of Article 3.4.g;
Recommends that Contracting Parties ensure that their public authorities, football authorities, clubs and police work together to identify the most appropriate and effective mechanism for spectator searches.

40.11. Recommendation on police co-operation (87/3)
Adopted by the Standing Committee of the European Convention on Spectator Violence and Misbehaviour at Sports Events and in Particular at Football Matches during their 2nd meeting, 1987

The Standing Committee,
Recommends:

a. that, in order to ensure the effective bilateral and multilateral co-operation called for under Article 3.1.b and, in particular, Article 4 of the Convention, and in particular with the group of permanent correspondents (central contact point within the police for potential problems of football hooliganism), nominated within the European Communities:
    i. those Contracting Parties not members of the European Communities, nominate a correspondent with similar functions, and
    ii. that all Contracting Parties inform the Secretary General of the name, address and communication numbers of its correspondent, so that a list may be prepared for circulation to every government, in order, in particular, to facilitate speedy bilateral contacts when necessary;
b. that the group of permanent correspondents within the European Communities be invited to send a representative to attend, as an observer, the next meeting of the Standing Committee.

40.12. Recommendation No. 2/88 on preparations for major events

The Standing Committee recommends Contracting Parties:
On police co-operation:
That the relevant police authorities consider organising before major international competitions training seminars for senior police officers on the organisation of crowd control measures (before, during and after matches).

40.13. Recommendation on police co-operation (88/1)
Adopted by the Standing Committee of the European Convention on Spectator Violence and Misbehaviour at Sports Events and in Particular at Football Matches during their 4th meeting, 1988

1. On the use of advisory police "spotters"
That, on the occasion of major international sports events where spectator violence is to be feared, the police authorities from the countries of the participating teams discuss the possibility of arranging for advisory plain-clothes policemen from the visiting country(ies) to assist the police force(s) responsible for the match(es) on potential problems from the visiting supporters (for example, help in identifying known troublemakers, advice on signs of trouble developing).
2. On preparations for major events
That the relevant police authorities consider organising before major international competitions training seminars for senior police officers on the organisation of crowd control measures (before, during and after matches).

40.14. Recommendation on guidelines for ticket sales (89/1)

The Standing Committee of the European Convention on Spectator Violence and Misbehaviour at Sports Events and in particular at Football Matches,
Under the terms of Article 9.1.c of the Convention;
Having seen Articles 1 and 3.4.c of the Convention;
Concerned by occasions when the free availability of tickets has contributed to outbreaks of spectator violence;
Aware of the need to institute a closer control of the distribution and sale of tickets for football matches where spectator violence is to be feared;
Wishing to build common guidelines on the basis of the experiences gained by contracting parties and signatory states;
Recommends that the Parties to the Convention consider the formulation and implementation of appropriate measures to give effect to the principles set out in the attached guidelines for ticket sales;
Instructs the Secretary General to transmit this recommendation to the other member states or states party to the European Cultural Convention for information.

Appendix
Guidelines
When spectator violence is to be feared in association with a match, the organising authorities could consider implementing one, several or all of the following suggestions as appropriate to control the sale of tickets with a view to reducing the possibility of spectator violence.
1. Ensuring that the production of tickets helps the supervision and control of spectators and investigation afterwards of possible sources of trouble. This can be done by:
   a. numbering tickets and strictly controlling production and sale to the number agreed at 7 below;
   b. colouring tickets so that they correspond to particular sectors of the ground and particular entries;
   c. printing a plan of the stadium, with the sectors printed in the appropriate colours, and of its vicinity, onto the back of the ticket as information for visiting spectators and to help segregate groups of rival fans;
   d. recording the allocation of each ticket or batch of tickets;
   e. envisaging machine readable tickets so that forgeries can be detected and entering spectators more easily controlled;
   f. strictly controlling ticket holders at entry points and ensuring they have an appropriate ticket.

2. Envisaging where possible the creation by the organisers or stadium owners of obligations or conditions for the purchase of tickets, which could be applicable also to any subsequent purchase. These conditions would help ensure a better control of the "second-hand" market and could allow organisers or stadium owners to exclude undesirable spectators from future matches. Such obligations or conditions would derive from private law.
3. Football associations, clubs, and other organisers could also envisage creating a licensing system to authorise some persons or agencies to sell tickets with conditions (such as the observance of instructions, or limitations – such as places or times of sale, only to members or subscribers, etc. – which the organiser or competent authority might issue from time to time and notify the licensee) that would allow them to withdraw the licence in case of trouble with ticket holders from their allocation.
4. When national football associations act as distributors of tickets for major international events, they should add their own distinguishing mark to their batch of tickets.
5. Restricting the number of tickets which any one individual can purchase.
6. Reducing the number of tickets available to away supporters.
7. Deciding the number of tickets which will be sold for a match (not necessarily the full theoretical capacity of the ground); where advisable, reducing the capacity and the number of tickets sold for each sector by a certain percentage, bearing in mind safety, control and public order factors.
8. Restricting the number of tickets available for purchase in bulk (to be defined bearing in mind the match) by:
   a. i. tour operators or other licensed outlets
      ii. supporters' clubs
      to correspond with their effective travel capacity, so that unaccounted-for tickets do not circulate;
   b. companies and firms buying tickets for commercial entertainment, or sponsors of a club. Companies should be asked to show how they distributed their allocation of tickets, and warned beforehand of any areas where distribution might be undesirable.
9. Not allowing the sale of tickets in a period before a match (12 hours, 24 hours, etc.), and certainly not in the period immediately preceding the match (e.g., 4 hours).
10. When particularly large numbers of visiting supporters from several countries are to be anticipated, to introduce a voucher system by which potential spectators apply for the tickets they desire, and after due examination, may later exchange their voucher(s) for the tickets allocated to them.
11. At multi-round events, the organising committee may take over or make arrangements for purchasing unwanted tickets and selling tickets that are wanted, in order to introduce some order into the second hand market and reduce opportunities for the black market.

Guidelines for ticket sales

Explanatory memorandum

Background

1. Experience in the Standing Committee shows that some outbreaks of hooliganism are caused by tickets falling into the hands of "undesirable" spectators. This may be the fault of the organisers (for example, if tickets are sold on the day of a high-risk match), or because of the lack of supervision by third parties, such as tour operators or others,

over the distribution of their allocated tickets, so that undesirable spectators obtain their tickets indirectly and without the organisers being able to prevent this. Furthermore, the black market is an ancient and persistent sphere of economic activity which contributes an additional element of unforeseeable chance. There is also a small contribution from forged tickets.

2. The Standing Committee is aware that the laws of contracting parties concerning contract, the rights of the individual purchaser of a ticket, and the relationships between organiser, agent and spectator vary quite considerably. Some measures which are applicable in one country are not possible in another (for instance, the powers of the organiser to forbid entry to a person holding a valid ticket). The plans to introduce membership schemes in some countries may additionally complicate the legal situation.
3. The guidelines draw on the collective experience of the Standing Committee, but it is conscious that they can and will be followed only in so far as it is legally possible in each country. The sharing of experience does not impose an obligation to imitate: but it provides insights into the sources of problems, which may then be tackled in whatever will be the most appropriate fashion.
4. The Standing Committee does not consider that this problem is one which is likely to be solved by (new) legislation: it is in the realm of improved operational supervision and practical management that progress is likely to be made. This raises the question of responsibility, which also varies from country to country: each will assign primary and secondary responsibilities to whichever authority is most appropriate, whether by law or by custom.
5. The guidelines should therefore be interpreted in accordance with Article 1 of the Convention ("The Parties ... undertake, within the limits of their respective constitutional provisions, to take the necessary steps to give effect to the provisions of this Convention.") and Article 3.4 "... sports organisations and clubs, together with, where appropriate, stadium owners and public authorities, in accordance with responsibilities defined in domestic law, take practical measures at and within stadia to prevent or control [spectator] violence and misbehaviour, including: ... c. to ensure [] segregation by strictly controlling the sale of tickets and to take particular precautions immediately preceding the match; ..."

40.15. Recommendation on comprehensive report on measures to counter hooliganism (89/2)

Adopted by the Standing Committee of the European Convention on Spectator Violence and Misbehaviour at Sports Events and in Particular at Football Matches during their 5th meeting, 1989

Introduction

I. At their 13th Informal Meeting (Athens, 1 and 2 June 1988), the sports ministers asked the Standing Committee to "produce a practical report on a comprehensive package of control measures". (MSL-GT 13 (88) 14 rev., paragraph 30.)

II. The first draft of such a report, based on experiences/measures which had been brought to the attention of the Standing Committee, was examined at the 4th meeting on 19 and 20 July 1988. A revised draft was submitted for later comments and the final draft included lessons learned from the European Football Championships (Federal Republic of Germany, June 1988). This report therefore incorporates some of the latest examples of good practice (13 April 1989).

III. It should be stressed that this report lists all the measures used in all countries and organisations which participate in the work of the Standing Committee. Not all these measures however will be applicable in each and every country: the measures adopted will depend on their football history, legal and administrative traditions and structures, as well as the level of spectator violence they are faced with. The method and tactics of policing of potential hooliganism will also be a matter for each country to decide and they are not dealt with in this report. The list of measures should therefore be seen as a "menu", from which choices may be selected. It is for the same reason that the report lists measures to be taken and does not always specify the authority which should take them. Furthermore, some measures can only be implemented within the limits of existing domestic legislation and the powers conferred upon the relevant authorities.

IV. These measures will also be applicable, pari passu, for measures to be taken in international (bilateral or multilateral) co-operation.

V. The report is divided into five parts:

A. Permanent measures to prevent spectator violence
B. Measures to be taken before a high-risk match
C. Measures to be taken during a high-risk match
D. Measures to be taken after a high-risk match
E. Long term measures

VI. As some of the measures may appear to be of a rather general nature, it is important to stress that preparation, planning and the exchange of views and information – in short co-ordination and co-operation – is probably the vital ingredient of success. The main lesson which the Standing Committee draws from its experience is that without full and willing consultation, co-operation and co-ordination between football authorities and public agencies at club and national level, measures to control spectator violence will not be effective. This aspect is equally important when international matches or tournaments are arranged and the parties should arrange for such co-operation on a bi- or even multilateral basis between whatever will be the most appropriate bodies in good time before such events.

VII. It is also relevant to point out that some of these measures refer also to the safety and security of football spectators.

A. Permanent measures to prevent spectator violence
(For adoption as appropriate at local, national, international levels)

1. Are there channels for consultation, co-operation and co-ordination, and for the exchange of information and intelligence between:
   a. football clubs, football associations
   b. local, national and transport police forces
   c. between football and police authorities?

   This exchange of information should take advantage of the experience gained by associated groups such as supporters' clubs, tour operators, etc.

   It will cover problems raised not only at the origin and destination of potential hooligans but also during their transit.

   For major tournaments, co-operation machinery should be established early and cover all aspects of preparation.

Co-ordination

2. Is there a national co-ordination committee on hooliganism?
3. Is there a system for the co-ordinated collection of national information on hooliganism?

4. Has a machinery been developed for identifying high-risk national matches and implementing counter-strategies? This machinery should take into account the criteria used by UEFA for deciding high-risk matches.

Grounds

5. Are adequate barriers, grilles, fencing, tunnels etc. provided at grounds for public safety and control, the segregation of supporters, and protection of players, officials, etc.? A sufficient space between pitch and stands is desirable. Emergency exits through fencing on to the pitch are desirable.
6. Are there facilities including a command and control post at grounds for police/security forces, medical care, etc.?
7. Are there facilities to control entry of spectators into grounds (for example machines for reading passes or tickets, metal detectors, breathalysing equipment, etc.)? Clubs should assume, where appropriate, powers to use these facilities.
8. Do grounds comply with the provisions of UEFA's brochure "order and security in the stadia" and, when appropriate, with its security checklist?
9. Have national public and football authorities prepared and do they implement either legislation or a national handbook on crowd safety and control providing clear standards and guidelines for stadium owners and managers?
10. Have clubs, owners or managers improved the quality of spectators' areas and terraces at grounds (small sections; seating; family enclosures; other facilities)?

Clubs

11. Are clubs aware of their own responsibilities in matters of security, etc.? Each football association and, ideally, large club should have its own security committee. Clubs should acknowledge the priority of safety and security of spectators over gate receipts and profit.
12. Do football clubs give adequate encouragement for the organisation of responsible supporters' clubs, including the proper training of adequate numbers of stewards and marshals and their liaison with the local police; and for responsible tour operators etc.?
13. Has the need for membership schemes (whether complete or partial) been considered, with special attention for domestic away matches (for example, "pass system" cf. 7), or measures to encourage peaceful fans and identify and exclude troublesome ones.
14. Have clubs designated a spectator safety/control/security liaison officer? Have national football associations designated a similar national official?

Regulation, legislation, etc.

15. Is there a strategy for the production of tickets and control of ticket sales, including:
    a. numbering and colouring of tickets;
    b. clear conditions for sale and resale;
    c. devising a system for checking and tracing purchases of tickets where appropriate (eg voucher scheme);

- d. defining the role of clubs or FAs or supporters' clubs in supervising the distribution of allocated tickets;
- e. making, where appropriate, provision for all-ticket matches;
- f. restricting opportunities for black-market sales and/or forgeries;
- g. implementing the recommendation and guidelines for ticket sales adopted by the Standing Committee (Recommendation N° 1/89).

16. Are there legislative or administrative powers (for application nationally, locally or by the police as appropriate) permitting:
    - a. the control or ban of alcohol sales and distribution in and around matches;
    - b. banning possession of pyrotechnic devices at grounds (or projection when a match is in progress);
    - c. high risk matches to be banned, played elsewhere, or at a different time, or under certain conditions?
17. Has consideration been given to the adoption of legislation providing an adequate definition of hooliganism (including disorderly conduct and/or frightening behaviour at a sports event) with appropriate punishment, including exclusion from future matches, of offenders?
18. Has consideration been given to granting powers where possible to exclude undesirable spectators from grounds; from travelling in organised supporters' journeys, etc.?
19. Have public authorities powers to license grounds for high-risk matches and to approve the holding of them?

B. Before high-risk matches

20. Are known troublemakers prohibited/discouraged from leaving home territory for away matches; or can conditions for travel be imposed?
21. Is consideration given to the organisation, particularly for international matches, of seminars with participation from appropriate authorities, to ensure the precautions and measures used employ the latest examples of good practice (Recommendation N° 1/88)?
22. Is information, publicity, etc. on good behaviour provided, in the language of the visiting supporters, explaining inter alia the standards that the host will expect?
23. Have the police developed contacts with local citizens and regular supporters to explain measures taken for ordinary and for exceptional matches?
24. Have police forces been given training in methods for welcoming and helping visiting supporters?
25. It is advisable to anticipate the degree of likely press and media interest in a match or tournament, and to prepare policies for press conferences and to plan for consequences of possible events; have football and police press officers been trained in this aspect (cf. 39)?
26. Is there a ticket sale policy for the match? (cf. 15) for example:
    - a. limits on number of purchases;
    - b. no sale on day;
    - c. not necessarily selling tickets for all the capacity available (reduction overall and for each sector proportionately);
    - d. restricting black-market sales.

27. Are ticket sales compatible with and do they contribute to the effective segregation of supporters in distinct, designated and separated areas, and allow, where necessary, adequate police supervision?
28. Do clubs/FAs prepare co-ordinated travel-ticket arrangements for their visiting supporters?
29. Do clubs/FAs consider preparing appropriate accommodation, when necessary, for visiting supporters, especially at international events?
30. Are travel and approach routes (including car and coach parks) of rival supporters segregated?
31. Do visiting supporters arrive just before, and leave immediately after, the match?
32. Do clubs provide adequate trained stewards and marshals for home and away supporters respectively? Do organisers consider recruiting/hiring additional stewards for particular matches? (cf. 12)
33. Is consideration given to banning alcohol distribution or sale during organised travel to matches. (Recommendation N° 1/87).
34. Is consideration given to banning alcohol distribution or sales in the vicinity of the grounds before, during and after a match? (Recommendation N° 1/87).
35. Is there specific pre-match planning, liaison and co-ordination and regular, including eve-of-match, briefings for all parties concerned? Are there contingency plans agreed by the police and the referee?
36. Have public authorities taken account of UEFA's measures for security?
37. In accordance with Article 3.1 of the Convention, will "adequate public order resources" be secured?
38. Have arrangements for sharing the costs involved of securing these resources been considered?
39. Has the use of police 'spotters', knowing the visiting supporters, to advise the 'home' police been considered? (Recommendation N° 1/88)
40. Has providing simultaneous watching facilities at the home ground for an away game (or additional watching facilities nearby the match) been considered?
41. Are there regular searches for, and removal of, dangerous objects (for example, building materials, rubble, or other rubbish) inside and in the vicinity of the stadium in good time before it is opened?

C. At high-risk matches (while spectators are in the stadium)

42. Are UEFA's Binding Instructions followed?
43. Are turnstiles opened in good time, giving spectators ample opportunity to enter before the start of the match?
44. Are police, stadium speaker, stewards (including fire stewards) and pre-match entertainers at their respective places of duty, or ready, when turnstiles are opened?
45. Do clubs, and/or police as appropriate, control entering spectators with a view to:
    a. excluding those "under the influence";
    b. excluding known trouble makers;
    c. excluding holders of doubtful tickets;
    d. excluding dangerous objects, pyrotechnics, alcohol;

e. providing random searches, frisks, etc.? (Recommendation N° 2/87).

46. Are spectators found in a wrong area or sector moved to the correct one, or, at the discretion of stewards or police, expelled?
47. Is segregation effective?
48. Is the distribution, sale or consumption of alcohol at the ground banned or restricted?
49. Are all goods for consumption sold in soft containers?
50. Are adequate trained marshals and stewards provided? (cf. 12)
51. Is the size, material and use of slogans on flags, banners, rattles, musical instruments, etc. controlled (including for fire risk)?
52. Are any outbreaks of hooliganism recorded on closed-circuit television (CCTV) or video?
53. Is a public address system used and a pre-match and interval programme of events or entertainment provided?
54. Are adequate public order resources at the ground (cf. 37) secured?
55. Are all exit doors/gates during the time any spectators are in the ground adequately staffed? Are all exits capable of being opened at any time in an emergency from the inside (ground side)? (The locking of exits – even when a steward with a key is present – is unsatisfactory.)
56. Are adequate medical care staff present?

D. After matches

(See also Nos 28-32.)

57. Do away spectators return rapidly (especially if team is defeated), and are they separated from home spectators on dispersal from the ground?
58. Are spectators who commit acts of violence or other criminal behaviour identified and prosecuted in accordance with the due process of the law in accordance with Article 5.1 of the Convention?
59. Do clubs regularly review their list of undesirable spectators?
60. Do clubs review measures taken and draw lessons?
61. Do the agencies involved in co-operation continue to consult and co-ordinate and profit from experience?

E. Long-term measures

62. Are there appropriate educational and sporting programmes on the teaching and practice of fair play at clubs, schools; is there training in fair play?
63. Do clubs/FAs encourage the development and pursuit of community schemes with various age-groups and talents?
64. Are there ad hoc socio-cultural programmes suitable for visiting supporters, and permanent ones for regular supporters, including those on the fringes of hooliganism?
65. Do clubs develop ways of making their fans important for them?
66. Do the agencies involved discuss with and consult the media on their role in the portrayal of hooliganism, fair play, etc.?
67. Do clubs/FAs take a strong line against cheating and violence on the field of play; do they ensure that match officials are adequate for the task?

68. Do clubs take a strong line against troublesome 'supporters' and encourage more responsible supporters' clubs?
69. Do local authorities encourage the development of the educational role of football clubs, for example in schools?
70. Is co-ordinated research into the causes and origins of football hooliganism, its role in society and into strategies to counter it, encouraged?

40.16. Resolution on Spectator Violence (89/3)

The European Ministers responsible for Sport, meeting in Reykjavik from 30 May to 1 June 19 for their 6th Conference,
Note with pleasure that fifteen member states are Contracting Parties to the European Convention on Spectator Violence and Misbehaviour at Sports Events and in particular at Football Matches and urge as many other member states as possible to sign and/or ratify the Convention rapidly;
Note that the problems of spectator violence remain a cause for serious concern, particularly in the aftermath of important matches and that public and football authorities must continue to be vigilant and to act together in the closest possible co-operation;
Thank the Standing Committee of the European Convention for the work it has undertaken and for the report presented to this Conference;
Note with pleasure, subject only to the regrettable behaviour of a small number of supporters, the successful outcome of the work of the responsible authorities of the Federal Republic of Germany, UEFA and the national authorities concerned with the European Football Championships in 1988;
Approve the guidelines for the control of ticket sales prepared by the Standing Committee;
Approve the Comprehensive Report on Measures to combat Hooliganism prepared by the Standing Committee at the request of the Sports Ministers at their 13th informal meeting at Athens;
Agree to work for the implementation of the controls and of such measures which are or may be appropriate at national level and to bring them to the attention of the relevant national authorities and organisations;
Consider that the following subjects merit particular attention and further study, and that the Standing Committee would be the most appropriate forum for this work:

1. the continuation of close co-ordination with the bodies concerned with the preparation of the World Cup in 1990 and the next European Football Championships in 1992, and to pay particular attention to the problems posed by spectators travelling through or staying in countries other than their own;
2. the evaluation of the behaviour of spectators at the European Football Championships in 1988 and during international matches during the 1989-90 season;
3. the evaluation of social, cultural and educational projects carried out in member states of the CDDS in order to develop practical preventative measures aimed at hooligans and potential hooligans;
4. the further development of practical working relationships with the group of permanent correspondents on football hooliganism in the European Community, bearing in mind the separate but complementary nature and responsibilities of the two bodies;

Instruct the Secretary General to inform the Standing Committee of this Resolution.

40.17. Resolution on Safety (89/4)

The European Ministers responsible for Sport, meeting at their 6th Conference from 30 May to 1 June 1989 in Reykjavik,
Express their heartfelt sympathy for the victims of and to those bereaved by the tragic events on 15 April 1989;
Reaffirm their belief that sports events should be the occasion for friendly, peaceful and enjoyable meetings for spectators and participants;
Recall that the European Convention on Spectator Violence did not ignore the importance of measures for spectator safety;
Note that international sports events are constantly increasing in number and size;
Resolve that a necessary complement to the European Convention on Spectator Violence is the preparation of a text incorporating the principles and appropriate measures to guarantee spectator safety at sports grounds and events;
Consider that the Standing Committee should be able to make proposals for such a text;
Instruct the Secretary General to inform the Standing Committee of this Resolution;
Invite the Committee of Ministers of the Council of Europe to instruct the CDDS to prepare, in conjunction with the Standing Committee, the draft of such a text.

40.18. Recommendation on guidelines to the Parties for the implementation to Article 5 of the Convention: identification and treatment of offenders (90/1)

Adopted by the Standing Committee of the European Convention on Spectator Violence and Misbehaviour at Sports Events and in Particular at Football Matches during their 7th meeting, 1990

The Standing Committee:
Recalling that Article 5 of the Convention creates obligations for Parties to identify persons involved in wrongdoing as spectators at sports events, and, subject to existing legal procedures and the principle of the independence of the judiciary, to prosecute them in accordance with the due process of the law;
Encouraging Parties to act vigorously on the basis of this article;
Recalling that the Union of European Football Associations has laid down "binding instructions" to the organisers of certain matches on the exclusion of troublemakers;
Recalling that sports organisations, clubs, stadium owners and others concerned, including police forces, may have a range of possible powers enabling them to exclude from grounds various categories of potential spectators;
Aware that the use of video-recorders and closed-circuit television greatly facilitates the possibility of acting in accordance with the terms of Article 5.

Recommends the Parties:

1. that those Parties which have not yet ratified the European Conventions referred to in Article 5.2 namely:
    a. European Convention on the Transfer of Proceedings in Criminal Matters;
    b. European Convention on Extradition;
    c. Convention on the Transfer of Sentenced Persons should consider the early ratification of each of these instruments;
2. that they, where appropriate in conjunction with the local organising committees of major sports events, particularly international events, draw the attention of the appropriate

police and prosecuting authorities to Article 5 of this Convention, and to this recommendation, and encourage them to make contingency plans for the use of some or all of the various measures advocated, should acts of spectator violence or misbehaviour be committed;

3. that for events when visiting foreign spectators are to be expected, the appropriate authorities of the visiting country or countries contact the local organising committee with a view to the preparation of ad hoc, bilateral agreements for the identification of offenders in accordance with Article 5;
4. that, in those states where the temporary police detention of troublesome supporters is possible, on the grounds, for example, of helping to maintain public order, such temporary detention should not be seen as an alternative to the prosecution of offenders if such prosecution is considered sustainable;
5. that, in the case of successful prosecution of offenders, courts should be empowered to give consideration to the imposition of non-custodial penalties, such as community service, exclusion orders or other measures which have the effect of preventing individual offenders from attending sports events or particular sports events for a stated time, (for example, having to report to a police station at certain times) or forbidding access to grounds where such events take place.

Instructs the Secretary General to transmit this recommendation to the other member states and to the non-member states party to the European Cultural Convention.

40.19. Recommendation on the promotion of safety at stadia (91/1)

Adopted by the Standing Committee of the European Convention on Spectator Violence and Misbehaviour at Sports Events and in Particular at Football Matches during their 9th meeting, 1991

The Standing Committee recommends the Parties:

1. to encourage and actively promote safety in all sports stadia (sports grounds, sports halls, sports centres, etc.) in co-operation with sports organisations and stadium owners;
2. to this end, to take all the necessary steps including legislation, at the appropriate national, regional or local level, in order to ensure the application of the guidelines set out in the appendix to this recommendation and of any other international or national norms and regulations, in particular for the construction of new stadia;
3. to ensure as a minimum that the regulations adopted by UEFA for its competitions are met for new stadia, and that existing ones are renovated to meet them by the year 2000;
4. to set up national supervisory and advisory bodies, where such bodies do not exist, to monitor progress in the areas covered by the present recommendation;
5. to support efforts to study measures designed to improve spectator safety in stadia and the financing of such improvements;
6. to ensure that the design of new or renovated stadia in accordance with this Recommendation,
    a. pay attention to the surroundings in which they are situated;
    b. permit access by persons suffering from disabilities;
    c. provide attractive facilities for spectators.
7. to determine, at national and/or regional level, and in accordance with appropriate priorities, a timetable for the progressive implementation of this recommendation and

its Appendix, in particular with regard to the renovation of existing sports stadia; this timetable may take account of criteria based on the type and the capacity of stadia and appropriate management considerations.

Appendix

Safety in stadia: principles and rules

A. General principles

I. Safety in stadia is a function of several risk factors which can be divided into three main categories: the danger of fire, the possibility of structural failures (whether through design faults or through functional inadequacies); and problems inherent in the presence of large crowds (operational factors). Thus the main issue is how to minimise these risks. This can be done through preventive actions on the one hand and the preparation of efficient responses to those accidents that cannot be avoided or foreseen on the other.

II. Furthermore, many of the measures set out in the Convention and taken by Parties to combat hooliganism can and should also be used to promote spectator safety: for example controls on tickets sales, checks on entry to the stadium, closed circuit television etc. Other measures designed to prevent violence and misbehaviour by spectators should in no case impair the safety of spectators.

B. Preventive measures

Fire – both immediately and nearby

III. The appropriate public authorities should ensure that the use and supply of gas, electricity and other inflammable substances is in accordance with the appropriate legislation for public outdoor places of the size and capacity of the stadium under consideration.

IV. Any inflammable substance should be stocked only if strictly necessary for the functioning of the facility and in any case well away from spectators and athletes, in accordance with the existing regulations on the stockage of such substances.

V. Kitchens, heating systems, generators should be kept in separated parts of the buildings with adequate insulation; in stadia where it is not possible to separate such facilities, the areas must be stringently fire-proofed.

VI. The design and the materials used in the construction of stadia should be of the type and quality required to ensure a good protection from fire and to minimise the risk of fire spreading. Fire-doors should be installed and fire-extinguishing devices must be of an approved type, in sufficient numbers, and located at easily accessible and visible places. Where appropriate, the European Standards (ENs) prepared by the European Committee for Standardisation should be followed.

VII. Adequate fire-fighting equipment and material should be pre-positioned bearing in mind the type and structure of the stadium and the number of spectators present, and sufficient manpower should be available to be called upon locally.

Structural questions

VIII. A maximum capacity, in terms of seats or persons, should be given for each stadium and for each sector of a stadium. This capacity will be a function of several factors, inter alia the maximum amount of stress that can be supported by the existing structure as indicated by the applicable regulations, including the European Standards (ENs) prepared by the European Committee for Standardisation. Technical norms laid down by such regulations should take into account the dynamics of crowd effects, the minimum size of seats, the type of partitioning between the sectors. Ideally, there should be no standing places in stadia of more than 10,000 places. In all stadia where standing places are authorised, the maximum capacity for standing places should be fixed in terms of persons per square metre. The safety of spectators inside the stadium depends largely on the respect of this maximum number of spectators.

IX. All accesses to the stadium, circulation paths inside it, and exits from it, should be as linear as possible, whether they be for spectators or for emergency vehicles. In particular doors should have the same width as corridors, staircases and landings leading up to them, in order to allow a regular flow of people. Such areas should be kept free of objects or people and possibly painted in a different colour to be easily identified. Each door should be used at any one time only as an entrance or as an exit and each sector should be equipped with a sufficient number of entries and exits (at least two) to allow a satisfactory flow of persons per minute, enabling it to be emptied in the time required for a rapid emergency evacuation of a threatened sector. Such flows should be pre-determined for each sector and stadium by an appropriate authority.

X. The size and shape of the areas immediately outside the stadia foreseen for the approach, access and egress of spectators, whether on foot or by motorized vehicle, should be such as not to create bottlenecks. All types of access and egress routes should be clearly indicated and lend themselves to the separation of supporters of different teams.

XI. Special separate parking areas for emergency vehicles should be available and be located so as to give them easy and quick access to the inside of the stadium. hey should be spacious enough to allow manoeuvring as well as parking, taking into account the number of vehicles required for the capacity of the stadium and the shape of the emergency areas. Such numbers should be pre-determined (see 23 below).

XII. The state of the structure should be the object of regular checks before matches to identify weaknesses and/or damage due to age, corrosion or human factors. Such checks should be a condition sine qua non for the grant of a "safety certificate" (permission granted by an appropriate public authority for a stadium to accommodate a pre-determined number of members of the public) by a competent "licensing authority" (authority which grants the safety certificate or permission to arrange a match to which paying members of the public are admitted (Article 6.2 of the Convention)).

Crowd management

XIII. Sufficient spaces inside stadia should be designed for the free movement of large crowds. Their size and shape should vary proportionately to the maximum number of spectators allowed into the stadium.

XIV. Each ticket should bear instructions to locate the allotted sector and, where appropriate, the seat within it and be controlled, preferably by a computerised system. Paths to find a given seat or sector should be clearly signposted, possibly with colours to be repeated on the ticket itself.

XV. The number of tickets available should not exceed the maximum designated capacity of any given sector, and for stadia where standing places are allowed, this will be fixed in terms of persons per square metre (see 13 above).

XVI. It should be possible for each sector to be closed off rapidly as this maximum number is about to be reached. To this end a device, whether electronical, mechanical or by means of a video, to control/count effectively the number of people entering the stadium, and a given sector, should be installed.

24. Crush barriers and other obstacles meant to protect players and/or spectators from violent actions by hooligans should be designed so as not to slow down or make difficult the entry or exit of spectators. In any case a minimum and maximum size and resistance load should be set by the authorities concerned. (see 6 and 8 above).

25. Where fences separating the terraces from the pitch exist they should have easily operated openings in order to allow emergency evacuation into the open space.
26. Co-ordination among all security and emergency forces concerned should be ensured by preliminary briefing and full information on the specific risks of the match, the structure of the facility, the plans and the location of the grounds. Such briefing should be addressed to both public and stadium emergency and policing staff. It should pay special attention to the co-ordination between them all.
27. The stadium owner or manager should provide the police with a well placed, well equipped and spacious control room. It should in particular allow a full view of the whole pitch, and of as much of the spectators' area as possible, and provide closed circuit television screens.
28. An efficient device for addressing the crowd should be installed. Communication between various police officers in charge, whether on the grounds or in the control room, should be ensured by reliable and constant radio/telephone lines.
29. A number of police officers and stadium staff should be specially trained to evaluate crowd densities and behaviour (in particular for signs of trouble), and be placed in sufficient numbers on the ground so as to supervise all sectors.
30. Adequate medical staff, ambulances, equipment and rooms should be present in the stadium to deal with emergency situations. The number should be fixed by the appropriate public or licensing authority which should aim to ensure that at least one person trained in first aid per 1,000 spectators should be present, and at least one doctor and one ambulance should be present on the ground, from the opening to the closing of the stadium, at all events at which 5,000 or more spectators are expected.

C. Responses

31. Good co-ordination and communication among all services concerned should be ensured as it is essential for an efficient response to any emergency situation. Contingency plans should be carefully studied, tried out and publicised among all services concerned in order to save time and energy, and to limit casualties and damage.
32. Police officers posted at the entrances to the stadia should be informed when emergency services are called, specifying which service, for what reason and where it is needed so that they can efficiently direct vehicles on their arrival.
33. Officers or stewards charged with supervising conditions in the individual sectors should readily release spectators in distress by opening the perimeter fences, after informing the co-ordinating centre, with which they should be constantly in contact. Therefore they should be capable, authorised and equipped to do so.
34. The crowd should be kept informed of the situation by means of powerful loudspeakers and, whenever possible, illuminated advertising or score boards for the transmission of messages. For this reason such boards should be clearly visible from all sectors.

40.20. Explanatory memorandum on Recommendation on Article 4 of the Convention: international co-operation (91/2)

Guidelines for co-operation in the policing of international football matches, implementing Article 4 of the Convention

1. The Standing Committee has approved the attached guidelines on international police co-operation. The detailed arrangements for international police co-operation in individual cases is primarily for bi-lateral negotiation between the parties concerned. These guidelines are intended to assist that process by offering suggestions based on proven

good practice, but are not intended to constrain. It should be noted that the guidelines describe the scope of international co-operation, the procedures by which it may be realised, and the problems which may arise. As identified in paragraph 4 of the document, the guidelines are consistent with the framework of the Convention, and in particular Article 4.

2. Article 4 of the Convention obliges parties as follows:

"4.1 The parties shall co-operate closely on the matters covered by the Convention and encourage similar co-operation as appropriate between national sports authorities involved.

4.2 In advance of their international club and representative matches or tournaments, the parties concerned shall invite their competent authorities, especially the sports organisations, to identify those matches at which violence or misbehaviour by spectators is to be feared. Where such a match is identified, the competent authorities of the host country shall arrange consultations between those concerned.

Such consultations shall take place as soon as possible and should not be later than two weeks before the match is due to take place, and shall encompass arrangements, measures and precautions to be taken before, during and after the match, including, where necessary, measures additional to those included in this Convention."

3. The guidelines have been derived from experience in international police co-operation during the European Championships in the Federal Republic of Germany (FRG) in the Summer of 1988; and from consideration by Working Group II of TREVI (the European Community group of law enforcement ministers and officials) – especially a conference organised by the Federal Republic in Münster, in March 1989.

Guidelines for co-operation in the policing of international football matches

1. These guidelines have been prepared by drawing on the practical lessons of international police co-operation during the European Football Championships in the Federal Republic of Germany in 1988. The guidelines do not prescribe in detail how individual states should liaise on police matters. Instead they suggest a framework based on proven good practice, and recommend that states negotiate detailed arrangements acceptable to each other and appropriate to the match or championship in question. Prime responsibility for organising this rests with the host country where the event is to take place. The larger the event the more there is a need for plans to be made early and in detail.

2. The objectives of policing an international football event may be stated as:
   a. to promote good behaviour and peaceful enjoyment of good sporting competition;
   b. to take account of the various cultures and traditions of visiting supporters, consistent with acceptable behaviour in the host and transit countries;
   c. to deal firmly, fairly and effectively with troublemakers;
   d. to make efficient use of police resources.

3. These guidelines cover the following topics:
   a. Assessing scale and importance (paragraphs 5 to 7);
   b. Initial police liaison (paragraphs 8 to 10);
   c. Pre-event conference (paragraph 11);
   d. The role of visiting police in the host country (paragraphs 12 to 19);
   e. Traffic management (paragraphs 20 to 22);
   f. Finance (paragraph 23);

g. Football authorities (paragraph 24);
h. Media and publicity (paragraphs 25 to 27); and
i. Feedback and de-brief (paragraphs 28 to 30).

Appendix A presents a possible timetable for policing a major event; and Appendix B contains a summary of definitions and terms used.

4. The guidelines provide suggestions for implementing Article 4, and they may also prove useful in implementing Articles 2, 3.1a and b, and 5 of the European Convention on Spectator Violence. These guidelines are consistent with those articles.

Assessing scale and importance

5. The first action should be for the host state to assess the scale of the event and of the policing operation likely to be required: for example by reference to the number and geographical spread of matches, foreign countries, visiting spectators and the risk of violence or disorder. A questionnaire to contributing states may be helpful. This assessment should identify the extent to which major international co-ordination of police effort will be required – and therefore the extent to which these guidelines may be invoked. The assessment should be complete early to enable all relevant agencies to make appropriate arrangements. Where many contributing states are involved the host state should identify those where the greatest degree of liaison will be needed and concentrate attention accordingly.

6. There are many factors which may complicate the policing of international in comparison to domestic matches.
   a. The territory to be managed by the police is more extensive, both in area and time: visiting spectators will travel longer distances, gather earlier and disperse later – perhaps much earlier and later.
   b. Delays in handling information are increased: lines of communication are extended, more reference information has to be supplied by telephone or facsimile and not in person, and translation of documents (particularly large and/or urgent texts) can be difficult.
   c. The host police are unfamiliar with the behaviour of visiting fans – and vice versa.
   d. As the choice of participants in later rounds of a championship depends on the results of earlier matches, planned ticket allocation and spectator separation may be badly disrupted – many tickets bought before teams qualified are resold on the streets by defeated supporters, without regulation.
   e. Potential troublemakers may feel less inhibited, less responsible and more anonymous when holidaying in a foreign country, and may suffer from an exaggerated sense of national pride.

7. The remainder of these guidelines assumes that the initial assessment has shown the event to be of major significance, requiring extensive police co-operation. As a very general guide, a single match could be considered as ‘major’ if more than 1,000 visiting foreign supporters were expected or there were good indications of serious trouble; a championship involving several such matches would be of still greater significance. Clearly for lesser events these arrangements would be scaled down accordingly.

Initial police liaison

8. For the largest tournaments, early and detailed police liaison is required. Each state should designate a central national office for the overall co-ordination of that country’s

effort on the championship, with particular reference to advance planning. That office may be the national permanent correspondent on football in person, or some other representative (in which case the permanent correspondent should be copied all communications). The choice should be of someone who is directly assigned to the operational policing of the event, able to give immediate attention to servicing requests, and able to act as a central reference point within the country for the collation and distribution as necessary of information to all police units involved.

9. It may well be useful for a small delegation of officers from a participating country to visit the host country well in advance of the championship and for a return trip to be made by the host to the (or each) participating country. Delegations though small should include command and operational level officers – both can be relevant. Outline travel, accommodation and ticketing arrangements for spectators should also be considered at this stage with the relevant national football authorities.

10. The objective of the initial police liaison should be to familiarise each side with the practical detail of how the other country polices football matches: the police tactics and the behaviour (and misbehaviour) of supporters; to specify and plan as clearly as possible what each country can contribute and how officers from different countries will work together (see paragraphs 12 to 19); to identify and resolve potential difficulties; and to begin the flow of operational information and intelligence as soon as is relevant. The earlier this is completed the better, to allow maximum benefit to be obtained and to allow police operations to be influenced at the earliest stage of planning. For the largest events, this stage can be begun twelve months in advance and it is desirable to have achieved good progress six months before the event.

Pre-event conference (see Recommendation No. 1/88)

11. The host country should consider organising a conference for all participating police forces, perhaps or three months before a major international football championship. The objective is to familiarise all participants with each other's plans and intentions, establish contact with opposite numbers, and identify remaining difficulties while there is still time to resolve them. The host should invite relevant people from his country (for example his national football authority and the organiser of the championship) and should distribute appropriate reference information at the conference.

The role of visiting police in the host country (see Recommendation No. 1/88)

12. Responsibility for police action and the maintenance of public order in the host country must at all times remain with the host authorities only. Nevertheless, it is crucial that relevant information and intelligence is made available by visiting police officers to the host police quickly enough and at a sufficiently senior level. Such information can only be volunteered as advice, and it is for the host police to decide what action to take as a result.

13. Foreign police may be able to supply the host police with three types of information. For maximum effect all are necessary but are subject to any provisions of international and national privacy and data protection legislation:

a. traffic information on numbers of spectators, dates, routes, means of travel and arrangements for accommodation (see paragraphs 20 to 22);
b. intelligence identifying known troublemakers who may travel to the football event, their methods of operation, and known or suspected intentions (paragraphs 15 and 16);
c. tactical intelligence identifying known troublemakers who have travelled to the event and – of even greater importance – actual intentions to engage in violence

and disorder at particular times and places, and predictions from the mood of a group that violence is about to take place (see paragraph 17).

14. It is particularly important that the command structure in the host country makes effective use of foreign liaison officers. It is often good practice to establish a local co-ordinating office for an operation such as the policing of a key international football match, whether that office has direct operational command of all police officers involved, or simply acts as an information exchange for relevant police commanders. Otherwise there is no collective police understanding of what is occurring, and individual police units may take contradictory action. In a major championship several such local co-ordinating officers may exist, one for each centre at which matches are taking place. These would be in addition to the central national office referred to in paragraph 8.

15. Assuming some such co-ordinating office exists, there will be a key liaison role for a visiting police officer deployed there. He will be able to communicate effectively in three directions: to provide advice as required to the centre of the host police operations dealing with supporters from his country; to communicate with other liaison officers from his country who are working in the area; and to refer back to his own country for reference information (or even local police enquiries).

16. This therefore implies that support arrangements are made at home by participating countries to service requests for information or other action from their key liaison officer in the host country. It is important that such support includes undertaking local enquiries without the detailed involvement of the liaison officer, and that cover should be available 24 hours per day in case it is needed urgently.

17. Liaison officers in the host country may also be useful in observing at first hand the behaviour of supporters from their country. Even observing groups at a distance a liaison officer may be more able than the local police to judge when trouble is likely or imminent: for example when the mood turns from enjoyment to hostility or when tactics indicate preparations are being made for a fight (for example, by established behaviour in watching for opposing supporters or collecting objects for use as weapons). If suitably trained officers are available, close observation by plain clothes liaison officers among groups of supporters may reveal precise intentions for the time and place of planned disorder.

18. Another possible role for liaison officers, if so desired by the host police, is in dealing publicly with supporters, for example to appeal for sensible behaviour and to show that the local police in the host country are well prepared. This could include speaking over the public address system at stadia or speaking to supporters in the street. The officer may also advise the host police on tactics at stadia, with reference to the behaviour of supporters from his country.

19. In all these roles it is essential that liaison officers are true experts: familiar with the behaviour of their supporters, and skilled in the police activity they will perform (such as concealed observation). If effective use is to be made of their potential, clear agreement must be made in advance on how they will operate and on the facilities at their disposal including communications (telephone, facsimile and local radio), interpreters, transport and accommodation.

Traffic management

20. It is helpful if shortly before an event each source country sends a traffic telex advising the police in their own country, carriers and transit and host countries of the known travel plans of visiting supporters. This can only be achieved in detail if, well in advance, the unit which prepares this telex establishes effective contact with the

football authorities and others responsible for arranging travel. The telex forms a common reference document from which all concerned can plan advance action or consult for information on a particular group that may become involved in trouble during their journey. The normal point of receipt in European Community countries should be the TREVI permanent correspondent on football and, if different, the central national office described in paragraph 8.

21. As well as listing individual groups, tour operators, routes, accommodation and dates it is helpful to summarise this information at the start of the traffic telex to show the total number of supporters involved and sub-totals broken down by main travel route (air, sea ferry, coach, car, etc.). Where possible the summary and individual details should be categorised as follows:
a. No trouble expected.
b. Some slight possibility of trouble. Advise supervision and limitations on sale of alcohol by carriers.
c. Warning: possible risk of trouble. Advise close supervision and prohibition on sale of alcohol by carriers.

It is probably unrealistic to hope for more specific information on category c passengers. If clear intentions to cause serious problems were known, the advice would anyway be to refuse carriage. Moreover, those few who may intend serious trouble at an event may travel peaceably and may be careful to disguise their intentions and identity. The more effective response to such persons is likely to be in good police liaison and intelligence, with officers well informed about known troublemakers.

22. Advance co-ordination of travel plans can also help to reduce the policing task in supervising travel to the event. Experience has shown the considerable advantage of asking coaches and cars travelling to major events to carry a distinctive emblem on their windscreens. This enables the police to recognise supporters among the large number of other road users. Similarly, asking supporters to keep to agreed routes and overnight stops (if those are necessary) can make police supervision easier. Again, true 'hard-core' troublemakers can be expected to avoid such advised routes – the measure is more to improve the management of orderly supporters or those with more limited potential for trouble.

Finance

23. Since policing a major international football event may involve liaison work within and between countries on an exceptional basis, it is wise for each state to ensure early in the planning phase that the number of police officers to be deployed on liaison work is specified and a firm understanding is reached on precisely which country and agency (for example, national or local police agency, football authority, national or local government) will meet the salary, travel and accommodation expenses of each officer, It is proposed as a general rule, for prior agreement on each occasion, that the host country should pay for accommodation and other facilities made available locally and that visiting countries should pay for travel and salaries of the officers involved.

Football authorities

24. From an early stage the central police point in each state should establish close contact with the representative of his country's football authority for the event and/or with appropriate local clubs, so that each is properly aware of the other's plans, and of the parallel negotiations that are taking place between police and football agencies (see also paragraph 9). In the host country those responsible for licensing grounds or ap-

proving safety arrangements should similarly be involved. An important issue is how to achieve proper separation of supporters towards the end of a championship given that there may be extensive and unregulated re-selling of tickets on the streets, but this is principally for the football authorities and host police.

Media

25. Experience has shown that major international football events generate considerable press and TV interest. There is a history of sensational reporting, sometimes greatly exaggerating actual problems at the event. European football hooliganism – real or imagined – makes popular reading and viewing. The presence of the media can potentially influence the violence and disorder being observed for example if rowdy supporters cause disorder to show off to TV cameras or press photographers. Foreign liaison officers in the host country may be distracted from their operational police tasks by the close attention of their country's media, who may for example follow the officers, ask repeatedly for statements or interviews, or publish in newspapers photographs which identify plain clothes officers – such newspapers may then go on sale in the host country and be bought by visiting supporters.

26. Careful consideration is therefore important if heavy media interest is likely in a match or championship. Relations with the media is a specialist function. After listening to the views of contributing countries, the host country should make a conscious decision on how the media are to be handled and what assistance is to be sought from contributing countries. For example, there should be an agreed response to request for interviews with visiting officers, and the host country should decide how it would respond to untrue or distorted reporting. Host countries should be cautious about referring publicly to any concealed involvement of foreign police officers: while helping to demonstrate that the host police are well prepared, it may also direct unhelpful media attention onto the activities of these officers while the event is taking place.

Publicity

27. Positive use can be made of various forms of publicity, in advance, directed to visiting supporters. Given suitable co-ordination this can start within contributing countries. An example could be a short guidebook handed to supporters on departure containing useful information about the locations of matches; a few helpful phrases in the foreign language; a welcome from the hosts; and an encouragement to good behaviour with the warning that the host police are well prepared to deal with trouble and that information about troublemakers will be sent to their home countries (see also paragraphs 28 and 29). Newspapers could be offered stories emphasising that there was effective pre-planning of police tactics. Feedback: information from the host to contributing countries

28. It is of great importance that having received information and assistance from contributing countries, the host country reports back information about visiting spectators who are involved in trouble. Clear agreement should be reached on this before the event takes place. Feedback is not only of assistance to contributing countries but may be valuable to other host countries in the future. That may be through information (for example, that individual 'X' has caused trouble at home and when he last went to an international championship) or action that can be taken (for example, to refuse to sell special travel or match tickets to him, or even to restrict through the courts his foreign travel). Accurate identification of detained, arrested or convicted visitors is therefore essential.

29. Feedback is not only valuable after the event. Publicity before an event that information about troublemakers will be sent to the person's home country can encourage more responsible behaviour by visiting supporters. Without this supporters may feel that even if caught causing trouble in the host country, the consequences will be slight because any conviction will not be known by the authorities at home.

De-brief

30. Within a reasonable period of a major football event involving the use of these arrangements, the host state should consider whether there are lessons to be learned and whether recommendations should be made on how guidelines such as these, or any other standing arrangements, ought to be revised. If appropriate the host state may arrange for a de-briefing meeting and for recommendations to be prepared, within three months of the end of the event. It is in any case helpful for the host state to circulate contributing states with a short report assessing how well any joint policing worked in practice, within that period.

Appendix A

Possible timetable for co-operation in the policing of a major international football championship

Months before championship

TIME	ACTION	PARAGRAPH
12 – 9	Assess scale	5 – 7
12 – 6	Initial police liaison	8 – 10
9 – 0	Continue preparations, collect and forward information and intelligence, agree plans for media, publicity and feedback	13 25 – 29
3 – 2	Pre-event conference	11
1 – 0	Visiting liaison officers begin duty in host country	12 – 19
0	Championship	12 – 19

Months after championship

0 – 6	Feedback	28, 29
2 – 3	De-brief conference	30

Appendix B

Summary of definitions and terms used

DEFINITION\TERM	PARAGRAPH
TREVI, and Permanent Correspondent	1, 7, 18
Objective of policing an international football event	2
European Convention on spectator violence	3
Central national office	8
Objective of initial police liaison	10
Pre-event conference	11
Types of information and intelligence	13
Local co-ordinating office	14
Key liaison role for visiting police officer	15
Support arrangements at home	16
Observing supporters	17
Dealing publicly with supporters	18

Use of police uniform by visiting police officers	18
Traffic telex	20
Categories of supporter (A,B,C)	21
Finance	23
Football authorities and ticketing	9, 11, 24
Media and publicity	23,25
Feedback	28,29
De-brief	30

40.21. Recommendation on Article 4 of the Convention: international co-operation (91/2)

Adopted by the Standing Committee of the European Convention on Spectator Violence and Misbehaviour at Sports Events and in Particular at Football Matches during their 9th meeting, 1991

Guidelines for international police co-operation for international football matches and tournaments

The Standing Committee,

Recalling that Article 4 of the Convention creates an obligation for parties to identify beforehand matches at which spectator violence or misbehaviour is to be feared and, after consultation, to take the necessary precautionary measures;

Mindful of the need to ensure in good time planning for international co-operation between police forces on the occasion of major international sports events, and in particular of international football matches and tournaments;

Recalling its recommendations adopted in 1988 on police co-operation (on the use of advisory police 'spotters', and on preparations for major events);

Bearing in mind the experience gained during the European Football Championships in the Federal Republic of Germany, 1988 and the World Cup in Italy, 1990:

Recommends the Parties:

1. to follow the principles set out in the attached guidelines on co-operation in the policing of international football matches;
2. to negotiate their detailed specific bilateral, and, where appropriate, multilateral, agreements on the basis of these guidelines.

40.22. Recommendation on Measures to be taken by the Organisers of Football Matches and Public Authorities (93/1)

Strasbourg, 3-4 June 1993

The Standing Committee (T-RV) of the European Convention on Spectator Violence and Misbehaviour at Sports Events and in Particular at Football Matches

Whereas, in connection with football matches, the primary concern of all involved must be public safety both at matches and in "transit", and recalling that, without prejudice to the responsibilities of the organisers, the public authorities are ultimately responsible for public order;

Considering that such safety can only be ensured through observance by the organisers of safety rules and regulations, and close and effective co-operation by them with the public authorities;

Recalling the preventative work carried out by UEFA in connection with Order and Security in stadia;

Considering that the organisation of football matches is subject to the provisions of:

- Existing national legislation and local rules on the organisation of public events of the country where the match would take place, and of football matches in particular;
- (in States which are Party to it), of
- The European Convention on Spectator Violence and Misbehaviour at Sports Events and in Particular at Football Matches;

Whereas in this context the sovereign power of States to issue laws and regulations, binding on State organs and on individuals, concerning public order and safety in general and at football matches in particular must be borne in mind, together with their power and duty to ensure observance of such laws and regulations, notably by means of police forces;

Recalling its previous Recommendations on Guidelines for the control of Ticket Sales at high-risk matches (Recommendation N° 1/89) and on the Promotion of Safety at stadia (Recommendation N° 1/91);

Recalling the comprehensive Report on Measures to combat Hooliganism, approved with Resolution N° 3 of the 6th Conference of European Ministers responsible for Sport (Reykjavik – 1989);

Feeling it advisable to produce guidelines for an agreement, in the form of a standard check-list of measures to be taken, to be concluded between the organisers of a football match and the public authorities of the country where the football match was to be organised, the aim of the agreement being the definition of the obligations and responsibilities of the organisers of football matches on a European level (particularly within the framework of UEFA and FIFA competitions);

Recommends to Governments of Parties to the European Convention on Spectator Violence and Misbehaviour at Sports Events and in Particular at Football Matches:

I To make use of the Standard Checklist of measures to be taken by the organisers of football matches and public authorities, appearing in the Appendix to the present Recommendation, with a view to identifying respective roles and responsibilities of those involved in the organisation of football matches, and particularly high-risk ones.

II That the standard checklist, which is general in nature, be:
- adapted where necessary to local conditions on the basis of national legislation or local rules;
- applied principally to high-risk international matches, but also be used where appropriate for other events such as national championship matches or local events;
- used as the basis for agreements between the organisers and the public authorities, as early as possible before each match, on their respective role and responsibilities with regard to the measures included in the Checklist (which would not replace or supersede, but complement, other applicable legal provisions and regulations).

III That, wherever it is not already done, the public authorities draw up a comprehensive list of practical measures to be taken by the owners and managers of stadia and the organisers of football matches, including detailed technical provisions for structural matters, inspections and tests, terraces and stands, stairways and ramps, fire and medical facilities, communications, lighting, stewarding etc. Such national handbooks on crowd safety and control would provide clear guidelines for stadium owners and managers, and facilitate compliance by the organisers with desirable standards to be observed.

IV That the public authorities invite the organisers or the national football association or other responsible bodies to take all educational and social preventative measures that could contribute to a sporting match.

Appendix

Standard Checklist of Measures to be taken by the organisers of Football Matches and Public Authorities

Directions for Use

1. Those responsible for specific measures listed below should be identified with a cross in the appropriate column(s).
2. Wherever possible, the person(s) responsible should also be identified by name, and deadlines given for completion of the suggested measures.
3. Wherever possible, only one should be indicated as being responsible for each suggested measure.
4. Additions or modifications to the standard checklist measures should appear on the checklist itself.

MEASURES	A	B	C	D	E	F
I. To ensure the safety of spectators within and around the Stadium, all measures necessary to ensure the orderly preparation of the match will be taken, including:						
Structural Measures 1. Verification of the stadium's structure and deliverance of a safety certificate by public authorities (the facilities will have to meet the requirements of public authorities on stadium infrastructure and safety of facilities; this will particularly apply to temporary stands where their use is permitted).						
2. Careful upkeep of the facilities used for such matches, which will have to be cleaned and repaired where necessary, their structural stability and conformity to safety regulations being checked and certified regularly in accordance with the requirements of the public authorities.						
3. Searches before the match for, and removal of, dangerous objects (for example, building materials, rubble, loose seats, glass or other rubbish) inside and in the vicinity of the stadium in good time; eliminating or sealing off any construction site within or in the vicinity of the stadium.						
4. Running a thorough check on the morning of the day of the match for bombs, smuggled smoke grenades, fire works and/or other dangerous or suspicious objects; after this check only controlled access to the stadium is to be permitted.						
5. Checking the existence of or erecting appropriate barriers, grilles, fencing, crush barriers and other obstacles meant to ensure public safety and control, avoid undesired spectator movements, facilitate the separation of supporters, protect players, officials and spectators, constructed in such a way as not to impede emergency evacuation of the stadium.						
6. Protection of the playing field or pitch (by appropriate means, to be specified by the representative of public authorities) and prevention of unauthorized access to it; creation where appropriate of adequate emergency exits and passages onto the pitch.						

MEASURES	A	B	C	D	E	F
7. Where there are emergency gates leading from the spectator areas into the playing area, no form of obstruction which would prevent the outward opening of such gates shall be permitted.						
8. Protection of players (including protection of guest team during training sessions and transfers to and from the stadium), officials and referees, also providing them with guarded parking spaces for their vehicles and protected access to the playing field with a retractable tunnel, where necessary; protection of supporters' means of transport.						
9. Providing police forces with the facilities necessary for them (including where possible a command and control post equipped with a TV surveillance system), in accordance with national/local regulations.						
10. When this is felt to be necessary, constructing fine-mesh nets behind the goals where these are close to the stands, to protect players from any objects thrown; these nets should be fireproof and not impede the evacuation of supporters in case of emergency.						
11. Where appropriate, separation of opposing teams' supporters (including where necessary through the construction of separation barriers to be approved by the public authorities), if possible in sufficiently distant areas of the stadium.						
12. Verifying the existence of adequate entrances and exits to the facilities (with doors opening towards the exterior) and their efficient permanent staffing to ensure easy access and evacuation by the public; all exit doors should always be in a non-locked condition when there are spectators in the stadium and should be permanently staffed to guard against abuse.						
13. Facilitating access by spectators to their seats with clear indication of the various stands, and their exits.						
14. Improving as far as possible the quality of spectators' areas and terraces at grounds (small sections; seating; family enclosures; other facilities including sanitary ones and public refreshment bars).						
Security Measures 15. Giving the public authorities as early as possible all relevant information on the planned match, and in particular the names of the teams involved and of the organisers, the date, hour and place of the match, and any other information that might assist the authorities in evaluating the level of risk of the match.						
16. Alerting the public authorities to the possible needs for public order resources, to counter outbreaks of violence and misbehaviour, both in the immediate vicinity of and inside stadia, and along the transit routes used by spectators.						
17. Forwarding relevant information to the Police forces of the different localities involved or likely to be involved, including transit countries; (If appropriate, these could then set up a hooligan intelligence centre and/or a register of convicted hooligans, or other co-operation measures).						
18. Inspection of the stadium in good time before the match, by representatives of the owners, the organisers (Including the Safety Manager – see below) and those of the public authorities, to ascertain possible technical or material deficiencies and provide solutions to them; a final inspection will take place the day before the match.						

MEASURES	A	B	C	D	E	F
19. Arranging for Security services within the Stadium, in agreement with the Police Authorities; verifying that all safety and security personnel are clearly identifiable and in their allotted position in and around the stadium before the stadium is opened to the public, and that they are appropriately trained and aware of their duties.						
20. Providing rapid information of police emergency forces, enabling them to act quickly in case of need.						
21. Controlling the movement of spectators within the Stadium; providing a sufficient number of trained stewards to assist spectators.						
22. Public address system for crowd safety, and to enable Safety Manager, the Police and Emergency Services to inform or give directions to the spectators; instructions to speakers (who should be able to express themselves in the language of foreign supporters) to avoid undesirable comments liable to excite the public against the opposing team and its supporters, referees, officials and police forces.						
23. Preferably, a closed-circuit video equipment (CCTV) should be present to monitor the situation, ensure crowd safety and identify offenders.						
24. Determining that the accommodation for spectators in the stadium is suitable for the match concerned.						
25. Verifying the correct application by the Club or National Football association of UEFA guidelines and instructions, in as much as they do not contradict rules and instructions by local and national public authorities.						
26. Arranging for adequate medical and first aid assistance, fire prevention and other emergency services, and facilities for them; organising a radio-telephone link between the emergency services, the police forces and the Safety Manager.						
Entry Controls 27. Entry controls on spectators (including where necessary body checks, use of metal detectors and crowd searches).						
28. Providing safe storage for confiscated dangerous items, and personal belongings which are to be returned after the match.						
29. Where appropriate, controlling approaches to the stadium with removable barriers.						
30. Excluding, in so far as it is legally possible, known and potential troublemakers from grounds.						
31. Preventing access to the stadium to any person in possession of dangerous objects, alcoholic drinks, pyrotechnics, smoke grenades etc.; preventing access to any intoxicated person (alcohol, drugs).						
32. Preventing access to the stadium of any person in possession of racist or other offensive banners or signs and banners inciting to violence, and their display in the stadium or its vicinity.						
33. Prohibition of sales of drinks in glass bottles, restriction and preferably banning of alcohol sales and distribution in the stadium, and where appropriate restriction or preferably banning of their sale and distribution out of the stadium and particularly in its vicinity; ensure that all beverages available are in safe containers.						

MEASURES	A	B	C	D	E	F
II. Providing assistance and guidance for spectators to and from the Stadium, including, where possible: 34. Presence of staff at train stations and parking lots and at main crossroads near the Stadium, and information on travel possibilities; in train stations, signs indicating means of transport to/from stadium.						
35. Where appropriate, separation of travel and approach routes of rival supporters (including car and coach parks).						
36. Co-operation with transport authorities, tour operators and transport companies, whose personnel should be specially trained.						
37. Informing public authorities of the host country and of transit countries on travel plans of groups of spectators. When possible, provide travel information on individual and casual supporters (including supporters likely to be without tickets).						
38. Facilitating the work of accompanying police forces (escorts) through exchange of information on supporters' movements.						
39. Providing after-match vigilance on supporters' activities (in city centres, on return means of transport, especially trains, etc..) and entertainment.						
40. Providing information, publicity, etc. on desirable behaviour in the language of the visiting supporters, explaining inter alia the standards that the host will expect.						
41. Arranging a meeting point outside the stadium, a lost children service and a lost and found service to be manned at all times.						
42. Developing contacts with local citizens and regular supporters to explain measures taken for ordinary and for exceptional matches.						
43. Anticipating the degree of likely press and media interest in a match or tournament, preparing policies for press conferences and planning for consequences of possible events; training football and police press officers in this respect.						
44. Co-ordination with police 'spotters', knowing the visiting supporters.						
III. Controlling ticket sales (their quantity being agreed with UEFA and public authorities beforehand, bearing in mind the safe capacity of the stadium and the need to ensure where appropriate optimal separation of the different fan groups), including:						
45. Ticket distribution, and organising ticket sales so that they take place without disturbances (Ticket sales at the stadium on the day of the match may take place only with the agreement of the police authorities).						
46. Producing tickets in such a way as to render production and use of counterfeit or bogus tickets difficult, simplify control (for ex. by making them machine readable, using appropriate numbering and colour codes, etc.), direct and canalise spectators to their seats and avoid exceeding the authorised capacity of the stadium.						
47. Devising a system for checking and tracing purchasers of tickets where appropriate (eg voucher scheme) and defining the role of clubs or Football Associations or supporters' clubs in supervising the distribution of allocated tickets, and particularly free and reduced price tickets; wherever possible, the sale of tickets will be computerised.						

MEASURES	A	B	C	D	E	F
48. Reducing the number of tickets which any one individual may purchase and the number of tickets available to away supporters, and restricting the number of tickets available for purchase in bulk.						
49. Where necessary, reducing the overall number of tickets for sale, bearing in mind safety, control and public order factors.						
50. Controlling tickets at the entrances and preventing illegal entry.						
51. Informing would-be spectators as soon as possible, through the appropriate national and international channels, when a match is sold out.						
52. Regular review by Football Associations, Clubs and the Police of their lists of known and potential troublemakers.						
IV. Planning of all financial matters related to the match, and particularly matters relative to security and safety well in advance, including:						
53. Contracting adequate insurance cover for medical, fire, and general accident hazards, and damage caused by supporters within the stadium.						
V. Any other matter related to the organisation of the match, such as:						
54. Preliminary contact between the police and the guest team's country's embassy/consulate, in order to ensure rapid communication in case of need.						
55. Providing ad hoc entertainment programmes suitable for visiting supporters.						
56. Co-operation with supporters' clubs to obtain their help in avoiding incidents, and making football clubs aware of their own responsibilities in safety and security matters.						
57. Publishing lists of prohibited objects.						
58. Making useful information available to the fans (bus and other public transport lines to and from the stadium, parking facilities, customs provisions and visa requirements, accommodation and eating possibilities and their average prices etc.); where possible, providing appropriate accommodation for visiting supporters.						
59. Liaising with the media in a spirit of co-operation, particularly concerning information for supporters and the number of media representatives circulating near the playing field.						
60. Distraction and entertainment of spectators before the game (curtain-raiser match, music parade etc.).						
VI. Co-ordination measures 61. To ensure appropriate co-ordination, before the match the organisers shall nominate a Safety Manager, in charge of contacts with the public authorities and their consultation, and liaison with the Police and Emergency Services, granting him/her the necessary resources to carry out the tasks for which he/she is responsible, including access to and radio communication with the command post.						
62. The Safety Manager will evaluate on behalf of the organisers the degree of risk which the match presents, and supervise on their behalf the application of the safety measures mentioned above, and the dissemination of information to spectators on safety measures, particularly concerning objects which may not be introduced in the stadium.						

MEASURES	A	B	C	D	E	F
63. The Safety Manager, in liaison with the representative of the public authorities empowered to authorise the staging of the match and with the police, will ensure the implementation of those safety measures which are the organisers' responsibility. For high-risk matches, the Safety Manager will ensure that there are a sufficient number of coordination meetings with all parties involved in planning and supervising the staging of the match.						
64. The Police Department, the Fire Department, and Medical Emergency bodies will each name a representative, who will attend the coordination meetings.						
65. After the match, the Safety Manager will draw up a report on the effectiveness of preventative measures taken, to be sent to the appropriate authorities.						
66. The Police Commander and the Safety Manager will make contact with the Referee before the match.						
67. Where appropriate, the public authorities will authorise the match after checking compliance by the organisers with applicable legislation (if any) on the staging of public events, and any other obligation of the organisers, including those listed above.						
68. The organisers will be informed by the public authorities as soon as possible of any objection to the staging of the match(es) and/or of any particular condition which would have to be fulfilled before the match(es) could take place.						
69. A Crisis Group, including the Safety Manager, senior representatives of the Police, Fire Department, Medical Emergency, the competing teams, the Stadium authority and the Public Authorities, will meet in case of need before or during the match, to take urgent decisions where appropriate; arrange a key word known to Crisis Group members only, to be used through the public address system as call in case of need.						
70. After the match, examine measures taken and draw lessons.						

A = Stadium Owner
B = Organiser (Specify)
C = National Football Association
D = UEFA
E = Public Authorities (Local or National – Specify which)
F = Others (Specify whom)

40.23. Recommendation on measures to be taken by organisers and public authorities concerning high-risk indoor sports events (94/1)

The Standing Committee (T-RV) of the European Convention on Spectator Violence and Misbehaviour at Sports Events and in Particular at Football Matches

Recalling its Recommendation N° 1/93 on Measures to be taken by the Organisers of Football Matches and Public Authorities;

Considering that indoor sports facilities give rise to specific safety problems requiring particular measures to be taken;

Whereas, in connection with all sports events, the primary concern of all involved must be public safety both at the event itself and, when necessary, in "transit", and recalling that, without prejudice to the responsibilities of the organisers, the public authorities are ultimately responsible for public order;

Considering that such safety can only be ensured through observance by the organisers of safety rules and regulations, and close and effective co-operation by them with the public authorities;

Recalling the preventative work carried out by international sports federations in connection with safety measures at indoor sports events;

Noting also the standard-setting work carried out by European Committee for Standardisation concerning the accommodation of spectators and hoping that this work will soon help in ensuring a maximum of security for them throughout Europe;

Considering that the organisation of sports events is subject to the provisions of:

- Existing national legislation and local rules on the organisation of public events of the country where the match would take place, and of sports events in particular; and (in States which are Party to it), of
- The European Convention on Spectator Violence and Misbehaviour at Sports Events and in Particular at Football Matches;

Whereas in this context the sovereign power of States to issue laws and regulations, binding on State organs and on individuals, concerning public order and safety in general and at sports events in particular must be borne in mind, together with their power and duty to ensure observance of such laws and regulations, notably by means of police forces;

Recalling its previous Recommendations on Guidelines for the control of Ticket Sales at high-risk matches (Recommendation N° 1/89) and on the Promotion of safety at stadia (Recommendation N° 1/91);

Feeling it advisable to produce guidelines for an agreement, in the form of a standard checklist of measures to be taken, to be concluded between the organisers of a high-risk sports event and the public authorities of the country where the event is to be organised, the aim of the agreement being the definition of the obligations and responsibilities of the organisers of high-risk indoor sports events on a European level, and recognising that some sports and high-risk sports events might require additional or different measures;

Recommends to Governments of Parties to the European Convention on Spectator Violence and Misbehaviour at Sports Events and in Particular at Football Matches:

I To make use of the Standard Checklist of measures to be taken by the organisers and public authorities concerning high-risk indoor sports events, appearing in the Appendix to the present Recommendation, with a view to identifying respective roles and responsibilities of those involved in the organisation of events and particularly high-risk ones.

II That the standard checklist, which is general in nature, be:

- adapted where necessary to local conditions on the basis of national legislation or local rules;
- applied principally to high-risk international events, but also be used where appropriate for other events such as national championship events or local events;
- used as the basis for agreements between the organisers and the public authorities, as early as possible before each event, on their respective role and responsibilities with regard to the measures included in the Checklist (which would not replace or supersede, but complement, other applicable legal provisions and regulations).

III That, wherever it is not already done, the public authorities draw up a comprehensive list of practical measures to be taken by the owners and managers of sports halls and the organisers of events including in particular detailed technical provisions for structural matters, regular inspections and tests of the roof and stands (particularly in the case of moveable structures), special checks in the case of severe weather (e.g. snow-loads), extreme temperature variations, use of chemical agents or other extraneous events which could impair structural safety; stairways and ramps, the provision of unobstructed assembly areas around the hall, fire and medical facilities, communications, lighting (emergency alternative electricity supply for communications and lighting), stewarding etc. Such national handbooks on crowd safety and control would provide clear guidelines for sports hall owners and managers, and facilitate compliance by the organisers with desirable standards to be observed.

IV That the public authorities invite the organisers or the competent national sports association or other responsible bodies to take all educational and social preventative measures that could contribute to a sporting event.

Standard Checklist of Measures to be taken by organisers and public authorities concerning high-risk indoor sports events

Directions for use

1. Those responsible for specific measures listed below should be identified with a cross in the appropriate column(s).
2. Wherever possible, the person(s) responsible should also be identified by name, and deadlines given for completion of the suggested measures.
3. Wherever possible, only one should be indicated as being responsible for each suggested measure.
4. Additions or modifications to the standard checklist measures should appear on the checklist itself.

MEASURES	A	B	C	D	E	F
I. To ensure the safety of spectators within and around the Sports hall, all measures necessary to ensure the orderly preparation of the event will be taken, including:						
Structural Measures 1. Verification of the hall's structure and deliverance of a safety certificate by public authorities (the facilities will have to meet the requirements of public authorities on the infrastructure and safety of facilities; this will particularly apply to temporary or "telescopic" stands and opening roofs where their use is permitted); assurance of all-seater capacity and provision for persons with disability.						
2. Careful upkeep of the facilities used for such matches, which will have to be cleaned and repaired where necessary, their structural stability and conformity to safety regulations being checked and certified regularly in accordance with the requirements of the public authorities, including seismic safety precautions in regions where earthquakes are a risk.						
3. Searches before the event for, and removal of, dangerous objects (for example, building materials, rubble, loose seats, glass or other rubbish) inside and in the vicinity of the sports hall in good time; eliminating or sealing off any construction site within or in the vicinity of the sports hall.						
4. Running a thorough check on the morning of the day of the match for bombs, smuggled smoke grenades, fireworks and/or other dangerous or suspicious objects; after this check only controlled access to the hall is to be permitted.						

MEASURES	A	B	C	D	E	F
5. Protection of the sports area (the term 'sports area' in the present text includes sports floors, ice-rinks, pool, ring, court or other area/surface required by the sport in question.) and access to it (by appropriate means, to be specified by the representatives of public authorities and the relevant sports federations.						
6. Protection of players (including protection of guest team during training sessions and transfers to and from the hall), officials and referees, also providing them with guarded parking spaces for their vehicles.						
7. Providing police forces with the facilities necessary for them (including where possible a command and control post, placed so as to get a good overall view of the hall, and equipped with a TV surveillance system), in accordance with national/local regulations.						
8. Appropriate measures to be taken by the organisers and public authorities to: a. protect spectators from hazards occasioned by the sports concerned (e.g. flying ice hockey pucks); and b. protect as far as possible, the players and playing area from objects thrown by spectators.						
9. Where appropriate, separation of opposing teams' supporters (including where necessary through the construction of separation barriers to be approved by the public authorities), if possible in sufficiently distant areas of the hall, equipped with separate sanitary facilities.						
10. Verifying the existence of adequate separate entrances and exits to the hall (with doors opening towards the exterior) and their efficient permanent staffing to ensure easy access and evacuation by the public; all exit doors should always be in a non-locked condition when there are spectators in the hall and should be permanently staffed to guard against abuse. There should be adequate, unobstructed areas around the hall to act as assembly areas in the case of evacuation. Exits should be designed to facilitate evacuation of handicapped people without impeding the evacuation of other spectators.						
11. Facilitating access by spectators to their seats with clear indication of the various stands, and their exits.						
12. Improving as far as possible the quality of spectators' accommodation in halls (including that for people with disabilities) (small sections; public refreshment bars and sanitary facilities).						
13. Ensuring good air quality, including a ban on smoking and the possibility of monitoring smoke density; and control of humidity and temperature.						
Security Measures 14. Giving the public authorities as early as possible all relevant information on the planned match, and in particular the names of the teams involved and of the organisers, the date, hour and place of the match, and any other information that might assist the authorities in evaluating the level of risk of the match;						
15. Alerting the public authorities to the possible needs for public order resources to counter outbreaks of violence and misbehaviour, both in the immediate vicinity of and inside sports halls, and along the transit routes used by spectators.						

MEASURES	A	B	C	D	E	F
16. Inspection of the hall in good time before the match, by representatives of the owners, the organisers (Including the Safety Manager – see paragraph 58 below) and those of the public authorities, to ascertain possible technical or material deficiencies and provide solutions to them; a final inspection will take place the day before the match.						
17. Arranging for Security services within the hall, in agreement with the Police and other emergency authorities; verifying that all safety and security personnel are clearly identifiable and in their allotted position in and around the hall before it is opened to the public, and that they are appropriately trained and aware of their duties.						
18. Providing rapid information for police emergency forces, enabling them to act quickly in case of need.						
19. Controlling the movement of spectators within and around the hall; providing a sufficient number of trained security personnel to assist spectators.						
20. Using the public address system and the score boards for crowd safety, enabling the Safety Manager (see paragraph 58 below), the Police and Emergency Services to inform or give directions to the spectators; instructions to speakers (who should be able to express themselves in the language of foreign supporters) to avoid undesirable comments liable to excite the public against the opposing team and its supporters, referees, officials and police forces; siting of the communication centres in such a way as it is protected from being taken over by unauthorised persons; provision of alternative emergency electricity supply to maintain visual and sound communications (as well as lighting) in an emergency.						
21. Installing closed-circuit video equipment (CCTV) should be present to monitor the situation, ensure crowd safety and identify offenders;						
22. Determining that the accommodation for spectators in the hall is suitable for the match concerned.						
23. Verifying the correct application by the Club or national sports association of relevant international federation guidelines and instructions.						
24. Arranging for adequate material and first aid assistance, fire prevention and other emergency services, and facilities for them; organising a radio-telephone link between the emergency services, the police forces and the Safety Manager (see paragraph 58).						
Entry Controls 25. Entry controls on spectators (including where necessary body checks, use of metal detectors and crowd searches).						
26. Providing safe storage for confiscated dangerous items, and personal belongings which are to be returned after the match.						
27. Where appropriate, controlling approaches to the hall with removable barriers.						
28. Excluding, in so far as it is legally possible, known and potential troublemakers from halls.						
29. Preventing access to the hall by any person in possession of dangerous objects, alcoholic drinks, pyrotechnics, smoke grenades, etc.; preventing access to any intoxicated person (alcohol, drugs). Taking into account the grave danger represented by fire in sports halls, ensuring strict control over the possession, even innocently, of flammable or combustible materials.						

MEASURES	A	B	C	D	E	F
30. Preventing access to the hall of any person in possession of racist or other offensive banners or signs and banners inciting to violence, and their display in the sports hall or its vicinity.						
31. Prohibition of sales of drinks in glass bottles, restriction and preferably banning of sale and distribution in the hall of alcohol and smoking materials and where appropriate restriction or preferably banning of alcohol and tobacco sales and distribution outside the hall and particularly in its vicinity; ensure that all beverages available are in safe containers.						
II. Providing assistance and guidance for spectators to and from the Sports hall, including, where possible: 32. Presence of staff at railway stations, airports, car parks and at main crossroads near the hall, and information on travel possibilities; in stations, signs indicating means of transport to/from hall;						
33. Where appropriate, separation of travel and approach routes of rival supporters (including car and coach parks).						
34. Co-operation with transport authorities, tour operators and transport companies, whose personnel should be specially trained.						
35. Facilitating the work of accompanying police forces (escorts) through exchange of information on supporters' movements.						
36. Providing after-match vigilance on supporters' activities (in city centres, on return means of transport, especially trains, etc.) and entertainment.						
37. Providing information, publicity, etc. on desirable behaviour in the language of the visiting supporters, explaining inter alia the standards that the host will expect.						
38. Arranging a meeting point outside the hall, a lost children service and a lost property service to be manned at all times.						
39. Developing contacts with local citizens and regular supporters to explain measures taken for ordinary and for exceptional matches.						
40. Anticipating the degree of likely press and media interest in a match or tournament, preparing policies for press conferences and planning for consequences of possible events; training sports and police press officers in this respect.						
41. Co-ordination with police 'spotters', knowing the visiting supporters.						
III. Controlling ticket sales (their quantity being agreed with the organisers and public authorities beforehand, bearing in mind the safe capacity of the sports hall and the need to ensure where appropriate optimal separation of the different fan groups), including: 42. Ticket distribution, and organising ticket sales so that they take place without disturbances.						
43. Producing tickets in such a way as to render production and use of counterfeit or bogus tickets difficult, simplify control (for ex. by making them machine readable, using appropriate numbering and colour codes, etc.), direct and canalise spectators to their seats and avoid exceeding the authorised capacity of the hall.						
44. Devising a system for checking and tracing purchasers of tickets where appropriate (eg voucher scheme) and defining the role of clubs, sports associations or supporters' clubs in supervising the distribution of allocated tickets, and particularly free and reduced price tickets; wherever possible, the sale of tickets will be computerised.						

MEASURES	A	B	C	D	E	F
45. Reducing the number of tickets which any one individual may purchase and the number of tickets available to away supporters, and restricting the number of tickets available for purchase in bulk.						
46. Where necessary, reducing the overall number of tickets for sale, bearing in mind safety, control and public order factors.						
47. Controlling tickets at the entrances and preventing illegal entry.						
48. Informing would-be spectators as soon as possible, through the appropriate national and international channels, when a match is sold out.						
49. Regular review by sports associations, Clubs and the Police of their lists of known and potential troublemakers.						
IV. Planning of all financial matters related to the match, and particularly matters relative to security and safety well in advance, including : 50. Contracting adequate insurance cover for medical, fire, and general accident hazards, and damage caused by supporters within the hall.						
V. Any other matter related to the organisation of the match, such as: 51. Preliminary contact between the police and the guest team's country's embassy/consulate, in order to ensure rapid communication in case of need.						
52. Providing ad hoc entertainment programmes suitable for visiting supporters.						
53. Co-operation with supporters' clubs to obtain their help in avoiding incidents, and making clubs aware of their own responsibilities in safety and security matters.						
54. Publishing lists of prohibited objects.						
55. Making useful information available to the fans (bus and other public transport lines to and from the hall, parking facilities, customs provisions and visa requirements, accommodation and eating possibilities and their average prices etc.); where possible, providing appropriate accommodation for visiting supporters.						
56. Liaising with the media in a spirit of co-operation, particularly concerning information for supporters and the number of media representatives circulating near the playing field.						
57. Distraction and entertainment of spectators before the game (curtain-raiser match, music, etc.).						
VI. Co-ordination measures 58. To ensure appropriate co-ordination, before the match the organisers shall nominate a Safety Manager, in charge of contacts with the public authorities and their consultation, and liaison with the Police and Emergency Services, granting him/her the necessary resources to carry out the tasks for which he/she is responsible, including access to and radio communication with the command post.						
59. The Safety Manager will evaluate on behalf of the organisers the degree of risk which the match presents, and supervise on their behalf the application of the safety measures mentioned above, and the dissemination of information to spectators on safety measures, particularly concerning objects which may not be introduced in the hall.						

MEASURES	A	B	C	D	E	F
60. The Safety Manager, in liaison with the representative of the public authorities empowered to authorise the staging of the match and will ensure the implementation of those safety measures which are the organisers' responsibility. For high-risk matches, the Safety Manager will ensure that there are a sufficient number of coordination meetings with all parties involved in planning and supervising the staging of the match.						
61. The Police Department, the Fire Department, and Medical Emergency bodies will each name a representative, who will attend the coordination meetings.						
62. After the match, the Safety Manager will draw up a report on the effectiveness of preventative measures taken, to be sent to the appropriate authorities.						
63. The Police Commander and the Safety Manager will make contact with the match officials before the match.						
64. Where appropriate, the public authorities will authorise the match after checking compliance by the organisers with applicable legislation (if any) on the staging of public events and the safety of public buildings, and any other obligation of the organisers, including those listed above.						
65. The organisers will be informed by the public authorities as soon as possible of any objection to the staging of the match(es) and/or of any particular condition which would have to be fulfilled before the match(es) could take place.						
66. A Crisis Group, including the Safety Manager, senior representatives of the Police, Fire Department, Medical Emergency, the competing teams, the Sports hall authority and the Public Authorities, will meet in case of need before or during the match, to take urgent decisions where appropriate; arrange a key word known to Crisis Group members only, to be used through the public address system as call in case of need.						
67. After the match, examine measures taken and draw lessons.						

A = Sport Hall Owner
B = Organiser (specify)
C = Competent national sports association (specify)
D = Competent international sports federation (specify)
E = Public Authorities (local or national – specify which)
F = Others (specify whom)

40.24. Recommendation on the use of standard forms for the exchange of police intelligence concerning high risk sports events (T-RV/97/1)

The Standing Committee of the European Convention on spectator violence and misbehaviour at sports events and in particular at football matches;
In accordance with Article 9.1.c of the Convention;
Having regard to Articles 1, 3.1.b and 4 of the Convention;
Recalling its 1988 Recommendation on police co-operation (use of advisory police "spotters", preparations for major events);
Recalling its 1991 Recommendation concerning Article 4 of the Convention: international co-operation;

Recalling its Recommendations on measures to be taken by the organisers of football matches and public authorities (Recommendation N° 1/93) and measures to be taken by organisers and public authorities concerning high-risk indoor sports events (Recommendation N° 1/94);
Recalling the Convention for the protection of individuals with regard to automatic processing of personal data (ETS 108);
Recalling Recommendation N° R(87) 15 of the Committee of Ministers to member States regulating the use of personal data in the police sector;
Aware of the need to strengthen measures for combating hooliganism and to improve international co-operation between police forces in connection with major international sports events, in particular international football matches and championship fixtures;
Considering that police co-operation and the exchange of information between police forces in the different localities concerned are key elements of prevention measures aimed at combating spectator violence and misbehaviour;
Noting that the Council of the European Union adopted a Recommendation on 22 April 1996 on guidelines for preventing and restraining disorder connected with football matches;
Anxious to avoid the adoption of two different texts in this sphere;

Recommends that the Parties to the Convention:
1. use the same standard forms, set out in Appendix 1 to the present Recommendation;
2. process the personal data collected on the basis of these forms only for the purposes for which these forms were designed; and
3. destroy the data when they are no longer needed for the purposes for which they were collected, and in any case within 5 years.

Appendix 1
STANDARD FORMAT FOR THE EXCHANGE OF POLICE INTELLIGENCE AIMED AT REDUCING SPECTATOR VIOLENCE AND MISBEHAVIOUR

COMPETITION FIXTURE
. . . . V. . . . .
COMPETITION: . . . .
DATE: . . . .
VENUE: . . . .
KICK-OFF TIME: . . . .

ASSESSMENT AND CATEGORIZATION OF SUPPORT
Please indicate estimated numbers of supporters in brackets.
A = peaceful [ ]
B = some potential for confrontation or disorder especially alcohol-related [ ]
C = violent or organizers of violence [ ]

INTELLIGENCE:
. . . .
. . . .
. . . .
. . . .

Theses forms should not include names or photographs of individuals or groups.

TRAVEL INFORMATION

. . . . V..

AIR TRAVEL
OUTWARD/RETURN JOURNEY
(Please delete as necessary)

Scheduled or Charter Flight:..
Name of the Travel company:..
Name of Airline or Air Operator and Flight number: ....
....
Date/time of departure: ....
Departure airport :...
Number of supporters on flight:...
Categorization of Supporters on flight:...
Organized or Independent travellers:..
Date/time of arrival (show local time if appropriate): ....
Arrival Airport: ....
Stop-overs if applicable ....

ACCOMMODATION
Stop-overs en route if applicable and name of Hotel/Pension/Campsite:...................................
....
....
....
....
Hotel/Pension/Campsite at Venue:..
....
....
....
....

COMMENTS

TRAVEL INFORMATION

. . . . V..

PRIVATE CAR/MINIBUS/CAMPERS/VAN, ETC.
OUTWARD/RETURN JOURNEY
(Please delete as necessary)

Description of vehicle:..
Make/colour:...
Registration Number (where possible): ....
Number of Passengers: ....
Categorization of passengers: ....
Organized or independent travellers:..

Date/time/place of departure:..
Ferry Company/Ferry Crossing/Date/Time of crossing: ....
....
Channel tunnel/dates/times:...
Motorways or other routes:..
Border Crossing points/times:...
Time of arrival at venue:...

ACCOMMODATION
Name of Hotel/Pension/Campsite, etc.:...
....
....
....
....

COMMENTS

TRAVEL INFORMATION
. . . . V...

RAIL TRAVEL
OUTWARD/RETURN JOURNEY
(Please delete as necessary)

Date/time of train:..
Departure station:...
Number of Supporters travelling: ....
Organized of Independent travellers:..
Ferry company/Date/Time of crossing: ....
Channel tunnel/date/time: ....
Departure station after crossing: ....
Date/time of train:..
Date/time of arrival:..

ACCOMMODATION
Stop-overs en route if applicable and name of hotel/pension/campsite:...................................
....
....
....
....
Hotel/pension/campsite at venue: ....
....
....
....
....

COMMENTS

TRAVEL INFORMATION
. . . . V..

COACH TRAVEL
OUTWARD/RETURN JOURNEY
(Please delete as necessary)

Name of Company: ....
Number of coaches: ....
Description of vehicles/Livery: ....
Registration numbers (where possible): ....
Number of passengers on each vehicle: ....
Categorization of Passengers on each vehicle: ....
Organized or independent travellers: ....
Date/time/place of departure: ....
Ferry company/date/Time of crossing: ....
Channel tunnel/dates/times: ....
Motorways or other routes showing border crossing points/dates/times: ....
....
Stops/Locations/Times: ....
Estimated time of arrival at venue: ....

ACCOMMODATION
Stop-overs en route if applicable and name of hotel/pension/campsite: ....
....
....
....
....
Hotel/pension/campsite at venue: ....
....
....
....
....

COMMENTS

APPENDIX 2 to the Recommendation

Explanatory memorandum on Recommendation (T-RV/97/1)

1. European Convention on spectator violence and misbehaviour at sports events and in particular at football matches (1985):
The States Signatories express their determination to control spectator violence and misbehaviour at sports events in the Convention's very first article:
"The Parties, with a view to preventing and controlling violence and misbehaviour by spectators at football matches, undertake, within the limits of their respective constitutional provisions, to take the necessary steps to give effect to the provisions of this convention".
In this connection, Article 3.1.b stipulates that:

"[The Parties undertake]...to facilitate close co-operation and exchange of appropriate information between the police forces of the different localities involved or likely to be involved".

This provision is supplemented by Article 4 of the Convention, which provides for international co-operation in this sphere.

On the basis of the principles of the Convention, a number of initiatives have already been taken by the Standing Committee.

2. Activities of the Standing Committee (T-RV):

In accordance with Article 9 of the Convention, the Standing Committee has made recommendations and proposals to the Parties on measures to be taken in order to implement the Convention.

In its 1988 Recommendation on police co-operation, the Standing Committee advocated the use of police "spotters" working in an advisory capacity to identify troublemakers or provide advice as to signs of trouble developing at major international sports events:

a. On the use of advisory police "spotters"

That, on the occasion of major international sports events where spectator violence is to be feared, the police authorities from the countries of the participating teams discuss the possibility of arranging for advisory plain-clothes policemen from the visiting country(ies) to assist the police force(s) responsible for the match(es) on potential problems from the visiting supporters (for example, help in identifying known troublemakers, advice on signs of trouble developing).

b. On preparations for major events

That the relevant police authorities consider organising before major international competitions training seminars for senior police officers on the organisation of crowd control measures (before, during and after matches).

In the area of international police co-operation and in accordance with Article 4 of the Convention, comprehensive guidelines were adopted by the Standing Committee in its 1991 Recommendation. These guidelines include numerous suggestions for co-operation in maintaining order at international football matches.

Two topics focused more specifically on the exchange of information:

1. The role of visiting police in the host country

It is suggested that the foreign police authority may be able to supply the host police with three types of information, while bearing in mind that this information is subject to any international and national provisions with regard to the right of privacy and data protection:

i. traffic information on numbers of spectators, dates, routes, means of travel and arrangements for accommodation;

ii. intelligence identifying known troublemakers who may travel to the football event, their methods of operation, and known or suspected intentions;

iii. tactical intelligence identifying known troublemakers who have travelled to the event and – of even greater importance – actual intentions to engage in violence and disorder at particular times and places, and predictions from the mood of a group that violence is about to take place.

2. Traffic management

It is suggested that, shortly before an event, each source country send a traffic telex advising the police in their own country, carriers and transit and host countries of the known travel plans of visiting supporters.

As well as listing individual groups, tour operators, routes, accommodation and dates, it is helpful to summarise this information at the start of the traffic telex to show the total number of supporters involved and sub-totals broken down by main travel route (air, sea ferry, coach, car etc.). Where possible the summary and individual details should be categorised as follows:
A – No trouble expected;
B – Slight possibility of trouble;
C – Warning: possible risk of trouble.

Police co-operation and information exchange also form part of the security measures set out in two more recent Recommendations adopted by the Standing Committee (Recommendations Nos 1/93 and 1/94):
"Facilitating the work of accompanying police forces (escorts) through exchange of information on supporters' movements."
The more specific initiatives of the Council of the European Union in the sphere of information exchange, inter alia by adopting standard forms for the uniform presentation of police intelligence reports, are appreciable and may be considered as complementing the efforts of the Council of Europe.
However, it must be remembered that the Recommendation of the Council of the European Union is limited to the fifteen members of the Union and not easily applicable, therefore, to those States Parties to the Convention which are not EU members.
It would be sensible to avoid adopting two different texts in this sphere.
In this respect, the adoption of the standard forms set out in Appendix 1 to the present Recommendation could facilitate the exchange of information advocated in the Convention and the Standing Committee's recommendations.
These forms have been slightly modified further to the suggestions made, by the Project Group on data protection, within the context of the Convention for the protection of individuals with regard to automatic processing of personal data (ETS N° 108).

Resolution No. 1/97 on the use of non-discriminatory terms

The Standing Committee (T-RV) of the European Convention on Spectator Violence and Misbehaviour at Sports Events and in particular at Football Matches;
Having regard to Article 9 of the Convention;
Having regard to its recommendations of 1989, 1991, 1993 and 1/94;
Bearing in mind the progress made in controlling spectator violence and misbehaviour since the Convention came into force in November 1985;
Decides that:
In the explanatory reports to its 1989 Recommendation on Ticket Sales and its 1991 Recommendation on Police Co-operation and in the standard checklists of measures to be taken, set out in the appendices to Recommendations Nos.1/93 and 1/94,
The term "segregation" shall be replaced by "separation" wherever it occurs.

Statement on fences and barriers (1997)

The Standing Committee of the European Convention on Spectator Violence and Misbehaviour at Sports Events and in particular at football matches at its 17th meeting at Strasbourg on 5-6 June 1997, adopted the following statement on fences and barriers:

"The consequences of major outbreaks of spectator violence and misbehaviour in the 1980s included, inevitably, restrictive measures such as the erection of perimeter fences and obstacles to protect the playing area. This has led to restricted views and a less welcoming environment.

Certain measures which could eventually make it possible to remove perimeter fences have been identified.

The Standing Committee notes these with satisfaction and looks forward to the day when such fences and barriers will no longer be needed.

The Standing Committee considers that the basic prerequisites for this, developed to a sufficient standard, include:

- The introduction of all seater and numbered seats stadia, equipped with closed-circuit television and command and control posts.
- Adequate management of ticket sales.
- The improvement of crowd control management techniques (both by police forces and by football bodies), with a growing role for stewards illustrating the shift towards self-policing and self-responsibility.
- Better national and European police cooperation for the identification of potential trouble makers and better security.
- The introduction of appropriate legislation, with effective sanctions for convicted offenders.

All Parties to the Convention agree to work in the same direction so that major matches can be sources of peaceful enjoyment.

The example of Euro '96 shows that if all other measures are in place, perimeter fences can be removed and police presence reduced in stadia.

At its next meeting, the Standing Committee aims to adopt a strategy to achieve this."

40.25. Written declaration No. 276 on Football Hooliganism

Adopted by the Assembly on 22 June 1998

This written declaration commits only the members who have signed it.

The undersigned members of the Parliamentary Assembly of the Council of Europe strongly condemn the acts of violence perpetrated by hooligans in Marseille and in other French cities hosting the 1998 Football World Cup.

Although this violence is the action of a very small minority among the huge crowds of peaceful football fans, its coverage by the media, and in particular television, gives a distorted image which is detrimental to sport as a whole.

The European Convention on Spectator Violence and Misbehaviour at Sports Events and in Particular at Football Matches of 1985 has contributed to the decrease of spectator violence, in particular inside stadia, and continues to be the appropriate framework for European co-operation in this field.

Although hooliganism – as well as violence in general – are the consequence of social problems the solution of which cannot be found in the field of sports, we feel that more should be done to avoid the deplorable scenes we have been witnessing recently and therefore call on those responsible, including the Standing Committee of the European Convention on Spectator Violence, to:

1. adopt a more appropriate policy regarding ticketing, in particular in order to increase security through separation;
2. develop more effective exchanges of information and intelligence;

3. ensure that those arrested for hooliganism are charged and brought before a court and, if found guilty, are given custodial sentences which could be served in their countries of origin;
4. take more effective measures to keep known hooligans away from sensitive football matches, including those taking part in other countries.

40.26. Recommendation on the identification and treatment of offenders and the exchange of intelligence at the European Football Championships (EURO 2000) (T-RV/99/3)

The Standing Committee of the European Convention on spectator violence and misbehaviour at sports events and in particular at football matches (T-RV);
In accordance with Articles 1 and 9.1.c of the Convention;
Having regard to Article 5 of the Convention and Recommendation No. 1/90 on the identification and treatment of offenders;
Having regard to Article 3.1.b of the Convention in respect of the exchange of intelligence and Recommendation No. 1/97 on the use of standard forms for the exchange of police intelligence concerning high risk sports events;
Bearing in mind the experience gained in the course of the World Cup (France 1998), notably with an eye to the preparations for the European Football Championships in Belgium and the Netherlands (EURO 2000);
In view of cross-border activities and/or attempts by hooligans to organise at international level;
Considering the draft treaty on cross-border co-operation of police forces in both organisers' countries of EURO 2000;
Recommends that the Parties, for the purposes of the European Football Championships EURO 2000,

I. concerning the identification and treatment of offenders,
1. introduce, within the limits of their respective constitutional provisions, preventative measures to impede known violent fans from leaving their home country and/or entering the territory of the organising countries;
2. take legislative or other regulatory measures, where appropriate, allowing for the preventative or temporary arrest of suspected persons in order to isolate dangerous elements in time;
3. contemplate, where appropriate, the temporary reinstatement of border controls, making use of the possibility offered under section 2, subsection 2, of the Convention of 19 June 1990 applying the Schengen Agreement;
4. provide appropriate sentences for persons found guilty of football-related offences, such as prohibition of access to stadiums for a specific period, prohibition on entering the national territory of the organising country or expulsion through a procedure for very urgent cases;
5. recognise and take into account, to the fullest extent possible, national stadium bans or other exclusion orders, and any other sentence handed down following football related offences by courts in other countries.

II. concerning the exchange of intelligence and information,
1. install effective systems for the exchange of intelligence and information in order to prevent the movement of known troublemakers when EURO 2000 is held:

2. introduce appropriate measures for constituting files of administrative and/or judicial sanctions, such as national stadium bans or exclusion orders, etc. and contemplate the exchange of such data between the bodies concerned (police, judicial authorities, match organisers etc.) in the States parties to the Convention;
3. use the available channels, appropriate for exchange of intelligence and information related to the field of hooliganism, such as specialised national bodies, the Schengen Information System, Europol, Interpol, and/or conclude, if the case arises, bilateral agreements in order to facilitate the exchange of good quality information and intelligence;
4. make sure that information and intelligence transmitted be detailed enough to be of practical use;
5. see that the services concerned transmit sufficiently early information and intelligence capable of being taken into account in the planning and operational stages of the EURO 2000;
6. seek means of identifying spectators, who while not appearing on police lists, may become violent at major matches;
7. make use, for the exchange of information, of the list of national correspondents created by the Standing Committee for bilateral contacts on matters connected with football hooliganism.
8. The exchange of information referred to in section II above must take place bearing in mind the provisions of the Convention for the protection of individuals with regard to automatic processing of personal data and other criteria set by the Council of Europe.

III. concerning the implementation of these measures,
1. implement the measures advocated in this Recommendation for the preparatory phases and during the European Football Championships EURO 2000;
2. develop and implement a system to evaluate the use and effectiveness of this Recommendation.

40.27. Recommendation 1434(1999) on Football hooliganism

1. The Assembly considers that football hooliganism is a threat to the sport and that more efforts will have to be made to reduce hooliganism and prevent the occurrence of incidents such as those at the 1998 World Cup in France.
2. It believes that the European Convention on Spectator Violence and Misbehaviour at Sports Events and in particular at Football Matches of 1985 is the appropriate framework for cooperation in this field. According to Article 1 of the convention, the Parties are obliged to take the necessary steps to prevents and control violence and misbehaviour by spectators at football matches and other sports event in which violence or misbehaviour by spectators is to be feared.
3. Since the adoption of the convention hooliganism has changed gradually. Changes include:
   i. a more deliberate seeking out of confrontations by hooligans. The use of weapons and drugs illustrate the deliberateness of the hooligans;
   ii. an increase in hooligan planning, mobilisation, co-ordination and organisation. More experienced hooligans play an important role, as do modem means of communication (mobile phones, internet). Pan groups may form coalitions. Representatives of rival fan groups may contact one another to discuss arrangements;

iii. a shift in place and time. Confrontations increasingly occur outside football stadia and apart from football matches.

4. The Assembly considers that, to succeed. safety measures should be complemented by social preventive measures and an increased effort in the field of education.
5. A long-term integrated approach, in which all parties concerned make binding arrangements, is crucial for the reduction of hooliganism. Both clubs and national and international football authorities have to assume their responsibilities.
6. Players and clubs have a responsibility to prevent any behaviour on the playing field that might provoke violence among fans.
7. For an atmosphere conducive to tolerance and fair play, a balance has to be sought between security and safety on the one hand and friendliness and hospitality on the other.
8. Co-operation and co-ordination during international events are still far from optimal in that many countries are not able to provide the necessary information and countries with a lot of experience in dealing with hooligans often feel that their experience is not used to the full.
9. Sensationalist or exaggerated press reports, sometimes enhancing nationalist tendencies, contribute to a climate conducive to hooliganism, especially in the periods leading up to championships.
10. Communication is a key factor in the prevention or escalation of incidents and this does not apply only to communication within and between those involved in security. Communication with fans by police officers. stewards and fan coaches contributes to the prevention of incidents, especially if people familiar to them address fans in their own language
11. An important contribution to the prevention of hooliganism is by excluding known hooligan from attending matches. Alcoholic drinks should be banned from stadia.
12. The possibilities to manage a temporary event such as a championship safely are constrained by the long term policies (or lack of them) in the participating countries.
13. The Assembly recommends that the Committee of Ministers continue and reinforce its work against hooliganism in sport on the basis of the European convention, in association with governments and the relevant sports bodies, clubs, associations and stadia owners, and in particular by:

With regard to hooliganism in general:

- Strengthening educational, social and cultural measures and strategies to prevent hooliganism;
- Requiring the taking of responsibilities by clubs, and national and international football authorities by making it compulsory for them to make integrated safety plans, including measures for the prevention of hooliganism. the appointment of fan-coaches and a media strategy;
- Stimulating user-friendly stadia in which social control is made easier (for example by encouraging family participation) and hospitality has priority (for example in the form of seats, shelter, sanitation and the possibility to buy food and non-alcoholic drinks;
- Stimulating a more active involvement of fans and fan-societies, (for example in the allocation of tickets):
- Developing a European approach to fan coaching;
- Stipulating that all football matches in national competitions, in countries where this is necessary, have to be played simultaneously;

- Stimulating international co-operation and co-ordination along the lines of the European Union "Handbook for international police-co-operation and measures to prevent a control violence and disorder around football matches";
- Establishing permanent football intelligence units in each country and facilitating regular consultations between them;
- Looking for ways to apply stadia bans internationally.

With regard to the organisation of Euro 2000 and future international sports events:

- Stimulating international co-operation and co-ordination before and during the event by complementing arrangements made in the organising countries, by providing feedback and by a matching communications strategy;
- Encouraging all participating countries to send stewards and fan-coaches in large numbers;
- Stimulating an active and open media policy to help prevent exaggerated and unfounded media coverage;
- Continuing research on "best practices" and the effectiveness of measures taken to prevent hooliganism and evaluating international co-operation and co-ordination before and during the event;
- Establishing international centres for visiting fans ("fan-homes") in places where matches are to be played in order to inform and help fans in their own language;
- Organising publicity campaigns in each participating country, with the participation of popular players, to encourage an atmosphere of festivity and tolerance.

40.28. Recommendation on Stewarding (99/1)

Adopted at the 19th meeting, 9-10 June 1999, of the Standing Committee of the European Convention on Spectator Violence and Misbehaviour at Sports Events and in particular at Football Matches

The Standing Committee (T-RV) of the European Convention on Spectator Violent and Misbehaviour at Sports Events and in particular at Football Matches;
Having regard to the need to ensure the safety of spectators and the creation of an environment which discourages violence and misbehaviour;
Recognising that the great majority of spectators do not misbehave;
Considering that the resources of the police should be employed most effectively to maintain public order, prevent and detect crime and arrest lawbreakers;
Seeing a need for stewards to welcome and care for spectators and ensure their safety and well-being as foreseen in Article 3.2 of the convention;
Considering that these stewards should be properly selected, trained, equipped and directed;
Recognising the value of stewards in enabling the stadium management or the organisers of the match to identify and exercise their responsibilities for enforcing the regulations of the stadium by the most appropriate means;
Having regard to the increase in matches at European level, the greater ease of travel and the importance of treating all spectators in a suitable and consistent manner;
Recognising the potential safety benefits of collaboration between stewards from different parties to the convention with compatible stewarding systems;
Considering that this could best be achieved by introducing common minimum standards of recruitment, selection, training and assessment;

Having identified certain principles which are valid in all states party to the convention, notwithstanding their different history, culture and legal systems;
Considering that these are best applied by means of clear requirements imposed by the public authorities or with their agreement;
Having regard to the study on stewarding in sport conducted by the Clearing House (T-RV(97)Inf1);
Recommends to governments of parties to the European Convention on Spectator Violence and Misbehaviour at Sports Events and in particular at Football Matches that they encourage clubs, stadium owners and/or other appropriate bodies in football and other sports to develop a system of stewarding at sporting events with large attendances, based upon the following principles:

1. Stewards should be provided by whoever is responsible for the safety of spectators at the match; this may be either the management of the stadium or the organiser of the event.
2. The nature, role and functions of stewards should be clearly defined; these functions, which should be distinct from, but complement those of the police, should include:
   a. searching the stadium before, during and after the match as necessary;
   b. welcoming, directing and caring for all spectators, whatever their age, race, sex, disability or the team they support;
   c. responding to any complaints from spectators;
   d. informing spectators of the arrangements and facilities at the stadium and of any safety requirements laid down by the organisers or the emergency services;
   e. assisting in the safe operation of the stadium, in particular supervising and ensuring the safe entry and exit of spectators;
   f. enforcing the regulations of the stadium;
   g. keeping spectators out of those parts of the stadium to which the public does not have access;
   h. observing all areas of potential danger and preventing overcrowding;
   i. responding to incidents and emergencies and taking the necessary action to deal with them;
   j. assisting the police or emergency services as required.
3. Recruitment procedures should ensure that all stewards are fit and active and can demonstrate that they have the necessary good character, temperament and ability to perform their duties.
4. Thorough training should be provided to all stewards, leading ultimately to the issue of an appropriate certificate. This training should be both theoretical and practical, and cover, inter alia:
   a. the legal status, responsibilities and duties of stewards;
   b. the requirements in force at the stadium;
   c. the organisation and management of safety at the stadium;
   d. the principles of crowd management, including how to monitor spectators and to respond to hazards;
   e. how to deal with unsafe or unacceptable behaviour;
   f. taking care of spectators;
   g. the configuration of the stadium, in particular the entrance and exit routes and the location of the alarm and communications systems;
   h. what action to take in the event of a spectator being injured;
   i. what action to take in the event of a fire or other emergency;
   j. evacuation of the stadium.

5. A system for the ongoing assessment of each steward should be maintained, including records of his or her:
    a. qualifications or skills;
    b. suitability and fitness for the task;
    c. attendance at matches and duties performed;
    d. standard of performance;
    e. training received and further training needs.
6. All stewards should be required to comply with a code of conduct as a condition of their employment. This code should include provisions that all stewards should, inter alia:
    a. be polite, courteous and helpful to all spectators at all times, without discrimination;
    b. be suitably dressed with no display of team colours;
    c. concentrate on their duties at all times and refrain from watching the match or celebrating a goal;
    d. never work under the influence of alcohol, drugs or medicines which may affect their behaviour.
7. All stewards should be clearly identifiable. This entails the wearing of suitable clothing so that they may be quickly and easily recognised by spectators, by the stadium management, the police and other authorities.
8. Procedures should be established for determining the minimum number and location of stewards, including supervisory stewards, to be deployed at each match and for ensuring that the stewards are so deployed.
9. Arrangements should be put in place for the effective use of stewards, in particular through:
    a. the establishment of a clear hierarchical command and safety management structure with appropriate means of communication;
    b. detailed briefing and debriefing before and after each match;
    c. the issue to all stewards of a check list and/or handbook summarising their duties;
    d. refresher training at periodic intervals.
10. By agreement between the two clubs or countries concerned, suitably qualified stewards from the visiting club or country should be invited by the organisers to accompany the visiting supporters so as to assist the local stewards to provide for their safety, welcome and care.

40.29. Recommendation on the removal of fences in stadiums (99/2)

Adopted at the 19th meeting, 9-10 June 1999, of the Standing Committee of the European Convention on Spectator Violent and Misbehaviour at Sports Events and in particular at Football Matches

1. The tragic events of the 1980s in football stadiums led European countries to take practical steps to prevent and control spectator violence and misbehaviour at football matches. Fences and other barriers were installed in football stadiums to separate rival teams' supporters in the stands and/or prevent spectators from invading the pitch.
2. These fences and barriers created a cage-like environment in Europe's stadiums. Being unsightly and having negative connotations, they are not conducive to the creation of a harmonious and festive spirit at football matches. Indeed, they heighten the tension and

the feeling of alienation among spectators. Furthermore, fences can be a safety hazard, particularly when crowds panic. Fences around pitches, for example, hinder evacuation in an emergency.

3. Since the period when fences were installed, stadium design and crowd control techniques have progressed. Renovation work on many football grounds has considerably improved spectator facilities, for example in terms of refreshments, ladies' lavatories, etc., making stadiums pleasanter and more attractive places for the whole family. Another major improvement in spectator safety has been the introduction of numbered seating-only arrangements. In addition to these innovations, modern information and communication technologies and high-powered video surveillance systems have been installed, the ticket sales system has been improved, a better method of controlling access to the stadiums developed, appropriate legislation with effective sanctions introduced and better European police co-operation instigated. Enhanced stewarding techniques have also improved conditions for the reception of spectators and helped to create an environment that discourages violence. Lastly, police forces are now more experienced in crowd control.

4. The last European championship (Euro 96) and the 1998 World Cup championship in France were held mainly in stadiums with no fences. The removal of fences from most grounds has not led to any increase in spectator violence, except for a few minor incidents. This state of affairs prompted the Standing Committee to reconsider its policy in this matter. On the basis of the experience of Euro 96, it adopted a statement on fences and barriers (appended) at its 17th meeting, on 5 and 6 June 1997.

5. The same applies to the 1998 World Cup in France where the removal of fences in most stadiums had no adverse effect on safety, except in a few isolated incidences.
In its evaluation report on the 1998 World Cup, FIFA concluded:
"The removal of perimeter fences in most of the stadia did not exacerbate the safety situation at all, except in a very few isolated cases. The crowd fully respected the fact that the field of play is sacred. This should further encourage FIFA and the national associations to continue to dismantle perimeter fences, even for league matches. Of course the undersigned is perfectly aware that World Cup spectators are quite different from those who attend normal first division matches in most European countries." (cf T-RV (98) 16).

6. In the national reports to be presented to the Standing Committee at its 19th meeting, one of the questions concerns fencing. A total of 20 delegations supplied information on the situation and trends in their countries concerning the removal of fences. In 5 of these countries there are no fences in football grounds, while another 2 have fencing in only a third of their stadiums. Nine countries are gradually removing fences or replacing them with lower, more attractive barriers or transparent Plexiglas. Only 4 countries are in favour of keeping fences. This means that a large majority of European countries have already set about removing fences from their stadiums.

7. It is interesting to note that countries, like England and France, that recently staged major international championships (Euro 96 and the 1998 World Cup) pioneered the move to dismantle fences in stadiums in the wake of this experience. The international championships they hosted provided these countries with an incentive to improve their systems of safety, crowd control, stadium design, stewarding (see Recommendation No.1/99 on stewarding) and so on. Their examples show that the removal of fences should be one of the measures taken to improve safety arrangements as well as conditions for the reception of spectators in football stadiums.

8. The removal of fences also seems to go hand in hand with the development of a more festive, family-friendly atmosphere. Removing physical barriers undoubtedly helps to get rid of mental barriers: "good treatment breeds good behaviour".
9. In the light of these considerations, the Standing Committee recommends to the States parties to the Convention to proceed to the removal of fences in sports grounds. The removal of fences, which is primarily the responsibility of stadia owners and/or organisers of matches, could be carried out on a voluntary basis and gradually. The principle should be the removal of all fencing; but, where necessary, other measures or means of a less irksome nature could be used to keep spectators off the pitch, such as the installation of low, removable barriers and the adjustment of the height of terraces or of the first row of seats. Finally, this new strategy should be implemented in concert with the national and international football organisations, and Parties could offer incentives to help with improvements to the physical fabric of stadia.

Appendix to the Recommendation
STATEMENT ON FENCES AND BARRIERS
Adopted by the Standing Committee at its 17th meeting on 5-6 June 1997 in Strasbourg
"The consequences of major outbreaks of spectator violence and misbehaviour in the 1980s included, inevitably, restrictive measures such as the erection of perimeter fences and obstacles to protect the playing area. This has led to restricted views and a less welcoming environment.
Certain measures which could eventually make it possible to remove perimeter fences have been identified.
The Standing Committee notes these with satisfaction and looks forward to the day when such fences and barriers will no longer be needed.
The Standing Committee considers that the basic prerequisites for this, developed to a sufficient standard, include:

- The introduction of all seater and numbered seats stadia, equipped with closed-circuit television and command and control posts.
- Adequate management of ticket sales.
- The improvement of crowd control management techniques (both by police forces and by football bodies), with a growing role for stewards illustrating the shift towards self-policing and self-responsibility.
- Better national and European police cooperation for the identification of potential trouble makers and better security.
- The introduction of appropriate legislation, with effective sanctions for convicted offenders.

All Parties to the Convention agree to work in the same direction so that major matches can be sources of peaceful enjoyment.
The example of Euro '96 shows that if all other measures are in place, perimeter fences can be removed and police presence reduced in stadia.
At its next meeting, the Standing Committee aims to adopt a strategy to achieve this."

40.30. Recommendation Rec (2002) 1 on guidelines for ticket sales at international football matches (teams and nations)

The Standing Committee of the European Convention on Spectator Violence and Misbehaviour at Sports Events and in particular at Football Matches, under the terms of Article 9.1.c of the convention,

Having regard to Articles 1.1 and 3.4.c of the convention,
Bearing in mind the Standing Committee's Recommendation No. 1/89 on guidelines for ticket sales;
Bearing in mind the Resolution of the Council of the European Union (6 December 2001) concerning a handbook for international police co-operation and measures to prevent and control violence and disturbances in connection with football matches with an international dimension (Enfopol 128), and more specifically chapter 6 of the handbook;
Considering recent developments in the field of ticketing policy, ticket sales and ticket control, and the experience acquired on the occasion of various international tournaments and at national and international matches;
Considering the increasing number of football matches at international level, and the importance of different countries proceeding in the most consistent possible way as regards ticket sales;
Bearing in mind the need to distribute tickets in as fair, equitable and transparent a manner as possible, within the constraints of necessary security and safety requirements;
Bearing in mind different regulations applying in European countries;
Recognising the responsibility of the organiser of a football match and/or stadium owner as to the safe progress of the match;
In view of the importance of managing a football match with the necessary security arrangements, regardless of whether breaches of the peace are predicted or planned,

Recommend that the Parties to the convention:
1. formulate and implement appropriate measures to give effect to the principles on ticketing policy and sales set out in the attached appendix;
2. transmit this recommendation to the national sports organisations, match organisers, stadium owners, etc.

Instructs the Secretary General to transmit this recommendation to the observers to the convention.
Appendix
Principles on ticketing policy and sales
A. Ticketing policy should be based on the following requirements:
1. an effective and efficient separation of rival fans;
2. preventing black-market sales and ticket fraud;
3. giving support to the policy of stadium bans;
4. distinguishing the various responsibilities of the different people involved (organisers, other ticket distributors and ticket holders);
5. the identification of fans.

B. The separation of rival fans can be realised by:
1. concentrating the fans of a given team in the same sections and/or stands in the stadium;
2. the physical separation of rival fans;
3. if appropriate, taking measures at the time of sale to avoid the concentration of fans from a third party;
4. requiring applicants for tickets to identify the team they support;
5. where it is deemed necessary, making arrangements for a prescribed percentage of seats per section to be left unsold, so as to tackle possible problems should fans intermingle;

6. if appropriate, including regulations for accepting back tickets from competing teams which cannot distribute all the tickets among their own fans, for resale by the organiser;
7. providing efficient measures to prevent black-market sales and ticket fraud (see below).

C. Preventing black-market sales and ticket fraud may be achieved by:
1. as regards black-market sales:
   a. providing a legal mechanism for punishing black-market ticket sales;
   b. so far as circumstances permit, not putting tickets on public sale until the identity of the teams participating in a match is known. For group matches in a European championship or world championship, tickets allocated to supporters of the participating teams should only be sold after the draw. Tickets may be sold to the general public before the draw where a system of selling tickets for matches involving only specific teams is in place;
   c. match organisers limiting the number of tickets available to any applicant with a view to ensuring optimum security. A maximum of four tickets per applicant per match should be sufficient. A lower number may be decided by the competent authorities and tournaments organisers;
   d. preventing the sales of large quantities of tickets by travel organisations and tour operators;
   e. always closely monitoring all tickets sales, in particular those via the Internet;
   f. for all tickets sold directly to the public, always including the name of the purchaser on the ticket. The names of other user groups, such as sponsors or national associations, should be included on all tickets allocated to such groups on the understanding that the groups concerned would keep detailed records of those to whom the tickets are allocated and make these as soon as possible available to the responsible authorities;
   g. ensuring that the distribution of tickets by the organiser and those who are officially designated by them is controlled to a high standard by:
      i. the mandatory keeping up-to-date of the files concerning applications for tickets;
      ii. screening these files according to a number of parameters (alone or in combination) such as identity, address, date of birth and bank account number;
      iii. requiring the purchaser to provide the names of each person for whom he is applying for a ticket;
      iv. organising an efficient information exchange with regard to the aforementioned files between the organiser and the police services and/or competent authorities involved, making a joint intervention possible;
2. as regards ticket fraud:
   a. in order to guard against criminal abuse, to prevent overcrowding and to ensure that no one can enter the stadium by means of a fraudulent ticket, ensuring that the following measures are taken:
      i. using a series of security techniques in the ticket, such as the choice of paper, the printing techniques, codes, etc.;

      – providing the necessary control mechanisms so as to detect fraud, e.g. by briefing the supervising staff on the security techniques, automated admission controls, bar code controls, UV controls, etc.;

3. as regards both black-market sales and ticket fraud:
   a. organising ticket sales in such a way that all supporters, regardless of status, are given a fair and equal opportunity to purchase a ticket;
   b. providing the general public with the necessary information through the media, a fan guide, etc.;
   c. issuing the tickets as late as possible, unless particular circumstances justify that they be issued earlier;
   d. arranging prior discussion between all the relevant authorities of the strategies to be adopted in the event, possibly late in the day, of the emergence of false tickets or black market sales.

D. Support measures for the banning policy, insofar as this is permitted by law, could involve:
1. passing on among the different parties concerned, where this is legally possible, the data regarding banned individuals, including those who are the subject of stadium bans;
2. screening the files on banned people, to the extent that this is permitted by law, by the match organiser or the police forces of the country involved;
3. co-operating with the competent authorities over the setting-up, where the technology is readily available, of a technical system based for instance on the use of biometrical data (picture, voice recognition, colour of the eyes, hair colour, fingerprint code), which makes it possible to detect and/or to exclude banned people immediately and positively to the extent that this is permitted by law.

E. Defining the various responsibilities of the different persons involved (organiser, other ticket distributors and ticket holders) could be brought about by:
1. with regard to the authorised ticket distributors:
   a. making clear arrangements (whether contractual or not) concerning the distribution of tickets by the various authorised people so that they all operate a single and identical ticket distribution system;
   b. cancelling or limiting the supply of tickets to any authorised selling agent who has failed to observe the conditions of sale;
2. with regard to the holder of the ticket:
   incorporating in the conditions of sale that tickets are not transferable, unless the issuer has specifically approved this by a specified date. This non-assignability should constitute one of the terms of the contract between the organiser and the applicant for the sale and purchase of a ticket. The transfer of a ticket without approval would constitute and be reported as a breach of the contract. Selective controls, relying on concrete police information, can be used to check whether the ticket has been transferred without approval or not. The non-assignability can be mentioned on the ticket itself and will thus have a dissuasive function. The above mentioned rules on ?non-transferable? tickets aim to prevent persons who may pose a threat to public order from entering the stadium.

F. The identification of fans may be achieved by:
   1. recording the entitled ticket holder's name on the ticket;
   2. keeping up-to-date lists of ticket holders' names;
   3. linking the names of the ticket holders to a stand, section, row and seat number;

4. creating a ticket supervision system which can be scrutinized directly by the proper parties.

40.31. Recommendation Rec (2003) 1 of the Standing Committee on the role of social and educational measures in the prevention of violence in sport and handbook on the prevention of violence in sport

The Standing Committee of the European Convention on Spectator Violence and Misbehaviour at Sports Events and in particular at Football Matches;
In accordance with Article 9.1.c of the Convention;
Having regard to Article 3, paragraphs 2 and 5 of the Convention;
Recalling its Recommendation N° 2/89 on comprehensive report on measures to counter hooliganism;
Having regard to the Council of Europe's Integrated Project on 'Responses to violence in everyday life in a democratic society';
Noting that violence and misbehaviour amongst spectators at sports events, and in particular at football matches, have not been eradicated, and is moving increasingly from within stadia to town centres and other places;
Considering that such violence is part of a wider social phenomenon, which adversely affects genuine law-abiding supporters and local residents and that an integrated approach is needed to counter it;
Noting the many significant improvements since the Heysel tragedy, for example on police activity and co-ordination, stadia infrastructure, crowd management and video monitoring, organisation (most notably ticketing), stadium bans and the use of the criminal law at national and international level have had a real impact in reducing violence, particularly near and within stadia;
Noting various positive initiatives in different countries with regard to educational and social measures at national and international levels to prevent violence;
Drawing on the experience gained at recent major tournaments such as the World Cup in 2002 or the European Football Championship in 2000, which have demonstrated that making arrangements to accompany and welcome supporters is useful and effective;
Considering that the further development and use of such preventive measures will contribute to a further reduction of spectator violence and will provide structural support to those involved in the organisation and management of major sports events;
Aware of the need to place a greater emphasis on prevention within the framework of the overall international policy to fight hooliganism in order to supplement the necessary conventional security measures and to ensure that they are kept in balance;
Recommends to the Parties to the Convention:
That they take preventive social and educative measures aiming at improving the welcoming and coaching of supporters, with regard to their national circumstances, drawing inspiration from the principles and initiatives presented in the Handbook on prevention of violence in sport appended herewith, notably by:

1. setting-up a fan coaching policy, developing fan embassies and the use of accompanying persons;
2. encouraging clubs to develop closer relations with their supporters, to value the official supporters' clubs, to stimulate their setting up and to give them a role in the context of club management and life of the club;
3. making the clubs aware of the role that they can play in their social environment;

4. enabling national and local authorities, and also other bodies to play a major role in developing policy measures for preventing violence.

Calls upon all sport organisations, such as FIFA and UEFA and national football associations, to assist in these aims with all the means available to them.

Appendix to Recommendation Rec (2003) 1

Handbook on the prevention of violence in sport

CONTENTS

5. Finance
6. Accompanying persons
a. Role and tasks
b. Structure
c. Recruitment, selection and training
F. Activities for local people during international tournaments
a. Awareness-raising campaigns
b. Targeted prevention

Introduction

The prevention of spectator violence is a necessity for many sports events in every country of Europe.

The concept takes many forms and corresponds to widely differing realities in practice.

Preventive activities vary widely, ranging from evening remedial lessons for child supporters run by football clubs, to adventure sport activities organised for hooligans at weekends, to well-publicised fan embassies at major tournaments, and fair play campaigns. Activities are also organised by private associations on their own initiative, and others are run under government programmes carried out by public or semi-public institutions.

Even if the philosophies and the political lines behind them vary, these schemes as a whole prove highly useful and are definitely effective.

The promotion of a more consistent approach to problems that are common to many different countries is desirable. This is particularly important in the context of international matches or tournaments.

This manual is designed to identify and promote existing good practice so that individual countries may learn from each other's experiences. It is not intended to be prescriptive. It is a menu from which each member state may select according to its needs and circumstances.

Most incidents at sports events stem from either defective infrastructure, or inadequate organisation (sale of too many tickets, spectator areas with insufficient capacity) or the poor organisation, or actions of the security staff. It is now possible to take the view that, if national legislation and security regulations are complied with, the recommendations made in the European Convention on Spectator Violence and Misbehaviour at Sports Events are applied, and the crowd is well managed, the kind of disasters that happened in the 1980s and early 1990s can now be avoided (although the circulation of spectators and ticket management are still areas of concern, in the latter case especially where international tournaments are concerned, because of the existence of black markets).

I. General principles behind a prevention policy

A. The current situation as regards hooliganism

In this early part of the 21st century, spectator violence at football grounds still remains a topical and disturbing problem, in spite of all the efforts made and resources invested over the past twenty years or so.

Most European countries are affected to a greater or lesser extent. However, the problem takes different forms. In most countries, the situation has been stabilising, with violence shifting from inside football grounds to outside, including urban areas and city centres. In some countries the nature of those involved in such violence has also changed. Football fans include young people from difficult neighbourhoods and hooliganism is becoming linked to urban violence.

1. Clubs and leagues

Violence has occurred at football grounds ever since football became a spectator sport, namely since the 1870s in England and the early years of the 20th century on the continent.

Spectator violence, whether spontaneous or planned, is most closely associated with professional football, though in some countries it is also to be found in the amateur game and in a variety of other sports.

The contemporary football world also faces violence of a premeditated kind. This is group violence, in the form of physical aggression or vandalism, engaged in by hard-core groups of supporters. These hard-core groups follow a particular club and systematically seek confrontation with their counterparts from rival clubs. They regard themselves as elite supporters and their membership of a group of hooligans as a 'way of life' which helps to add value to their social identity.

This violence may take a relatively organised form. Some hard-core groups make use of new communications technologies (GSM, the Internet, and so on) when planning and carrying out their acts of violence.

2. International tournaments

International tournaments are one-off large-scale events where considerable spectator movements and significant crowds have to be managed over a fairly long period of time.

Over the years there have been a number of serious incidents of disorder.

In most places, virtually no incidents occur inside football grounds during such tournaments; most incidents happen in city centres, after matches or in the days between them.

B. The need for preventive measures to combat violence in sport

A large number of practical measures have been introduced since the Heysel tragedy to prevent violence, both by states and by international co-operation, relating to police activity, infrastructure improvements, crowd management and video monitoring, better organisation (ticketing). This has included the use of the criminal law.

In contrast, while many proactive educational or social initiatives have been launched at local level to prevent football supporters resorting to violence, there is no common or co-ordinated approach towards prevention at international or pan-European level.

It is therefore desirable that greater attention and emphasis should be given to proactive preventive measures at these levels. These should be seen as complementing conventional security measures. An appropriate balance needs to be maintained between these different measures.

While the constitutional arrangements will vary from country to country, in most of them local authorities are likely to have a major role to play in developing and providing the various measures described in this manual for preventing violence in sport. Indeed, the lowest tier of public institutions, particularly city councils, may need to be catalysts in prevention policies and to give impetus to activities involving sports organisations or associations.

II. Initiatives and preventive measures

A. Relations between clubs and supporters

1. Introduction

The relationship between clubs and supporters provides a framework for a number of preventive measures. The clubs should take responsibility for initiating such measures.

It would seem natural for sports clubs and federations to adopt a stronger fan support policy, thus starting a process by which they draw closer to their fans, forging a new social link.

2. Supporters' charter

In an ideal world, a joint charter should be drawn up by the club and the representatives of its supporters' associations, setting out the club's obligations to its supporters and the supporters' obligations towards the club and clearly defining each party's rights and duties. This would help to formalise the relationship between clubs and supporters.

A supporters' charter could cover membership, consultation and information, accessibility, ticketing policy, merchandise, community activity, and loyalty rewards. It should be based on communication with the club, and also involve partnerships with local authorities and the media, and be centred on the values of fair play in sport.

UEFA could encourage national associations to set out a possible way forward, using positive examples.

3. Club officials responsible for supporter relations and associations of fans

Clubs should value supporters' associations, encourage their setting up and consult them regularly on issues that affect supporters. The more such groups are involved in the club's decision making, the more they are likely to be committed to the creation of an enjoyable trouble-free environment for all spectators. This has been particularly noticeable in the anti-racism initiatives adopted by clubs and supporters' groups in many countries.

All professional clubs in Germany have successfully adopted a system whereby a club official with decision-making authority has been made responsible for relations with fans, so as to ensure that supporters' associations receive support and that the process of communication between club and fans is a concrete and permanent one. This is a requirement from UEFA for all clubs in international competitions.

4. Supporters' departments

Larger clubs could consider establishing specific 'supporters' departments' to manage all aspects of their relationships with supporters. These will vary from club to club but may include ticketing, fixture list, information, organisation of travel to matches and regulations. Many clubs employ supporters in these departments. Part of the club management structure, they provide a specific interface between the club and its supporters.

B. The club's role in its social environment

1. Working with the community

As clubs have a high symbolic value, they are uniquely placed to play a leading role within their neighbourhood, their community and the whole of their local environment throughout the week. The club can play a pivotal role in supporting broader social policies and can represent a genuine driving force for the promotion of sport and for encouraging the learning process for young people, and even for supporting good citizenship. Football's link with society cannot be limited to match days, or stop where the sporting competition ends.

There are various noteworthy examples which show the way and deserve adoption elsewhere.

One is the community programme run in England. This may typically comprise a partnership with the local authority's educational services, under which the club organises remedial lessons for children who have difficulties at school. Classes are taken by official teachers at the ground, to which pupils are brought in vehicles bearing the club's logo. A high level of voluntary participation has been achieved, as has a clear improvement in the children's school results.

Another example are the 'social units' to promote the playing of football in residential neighbourhoods, to organise amateur football tournaments and to get professional players involved in campaigns which highlight the value of engaging in sporting activities and of sporting ethics.

Some clubs in the Czech Republic, with the help of government programmes, have set up junior fan clubs, aimed at very young supporters (from 8 to 12 years), and these run sporting and educational activities, as well as offering social assistance with the help of a social worker, at a 'clubhouse' which is a centre for leisure activities. The aim is to highlight such groups of young supporters with a positive mentality and positive behaviour, thereby giving rise to a 'new' culture of sport and developing a new generation of fans who will remain loyal.

The numerous local initiatives deserve support and an international framework. It would be useful in this context to appoint within every national federation, and at UEFA and FIFA, a person to be responsible for 'prevention and social programmes', who would help develop such activities and provide institutional support for them.

2. The city at the stadium and the stadium in the city

The football ground is the place where many different kinds of people come together, and sport provides a potential link between all the various component parts of the urban community, encouraging positive group action.

The football ground should play a full part in the life of the city, so that the people who live in the city also feel a sense of belonging at the football ground.

During World Cups, for example, the stadia could help to foster the involvement of local people in the sporting sphere and to bring the sporting infrastructure into the heart of the city. Firstly, by taking advantage of the pool of jobs to which the World Cups give rise, in synergy with the social reintegration programmes being run with young people in the neighbourhoods; secondly, by organising tours of the stadium for local people to show that it remains accessible; and finally by organising multicultural days in the context of the sporting event in which all local associations and authorities take part.

C. Fan coaching

1. The social and educational coaching of fans

Having regard to the changing nature of hooliganism and to its particular local circumstances, several countries have concluded that it is necessary to ask social workers to carry out educational activities targeted specifically at supporters, and have taken steps towards this end. Supplementing both passive security measures connected with infrastructure or supervision and police action to manage events, fan coaching is part of an operational prevention policy extending over the medium and long term, based on ongoing grass-roots work with supporters.

2. Definition

Fan coaching is part of the effort described as 'proactive socio-prevention'. It is carried out wherever the target audience is to be found and requires such an approach. Promoting a positive fan culture and creating positive conditions for the stay of visiting supporters are key prerequisites.

The basic principle is one of active social and educational action in the field by skilled professionals who work in a targeted manner, focussing on groups of young football fans. It is essential to let projects evolve continually, ensuring that new staff are constantly brought in and provided with in-service training, so that activities do not become bogged down in tradition. The supporters' world is changing, so, by definition, fan-coaching projects have also to develop.

Fan coaching schemes are quality background activities that take on their full scope when they are part of the local environment, and they are run within a club or a city. Fan coaches' intervention in the specific area of football is part of a broader prevention or urban security programme implemented at municipal level.

In practice, fan coaching is carried out in many different ways, mainly because supporters have different profiles, but also because hooliganism itself differs as well, leading to the adoption in each country of different methods of action. Fan coaching is therefore a flexible concept, adapted to each situation on the ground, according to local needs and specific national cultures. The most structured and institutionalised efforts in terms of fan coaching have mainly been made in Belgium, Germany and the Netherlands.

In these countries, the activities are carried out by teams of professionals specialising in social or educational work and steeped in the supporters' culture. Due to the sensitive area in which the activities are conducted and the complexity of the psycho-social problems involved, the teams work in and among the fans.

As regards responsibilities and funding, governments have a role to play, with direct support from the clubs and local authorities concerning the organisational aspects and implementation.

3. The staff involved

'Fan coaches' usually work under an employment contract.

4. The method

Fan coaching involves a mobile effort, both home and away, also encompassing ongoing educational and social work during the periods of supporters' lives when they are not involved in football, thanks to the organisation of structured educational activities.

While some fan coaching takes place on match days, using a situation-based approach, its main focus is on educational and social activity, which is ongoing during the rest of the week.

a. Educational activities

The educational activities provide a valuable opportunity to carry out specifically targeted educational work with young supporters outside the particular context of matches, with their associated excitement.

The organisation of classical sporting activities (such as football on a full-sized or smaller pitch) as part of an educational project to involve young people and make them more responsible is also intended to prevent young supporters from finding themselves at a loose end in their cities, while at the same time enabling them to meet their need to be active. Some structure is offered through participation in amateur championships.

Adventure sports, such as rafting and climbing, prove very appropriate, enabling young supporters to prove their worth in a positive field, by meeting open-air sporting challenges, rather than through resorting to violence. They also enable young people to expend their pent-up energy, while providing them with the excitement they need. Significantly, they learn proper standards by participating in this kind of activity.

As the key to these efforts is learning to be actively involved and to be responsible, offering supporters consumer activities merely to keep them occupied is to be avoided, for the essential aim is to enable young supporters' positive resources and potential to be used and developed, and to express themselves through action.

b. Social support

The link with football may provide an opportunity to carry out social work targeted at certain disadvantaged groups. Fan coaching may thus enable individuals with social difficulties who are not helped by conventional institutions to be given assistance. When fans' social situations are improved, one step is thereby taken towards making them more independent, also as individuals.

c. Street work

Permanent contact with fans is important, providing the cement that binds the educational work that needs to be done.

Such contact may be maintained through street work carried out in residential neighbourhoods or on premises frequented by fans, such as bars, keeping in contact with them between matches and activities, and enabling a relationship of trust to develop.

Or it may take the form of a fan centre, an educational infrastructure open during the week and offering games and educational material, providing a place where fans can meet each other freely in an educational context. This kind of infrastructure provides a permanent interface between fan coaching and fans.

d. Match days

The main aim of fan coaching on match days is to ensure that a channel of communication is open between supporters and organisers.

When fan coaching services are provided by staff recognised by the authorities and accepted by the fans, the staff can be regarded as a link between organisers and fans. Thanks both to their special position at the heart of events and to constant dialogue, they can often defuse some conflicts and thereby help to avoid certain incidents.

5. Relations between fan coaching schemes and the police

Fan coaching taking place in a context of integrated prevention is of proven effectiveness. An uncoordinated approach could prove counter-productive. Positive co-operation between the police and 'fan coaches' is vital to a long-term structured prevention policy. While the methods differ, the objectives are identical: to reduce violence in sport.

Both partners therefore need to understand each other's roles and perspectives and to value their contributions, in particular on the defusing of tension on match days. Fan coaches can act as important channels of communication between the police/clubs and groups of supporters.

In successful projects, the police and fan coaches have established a formal mechanism for consulting each other and exchanging information, co-ordinated through the local authority. At the same time, while there is considerable merit in a formal police contribution to the management of the fan coaching project, some countries consider it inadvisable to integrate the police into the fan-coaching structure.

6. International co-operation in the field of fan coaching

With both football and hooliganism now having an international dimension, other countries may wish to adopt the fan coaching approach according to their local needs.

Each country, region and city has its own peculiarities, and activities must be tailored to these specific local features, in particular as regards the level of institutionalisation and dialogue between fan coaches, the club, the local authority and the police.

International relations between fan coaching schemes could focus on exchanges of specific experience, so as to reinforce and enrich each country's practice.

There is a strong case for local fan coaching activities to be interlinked via a national platform. Thus each country might wish to appoint a national fan coaching correspondent to help centralise information and disseminate it both locally and to counterparts in other countries. This could prove valuable when clubs are competing in international competitions (If this information is seen as useful for the guarantee of public order, the national fan coaching correspondent can pass it on to the national police football information point. The national police football information point can then in turn pass on the information to the national fan coaching correspondent whenever this could be useful to the correspondent's work.).

These correspondents might come together from time to time in an appropriate forum to analyse developments and share their experiences.

Fan coaching is a concept that is primarily aimed at club supporters. Any international fan coaching structure for fans of national teams should focus more on the concept of the use of 'accompanying persons' (see section E6), a concept that is more flexible and enables the work done to extend to all supporters. While the 'accompanying persons' may include some workers from the fan coaching schemes, not all need come from that source.

D. The role of local authorities and other agencies

1. Educational activities

Local authorities are best equipped to co-ordinate and support activities that use sport as a tool for prevention or reintegration, especially activities run in schools or targeting school pupils. In Austria, for example, some activities are organised to teach school pupils about fair play and tolerance, and to inculcate in them respect for other cultures, by making them aware of the need to combat racism. At the same time, the FARE network runs national and international campaigns against racism.

In the urban context, one of the main focal points for action is that of rough estates, to which priority is given where policies of prevention through sport are concerned. It is important to provide facilities to enable young people from disadvantaged communities to engage in sport on a regular basis and in a structured context, and for financial considerations not to constitute an obstacle to this.

Amateur sport is the basis of all sporting activity and has a key role to play. While the media focus first and foremost on professional sport, the problems of violence are also significant in day-to-day sport, including in amateur football.

In addition to awareness-raising campaigns, targeted action is needed among amateur clubs and those who take part in sport at that level.

French legislation provides for an 'officer responsible for the prevention of violence in sport' to be appointed in 26 départements. This officer acts as a resource person and a facilitator for local sporting associations, institutions and other bodies, with a view to combating violence in amateur sport.

2. The role of advisory committees for the prevention of violence in sport

Local authorities need to establish appropriate structures for addressing the problem of violence in sport and for co-ordinating activities. These could take the form of a committee made up of members who play an active part in fan coaching, the police, the football club and the courts, in combination with youth and sports associations and institutions of higher education.

The committee could also be responsible for offering opinions and sending proposals to the local authority on the form to be given to prevention policy and to its programmes. It could act as a direct intermediary between those who work in the field and policy-makers. It could also give impetus to specific projects involving the partners, either in the form of awareness-raising campaigns or through targeted action meeting real needs.

Finally, it could identify new trends, with a view to ensuring speedy, appropriate and effective responses. In some countries, such committees already exist at national level.

E. Fan embassies

1. The atmosphere of the tournament

The fundamental principle underlying the organisation of a sports event must be the priority given to spectator and public safety. Thus the major challenge during sports events is that of striking a balance between the strict requirements of safety and security in the light of actual risk factors and the need to maintain the festive and convivial nature of the event.

The event must remain a welcoming and festive one, with local and foreign fans being treated correctly and with respect. As far as hospitality in connection with the matches is concerned, there is a need for a clear, well-understood and, where possible, consistent approach to the way in which supporters are treated, to the reception facilities organised for them and to the transport and accommodation policy adopted.

This can only be achieved if there is an integrated strategy under which all the responsible parties work together with common aims and objectives. This partnership requires a consensus among all concerned and their involvement during both the planning stage and the event itself.

It is important to note that the work done before matches take place, in the hours and even days preceding games, is vital. Well organised events preceding matches invariably have a positive effect on supporter behaviour and on the atmosphere in the ground.

A fundamental aim of such preventative arrangements is to create a partnership with the police, and to relieve them of some of their workload (in respect of the secondary task of providing public information), thus enabling them to concentrate on their main task of maintaining public order. The prevention programme also plays a significant role in creating a calm atmosphere and hence limiting the number of situations that might require police action.

2. Purpose

Fan embassies are intended to offer a point to which foreign supporters can go, and they focus on fan culture and on supporters' specific needs during the tournament. They provide supporters with an opportunity to talk in their own language to people familiar with the supporters' specific environment, and who have the necessary skills to help solve their individual difficulties. Fans can also obtain information and assistance relating to matches, to ticket sales, to accommodation, to travel, to leisure activities, to any planned screenings of matches, to the theft or loss of documents and to health care, and a wide variety of information about such matters as currency exchange or alternative activities.

The aim is thus to provide a channel of communication between supporters and the local and national authorities and the tournament organisers, particularly so that up-to-date information can be rapidly and efficiently disseminated, for a tournament, by definition, has a life of its own and can undergo constant change, with situations altering considerably and speedily. As the tournament itself is not fixed and immoveable, it is essential to have a facility directly linked to the situation in the field, and able to adapt to changing situations.

Fan embassies can also represent the views of the supporters to the authorities if problems arise and take proactive initiatives to build good will between different supporter groups and with local ethnic groups.

3. Functioning

a. Structure

During any international tournament, each host city should have a fan embassy scheme. Various formats are possible: a single embassy, or two embassies – one for each of the countries concerned – possibly even with a third information centre for other foreign fans in transit. The degree of professionalism and the structure's autonomy differ according to national cultural tendencies. Fan embassies are sometimes set up by the organising public authorities or alternatively by the supporters themselves.

The key requirement is that the structure should be capable of dealing with supporters in an appropriate manner, in particular fans of visiting teams.

b. Staffing and human resources

Clearly it is desirable for those involved in fan embassy provision to be adequately resourced and to possess the skills required to fulfil the functions described above.

In some cases, these can be paid staff contracted to an institutional authority or appointed association. In other cases, the involvement of committed volunteers from supporters' organisations has also proved effective.

The staff of a fan embassy should collectively possess an understanding of the fan culture of its target groups; detailed local knowledge; close contact with all relevant local, national and international agencies; and good knowledge of the languages of the target groups and the host nation.

c. Opening hours

Fan embassies should be accessible and contactable by telephone during the greatest possible number of hours. Experience has shown that permanent opening throughout the tournament may be desirable. The embassies must be open for as long as possible on the day before, the day of and the day after each match. One of the advantages of fan embassies is their accessibility, and another is their flexibility, enabling them to adapt to the situations that arise and also to tailor their activities to the lifestyles of visiting supporters.

d. Location and access

Choosing a location is a sensitive part of the preparations, as fan embassies should be accessible, visible and in a place that is easy to get to. This question of location needs to be the subject of close consultation between prevention services, supporters' associations, police and local authority, in the light of specific local characteristics. Ideally, it is useful for fan embassies to be located in city centres, enabling a considerable amount of work to be done in advance of the match and making the embassies accessible to the greatest possible numbers, for supporters as a whole traditionally go to the ground only an hour or two before kick-off.

It is useful, as was done at Euro 96, to set up a fan consulate near the ground, so that supporters have an alternative point of reference during the periods immediately before and after each match.

The way to fan embassies should be indicated by means of effective and visible signs, making it easy for supporters to find them and making them accessible at any time. It helps if the signs contain a logo that is common to all the host cities, making identification easier. The literature distributed to supporters in their own countries before the tournament should give the addresses and other details of the fan embassies. Printing special posters with city maps showing the location of fan embassies (and other useful information such as where to find bus stops, cash dispensers, etc.) for display in the windows of shops and cafes will enable supporters to establish their own location or to find out where their fan embassies are.

e. Reception facilities, services and information

As fan embassy staff are in constant touch with the organiser, local and national authorities, the police and the security services, they are able to provide supporters with up-to-date and accurate information. They must make sure that this information is definite and reliable, and constantly check its accuracy, so that no misleading information is provided to supporters.

An associated aim is to nip rumours in the bud. The widest variety of quite fantastic rumours circulates among supporters during tournaments, and these may create difficulties that are not easy to deal with. As fan embassies combine an official position at the heart of the network of organising bodies with special and immediate relationships with supporters on the spot, they are able rapidly and definitively to help put a stop to such kinds of rumours.

Matches and arrangements for the tournament

Fan embassies distribute brochures containing information about football grounds, their location, access to them, local public transport and the kick-off times of matches. This information should include legislation or regulations relating to the tournament or to crowd management and the rules applied within each ground, including any items that are prohibited and forms of behaviour which are regarded as anti-social. Regulations vary from country to country and even from match to match, as far as items such as banners, fireworks, cameras, mobile telephones, video cameras and umbrellas are concerned.

Tickets and their distribution

Tournament organisers should make accurate and up-to-date information available to fan embassies about pricing, sales outlets, the numbers of tickets remaining (if any) and the time limits and conditions applying to sales or provide a point of contact for them to obtain this information. It is important for fans to be told at a sufficiently early stage – and to know that this information is reliable – when a match has sold out, or how many tickets are still available and at what prices, or when ticket sales have finished. Fan embassies do not, however, sell tickets.

Accommodation

Generally speaking, fan embassies complement or back up conventional tourist offices, which provide information about various types of accommodation and services. It is important that information should be provided not only about hotels, but also about more economical accommodation, such as campsites or bed and breakfast establishments, and accurate information should also be supplied about public transport services to these places (location, cost and timetable).
When all local accommodation is taken, supporters must be able to be pointed towards more distant accommodation and told about the means of transport they can use to get there. When more critical cases arise, fan embassies may, in consultation with the local authority or police, identify the need for emergency and temporary accommodation for supporters, directing them to improvised campsites, gymnasia with camp beds, and so on.

Travel

Moving around the country, within its cities and to and from its football grounds, is a major challenge during tournaments, and the quality of information provided on the subject is particularly important. Not only city maps, but also public transport timetables (for trains, buses, trams and underground railways) should be available, and supporters should be provided with information corresponding to their personal needs. Information similarly needs to be provided about public and privately owned parking areas in the city or near the ground, park-and-ride facilities and the timetables of shuttles to the ground (ideally with a stop at the 'fan embassy').

Theft or loss of documents

Official documents, such as identity cards, passports and social security documents, as well as airline tickets and match tickets, among other things, are frequently lost or stolen during tournaments, causing dismay to the supporter who feels lost in an unknown environment and has to try to cope with a foreign language. Supporters need the benefit of a direct link or of having their problems

dealt with directly by the 'fan embassy', the reception facilities and hospitality of which come into their own when this kind of problem has to be solved.
In this context, the presence of a consular official in the vicinity of the fan embassy proves a considerable bonus and is therefore recommended.

Health care
Fan embassies need to be able to supply information about hospitals, ordinary or emergency medical services, emergency dentists and social welfare systems, so that supporters can be pointed in the right direction.

Activities
Fan embassies are a major source of information about leisure, sports and cultural activities organised for local people, or specifically for supporters, in the city or in other parts of the country, as well as details of how to get there. Such activities are sometimes even organised by 'fan embassies' themselves, by or for supporters, and these extend to concerts, games and other activities.
It is important that information should be up-to-date, and that the very latest news should be passed on, for many activities are organised too late to be publicised in official literature, or, alternative activities may not be included in this. Other activities, news of which should be circulated mainly by the fan embassy, include public screenings of matches, which are not always planned in advance and sometimes provide a last-minute solution to the problem of channelling the movements of spectators who cannot be accommodated at a sold-out match.

4. Other aspects
   a. Embassies in transit cities
      As well as setting up the basic fan embassies in host cities, additional facilities can usefully be set up in those cities through which large numbers of fans will pass, or where large numbers will be staying. Such cities are those which have tourist attractions, are centres of entertainment, offer attractive activities or have large numbers of hotel rooms likely to be used by many supporters, or cities located in such a geographical position that supporters will inevitably pass through.
      These scaled-down facilities can easily be placed within ordinary official services, such as tourist offices. One of their roles is also to provide information about the tournament's host cities.
   b. Local information centres
      It is useful if local organisers or local authorities can establish an information centre for local fans at the ground, so that they can obtain information. This would complement but not supplant the classic fan embassies. A classic fan embassy in the city with large numbers of staff is not justified over the whole period of the tournament.
5. Finance
   If it is to operate effectively, a fan embassy will incur significant logistical and staff costs.
   In view of the one-off nature of the event, part of the needs may be met with equipment, premises and staff made available by local authorities and associations. However, special funding is essential.
   Governments and tournament and match organisers will need to play their part in providing the necessary funding and support for the facility.

6. Accompanying persons

a. Role and tasks

Some countries also find it useful to send 'accompanying persons' with their supporters who travel to other countries or to request that such persons accompany supporters coming from other countries. These persons come from the fans' countries of origin, speak the host nation's language and are familiar with the culture of the national supporters.

They travel with their national supporters wherever they go within the host country, basing their movements on the dates of the fixtures. They are present in the host city on the day before, the day of and the day after the game. They also travel to other places if large numbers of fans are present there.

They may either be based in the fan embassy and provide a form of outreach to spectators or they may act as stewards, escorting organised groups from their home countries to the stadium and home again. This latter form is more commonly adopted for the supporters of clubs playing in international competitions.

Such 'accompanying persons' have no legal status outside their own country so their role must by definition be limited.

Their main duty is to look after the visiting supporters and to provide appropriate services so as to improve the reception that they receive and to optimise the hospitality shown to them. They can provide the fans with information and help them to solve problems, in close consultation with the fan embassy.

They play a roving fan ambassador role, helping to develop and strengthen a positive fan culture based on respect and tolerance. In some circumstances and in some countries, they may also be able to facilitate dialogue between police and supporters, so as to defuse tension and settle disputes without the need for police intervention.

In some circumstances, by agreement between the two countries concerned, they may be able to perform the tasks undertaken on match days by fan coaches (see section C). In this case the same considerations apply as at the local level.

b. Structure

The size of the team and the means of liaison with the organisers, police and local authorities will vary according to local needs and circumstances. It is important to ensure that there are clear lines of communication and that the responsibilities of each party are agreed and clearly understood.

c. Recruitment, selection and training

Host countries may also find it helpful to recruit welcoming staff and interpreters from among the nationals of visiting countries who already live there. Some countries, such as Turkey and Yugoslavia, may have many supporters resident in the organising country or neighbouring states. Other nations also have a considerable number of immigrant fans on the spot, among them Spain, Italy and Portugal.

The desired profile for accompanying persons does not necessarily have to be that of someone who does the work professionally or of someone who works in the education sphere with hooligans or with juvenile delinquents. As their tasks are mainly those of primary prevention aimed at all supporters, it may be beneficial not to be led by professional reflexes or different work practices.

F. Activities for local people during international tournaments

a. Awareness-raising campaigns

Related activities need to be held to raise awareness among local people and encourage them to get involved in the event, so that the festive dimension of the tournament and the concept of hospitality come right to the fore. If this is done, a convivial atmosphere will bind everyone together in the spirit of fraternity everyone expects during the tournament.

The tournament, with all its heavy symbolism, can act as a catalyst for larger-scale preventive activities. The dissemination of the values of tolerance and respect is encouraged through multicultural activities and awareness-raising campaigns.

Awareness can be raised among local people through preventive campaigns. One example of a very worthwhile initiative is that of the primary prevention activities undertaken in the 'Welkom!' schools project in the Netherlands.

It is necessary to emphasise the festive side of the event, as well as the concept of fair play, and, in particular, to demystify the mood of panic inevitably generated by the media in the preparatory phase of such tournaments, to help reduce tension in the local population, and to get ready for a fraternal festival of football, rather than for confrontations with foreign invaders with a thirst for both beer and violence.

People who run pubs and bars are a specific target, for they play a vital part in preventing over-consumption of alcohol. Both staff and management of alcohol outlets need to be made aware of their responsibilities. Information needs to be targeted at them so as to reduce the likelihood of incidents occurring.

b. Targeted prevention

An effort must be made to avoid making an already socially vulnerable group of the population feel excluded. It is undesirable for the tournament and all that goes with it to become the preserve of a few privileged people. Preventive activities need to be carried out in local estates, especially those considered difficult.

Such activities should take further local policies on integration through sport and on intercultural prevention, and should be organised in co-operation with associations and similar bodies that have experience of socio-preventive work. Alternative activities can be organised to avoid leaving people at a loose end or bored, a situation which often leads to offences being committed, examples of such activities being sporting tournaments, 'taster' sessions in certain sports, themed evenings, concerts and educational activities. Such activities also have a structuring function if they are part of a carefully considered educational project. And they distract the attention of young people from their potential interest in possible conflict areas and from taking part in clashes.

40.32. Congress of Local and Regional Authorities of the Council of Europe Recommendation 144 (2004) on the prevention of violence in sport, in particular at football matches: the role of local and regional authorities

The Congress,

1. Thanks the municipality of Lisbon for its warm welcome and hospitality and the National Association of Portuguese Municipalities (ANMP) for its support in the organisation of the first conference on "the role of local and regional authorities in preventing

violence at sports events, in particular football matches" (Lisbon, 23-24 June 2003);

2. Expresses satisfaction at the backing given to this conference by the Council of Europe's integrated project "Responses to violence in everyday life in a democratic society" and the close cooperation established on that occasion with the Council of Europe's Directorate of Youth and Sport (DG IV);
3. Reasserts the principles set out in its Recommendation 16 (1996) and Resolution 27 (1996) on sport and local authorities;
4. Points out that:
   a. sport fosters social integration and participation and, in this respect, makes a valuable contribution to the democratic process;
   b. sport plays an important role in promoting understanding between European citizens;
   c. sport has significant economic benefits at the local, regional and national levels;
   d. sport, an important activity in our societies, is an integral part of local community activities, and local and regional authorities should therefore endeavour to promote and support it;
5. Concerned at the violence and misbehaviour in and around stadiums and on the streets of cities hosting sports events, particularly football matches, considers that appropriate policies must be implemented to prevent such behaviour, often the result of the excessive abuse of alcohol and drugs;
6. Considers that:
   a. players and athletes contribute to the prevention of violence by their "fair play",
   b. coaches, trainers and managing directors of teams have an essential role to play in the prevention of violence;
7. Bearing in mind:
   a. the work of the Council of Europe, which for over twenty years has been promoting a global approach to the prevention of violence at sports events, and in particular;
   b. the recent recommendations by the Standing Committee of the Council of Europe Convention on Spectator Violence (ETS No. 120), which highlight the greater role that should be played by local authorities in preventing violence at sports events, notably through socio-educational action and fan coaching measures;
   c. the implications for local and regional authorities of the European Union's initiatives and decisions concerning police cooperation to improve safety and security at international football matches;
   d. the measures devised by FIFA (the International Federation of Football Associations), UEFA (the European Union of Football Associations), national football associations and the FESU (European Forum for Urban Security);
8. Aware of the diversity of situations in the countries of Europe as regards the degree of centralisation of public policy-making (policing and prevention);
9. Underlines:
   a. the major role that local and regional authorities can and must play in preventing violence at sports events, whether as regulators, coordinators of safety or security measures, owners of sports facilities, employers of the staff running those facilities, protagonists in policies for the promotion of amateur or school sport or instigators of prevention-oriented social and educational measures;

b. the importance of good cooperation between local/regional authorities and police and security services;

10. Invites the Committee of Ministers to take note of the following principles asserted at the Lisbon Conference and bring them to the attention of the Committee for the Development of Sport (CDDS), the Standing Committee of the Council of Europe Convention on Spectator Violence and the relevant ministries in the member states:

 a. As regards all sports events, local and regional authorities have a fundamental role to play in preventing violence in sport:

  i. preventing violence is not merely a matter for the police. It is not confined to security measures and logistics. Prevention of violence in general, and violence in sport in particular, has a significant social and educational dimension. In this connection, in view of the exclusion of certain young people, local and regional authorities can help to promote the social integration and participation of young people;

  ii. before any sports competition it is essential to adopt an integrated approach whereby all the authorities and bodies involved in the smooth running of the event are encouraged to cooperate in applying a common strategy. Each party (public or private) must be made aware of its own responsibilities and those of its partners;

  iii. local and regional authorities can assume the role of mediating between the diverging interests of competition and match organisers, stadium managers, football clubs, the police, fans and local inhabitants. In some countries this role has probably not been paid sufficient attention so far, and this state of affairs should now be remedied;

  iv. spectators should be treated as visitors to be welcomed and entertained. Local and regional authorities should recognise fan embassies' useful role in providing spectators with assistance and information and the positive influence they can have on their behaviour;

  v. measures should be taken to deal with the misbehaviour of a small minority of individuals. In some cases these measures may be very strict, but they must remain proportionate to the problem being tackled and be carefully targeted so as not to penalise the vast majority of law-abiding fans who merely wish to enjoy the sports event;

  vi. local and regional authorities should strive to create a festive atmosphere not only for visitors but also for local inhabitants;

 b. As regards major sports events and competitions, in particular big football matches:

  i. local and regional authorities should plan the event carefully well in advance. They should, in particular, provide for appropriate means of transport to be made available at the proper time;

  ii. a major competition affords local and regional authorities an opportunity to promote their city or region, to show a positive image at the national and international levels, to boost the local economy and, in the longer term, to endow themselves with new infrastructure and facilities;

11. Invites those members states which have not yet done so to ratify the Council of Europe Convention on Spectator Violence and Misbehaviour at Sports Events (ETS No. 120);

12. Invites the Committee of Ministers and the relevant ministries to continue their support for the work of the Standing Committee of the Council of Europe Convention on Spectator Violence and Misbehaviour.

40.33. Congress of Local and Regional Authorities of the Council of Europe Resolution 172 (2004) on the prevention of violence in sport, in particular at football matches: the role of local and regional authorities

The Congress,

1. Referring to its Resolution 27 (1996) on sport and local authorities and to the Lisbon Declaration adopted at the first conference on "the role of local and regional authorities in preventing violence at sports events, in particular football matches" ((Lisbon, 23-24 June 2003);
2. Bearing in mind the conclusions of the various workshops held at the Lisbon conference (CG/CULT (10) 6) and the work and recommendations of the Standing Committee of the Council of Europe Convention on Spectator Violence and Misbehaviour at Sports Events;
3. Invites local and regional authorities in Europe during the preparation and organisation of major sports events, (especially football matches) to take into account the positive experiences ("good practices") presented at the Lisbon Conference and in particular the following principles:
   a. Concerning security and safety in and around stadiums:
      i. take care of good stadium design and maintenance;
      ii. contribute to the co-ordination between the different services and levels of authority involved (national, regional, local), with a view to proper preparation of sports events;
      iii. take into account the role of the media in crisis prevention and management;
      iv. take into account the violence prevention role of supervisory staff (stewards) inside stadiums, entailing proper training of these staff;
      v. take care of well-conceived seat allocation in stadiums (separating fans of rival teams) through a good system for the sale and control of tickets;
   b. With regard to welcoming and accompanying spectators:
      i. take care of the appropriate supervision of spectators by:
         – reception points ("fan embassies") for visiting fans in cities hosting matches;
         – year-round socio-educational measures ("fan-coaching"). This coaching helps to keep misbehaviour in check and is also aimed at combating racism and xenophobia;
      ii. learn the lessons of "good practices" in this field disseminated via the "Eurofan" European network;
   c. Concerning participation of local inhabitants, conceive sports events as festive occasions, involving local people in socio-cultural events organised in host cities;
4. Invite the local and regional authorities to bear in mind Recommendation No. 1/2003 concerning the role of social and educational measures in the prevention of violence in sport of the Standing Committee of the Council of Europe Convention on Spectator Violence and the detailed handbook of good practices appended thereto;
5. Instructs its Culture and Education Committee to continue its work in this field, in particular with regard to policies for the prevention of violence in and around sports venues, inter alia by:

a. preparing and distributing a guide to good practices, at the local and regional levels, for the prevention of spectator violence at sports events;

b. regularly updating this guide.

Chapter 41
VISAS

41.1. Recommendation No. R (99) 10 of the Committee of Ministers to Member States on the Granting of Visas to Sportsmen and Sportswomen
Adopted by the Committee of Ministers on 22 April 1999, at the 669th meeting of the Ministers' Deputies

The Committee of Ministers, under the terms of Article 15.b of the Statute of the Council of Europe,
Considering that the aim of the Council of Europe is to achieve a greater unity among its members for the purpose of safeguarding and realising the ideals and principles which are their common heritage and facilitating their economic and social progress, and that this aim may be pursued, inter alia, through common action in cultural matters;
Having regard to Recommendation No. R (92) 13 on the European Sports Charter, in particular paragraph 6 of the preamble thereto and Article 8 on supporting top-level and professional sport;
Noting that the European Ministers responsible for Sport, reaffirming the importance of ethical values in sport and sport's role in social integration at their 15th informal meeting (Nicosia, 1998), proposed that means should be sought to arrange "easier visa procedures for sports people participating in international sports events";
Underlining the importance of the contribution sport makes to international understanding and European co-operation;
Considering that sport is also a cultural activity that enriches society and friendship between nations and that, given the intense media coverage, major European and international sports events offer a splendid opportunity for conveying messages of tolerance, fair play and solidarity;
Aware of the need to facilitate participation by sportsmen and sportswomen in major international sports events and noting that some member States have already introduced measures (such as granting free visas) in this area;
Considering that it is important for visas to be granted in time to enable competitors or teams, and the accompanying entourage, officially invited by the organisers, to take part in official sports competitions such as European or international championships, Olympic or regional games, qualifying rounds or bilateral sports meetings,
Recommends that the governments of the member States take all possible steps to speed up and/or facilitate the granting of visas to official sports delegations from other member States or Parties to the European Cultural Convention taking part in international sports events held on their territory or, where applicable, crossing their territory, and, if possible, issue them free of charge or at least at reduced costs to such official sports delegations;
Instructs the Secretary General to bring this recommendation to the attention of the governments of those states party to the European Cultural Convention that are not members of the Council of Europe and to the Executive Committee of the Schengen Agreement.

Chapter 42
WOMEN

42.1. Resolution on the Greater Involvement of Women in Sport (81/3)

The European Ministers responsible for Sport, meeting in Palma de Majorca from 8 to 10 April 1981 for their 3rd Conference;

Accepting that although women have traditionally been less involved in sport than men, they have an equal right to participate, to decide for themselves the type and level of sport which they wish to practise, and to be equally involved in the promotion and management of sport;
Recognising that the present unequal rate of participation of the sexes is the result of sociological patterns and traditional attitudes rather than physiological factors;
Aware that sport can offer enriching forms of leisure activity to those women particularly exposed to the difficulties of dual responsibility of family and work, and to the stresses of urban living;
Concerned to encourage teachers and parents to contribute to girls' awareness, through childhood and adolescence, of the continuing usefulness and value of the practice of sport at all ages;
Considering that the continued existence in certain member states of sport clubs which refuse to offer membership, or offer only restricted membership, to women is contrary to the ideals and spirit of sport and fair play;
Resolve to take all appropriate active policy measures in their countries to encourage greater involvement of women in sport, in particular by:

1. encouraging public authorities, sports federations and other parties involved to recognise and accept their individual responsibilities in facilitating a fundamental change of attitude towards women's participation in sport;
2. promoting a greater use by women of the existing opportunities available to them to take part in sport;
3. making available additional resources, or where this is not possible giving priority out of existing resources, in order to improve facilities for those sports in which women particularly wish to participate;
4. reviewing the position of women in the promotion and administration of sport as a public service, at national, regional and local levels, including the introduction of an active policy of recruitment of women to posts of responsibility;
5. encouraging the provision of crèches in public sports facilities;
6. encouraging the organisation of programmes and facilities to enable all members of families to participate in sport together;
7. considering all possible measures to eliminate sexism in sport and physical education both in and out of school;

Request the Committee of Ministers of the Council of Europe to instruct the CDDS to study as a priority:

1. arrangements for removing sex discrimination as regards membership of public and private sports clubs;
2. the level of the provision of crèches or other child-care facilities in association with sport centres;

3. the number and position of women in administrative and decision-making posts connected with sport;
4. the problem of exploitation (for example, by unduly intensive training) of young athletes – girls in particular – in certain competitive sports;
5. the consequences of national Sport for All policies on the participation of women;
6. the impact of national campaigns designed specifically to increase the involvement of women in sport;

Call upon the International Sports Federations to issue policy statements concerning the provision of resources for those sports in which women wish to participate, to take active measures against existing discriminatory practices, and to consider the urgent need to ensure that women are represented on their policy-making bodies;
Invite the mass media, bearing in mind their editorial independence, to analyse their treatment of sports affairs and the proportion of attention given to men in sport as opposed to women, with a view to redressing the present bias towards 'masculine' and competitive sport.

42.2. Resolution 1092 (1996) on discrimination against women in the field of sport and more particularly in the Olympic Games

The Assembly is concerned about the many instances of discrimination against women wishing to practise sport and more especially about the policy of discrimination with regard to their participation in the Olympic Games.
At the Barcelona Olympic Games in 1992, thirty-five countries had no women athletes in their teams, and one of those teams refused to walk behind a Spanish woman athlete at the opening ceremony.
Some Islamic countries organised women-only games in Teheran in 1993. Men were barred from these games, as were photographers (male and female) and television cameras. Apparently, the International Olympic Committee supports these games which, it has been announced, are to be held for a second time.
The Assembly recalls that the Olympic Charter states that "any form of discrimination with regard to a country or a person on grounds of race, religion, politics, sex or otherwise is incompatible with belonging to the Olympic Movement".
Wherever fundamental human rights are infringed, the Assembly considers it has a duty to intervene in the internal affairs of any state, irrespective of whether it is a member of the Council of Europe. Even if there are cultural differences and traditions, this should be no argument for accepting any policy of discrimination against women in sport.
It welcomes the creation of the Atlanta Plus Committee and its action against such situations.
The Assembly recalls the positive, leading role played by the International Olympic Committee in moral or ethical issues, particularly with regard to the fight against apartheid in South Africa.
The Assembly therefore requests that the International Olympic Committee:
1. firmly and clearly oppose any discrimination against women in sport;
2. refuse to support any sports event based on discrimination, such as the "Solidarity Games for Women in Islamic Countries".

42.3. Resolution on the prevention of sexual harassment and abuse of women, young people and children in sport (3/2000)

The European Ministers responsible for Sport, meeting in Bratislava for their 9th Conference from 30-31 May 2000,

Referring to the Final Declaration and Action Plan resulting from the Summit of the Heads of State and Government meeting in Strasbourg, on 10 and 11 October 1997 which speaks of the need to strengthen "the legal protection of children" and encourages "the adoption of a programme to promote the interests of children".

Conscious of Article 7 (10) of the Revised European Social Charter (1996) which affirms the rights of children and young persons to special protection "against physical and moral dangers to which [they] are exposed..."

Recalling Article 1 of the European Sports Charter (R. (92) 13) which states that "Governments .....shall take the steps necessary ......to ensure that everyone should have the opportunity to take part in sport ... in a safe and healthy environment.......[and] to protect .....the moral and ethical bases of sport and the human dignity and safety of those involved .... by safeguarding sports, sportsmen and sportswomen ...from practices that are abusive or debasing"

Bearing in mind Recommendation 1121 (1990) of the Parliamentary Assembly whereby the Assembly considers that "the right of children to special protection imposes obligations on society and on the adults normally dealing with them such as parents, teachers, social workers, doctors and others";

Noting that the "Windhoek Call for Action" of 22 May 1998 stresses the need to take action to "Ensure a safe and supporting environment for all girls and women participating at all levels by taking steps to eliminate all forms of harassment and abuse, violence, exploitation....";

Mindful of the United Nation's Convention on the Rights of the Child, particularly Article 34 which calls on the States Parties "to undertake to protect the child from all forms of...sexual abuse";

Taking note of the work of the Committee for the Development of Sport already done in this area, especially the two reports on "The problems women and children face in sport with regard to sexual harassment" and the "Analysis of codes of practice for preventing sexual harassment and abuse to women and children in sport";

A. Resolve to:

1. commission research and collect data at national level, in co-operation with national or international organisations and researchers, to ascertain the scale and importance of this problem in sport in their countries;
2. prepare a national policy which would:
   - make a clear statement about the absolute need to safeguard and promote the welfare of children, young people and women in sport;
   - define harassment and abuse of women, young people and children in sport, and provide specific guidance on what is appropriate and inadmissible behaviour;
   - explain that the principles apply to all, regardless of ethnic origins, age, gender, religion, disability or sexual orientation;
   - promote awareness of concern over behaviour which may be harmful either physically or psychologically to children, young people or female athletes;

– set out the responsibilities of sports organisations and individuals, including all those in relationships based on trust and/or power;
– list procedures that should be put into place and followed in order to protect children, young people and women athletes;
– stress the need for confidentiality and sensitivity in a delicate area;
– agree on sanctions and provide information on them.

3. agree that the implementation of the policy within the context of an overall framework of support and protection for children, young people and women in sport, could include such actions as:
   12. drawing up a basic code of conduct for coaches, trainers and leaders, incorporating the suggestions contained in the discussion document MSL-9 (2000) 3), which has been submitted to the Conference;
   13. encouraging national sports organisations to draw up codes of conduct based on the same principles;
   14. developing and disseminating information materials for families, athletes and coaches, trainers and leaders;
   15. setting up of independent telephone help lines;
   16. introducing specific courses on child protection in the education of coaches and trainers.
4. to draw up a timetable for the rapid implementation of these measures.

B. Invite the Committee of Ministers of the Council of Europe to ask the Committee for the Development of Sport to:
– promote research in the monitoring and evaluating of the measures (codes, help lines etc.) set up to combat sexual harassment and abuse among women, young people and children in sport;
– draft a specific reference to the prevention of sexual harassment and abuse for inclusion in a revised European Sports Charter (R (92) 13) and a revised Code of Sports Ethics (R (92) 14).

42.4. Recommendation 1701 (2005)[11] Discrimination against women and girls in sport
Text adopted by the Assembly on 27 April 2005 (13th Sitting)

1. Almost ten years after its Resolution 1092 (1996) on discrimination against women in the field of sport and more particularly in the Olympic Games, the Assembly is distressed to observe that women still suffer frequent discrimination in their access to, and practice of, both amateur and professional sport. This discrimination manifests itself in the persistence of stereotyping, the lack of a back-up and support structure for sportswomen and for girls who show potential in their sport, the difficulty of reconciling work/sport and family life, the problem of reintegrating into the world of work, inadequate media coverage of women's sport and the limited nature of private funding.
2. The lack of women on sport's ruling bodies constitutes a particular obstacle to the achievement of equality between women and men in sports activities. Notwithstanding the efforts made by the International Olympic Committee (IOC), women's participa-

[11] Assembly debate on 27 April 2005 (13th Sitting) (see Doc. 10483, report of the Committee on Equal Opportunities for Women and Men, rapporteur: Ms Aguiar).

tion in ruling bodies remains marginal in most Council of Europe member states.

3. This clearly constitutes a discrimination against women and girls which is contrary to the principles of the Council of Europe. In fact, the European Sports Charter, adopted by the Council of Europe in 1992 and revised in 2001, guarantees the promotion of the practice of sport for all parts of the population (Article 6) and expressly mentions the prohibition of discrimination (Article 4). In its first article it lays down certain principles, among them the aim "to enable every individual to participate in sport" and "to protect and develop the moral and ethical bases of sport, and the human dignity and safety of those involved in sport".

4. Moreover, the 10th Conference of European Ministers responsible for Sport, held in Budapest on 14 and 15 October 2004, emphasised that the particular role played by the Council of Europe in the realm of pan-European co-operation relating to sport was linked to the cardinal values of the Council of Europe (human rights, parliamentary democracy and the rule of law). The combating of discrimination against women and girls in sports activities is one of these efforts to achieve equality between women and men and requires that effective measures be taken.

5. The involvement of the Council of Europe with the issue of women's participation in sport started, however, much earlier, in 1980, with the seminar entitled A Greater Involvement of Women in Sport, organised by the Committee for the Development of Sport (CDDS). As a result of this, and of other similar initiatives, the network European Women and Sport (EWS) was created. The subject was discussed in ministerial conferences under the aegis of the Council of Europe and UNESCO from 1981 to 2004. The IOC also organised three world conferences on the topic.

6. The Assembly welcomes the work of the Council of Europe (CDDS), UNESCO, the IOC, the EWS and of all bodies, at national, European and international level, to combat discrimination against women and girls and to promote their participation in sport. In this context it supports the Brighton Declaration (1994), the Windhoek and Paris Calls for Action (1998 and 2004 respectively) and the Berlin Memorandum (2002).

7. The Parliamentary Assembly therefore calls on the Committee of Ministers to:

   i. instruct the CDDS to continue, in co-operation with other relevant bodies, to promote the participation of women and girls in sport, to combat discrimination against women and girls in sport and to conduct an in-depth study of national sport policies and their impact on women's and girls' participation in sports activities and to work out a European strategy for women and sport which would ensure:

      a. that physical education is accorded more importance in school and that women and girls are encouraged to take part in sport from their schooldays onwards, while respecting the principle of co-education;

      b. that the responsible officials in the departments of sport, education and health are implicated in awareness-raising and information campaigns on the necessity of practising sport, in particular for women of all ages, including handicapped women;

      c. that gender is taken into consideration in the definition of public action to promote sport (gender mainstreaming) and in the allocation of funds intended for sports activities (gender budgeting);

d. that violence, racism, sexual harassment and sexual abuse, both in sport and amongst spectators, are combated, as well as doping amongst sportsmen and sportswomen;
e. that action is taken to promote women's sport, particularly in respect of highly popular sports;
f. support for women's participation in top-level sport;
g. equal treatment for women and men in terms of pay, prize money and bonuses derived from professional sport;
h. that women play a greater part in sport's ruling bodies;
i. that gender-specific statistics are collected relating to the granting of funds and the practice of sport, enabling the impact on women and men of sport promotion policies to be gauged;
j. increased media coverage of the sports played by women and representation of women athletes which is more in conformity with the spirit of sport;

ii. organise a European ministerial conference to launch this strategy.

42.5. Resolution 1494 (2006)[12] on stopping trafficking in women before the FIFA World Cup
Text adopted by the Assembly on 12 April 2006 (12th Sitting).

1. The Parliamentary Assembly is very concerned about the announcement made by certain NGOs who predict that between 30 000 and 60 000 women and young girls may fall victim to trafficking for the purposes of sexual exploitation during the FIFA World Cup, which will take place in Germany between 9 June and 9 July 2006.
2. The Assembly considers it important to avoid confusing the concepts of trafficking, prostitution and immigration, which must be dealt with separately and appropriately. It reiterates that trafficking in human beings is defined in international conventions as "the recruitment, transportation, transfer, harbouring or receipt of persons, by means of the threat or use of force or other forms of coercion, of abduction, of fraud, of deception, of the abuse of power or of a position of vulnerability or of the giving or receiving of payments or benefits to achieve the consent of a person having control over another person, for the purpose of exploitation. Exploitation shall include, at a minimum, the exploitation of the prostitution of others or other forms of sexual exploitation, forced labour or services, slavery or practices similar to slavery, servitude or the removal of organs."
3. It must be remembered that trafficking constitutes a violation of human rights and an intolerable infringement of the dignity of its victims. The Assembly strongly condemns this practice, which consists of treating human beings as objects, and calls for the protection of the victims of trafficking.
4. The Assembly reiterates its firm intention to eradicate this scourge, as reflected in the text of the Council of Europe Convention on Action against Trafficking in Human Beings (CETS No. 197). It therefore welcomes the adoption, on 3 May 2005, of this convention which sets out measures for the prevention of trafficking, the protection of victims and the prosecution of traffickers. In particular, it points out that the convention provides for a recovery and reflection period of thirty days and measures to assist the victims of trafficking.

---

[12] Assembly debate on 12 April 2006 (12th Sitting) (see Doc.10881, report of the Committee on Equal Opportunities for Women and Men, rapporteur: Mrs Vermot-Mangold).

5. However, it notes that to date only 26 member states of the Council of Europe have signed the convention and no state has ratified it. It deeply regrets the fact that the European Community has not acceded to it either.
6. It is delighted that FIFA supports various humanitarian causes, such as the protection of the rights of children and the fight against racism. In its capacity as World Cup organiser, FIFA must also assume its responsibility to condemn the exploitation of women, which sometimes, highly regrettably, accompanies the holding of sports events, and therefore to denounce any activities that threaten human rights.
7. With the World Cup imminent, and given the acute nature of the problem of trafficking, men and women politicians alike, as well as sports organisations, must immediately take all the necessary measures to prevent trafficking and to protect its victims. In order to achieve this, the Assembly favours a non-discriminatory and humane approach, and therefore rules out any proposal to set up a temporary visa system applicable only to women.
8. Consequently, it welcomes and supports the European Parliament's decision to promote the "Red card to forced prostitution" campaign run by the German National Council of Women and to ask the European Commission and the member states of the European Union to campaign throughout Europe so as to inform and educate the general public, and in particular football fans, about forced prostitution in the context of world sports events.
9. It backs the European Parliament's call for the states that will be affected by this problem, especially Germany, to set up a multilingual helpline to allow the victims of trafficking to request emergency assistance. The emergency phone number should be prominently displayed, with guidance in every language, in the various means of transport and on the various routes used by people who are travelling.
10. It urges the member states of the Council of Europe:
10.1. to sign, if they have not already done so, and ratify the Council of Europe Convention on Action against Trafficking in Human Beings as soon as possible, so that it may come into force at the earliest opportunity and have the broadest possible impact;
10.2. to implement without delay the main provisions of the convention, such as the victim identification process and the recovery and reflection period of thirty days for the benefit of victims, paying special attention to presumed victims who are in the process of being identified as such;
10.3. to help victims by setting up, for example, multilingual information, reception and assistance centres, and by ensuring that the police treat women victims of trafficking in human beings as victims, and not as illegal immigrants;
10.4. to consider the possibility of holding responsible those who use the services provided by victims of trafficking.
11. The Assembly calls upon the European Community to sign and ratify the Council of Europe Convention on Action against Trafficking in Human Beings as soon as possible. It urges the European Commission to initiate without further delay the internal procedure making it possible for the European Community to sign and ratify this convention. It asks the Council of the European Union to take the decision to sign and ratify the convention.
12. It asks the Congress of Local and Regional Authorities to join the fight against trafficking in human beings. It calls on the municipal authorities of the World Cup host cities to denounce trafficking and to put in place multilingual information and reception units for victims.
13. It calls on FIFA to commit itself to a strong condemnation of trafficking in women, supporting for instance the Council of Europe's campaign to combat trafficking in human beings.
14. Finally, it encourages the media and professional footballers to condemn trafficking in women and to take part in the above-mentioned campaign.

TREATIES, RESOLUTIONS AND RECOMMENDATIONS

TREATIES

RESOLUTIONS

Adopted by the European Ministers responsible for Sport

Adopted by the Committee of Ministers

SUBJECT INDEX